Progressing Tourism Research

Bill Faulkner, 1945–2002

ASPECTS OF TOURISM 9
Series Editors: Chris Cooper (*University of Queensland, Australia*),
Michael Hall (*University of Otago, New Zealand*)
and Dallen Timothy (*Arizona State University, USA*)

Progressing Tourism Research

Bill Faulkner

Collated and edited by
Liz Fredline, Leo Jago and Chris Cooper

CHANNEL VIEW PUBLICATIONS
Clevedon • Buffalo • Toronto • Sydney

ASPECTS OF TOURISM

Series Editors: Professor Chris Cooper, *University of Queensland, Australia,*
Dr Michael Hall, *University of Otago, Dunedin, New Zealand*
and Dr Dallen Timothy, *Arizona State University, Tempe, USA*

Aspects of Tourism is an innovative, multifaceted series which will comprise
authoritative reference handbooks on global tourism regions, research volumes, texts
and monographs. It is designed to provide readers with the latest thinking on tourism
world-wide and in so doing will push back the frontiers of tourism knowledge. The
series will also introduce a new generation of international tourism authors, writing
on leading edge topics. The volumes will be readable and user- friendly, providing
accessible sources for further research. The list will be underpinned by an annual
authoritative tourism research volume. Books in the series will be commissioned that
probe the relationship between tourism and cognate subject areas such as strategy,
development, retailing, sport and environmental studies. The publisher and series
editors welcome proposals from writers with projects on these topics.

Library of Congress Cataloging in Publication Data
Faulkner, H.W. (Herbert William)
Progressing Tourism Research/Bill Faulkner; edited by Liz Fredline, Leo Jago, and
Chris Cooper.
Aspects of Tourism: 9
Includes bibliographical references.
1. Tourism. 2. Tourism–Research. 3. Tourism–Australia. 4. Tourism–Research–
Australia. I. Fredline, Liz. II. Jago, Leo. III. Cooper, Christopher P. IV. Title. V. Series.
G155.A1 F32 2002
338.4'791'072–dc21   2002015975

British Library Cataloguing in Publication Data
A catalogue entry for this book is available from the British Library.

ISBN 1-853150-48-2 (hbk)
ISBN 1-853150-47-4 (pbk)

Channel View Publications
An imprint of Multilingual Matters Ltd

UK: Frankfurt Lodge, Clevedon Hall, Victoria Road, Clevedon BS21 7SJ.
USA: 2250 Military Road, Tonawanda, NY 14150, USA.
Canada: 5201 Dufferin Street, North York, Ontario, Canada M3H 5T8.
Australia: Footprint Books, PO Box 418, Church Point, NSW 2103, Australia.

This compilation copyright © 2003 The estate of Bill Faulkner.

All rights reserved. No part of this work may be reproduced in any form or by any
means without permission in writing from the publisher.

Printed and bound in Great Britain by the Cromwell Press.

Contents

Disaster Management

Part 4: Tourism Research Agendas

Chapter Sources

Chapter 1 first appeared in Faulkner, H.W. and Shaw, R. (eds) (1982) Evaluation of tourism marketing. *BTR Occasional Paper No. 13* (pp. 6–9). Canberra: Bureau of Tourism Research, Canberra.

Chapter 2 first appeared in 1997 in *Journal of Travel Research* 35 (4), 23–32.

Chapter 3 first appeared in 2002 in a report to the Cooperative Research Centre for Sustainable Tourism, Brisbane.

Chapter 4 first appeared in 1993 in *Bureau of Tourism Research Occasional Paper No. 16*. Canberra: BTR.

Chapter 5 first appeared in 2000 in *Annals of Tourism Research* 27 (3) 763–784. It was co-authored with Liz Fredline.

Chapter 6 first appeared in 2000 in *Event Management 6 (4),* 231–246. It was co-authored with Laurence Chalip, Graham Brown, Leo Jago, Roger March and Arch Woodside.

Chapter 7 first appeared in 1995 in *Tourism Management* 16 (1), 29–37. It was co-authored with Peter Valerio.

Chapter 8 first appeared in 2001 in *Journal of Travel Research* 40 (4), 162–171. It was co-authored with Carmen Tideswell and Trevor Mules.

Chapter 9 first appeared in 1997 in *Pacific Tourism Review* 1 (1), 93–102. It was co-authored with Roslyn Russell.

Chapter 10 first appeared in 1999 in *Tourism Management* 20 (4), 411–423. It was co-authored with Roslyn Russell.

Chapter 11 first appeared in 2001 in *Tourism Management* 22 (2), 135–147.

Chapter 12 first appeared in 2001 in *Tourism Management* 22 (4), 331–344. It was co-authored with Svetlana Vikulov.

Chapter 13 first appeared in 1991 in *BTR Tourism Update*, September, pp. 2–3.

Chapter 14 first appeared in 1994 in Faulkner, B., Davidson, M., Craig-Smith, S. and Fagence, M. (eds) *Tourism Research and Education in Australia*, Proceedings of the Australian National Tourism Research and Education Conference, BTR, Canberra. It was co-authored with Phil Pearce, Robin Shaw and Betty Weiler.

Chapter 15 first appeared in 2001 in a discussion paper for the Cooperative Research Centre for Sustainable Tourism.

Preface

Despite passing so young, Bill Faulkner made an impressive contribution to tourism research, not just in Australia, but to researchers around the world.

This collection of a dozen papers is but a peek into the reporting of a life's work. It is representative of some of the innovative and cornerstone pieces that helped to change the course of the Australian tourism industry and it provides tools and models which will continue to contribute to the national interest for Australian tourism for decades to come.

For almost 20 years, I was able to work with, and learn from, Bill as he moved from researcher to the foundation Director of the BTR, then to Griffith University and on to the Cooperative Research Centre for Sustainable Tourism (CRC). His work provided such a benchmark within the industry and academe that he was named the Director of Research for the CRC and its Deputy CEO.

So many academics over the years have built protective walls around their research projects and have been very cautious about sharing their ideas and expertise. Bill Faulkner was the exact opposite. He broke this isolationist mould and so many of his capstone research works were built on an inclusive and collaborative basis. This meeting of minds and open sharing of his ideas not only produced outstanding research, but also helped develop a new crop of tourism researchers.

Bill was at the peak of his productivity and inventiveness at the point of his untimely passing. His works in progress at this time have done much to change the course of tourism research in Australia. His creation of the 'Destination Australia' programme, for example, sets the research agenda for both the CRC and Australian Tourism research at the opening of the 21st century. Bill's work on Revisioning the Gold Coast as one of Australia's premier tourism destinations has changed the way that local government will engage with the industry for many years to come.

Above all, his quiet, thoughtful and smiling presence had a special capacity to calm difficult situations and to bring people together to achieve his own predetermined agenda.

I hope that this small selection of his research publications might inspire succeeding generations of young Australians to build upon and grow both themselves and the national effort for our industry.

Sir Frank Moore, AO

Bill Faulkner: Progressing Tourism Research And Beyond

Introduction

Professor Herbert William Faulkner, known always as Bill Faulkner, passed away on 28 January 2002 after losing a year-long battle with cancer. He left behind a loving family, including his wife Shirley, his children Joanne, Ben and Catherine, and his grandchildren Bridget and Myfanwy. He is also survived by an extended family of colleagues and students who will miss greatly Bill's friendship and inspiration.

From humble beginnings, of which he was fiercely proud, Bill went on to become the 'father of tourism research' in Australia. Bill's death at the peak of his career represents an enormous loss to tourism research; one can only but imagine what his contribution would have been in the next ten years. Bill regarded himself as lucky, being paid to pursue his passion, namely, tourism research. It was a series of happy coincidences that brought Bill to this career, rather than any form of childhood aspiration. His career path is a classic example of the principles of Chaos Theory, which Bill came to favour as an explanation for many tourism phenomena. However, once he had chanced upon tourism research, Bill adopted it with a passion and gave his all to the advancement of the field.

Bill was a visionary with an enquiring mind, and his enthusiasm for research was infectious. The fact that he was so eager to share his expertise with others played an important part in the development of a tourism research culture in Australia. Indeed, one of Bill Faulkner's great legacies is the fact that there is a generation of tourism researchers in Australia whose work will be a testament to his mentorship.

This book has been compiled from Bill's extensive writings on tourism research and represents a permanent legacy of Bill's work for the inspiration of current and future tourism researchers. The aim of this collection is not to mourn his loss, but rather to celebrate his legacy. The idea for the book came from a group of Bill's colleagues and has the blessing of Bill's family and the board of the Council of Australian University Tourism and Hospitality Education (CAUTHE). Whilst this collection lives on as a permanent memory of Bill, CAUTHE, where Bill worked, will use the proceeds of the book to fund a student scholarship in Bill's name. This will ensure that his inspiration in tourism research will live on to benefit promising young tourism researchers of the future.

The selection of papers and writings has been drawn together into four key themes to represent Bill's research. We have also added a brief introductory section to each theme to orient readers into the background and genesis of Bill's writing and thinking in the area. Reading the papers leaves no doubt that Bill was the 'father of tourism research' in Australia and his growing influence in driving Australian tourism research is clear throughout the book. We therefore hope that the book will be a valuable collection of research papers for the use and inspiration of tourism students and researchers alike. We are grateful to the publishers of the original papers and to Bill's co-authors for willingly allowing us to republish them. Mike Grover of Channelview deserves particular mention here for his ready willingness to publish the collection.

Bill Faulkner

Bill was born in Bowral on 19 April 1945. His tertiary education began with a Teacher's Certificate at Sydney Teachers' College, followed by an undergraduate degree in geography by correspondence at the University of New England (Armidale), which he completed in 1973 with first class honours. He was awarded the university medal for his honours thesis. Following this success, Bill was offered a scholarship to undertake a PhD at the Australian National University (ANU), which he completed in 1979.

Public Service and the Bureau of Tourism Research

After obtaining his PhD, Bill accepted a lectureship at the University of Wollongong teaching Welfare Geography and Social Behaviour in Urban Space. He left the university in 1981 to join the Bureau of Transport Economics as a principal research officer in the Social Factors Section, before moving to the Department of Sport, Recreation and Tourism as Director of Research and Development in 1983. It was during this period that Bill wrote his first paper on tourism research, a refereed conference paper presented at the Institute of Australian Geographers conference in Brisbane in 1985, entitled 'Policy Oriented Tourism Research: A View of Future Needs'. In April 1987, Bill was promoted to Acting Assistant Secretary, Sports Facilities and Events Branch. This position no doubt fostered his interest in event tourism, which later became one of his research specialisations and is an identified research theme in this volume (Chapters 4–6).

In September 1987, the Bureau of Tourism Research (BTR) was established as an intergovernmental agency jointly funded by the Commonwealth and States/Territories. Its primary functions were to provide a national focus for the collection, analysis and dissemination of tourism data, and to conduct or co-ordinate research on priority issues in the tourism field. Bill Faulkner was appointed as the inaugural Director of the BTR and his task was to set up the organisation and to ensure that it met its objectives. During Bill's six years as Director he established the BTR as the most authoritative source of tourism statistics and associated research in Australia and substantially enhanced the quality, availability and use of tourism statistics and research in Australia.

Although Bill enjoyed his time at the BTR, a growing sense of discontent in relation to the politics of running a government bureaucracy, funding, and the type of research that he was able to conduct, prompted him to seek a return to university life. His discontent was exacerbated in 1992 when an evaluation of the BTR's performance and future directions recommended that a substantial increase in resources was necessary to ensure delivery of quality tourism research to support the tourism industry. However, this increase did not eventuate and instead, additional funding was directed to destination marketing bodies. As a result, Bill used several outlets to vent his frustration at what he described as 'advertising fundamentalism'. One of these papers is republished in this volume (Chapter 13).

Griffith University

While at the BTR, Bill developed strong connections with academic researchers in tourism whom he had met at various conferences, and there were many that he came to regard as close friends. He actively sought a move into academic life where he would have more freedom to pursue his research interests. In early 1993, Bill accepted a position as Associate Professor and Head of School in the School of Marketing at Griffith University.

Soon after his appointment to Griffith, he moved to the School of Tourism and Hotel Management at the Gold Coast campus of the university. In this position, he specialised in teaching Tourism Research Methods, an area in which he had substantial theoretical and practical expertise. In this role he established the Centre for Tourism and Hotel Management Research at Griffith University, which enabled him to concentrate more heavily on research and consulting activities.

In the early 1990s, as a consequence of the increasing number of Australian universities commencing education programmes in the fields of tourism and hospitality, the Council of Australian University Tourism and Hospitality Education (CAUTHE) was formed. The prime purpose of CAUTHE is to consolidate and represent the needs and interests of the various universities. Bill became an active member of CAUTHE and was instrumental in its early development. Along with Phillip Pearce, Robin Shaw, Robyn Bushell, and Gary Prosser, Bill played an important role in having tourism research recognised under the Australian Research Council (ARC) funding programmes. These efforts were important in underpinning the subsequent successful application to fund the Cooperative Research Centre (CRC) for Sustainable Tourism. Bill became the national Chair of CAUTHE and convened two of its annual conferences in 1994 and 1998.

In the mid 1990s, Bill took on the primary supervision role for a number of honours and PhD students at Griffith and before long he had attracted a small but dedicated band of female students who became known as the 'Faulknerettes'. These students remember Bill with huge affection due to the important and willing role that he played as an inspirational mentor. As well as working with each of his PhD students individually on their specific topics, Bill took additional time out of his busy schedule to organise regular symposia, gatherings at which all of his students would come together to discuss conceptual and practical matters relating to research.

The Cooperative Research Centre for Sustainable Tourism

In July 1997, the Cooperative Research Centre (CRC) for Sustainable Tourism was established and based at Griffith University on the Gold Coast. Bill became actively involved in research projects during 1998 and was then invited to become Program Coordinator for a new research programme, 'Tourism Policy, Product and Business Research' that was introduced in late 1998. The decision of the CRC to become national in membership and focus meant that Bill was the ideal person to champion such a move given his expertise and contacts. It was also in 1998 that Bill's contributions to tourism scholarship and research at Griffith University were finally recognised with his promotion to Professor.

Bill's ability to draw together researchers from different disciplines and universities to form powerful research teams became well recognised and was a fundamental building block of the CRC. His creativity and capacity for sharing his expertise for the benefit of others helped develop collaborative research in a manner that had not existed previously in the tourism field. Bill liked to achieve but did not simply seek opportunities that would advance his own career; he was a master at creating opportunities for others and was extremely generous with his time for colleagues and students alike.

In March 2000, Bill was appointed by the CRC Board as Deputy CEO and Director of Research, a position that he held until shortly before his death. According to Bill, the CRC for him was like 'a dream come true'. It was large in scale, was founded upon the principle of collaboration, and had an exciting research agenda. Drawing upon Bill's research vision and his ability to form and facilitate multi-disciplinary research teams, the CRC expanded from a relatively small operation in South Eastern Queensland to a national programme involving university, government and industry partners in every state and territory of Australia. Although there was resistance in some areas to the formation of this national research entity, much of this resistance evaporated out of respect for the vision and research expertise of Bill Faulkner. The manner in which Bill was able to harness the research expertise of quite disparate groups and craft exciting research projects to draw upon such intellectual capital was inspiring to those around him. As Deputy CEO and Director of Research, Bill worked at a phenomenal pace; not only inspiring others to work together, but also playing a very active research leadership role in many of the CRC's projects.

Bill's passion was always research, and he had a most eclectic range of research interests. Indeed, one of his big problems was that with such an enquiring mind and creative outlook, if anything, he became involved in too many projects. However, if one had to list his three key research foci, they would be destinations (Chapters 1–3), events (Chapters 4–6) and chaos theory (Chapters 9 and 10). Although it is clear that Bill's role in the CRC as Director of Research was to craft a research agenda (Chapters 13 –15), he still played an active 'hands on' role in research. In this role he led two major projects that will shape future work in the field.

Firstly, Bill masterminded the ambitious 'Gold Coast Visioning Project' (Chapter 3). This project comprised five phases commencing with an audit of the destination's tangible and intangible tourism resources. This was then augmented with an assessment of stakeholder perceptions, and an analysis of broader trends to provide a context. Likely scenarios for the future were then identified, and the project culminated in a visioning workshop in which stakeholders worked together to describe their core vision for Gold Coast tourism over the next 20 years. This project was threatening to many as it involved the need for stakeholders with quite disparate needs and interests to work together. It was largely Bill's ability in this area that held the group together in the early stages of the project. The stakeholder consultation process used in this project will act as a template for other regions.

Secondly, he led a team examining the tourism impacts of the Sydney 2000 Olympic Games (Chapter 6). This is yet another example of the team-based approach to research that Bill was keen to foster, and included a suite of interrelated studies that examined short- and long-term tourism impacts from a range of perspectives. The project broke new ground providing the most comprehensive examination of the Olympics ever conducted, and lays the foundation for future work on the impacts of mega-events.

The Bill Faulkner Legacy

As Bill was a person who became passionately involved in all activities that he undertook, there are few tourism academics in Australia that have not had an association with and benefited from his expertise. Bill's leadership role in CAUTHE gave him a platform to engage with other academics from the time that he joined Griffith University and, in later years, his role in the CRC ensured that he interacted on a daily basis with academics around Australia. Irrespective of how busy he was, Bill was always prepared to spend time with students and academics alike and had that special ability to make the person to whom he was speaking feel special. His manner was never in any way condescending.

During the last 12 months of his life, Bill's poor health forced him to take more time away from the day-to-day activities of the CRC. Although this pained Bill greatly, it afforded him the opportunity to develop his visionary Destination Australia Research Agenda, which establishes a vision for tourism research in Australia over the first 20 years of the new millennium (Chapter 15). The drive for this vision arose during discussions that Bill had with senior management at the Australian Tourist Commission about the problems that Australia could face if the forecasts of inbound tourist numbers to Australia of 20 million by 2020 prove correct. The research vision that Bill created was adopted by the CRC to underpin its application for a second term of government funding. Although his health was declining quickly, Bill was not prepared to let his work stop. He set up his office in his lounge room at home and communicated with colleagues by phone or e-mail. His home became a branch office of the CRC and many meetings were held there when Bill was too ill to travel. When accused of being a workaholic, Bill replied that his work was also his hobby and he needed to pursue his hobby to keep his mind off his illness.

Until three days before his death, Bill refused to give in to the cancer that was devouring him. Even in those last days, with the help of his daughter, Bill contacted via e-mail a number of those colleagues and friends with whom he was most closely associated and tidied up loose ends. A friend and inspiration to many, his legacy lives on through the many colleagues that he mentored and the research agenda that he created. Although so many people have benefited from having known Bill Faulkner, his passing leaves a huge gap in Australia's tourism research capacity. During the eulogy at Bill's funeral, one of those endeavouring to cover some of his CRC tasks commented in relation to Bill's diminutive stature, that 'it was amazing that someone with such small feet would have shoes that are so big to fill'.

It is hoped that through this collection of some of his writing, the vision of Professor Bill Faulkner, the 'father of Australian tourism research', will live on.

Leo Jago, Liz Fredline and Chris Cooper
August 2002

Part 1
Tourism Destination Management

Introduction

Bill Faulkner's focus on destinations underpinned his approach to tourism research and provided a framework that was adopted by many other tourism researchers. This destination focus was apparent in Bill's work from the early 1980s when he was in the Department of Transport Economics and was an important theme until his death in 2002. Indeed, the title of his final contribution to Australia's tourism research agenda, published in late 2001, was 'Destination Australia'. Perhaps the many years that Bill spent working in government encouraged him to take a more macro perspective. He was strongly of the view that tourism must be managed at the destination level and that the performance of individual tourism operators would be influenced by setting appropriate structures at the destination level. A destination framework, Bill considered, encouraged a more holistic approach to tourism than is achieved by considering levels below the destination.

The first chapter in this section was written in 1992 while Bill was Director of the BTR (Bureau of Tourism Research). It examines the evaluation of tourism marketing at the destination level, underlining the great emphasis that Bill placed on the role of evaluation, particularly in relation to marketing. Having seen so many destinations waste enormous sums of money on ineffective marketing campaigns without even realising that the money had been wasted, Bill was a firm believer that all destination marketing programs must have specific and measurable objectives, and that all programs must be evaluated against those objectives after the program has been completed. This chapter describes the purpose and process of evaluation and shows how it applies to tourism promotion and marketing at the destination level.

During the 1990s, the awareness of tourism's economic potential increased substantially and was accompanied by escalating levels of competition between destinations for tourists. National, state and local governments were tending to spend substantially more on destination

marketing, notwithstanding, as Bill points out 'this increased commitment
… to tourism marketing … coincided with a general trend toward greater
fiscal restraint in the policy environment' (Faulkner 1997: 23). This
amplified the imperative to ensure appropriate, effective and efficient
marketing campaigns, which maximised return on investment. As a
consequence of this shift, Bill revised his thinking on evaluation and
applied it specifically to the marketing activities of national tourism
administrations (NTAs). This culminated in the second chapter in this
section.

In this chapter, the issues of 'appropriateness', 'effectiveness' and
'efficiency' have been added as key assessment criteria to the original
model. The chapter provides a thorough review of evaluation techniques
and presents a framework for the evaluation of NTA programs, based
upon the earlier model. In recognising that the substantial lead times
often involved in travel decisions make it difficult to assess the immediate
impact of advertising, the chapter highlights the importance of tracking
studies, conversion studies and market share analysis. Bill originally submitted this chapter to the *Journal of Travel Research* and was disappointed
to receive quite critical reports from referees. Although sorely tempted to
abandon it, after many months Bill decided to rework it taking into
account the reviewer comments. The paper was accepted and subsequently won the prestigious annual best paper award from the *Journal
of Travel Research* for its contribution to both academe and industry. Bill
was delighted with this result and used the story on many occasions to
lift the spirits of his students when they received critical reviews.

The final chapter in this section overviews Bill's most ambitious
destination-based research project, the Gold Coast Visioning Project. For
the past 30 years, the Gold Coast has been one of Australia's premier
tourist locations and there were concerns about the Gold Coast's ability to
meet the future needs of tourists. Bill's vision was to undertake a three-
year multi-disciplinary project that identified the key facilitators and
inhibitors of tourism on the Gold Coast and then to develop a suite of
strategies to assure the sustainability of this destination. The project
included 11 core studies and brought together more than 15 researchers
from a range of universities. In order to achieve a strong sense of ownership of the final result, Bill had to consult with, and coordinate the needs
and interests of four major industry and public sector sponsors and
a multitude of other stakeholders. The engagement process that was
developed as part of this project is now being used around Australia to
prepare destination visions and management plans. It was Bill's vision
and passion that convinced stakeholders to fund the CRC (Cooperative
Research Centre) to undertake this ambitious project and his persever-
ance that kept the project on-track over the three-year period.

Reference

Faulkner, B. (1997) A model for the evaluation of national tourism destination marketing programs. *Journal of Travel Research* 35 (3), 23–32.

Chapter 1

The Anatomy of the Evaluation Process

Bill Faulkner

Background

In developing an approach to the evaluation of specific marketing campaigns one needs to first consider four fundamental questions:

- What are we evaluating?
- Why are we evaluating?
- Who are we evaluating for?
- How are we evaluating?

The details of the approach (i.e. the answer to the last question) will vary according to the answers to the first three questions. However, there are certain ingredients which are fundamentally irrespective of the context of individual evaluations and which therefore provide the building blocks around which a generalised framework for the evaluation process can be structured.

The purpose of this chapter is to describe such a framework and thus address the 'how' question alluded to above. However, before doing so, it is important that we first consider briefly the 'what', 'why' and 'for whom' questions.

These questions will be addressed largely in terms of the application of evaluation procedures to government programs.

What is an Evaluation?

Evaluation is a systematic process for assessing, on the basis of objective evidence:

- The extent to which stated program objectives and priorities match the needs of the clients of the program (i.e. the appropriateness of the program);
- The extent to which the program achieves its objectives (i.e. its effectiveness); and

- The extent to which the program outcomes are achieved at a reasonable cost and within a reasonable time frame (i.e. efficiency).

Why and for whom should evaluations be carried out?

There are two basic reasons for carrying out evaluations – accountability and planning.

Evaluations are necessary for organisations to demonstrate to their stakeholders that they have fulfilled their functions appropriately, efficiently and effectively. In the public sector, the stakeholders include the responsible minister, parliament and, ultimately, the public in general. With deteriorating economic conditions and associated government policy settings aimed at containing public sector outlays, the need to rigorously account for, and justify, program expenditures has been accentuated.

Apart from the external factors which demand that evaluations be carried out, it is also being increasingly realised that evaluations should be an integral part of an organisation's management and planning process. On-going systematic evaluation procedures are necessary for ensuring that the most effective and efficient means of achieving corporate goals are adopted and thus provide a rational basis for resource allocation. This role of evaluation is being increasingly emphasised in the rationale for program evaluations:

> The case for undertaking program evaluation rests upon it improving the information base upon which managers take decisions. Program evaluation assists managers to refine program objectives and identify cost-effective options. It helps clarify program management information requirements, and to check that programs are achieving what they were set up to achieve. It helps managers prove the performance of their programs and justify their resource requirements.

A framework for the evaluation process

The basic ingredients of the evaluation process can be described in terms of the four overlapping segments identified in Figure 1.1:

- Program review
- Monitoring
- Causal analysis
- Cost-benefit assessment

Each of these areas is described separately below.

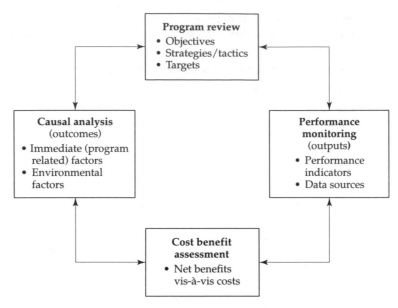

Figure 1.1 Framework for the evaluation of tourism promotion and marketing

Program Review

Objectives: what is the program meant to achieve?

In a tourism promotion and advertising program this would conceivably be, in general:

- to increase the level of visitation to the destination(s) concerned above to that which would have been experienced otherwise.

The time period over which a program aims to achieve this could be an important factor in the evaluation as not all programs can realistically expect to achieve immediate results.

The objectives of the program need themselves to be examined in the evaluation process in order to establish whether or not they are appropriate. If the stated objectives are inconsistent with the role or charter of the organisation, then the rationale of the program in question is obviously fundamentally flawed irrespective of how effective it has been.

Strategies/Tactics

What methods or approach have been adopted to achieve the objectives outlined above? This may involve a range of activities, or tactics, integrated to provide an overall strategy, e.g.

- a program of electronic and/or print media advertisements;
- the above supplemented by a toll-free information service;
- the distribution of pamphlets (distributed through the toll-free mechanism, direct mailing and/or travel centre outlets);
- organisation of, or participation in, trade shows;
- development of sales kits.

Targets

What outcomes are required if the program is to be considered a success? These may be expressed in such terms as:

- maintenance of or increase in market share;
- an increase in the representation of a particular market segment;
- an increase in awareness of, and/or interest in, the tourism product.

Monitoring

Performance indicators

How can the achievement of, or progress towards, the targets be objectively measured? This is, in effect, an operational definition of objectives and targets. In the context of tourism marketing, this requires the specification of the units for quantifying market share, awareness, etc.

Data sources (methods of data collection)

What sources of data can and will be relied upon for the evaluation? The specification of performance indicators also requires the nomination of existing sources of data which will be used to monitor progress towards targets and/or vehicles for collecting data which will be put in place. Existing sources, which might be used to measure, for instance, market share, include the Australian International Visitors Survey and Domestic Tourism Monitor. To monitor increases and awareness and inclination to travel to the destination in question, special tracking and conversion studies would need to be put into place.

An important consideration in the monitoring of impacts is the time horizon required to put in place instruments for measuring changes in attitudes/preferences and levels of activity. Not only is it necessary to allow sufficient lead times to develop and test survey instruments, but also these should ideally be in place well in advance of the program's initiation so that a before and after assessment can be made. In reality, this is seldom done because the evaluation process has not been generally viewed as an integral part of programs.

Causal analysis

A positive correlation between marketing or promotion initiatives and market trends is not, in itself, proof of a causal relationship. A range of factors which are quite independent of those under the control of the campaign have the potential to influence travel simultaneously. These need to be identified and factored into any assessment of the program. This phase of the evaluation therefore involves two steps:

- Assessment of the impact of immediate program related factors; and
- Identification and analysis of broader environmental factors which have the potential to impact on visitor numbers.

Immediate (program related) factors

In essence, most tourism marketing and promotion campaigns aim to influence consumers' predisposition to visit a destination, with the ultimate objective being to ensure that this is translated into actual visitation. Two aspects of the market's response therefore need to be measured if any direct link between the campaign and identifiable outcomes is to be established:

- Tracking and conversion studies are necessary to monitor changes in awareness, interest, preferences and intentions that may be attributable to campaign exposure; and
- Interception of actual visitors is necessary to establish the extent to which their decision to visit the destination was in fact motivated by changes in awareness, interest, etc. brought about by the campaign. It needs to also be established how important the influence of the campaign was relative to broader environmental factors.

Environmental factors

As noted previously, any change in the market's response which co-incides with a promotional or marketing campaign needs to be considered in the context of broader environmental factors which may also have a bearing on propensities and capacities to travel. The propensity or inclination to travel in a particular market, at a particular point in time, is dependent upon a combination of social and economic conditions which vary in the degree to which they can be quantified.

Relevant social conditions range from prevailing attitudes and tastes affecting holiday choices to more variable (in time) levels of consumer confidence, which in turn tend to reflect prevailing economic conditions, unemployment levels, etc. Also, the political climate at home or abroad can have a profound effect on the willingness to, or preferred destination of, travel.

Economic conditions in general affect both the capacity to travel, through disposable incomes, and the affordability of travel. The latter is governed by such factors as relative inflation rates and exchange rates. Economic conditions which have a more direct bearing on propensities to travel include such items as the availability of air services, fare levels, accommodation rates, etc.

Cost-benefit assessment

The bottom line in any evaluation is to establish and, if possible, quantify the net benefits arising from the program in question. If these benefits exceed the cost of the program, then it can be argued that the cost has been justified and the approach adopted is basically sound. However, as the relative contribution of specific factors influencing the outcome cannot necessarily all be quantified, it may be necessary to adopt a 'weight of evidence' approach.

Chapter 2

A Model for the Evaluation of National Tourism Destination Marketing Programs

Bill Faulkner

The increasing commitment of national governments to the funding of their tourism administrations' marketing activities abroad has been accompanied by demands for more rigorous evaluations of the effectiveness of these activities. More rigorous and comprehensive approaches to evaluation are also required to furnish a more solid foundation for strategic decision making. However, many evaluations to date have been ad hoc in the sense that they have relied on one or two techniques that address only part of the problem. A framework for systematically integrating a range of techniques is proposed as a way to overcome this deficiency while an alternative approach to market share analysis is described in an effort to add to the battery of techniques in this field.

With the emergence of tourism as a major growth sector in the global economy, national governments have become increasingly aware of the role this industry can play in enhancing a country's trade performance. Many have thus sought to improve their competitive position with respect to the international tourism market by either increasing funding allocations to their existing national tourism administration (NTA) or establishing and funding such bodies. Given the number and diversity of private sector concerns usually involved in the delivery of tourism product, NTA activities in general have involved a considerable emphasis on developing a coordinated approach to promoting their destination abroad. The fundamental objective of the NTA in this process, and the main parameter by which its performance is ultimately judged, is to increase the country's market share beyond that which might otherwise have been achieved.

The increased commitment of many governments to tourism marketing, however, has coincided with a general trend toward greater fiscal restraint in the policy environment. As a consequence, NTAs are under increasing pressure to carry out more systematic and rigorous evaluations of their activities so that the investment of public funds can be fully justified in terms of outcomes and competing priorities (WTO 1994). The stakeholders in this process are not just the government and the general public to whom it is ultimately accountable, but also the industry constituency with whom the NTA is working. This is particularly so where the NTA is involved in cooperative marketing programs with industry partners.

In one sense, evaluation can be construed as a tool for ensuring accountability in the use of public resources at a national level and, in this regard, it is in the NTAs' interest to develop credible methodologies for demonstrating their contribution simply because continued funding depends on them doing so. However, well-structured evaluation procedures also have an important internal role to play by virtue of the contribution they can make to the organization's ongoing planning and management processes. The introduction of systematic evaluation procedures as a routine component of an organization's activities provides a framework for monitoring and assessing its performance with respect to the environment within which it operates and a rational basis for the identification of priorities and allocation of resources. Evaluation keeps an organization in touch with changes in its environment and its performance with respect to this environment and is thus an essential prerequisite for responsiveness and adaptability.

Therefore, evaluation is important both as a proactive means of providing information for rational decision making and as a retrospective means of assessing the outcomes of decisions and their associated programs (Stufflebeam and Shinkfield 1985). This dual purpose of evaluation (i.e., accountability and management information enhancement) has been emphasized in national government guidelines on program evaluation (e.g., Australian Government Department of Finance 1989) and noted specifically in the tourism context by Burke and Lindblom (1989) and Davidson and Wiethaupt (1989). Meanwhile, the external pressures mentioned previously, combined with the growing recognition of strategic management requirements, have been instrumental in the growing interest in evaluation research in the tourism field noted by Cook and Azucenas (1994).

One of the problems confronting NTAs wishing to incorporate more rigorous evaluation procedures in their planning and management is that, in the tourism context, evaluation is of necessity a multilayered process. It is multilayered first because NTAs are generally engaged in a range of activities that are each intended to play a role in a loosely connected chain of events leading to decisions by consumers to visit a destination. A multilayered approach is also necessary because, at this stage, there is no single approach that can unequivocally substantiate and quantify the impact of tourism marketing programs on visitor numbers and, indeed, the limitations of individual approaches suggests that a combination of methods needs to be applied so that a composite picture can be produced. Another related problem arises from the complexity of the research necessary to investigate linkages between program initiatives and the market's response and the difficulties this creates in the translation of research into meaningful management information.

These problems imply that action is required on three fronts. First, a framework for structuring the evaluation process needs to be developed to enable relationships between individual facets of the process to be understood and to facilitate the application of a range of techniques in a way that enables their individual strengths and weaknesses to be appreciated. Second, the battery of available techniques needs to be expanded so that a range of techniques that are complementary in terms of their respective strengths and limitations can be applied. Finally, it is important that methods for presenting and explaining the information produced by these techniques be improved to make them more useful to decision makers.

This article takes a step toward addressing each of these requirements. After clarifying the principles, underlying dimensions, and structure of the evaluation process, a broad framework for evaluating tourism destination marketing programs is proposed. An alternative approach to assessing market performance outcomes is then described to add to the range of techniques available. This approach uses graphical techniques that enable the performance of individual countries in specific markets to be more readily compared.

The Dimensions and Structure of the Evaluation Process

As emphasized in public sector documents on the subject, evaluation can be simply defined as a systematic process for objectively assessing an organization's (or program's) performance (New South Wales Office of Public Management 1991). Three key criteria are used to assess an organization's (or program's) performance in this process.

(1) Appropriateness (i.e., the extent to which stated program objectives and priorities match the needs of clients and stakeholders);
(2) Effectiveness (i.e., the extent to which the program achieves its objectives); and
(3) Efficiency (i.e., the extent to which the program outcomes are achieved at a reasonable cost and within a reasonable time frame).

The basic ingredients of the evaluation process involve the four overlapping procedures described in Figure 2.1, where the appropriateness question is addressed mainly in the program review stage and effectiveness is assessed on the basis of examining outputs and outcomes in Stages 2 and 3. In these stages, one of the most challenging methodological issues concerns the establishment of causal linkages between the immediate impacts of the NTA's initiatives and the market's response. This issue is considered further in the next section. The bottom line in any evaluation is to establish and, if possible, quantify the net benefits of the program in question. However, as Hunt (1991) emphasizes, the general nature of NTA activities complicates this process:

> Measuring return on investment for governmental or public tourism organisations is complicated because most are unable to be particularly product-specific or narrow in their marketing efforts. Most of these organisations are required to develop and promote a rather generic or general destination product comprised of a large package of diverse products, services and attractions over which they have little or no control. (p. 2)

The appropriateness issue, specifically, requires some consideration at this stage because this helps define the orientation of NTA program activities and thus the focus of the discussion that follows. Most NTAs would view their overriding mission as being to boost their country's foreign exchange earnings by increasing its share of the international tourism market. However, a mission such as this is subject to several qualifications.

First, the focus on increasing international tourism market share

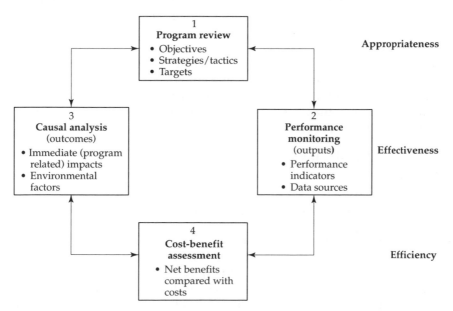

Figure 2.1 The structure of the evaluation process
Source: Faulkner (1992).

usually means that NTA activities tend to be preoccupied with promotional aspects of marketing to the exclusion of a broader marketing and management role (March 1994). However, there are inevitably situations where continuing growth of visitor numbers is inappropriate because the limits of the destination's social or environmental carrying capacity is being approached and, as a consequence, further increases are neither in the interest of the community nor consistent with long-term sustainability of the tourism industry (Cooke 1982; Getz 1994; Inskeep 1991; Woodley 1993; Zehnder 1976). This consideration has been recognized in the charter of some NTAs (e.g., the Australian Tourist Commission 1991), where responsibility for the minimization of adverse environmental and social impacts of international tourism is included.

Second, NTA international market share targets are generally expressed in terms of visitor numbers, even though a country's income from tourism can be increased by means other than simply increasing the number of visitors. Indeed, there is a strong case for using indicators other than this as a basis for evaluating results. Paraskevopoulos (1977), for instance, suggests that visitor nights is a more basic parameter for tourism demand, while O'Hagan and Harrison (1984) propose that the ultimate basis for measuring economic outcomes is clearly tourist expenditure. However, as comparable visitor expenditure data across many markets and destinations are not usually available, most discussion on international demand patterns is in terms of tourist numbers (Barry and O'Hagan 1972). Visitor numbers are thus emphasized in the following discussion, despite the limitations of this measure.

The application of the evaluation process described in Figure 2.1 to the NTA situation is outlined in the framework described in Figure 2.2. Here, a range of strategies that are commonly employed by NTAs are identified (Stage 1), along with corresponding performance or output indicators (Stage 2). Some of the issues associated with the analysis of outcomes are explored in the next section.

The Analysis of Outcomes

A meaningful evaluation of the NTA's overall marketing effectiveness eventually requires some conclusions to be drawn about the extent to which the market's response is actually attributable to the organization's actions. A positive relationship between marketing initiatives described in terms of the (Stage 2) outputs and favorable market trends (immediate impacts) is not, in itself, proof of a causal relationship. As emphasized by Hunt (1991), a range of factors that are quite independent of those under the control of the NTA and its various strategies have the potential to influence travel simultaneously. These need to be identified and factored into the assessment of the NTA's program. This phase of the evaluation might, therefore, involve two steps:

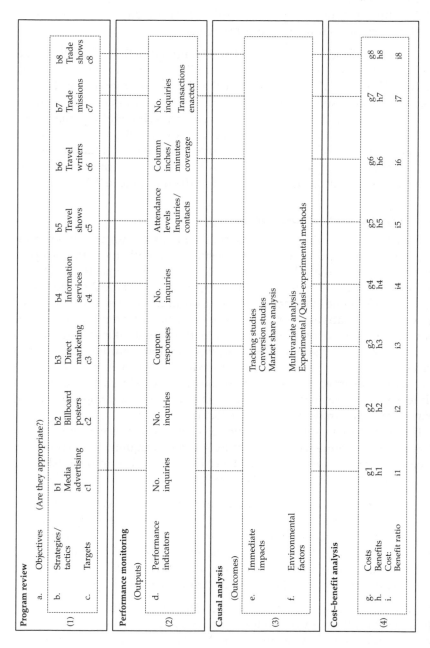

Figure 2.2 A framework for the evaluation of NTA programs

(1) Assessment of the impact of immediate program related factors (i.e., as identified by the output measures described in Figure 2.2); and
(2) Identification and analysis of broader environmental factors that have the potential to impact visitor numbers.

Most of the methods currently used and identified in Stage 3 of the framework (i.e., tracking studies, conversion studies, and market share analysis) are limited in terms of the second of the above requirements and, therefore, need to be used in conjunction with other methods (such as multivariate analysis and experimental or quasi-experimental approaches) if causal relationships are to be established. An examination of these aspects of evaluation research sharpens the appreciation of the limitations associated with these methods and, in the process, reinforces the argument for a multilayered approach such as that described in Figure 2.2.

Tracking and conversion studies

In the first instance, tourism marketing campaigns aim to influence the consumer's predisposition to visit a destination, while the ultimate objective is to ensure that this is translated into actual visitation. Output performance indicators, such as those referred to in Stage 2 of the framework, provide some evidence of the exposure and response levels achieved by various initiatives, but they provide little information about the influence these have on the consumer. Methods that take us a step closer to understanding these impacts include tracking studies, conversion studies, and market share analyses. Tracking and conversion studies are, in essence, concerned with identifying the immediate impacts of programs, while market share analysis is concerned more with isolating shifts in the marketplace that may or may not reflect these impacts.

Tracking studies attempt to monitor changes in the markets' awareness, interest, preference, and intentions as a consequence of exposure to advertising campaigns. The importance of such studies in the evaluation process is highlighted by Davidson (1994):

> In essence, the science of predicting human behavior – of which advertising evaluation research is a branch – is at best imprecise. The relationship between message and a change in the mind set is more direct and easier to study; and if the effect of advertising begins in the potential customer's mind then advertising evaluation research should also begin in the potential customer's mind. (p. 538)

Davidson also draws attention to the tendency of evaluation research to often focus on the immediate impact tourism advertising has on awareness of, and interest in, a destination, rather than on the final sales achieved. He attributes this to two factors that emphasize both the strengths and limitations of tracking studies.

(1) The lead times involved in travel decisions mean that the impact of advertising often takes a long time to be expressed. More immediate feedback on the effectiveness of the program is often required and tracking studies serve this purpose; and

(2) The final decision to travel to a destination is influenced by many other factors apart from the advertisement.

On the role of tracking studies, Siegel and Ziff-Levine (1994) therefore conclude that:

> It is only rarely that definitive conclusions can be drawn about the impact of advertising on travel behavior. Instead, tracking research is more valuable, from a diagnostic perspective, in pin-pointing the strengths and weaknesses of a campaign for the fine-tuning of creative development and media buying. (p. 563)

In finally assessing the impact of a campaign on the bottom line (i.e. increased volume of visitors), tracking studies play a necessary, but not sufficient, role. They are necessary if the first link in the causal chain is to be verified, but a change in the predisposition of the market toward a particular destination does not necessarily translate into actual trips.

Conversion studies can be seen as taking the evaluation process a step further, to the extent that they provide an estimate of the proportion of those responding to advertisement who actually travel to the destination. Considerable emphasis has been placed on the use of conversion studies as a basis for evaluating tourism advertising campaigns (Mok 1990). A common approach is linked with advertising campaigns where there is a direct response component that involves providing additional inform-ation to the public through mail coupons or toll-free telephone calls. This enables the researcher to contact respondents to ascertain the extent to which advertising material was, in fact, instrumental in stimulating their travel to the destination. Alternatively, random samples of the relevant population are carried out.

Many authors have drawn attention to methodological deficiencies in the application of conversion studies to the tourism field (e.g., Ballman *et al.* 1984; Burke and Gitelson 1990; Burke and Lindblom 1989; Davidson 1994; Ellerbrock 1981; Hunt and Dalton 1983; Mok 1990; Siegel and Ziff-Levine 1994; Sunday 1975; Woodside 1981, 1990), and several others have highlighted the tendency of the methods used to exaggerate the impact of the advertising program (Ballman *et al.* 1984; Ellerbrock 1981; Hunt and Dalton 1983; Woodside 1981). Common deficiencies itemized by Ballman *et al.* (1984) and later by Mok (1990) include:

(1) The failure to use proper sampling techniques and a tendency not to take the implications of sampling error into account in the interpretation of results.

(2) The failure to allow for the effect of non-response bias. As those who visit a destination are more inclined to respond to a survey than those who have not (Ellerbrock 1981), the lower the response rate the higher the potential for an inflated measure of conversion rates. The extent of inflation due to this factor has been estimated to be as high as 40 to 50% (Ballman *et al*. 1984; Hunt and Dalton 1983).

(3) In conversion studies associated with destination information services, there has been a tendency not to factor out those respondents who had decided to visit the destination prior to being exposed to the advertisements and for whom the advertisements simply facilitated the collection of information for planning purposes. Again, this results in conversion rates being inflated and, according to Ballman *et al*. (1984), highlights the need to put advertising effects into the context of various extraneous sources of information that influence decisions (e.g., word of mouth, relatives and friends who live at potential destinations, media news and events); and

(4) Failure to include all costs associated with the development of advertising campaigns.

With these limitations in mind, Burke and Lindblom (1989) and Burke and Gitelson (1990) have concluded that conversion studies provide useful diagnostic information for the destination marketer, but they are potentially misleading if relied on to produce figures on the return on investment.

Multivariate analysis

Multivariate analysis has the potential to provide the foundation to assess return on investment by providing the ability to identify and quantify the relative impact of a range of factors. Any change in the market's response coinciding with a promotional campaign or more general marketing initiatives needs to be considered in the context of broader environmental factors, which may also have a bearing on propensities and capacities to travel. The inclination to travel in a particular market at any point in time is dependent on a combination of social and economic conditions that vary in the degree to which they can be quantified.

Relevant social conditions range from prevailing social mores, attitudes, and tastes affecting holiday choices to more variable (in time) levels of consumer confidence, which in turn tend to reflect economic conditions, unemployment levels, and the political climate at home and abroad. In addition, events such as the Chernobyl disaster, the Gulf War, and various Olympic Games have demonstrated how ephemeral political, environmental, and hallmark events can have profound short-term effects on patterns of world travel (Faulkner 1990).

Among the range of factors that have a bearing on travel, economic factors have probably been the most systematically investigated and, as a consequence, their influence is arguably better understood. Economic conditions, in general, affect both the capacity to travel through their impact on disposable incomes and the affordability of travel. The latter is governed by such factors as relative inflation and exchange rates. Economic conditions that potentially have a more direct bearing on propensities to travel include those that affect such items as the availability of air services, fare levels, and accommodation rates.

In their review of more than 50 studies that have attempted to model international tourist movements over the past 30 years. Crouch and Shaw (1990) and Crouch (1994) have noted the general dependence on econometric and, to a lesser extent, gravity model approaches. According to Crouch (1994). the most frequently analyzed independent variables have been income levels (in 89% of studies), tourism product price levels (70%), costs of transportation (58%), and exchange rates (33%). Special events and terrorist incidents were incorporated as dummy variables in 58% of the studies examined. Although the possible influence of marketing variables (e.g., expenditure on marketing programs) has been frequently acknowledged, as Witt and Martin (1987) note, few studies have actually attempted to take this factor into account. Among those studies that have, however, the results have been inconclusive.

Uysal (1983) and Uysal and Crompton (1984) analyzed the impact of promotional expenditure by the Turkish Ministry of Tourism and Culture and concluded that, relative to other determinants of demand, promotional expenditure appeared to have minimal effect on tourist flows to that country. In their study of promotional effects on British tourism to Ireland, Barry and O'Hagan (1972) concluded that income and price were more important, while Uysal and O'Leary (1986) arrived at a similar conclusion in their analysis of tourism in Yugoslavia and Greece. On the other hand, Papadopoulos (1987) concluded that promotional expenditure by the Greek National Tourist Organization did have an impact on tourist arrivals, although the strength of this impact varied among the major markets. Similarly, Crouch, Schultz, and Valerio (1992) cite Clark (1978) as concluding that the impact of the Barbados promotional effort varied according to the class of hotel and origin of visitors.

Witt and Martin's (1987) critique of several of the above studies drew attention to such problems as the exclusion of potentially important explanatory variables (especially costs), multi-collinearity of data, and inaccuracies associated with the derivation of marketing expenditures. It was also noted that as promotional programs have impacts over periods beyond the units of time used for analytical purposes, the isolation of these effects is compounded. A similar problem has been referred to in relation to the interpretation of shift share analysis in the previous section.

In a more recent study, which included marketing expenditure among the variables used to model international visitor flows to Australia, Crouch, Schultz, and Valerio (1992) concluded that the international marketing of the Australian Tourist Commission played a statistically significant role in influencing inbound tourism to that country. However, the authors also emphasized that statistically significant relationships, such as those revealed by regression analyses, do not necessarily imply causal linkages. Industry Canada (1994) has since adopted a similar approach to the analysis of Tourism Canada's advertising programs and concluded that advertising has had a small but significant effect on the U.S. and Japanese markets.

In a non-econometric approach involving a comparison of 15 NTAs actively engaged in promotions in the U.S. market, Hunt (1991) noted that in general those with above average marketing expenditure achieved better growth rates in their share of this market. A similar, earlier study in the same market by Sunday (1975) concluded that the effect of advertising seemed quite small when compared with the array of factors that influence tourism. The same author, however, also observed that as the absolute magnitude invested by the individual countries concerned was relatively small, the amount invested could be justified by a very small number of additional visitors.

Experimental and quasi-experimental design

The myriad of external factors that impinge on the market's response, along with the interaction of specific promotions with other elements of the marketing mix (Park, Roth and Jacques 1988), highlights the complexities associated with the effort to link specific NTA initiatives with changes in the destination's performance. Under these circumstances, the experimental or quasi-experimental methodologies are potentially the more convincing approach to establishing cause and effect relationships.

To prove that a tourism marketing program has actually been responsible for a positive response in the market, it is necessary to demonstrate that the program preceded the supposed changes in the market, that the supposed cause and effect co-vary, and no alternative explanations of the effect exist apart from the assumed cause (Posavac and Carey 1992). The combination of methods described above satisfies the first two criteria, but is generally deficient with respect to the last one. Greater internal validity can only be achieved by adopting an experimental or quasi-experimental approach with the ability to:

(1) Observe individuals in the marketplace both before and after the implementation of the program in question;
(2) Observe additional people (i.e., control groups) who have not been exposed to the program; and

(3) Take into account a wide variety of variables to ensure that other factors with the potential to influence responses can be detected.

Experimental and quasi-experimental approaches involve a level of control that enables all three of the above conditions to be observed, with the main distinction between the two approaches being that the latter does not involve the random assignment of individuals to treatment and nontreatment groups (Cook and Campbell 1979).

Woodside (1990) has advocated the application of experimental methods to evaluate tourism marketing campaigns and has, in particular, argued that experimental design principles should routinely be built into marketing plans so that their impacts can be properly assessed. This approach draws on the principles of Caples' (1974) tested advertising methods, which have been applied more generally. In his evaluation of the effectiveness of Hawaii's print media destination advertising in 13 U.S. midwestern states, Woodside attempted to factor out extraneous effects by adopting a "quasi-experimental" approach involving comparisons with 16 other (non-targeted) states. He concluded that the program affected demand for trips to Hawaii only slightly, and the retentive effect was only evident after the second advertising campaign.

One problem associated with quasi-experimental design in this context is that the targeting of areas for promotion is itself influenced by an assessment of the likely responsiveness of populations in these areas, which in turn compounds comparisons with control groups in non-targeted areas. As Cook and Campbell (1979) observe, the challenge "confronting the persons who try to interpret the results from quasi-experiments is basically one of separating the effects of a treatment from those due to the initial incomparability between the average units in each treatment group" (p. 6).

Cost-benefit analysis

As emphasized earlier, the bottom line in any evaluation is, ultimately, the cost-benefit ratio achieved by the program. A useful overview of the issues involved in this aspect of the process is provided by Dwyer and Forsyth (1995). For the purposes of this study, it is sufficient to note that cost-benefit ratios have been produced at the broader level (i.e., with respect to advertising expenditures in general) in the form of elasticities derived from some regression analyses. Here, advertising expenditures were included as an explanatory variable (e.g., Crouch, Schultz and Valerio 1992; Industry Canada 1994; Papadopoulos and Witt 1985; Uysal and Crompton 1984). However, in view of the difficulties encountered in isolating and quantifying the final effects of individual strategies, it appears that the derivation of cost-benefit ratios to the degree depicted in the final phase of the figure is far from being achievable at this stage.

Market Share Analysis

As noted in previous sections, the role of market share analysis in the evaluation process is central as an indicator of the extent to which the NTA has achieved its fundamental objective, but it is limited as a basis for attributing outcomes specifically to the NTA's actions. Nevertheless, this form of analysis provides a useful basis for monitoring the performance of a destination vis-à-vis competitors and particular target markets and, in this sense, it also provides valuable diagnostic information for strategic planning. This is especially so when used in conjunction with other methods referred to in the framework.

Indices based on rankings provide a broad indication of the relative effectiveness of an NTAs programs, but there are several reasons for caution in the way they should be interpreted. First, the relative position of a destination is often largely a reflection of geographical and historical factors that are outside the control of the NTA and its programs. Second, partly for the same reason, infrastructure and/or carrying capacity constraints may put a ceiling on how far up in the rankings a particular destination should rise. Finally, in any case, it is not so much the destination's ranking at a particular point in time that is important, but rather the progress it makes over a period of time.

Following on from the last point, it would seem that what is required is an index that reflects the dynamics of the marketplace and changes in the destination's performance with respect to this market, while at the same time allowing for the "givens" that place broad limits on the destination's overall competitiveness. Toward this end, an approach analogous to shift-share analysis of regional economics is promising.

Shift-share analysis was originally widely applied during the 1960s to compare the economic development of regions vis-à-vis a larger reference group comprising the national or global economies (Houston 1967). Historically, this form of analysis has concentrated on supply side factors, such as employment, manufacturing output, and income (e.g., Andrikopolous, Bronx and Carvalho 1990; Beck and Herr 1990; Ledebur and Moomav 1983; Tervo and Okko 1983), as it has in the one application to tourism by Sirakaya, Uysal, and Toepper (1995). By contrast, since the focus of this article is on market share trends, this application will have a demand side emphasis.

The main strength of the shift-share approach with respect to the assessment of a destination's performance is that it depicts outcomes in terms of the change in market share achieved, and this is viewed in the context of overall change in the market. In addition, by focusing on change over a period of time, rather than by providing a snapshot as in the case of most other indices, the possibility of ephemeral or random events distorting the picture is reduced. Indeed, Vanhove and Klaassen

(1987) emphasize the importance of applying techniques such as shift-share analysis over a period of time to ensure that enduring trends can be isolated. Finally, long-term trends in the level and profile of international visitors are used as a basis for factoring in limits imposed by the geographical and historical context. This is not intended to imply that these limits are insurmountable. They merely allow comparisons to be made within realistic "aspiration levels".

For the purposes of explaining and illustrating this application of the shift-share approach, the following discussion will refer to visitor numbers only as a basis for analysis, even though this approach can be just as readily based on the other parameters. In general, data considerations make the definition of markets in terms of visitor numbers and country of origin most convenient, although as noted previously, other criteria (e.g., nights, expenditure, age, sex, purpose of trip, psychographic orientation) might be equally or more relevant for marketing purposes.

As implied by the term "shift-share," the primary objective of the approach is twofold:

(1) To enable a destination's position with respect to its share of a particular market to be established; and
(2) To provide an indication of the extent to which the destination is improving its position with respect to a particular market relative to overall movements in that market.

There are, therefore, two dimensions of the analysis:

(1) An index of market share with respect to each major market. To neutralize the scale of the destination's overall involvement in international tourism, this dimension is expressed in terms of a "market bias index" (B), which reflects the degree to which the destination's market share, with respect to a particular market, deviates from its share of visitors overall. The derivation of this index is as follows:

$$
B_{ik} = \frac{\left[X_{ijk} \Big/ \sum_{i=1}^{n} X_{ijk} \right] - 1.0}{\left[\sum_{j=1}^{n} X_{ij(k)n} \Big/ \sum_{i=j}^{} \sum_{j=i}^{} X_{ij(k)n} \right]}
$$

where

B_{ik} = Market bias index for destination i in year k,
X_{ijk} = Visitor numbers to destination i from market j in year k, and
n = Number of markets (origin) and destinations.

(Alternatively, B_{ik} can be described in the following terms: B_{ik} = Destination is market share with respect to market j in year k × 100/Destination is total market share with respect to all markets, j . . . n, in year k.)

Thus, if destination share of a particular market (j) is on a par with its share of visitors overall, $B_{ij} = 0$. If its share of another market (l) exceeds what would be received on a pro rata basis, then $B_{ij} > 0$.

The market bias index complements Hudman's country potential generation index (Hudman 1979, 1980; Hudman and Davis 1994) in the sense that where the latter is concerned with the relative propensity of a country to generate trips, the market bias index looks at the relative importance of a particular country of origin from the receiving country's point of view.

(2) An index of change (C) in the visitors received from each market relative to the change in that market overall.

$$C = \left[\left(X_{ijk} / X_{ij1} \right) - 1 \right] - \left[\left(X_{jk} / X_{j1} \right) - 1 \right]$$

where

Xijk   = Visitor numbers to destination i from market j in year k.
Xjk   = Total outbound visitors from market j in year k, and
1 . . . k = Years 1988 (1) to 1992 (k).

(Alternatively, B_{ik} can be described in the following terms: Bik = Destination is market share with respect to market j in year k × 100/Destination is total market share with respect to all markets, j . . . n, in year k.)

If the destination in question achieves a growth rate for market (V) that is consistent with the growth of that market overall, then $C_{ij} = 0$. If the growth achieved by the destination with respect to another market (0) exceeds the growth of that market overall. then $C_{il} > 0$.

To illustrate this approach to market share analysis, indices have been calculated for the top 40 countries in terms of tourism promotional expenditure as indicated by the WTO's survey of NTA budgets (WTO 1994). For the purposes of this exercise, it is assumed that these countries account for the whole international tourism market, whereas in fact they account for 87%. The change index is based on the average annual change over the period 1988 to 1992, while the reference year for the market bias index is 1992. There may be some merit in also using average annual figures for the latter index, as this would alleviate any problems associated with the sensitivity of the analysis to the base year used. However, there is also value in relying on the most recent picture of the market bias profile to assess the situation.

The potential value of these two indices in assisting in the assessment of an NTA's performance with respect to a range of markets lies in the way the results can be graphically represented. In Figure 2.3, Australia's status vis-à-vis the various markets is plotted on a graph that has the market bias index (B) on the horizontal axis and the change index (C) on the vertical axis. Within this framework, markets can be classified in the following way:

(1) Performing markets (Quadrant I: +B, +C), where the country's share of the market in question exceeds its overall share of the total market and where it has achieved a higher than average growth rate for this market;
(2) Emerging markets (Quadrant II: −B, +C), where an above average growth in the market has been achieved, but the share of this market still falls behind that expected on a pro rata basis;
(3) Declining markets (Quadrant III: +B, −C), where market share exceeds the pro rata level, but this position is being eroded by lower than average growth; and
(4) Stagnant markets (Quadrant IV: −B, −C), where the market share is below the pro rata level, and this situation is exacerbated by lower than average growth.

The presentation of the market share analysis in this format highlights the parallels between this approach and the applications of portfolio analysis to tourism by Calantone and Mazanec (1991) and McKercher (1995). Calantone and Mazanec plotted country of origin markets to a destination according to growth rate on the vertical axis and relative market share on the horizontal axis to produce a classification of markets comparable with that provided in Figure 2.3. The main differences between the two approaches are that the market bias and change indices referred to previously are modified to reflect relative position of the destination in the global market as a whole and the performance of different destinations can be more readily compared.

As far as Australia is concerned, Figure 2.3 reveals that Japan stands out as the market in which the best results have been achieved, while Australia's relatively strong historical position as a destination for the U.K. market has been maintained. On the other hand, Australia's position with respect to some of the other markets is more problematic. The WTO's survey of NTA budgets (WTO 1994) indicates that priority in the allocation of Australia's tourism promotional budget in 1991 was given to the United States, Europe, Asia, Japan, and the United Kingdom, respectively. The positions in the graph of the U.S. and European markets in particular, and to a less extent the Other Asia market, suggest a less than satisfactory outcome. However, some caution needs to be exercised in the interpretation of these results, because much of the reference period associated with the indices predates 1991 and allowance needs to be made for a gestation period for promotional effects. On the other hand, it is also relevant to note that Australia targeted the U.S. and European markets over much of the period from 1988 to 1992. The interpretation of analyses such as those presented in Figure 2.3 also need to take into account instances where resource allocation in the NTA concerned is motivated by strategic decisions aimed at arresting the stagnation of important markets. Whether this is an appropriate response is, of course, open to debate. Apart from these considerations, the discussion elsewhere in this article highlights the need to examine market share patterns in the context of a range of indicators before a proper understanding of their implications can be developed.

The graphical representation of indices also provides a useful basis for comparing a country's performance in relation to a specific market with that of competitors who have also targeted this market. This can be done by plotting the indices for the target market registered by the countries

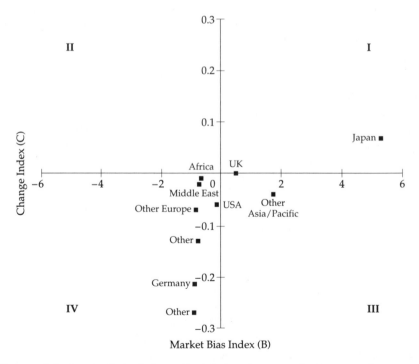

Figure 2.3 Australia's international tourism marketing performance, 1988–92

concerned on one graph. Thus, in Figure 2.4, the performance of countries that have assigned first or second priority to the U.S. market in the allocation of promotional funds (WTO 1994, Table 8) is compared with others.

Notwithstanding the above cautionary note regarding the gestation period for promotional effects and strategic considerations, the results are nevertheless somewhat disconcerting. Historically, those countries targeting the U.S. market have generally not been performing any better than the remainder. Indeed, if anything, the opposite is the case. However, it appears that Mexico has succeeded in consolidating its obvious geographical advantage with respect to the market, while China has gained ground. China, however, still has less than a pro rata share of the market. Although Canada, Bermuda, and Barbados each enjoy a relatively high market share by virtue of their geographical proximity, it appears that they are losing ground. It also appears that Greece, Switzerland, Italy, Portugal, and Australia have all registered mediocre results over the reference period, despite the priority they have each assigned to the U.S. market.

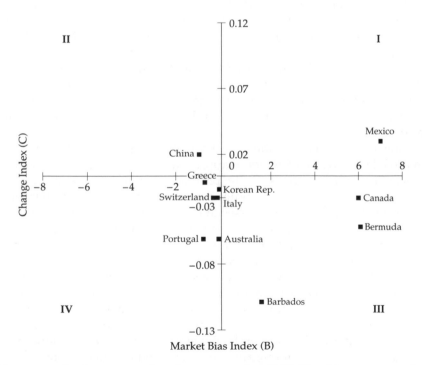

Figure 2.4 Performance of various countries 1988–92 with respect to the U.S. market

Conclusion

The range of activities in which NTAs engage constitutes just a few of the extensive array of factors that affect international tourism flows. Some of these factors are quantifiable and have thus been taken into account in conventional forms of analysis. However, many potentially important variables are excluded from analysis because adequate data are not available and/or they are simply not quantifiable. Those analyses that have been carried out have, therefore, been able to isolate the impacts of advertising and other contributing factors in a partial sense only, and attempts to identify the relative contribution of the NTAs' programs have been frustrated by this problem.

The process of attributing market trends to the actions of NTAs is further complicated by the fact that many of the variables influencing tourists' decisions in general, and the attractiveness of the destination in particular, are simply beyond the NTA's control. Therefore, whatever criteria are adopted as indicators of success in the marketplace, extreme caution must be exercised in the extent to which outcomes are attributed specifically to the NTA's actions.

After recognizing these problems, and the fact that any single method that might be employed is deficient in some respect and therefore "subject to numerous caveats," the Australian Tourist Commission (1991: 3) resolved to adopt a "weight of evidence" approach to the evaluation of its programs in 1991. This approach involved the conduct of several parallel studies that would each have a different set of strengths and limitations. It was thus believed that, in combination, collaborative results providing evidence of the benefits derived from the Commission's activities would be obtained.

One of the main implications of the analysis contained in this article is that while the weight of evidence approach is a step in the right direction, it is an incomplete response to the problem. A more systematic approach is necessary, with a range of studies being carried out so that each facet of the evaluation process is addressed and the chain of events in the marketing process is examined comprehensively. The model presented in Figure 2.2 represents an attempt to provide a framework for the more coherent methodology that is required to achieve this.

The other issue examined previously concerns the development of more techniques to fill gaps in the framework and to support the strategic planning role of the evaluation process by providing a basis for generating more diverse insights into aspects of the destination's performance. An important consideration in the development of these techniques is to devise means for communicating research findings that enhance their usefulness to decision makers. It is hoped that shift-share approach to market share analysis will be seen as a contribution in both these respects.

References

Andrikopolous A., J. Bronx and E. Carvalho (1990) Shift-Share Analysis and the Potential for Predicting Regional Growth Patterns: Some Evidence for the Region of Quebec, Canada. *Growth and Change*, 21 (1): 1–10.

Australian Government Department of Finance (1989) *Program Evaluation: A Guide for Program Managers*. Canberra: Australian Government Department of Finance.

Australian Tourist Commission (1991) *Evaluation of the Australian Tourist Commission's Marketing Impact*. Sydney: Australian Tourist Commission.

Ballman, G., J. Burke, U. Blank and D. Korte (1984) Toward Higher Quality Conversion Studies: Refining the Numbers Game. *Journal of Travel Research*, 22 (Spring): 28–33.

Barry, K., and J. O'Hagan (1972) An Economic Study of Tourist Expenditure in Ireland. *Economic and Social Review*, 3 (2): 143–61.

Beck, R. J. and W. McD Herr (1990) Employment Linkages from a Modified Shift-Share Analysis: An Illinois Example. *Review of Regional Studies*, 20 (3): 38–45.

Burke. J. L., and R. Gitelson (1990) Conversion Studies: Assumptions, Applications. Accuracy and Abuse. *Journal of Travel Research*, 28 (Winter): 46–51.

Burke, J. L. and L. A. Lindblom (1989) Strategies for Evaluating Direct Response Tourism Marketing. *Journal of Tourism Research*, 28 (Fall): 33–37.

Calantone, R. J. and J. A. Mazanec (1991) Marketing Management and Tourism. *Annals of Tourism Research*, 18 (1): 101–19.

Caples, J. (1974) *Tested Advertising Methods*. 4th ed. Englewood Cliffs, NJ: Prentice Hall.

Clark. C. D. (1978) *An Analysis of the Determinants of Tourism Demand in Barbados*. Ph.D. diss., Fordham University (as referred to in Crouch, Schultz and Valerio, 1992).

Cook, S. D. and V. Azucenas (1994) Research in State and Provincial Travel Offices: In *Travel Tourism and Hospitality Research: A Handbook for Managers and Researchers*, 2d ed., edited by J. R. Brent Ritchie and C. R. Goeldner. New York: John Wiley and Sons, pp. 165–80.

Cook, T. D. and D. T. Campbell (1979) *Quasi-Experimentation*. Boston: Houghton Mifflin.

Cooke. K. (1982) Guidelines for Socially Appropriate Tourism Development in British Columbia. *Journal of Travel Research*, 21 (Summer): 22–28.

Crouch. G. I. (1994) The Study of International Tourism Demand: A Survey of Practice. *Journal of Travel Research* 32 (Spring): 41–55.

Crouch. G. L., L. Schultz and P. Valerio (1992) Marketing International Tourism to Australia: A Regression Analysis. *Tourism Management*, 13 (2): 196–208.

Crouch, G. L. and R. N. Shaw (1990) Determinants of International Tourism Flows: Findings from Thirty Years of Empirical Research. *Proceedings of the 21st Annual Conference of the Travel and Tourism Research Association*. Lexington, KY: Travel and Tourism Research Association, pp. 45–60.

Davidson, T. L. (1994) Assessing the Effectiveness of Persuasive Communications. In *Travel Tourism and Hospitality Research: A Handbook for Managers and Researchers*, 2d ed., edited by J. R. Brent Ritchie and C. R. Goeldner. New York: John Wiley and Sons, pp. 537–43.

Davidson. T. L. and W. B. Wiethaupt (1989) Accountability Marketing Research: An Increasingly Vital Tool for Travel Marketers. *Journal of Travel Research*, 27 (Spring): 42–45.

Dwyer. L. and P. Forsyth (1995) Assessing the Net National Benefits from

Promotion in Inbound Tourism, *Proceedings of the 26th Annual Travel and Tourism Research Association Conference*. Lexington, KY: Travel and Tourism Research Association, pp. 123–33.

Ellerbrock, M. (1981) Improving Coupon Conversion Studies: A Comment. *Journal of Travel Research*, 19 (Spring): 37–38.

Faulkner. H. W. (1990) Swings and Roundabouts in Australian Tourism. *Tourism Management*, 11 (1): 29–37.

Faulkner, H. W. (1992) The Anatomy of the Evaluation Process, In *Evaluation of Tourism Marketing*, edited by H. W. Faulkner and R. Shaw. BTR Occasional Paper No. 13. Canberra: Bureau of Tourism Research, pp. 6–9.

Getz, D. (1994) Residents' Attitudes Toward Tourism: A Longitudinal Study in Spey Valley. Scotland. *Tourism Management*, 15 (4): 247–58.

Houston, D. B. (1967) The Shift-Share Analysis of Regional Growth: A Critique. *The Southern Economic Journal*, 34: 577–81.

Hudman. L. E. (1979) Origin Regions in International Tourism. *Weiner Geographische Schrifrum*, 53/54: 43–49.

Hudman, L. E. (1980) *Tourism: A Shrinking World*. Columbus: Grid.

Hudman, L. E. and J. A. Davis (1994) World Tourism Markets: Changes and Patterns. *Proceedings of the 25th Annual Tourism and Travel Research Association Conference*. Lexington, KY: Travel and Tourism Research Association, pp. 127–45.

Hunt, J. D. (1991) The Impact of National Tourism Organisation Advertising Expenditures on the United States Traveller Market. Appendix G in *Evaluation of the Australian Tourist Commission's Marketing Impact*. Sydney: Australian Tourist Commission.

Hunt, J. D., and M. J. Dalton (1983) Comparing Mail and Telephone for Conducting Coupon Conversion Studies. *Journal of Travel Research*, 21 (Winter): 16.

Industry Canada (1994) *An Economic Evaluation of Tourism Canada's International Advertising*. Unpublished internal report. Ottawa: Financial and Economic Analysis, Corporate and Industrial Analysis Branch.

Inskeep, E. (1991) *Tourism Planning: An Integrated and Sustainable Development Approach*. New York: Van Nostrand.

Ledebur, L. C., and R. L. Moomav (1983) A Shift-Share Analysis of Regional Labor Productivity in Manufacturing. *Growth and Change*, 14 (1): 2–9.

March, R. (1994) Tourism Marketing Myopia. *Tourism Management*, 15 (6): 411–15.

McKercher, B. (1995) The Destination-Market Mix: A Tourism Market Portfolio Analysis Model. *Journal of Travel and Tourism Marketing*, 4 (2): 23–40.

Mok, H. R. (1990) A Quasi-Experimental Measure of the Effectiveness of Destination Advertising: Some Evidence from Hawaii. *Journal of Travel Research*, 28 (Summer): 51–55.

New South Wales Office of Public Management (1991) *New Requirements and Guidelines for Program Management*. Sydney: NSWOPM.

O'Hagan, J. W. and M. I. Harrison (1984) Market Shares of U.S. Tourism Expenditure in Europe: An Economic Analysis. *Applied Economics*, 16 (6): 919–31.

Papadopoulos, S. and S. F. Witt (1985) A Marketing Analysis of Foreign Tourism in Greece. In *Proceedings of the Second World Marketing Congress*, edited by S. Shaw, L. Sparks, and E. Kaynak. University of Stirling, pp. 682–93.

Papadopoulos, S. (1987) Strategic Marketing Techniques in International Tourism. *International Marketing Review*, Summer: 71–84.

Paraskevopoulos, G. N. (1977) *An Economic Analysis of International Tourism*.

Lecture Series 31. Athens: Centre for Planning and Economic Research.

Park. C. W., M. S. Roth and P. F. Jacques (1988) Evaluating the Effects of Advertising and Sales Promotion Campaigns. *Industrial Marketing Management*, 17: 129–40.

Posavac, E. J. and R. G. Carey (1992) *Program Evaluation: Methods and Case Studies.* 4th ed. Englewood Cliffs, NJ: Prentice Hall.

Siegel, W. and W. Ziff-Levine (1994) Evaluating Tourism Advertising Campaigns: Conversion versus Advertising Tracking Studies: In *Travel Tourism and Hospitality Research: A Handbook for Managers and Researchers*, 2d ed., edited by J. R. Brent Ritchie and C. R. Goeldner. New York: John Wiley and Sons, pp. 559–64.

Sirakaya, E., M. Uysal. and L. Toepper (1995) Measuring Tourism Performance Using A Shift-Share Analysis: The Case of South Carolina. *Journal of Travel Research*, 34 (Fall): 55–61.

Stufflebeam. D. L. and A. J. Shinkfield (1985) *Systematic Evaluation.* Boston: Kluver-Nijhoff.

Sunday, A. A. (1975) Estimation of the Effectiveness of International Tourism Promotion by Selected Countries in American Media. Ph.D. diss., University of Illinois at Urbana-Champaign.

Tervo, H. and P. Okko (1983). A Note of Shift-Share as a Method of Estimating the Employment Effects of Regional Economic Policy. *Journal of Regional Science*, 23 (1): 115–21.

Uysal, M. (1983) Construction of a Model Which Investigates the Impacts of Selected Variables on International Tourist Flows to Turkey. Ph.D. diss., Texas A&M University (as reported in Crouch, Schultz and Valerio 1992).

Uysal, M. and J. L. Crompton (1984) Determinants of Demand for International Tourist Flows to Turkey. *Tourism Management*, December: 288–97.

Uysal, M. and J. T. O'Leary (1986) A Canonical Analysis of International Tourism Demand. *Annals of Tourism Research*, 13 (4): 651–55.

Vanhove, N. and P. Klaassen (1987) *Regional Policy: A European Approach.* Aldershot, England: Gower.

Witt, S. F. and C. A. Martin (1987) International Tourism Demand Models: Inclusion of Marketing Variables. *Tourism Management*, 8 (1): 33–40.

Woodley. A. (1993) Tourism and Sustainable Development: The Community Perspective. In *Tourism and Sustainable Development: Monitoring, Planning, Management*, edited by J. G. Nelson, R. Butler and G. Wall. Waterloo, Ontario: University of Waterloo Heritage Resource Centre, pp. 137–47.

Woodside. A. G. (1981) Measuring the Conversion of Advertising Coupon Inquiries into Visitors. *Journal of Travel Research.* 19 (Spring): 38–41.

—— (1990) Measuring Advertising Effectiveness in Destination Marketing Strategies. *Journal of Travel Research*, 29 (Fall): 3–8.

WTO (World Tourism Organisation) (1994) *Budgets of National Tourism Administrations.* Madrid: WTO.

Zehnder, L. E. (1976) Tourism and Social Problems: Implications for Research and Marketing. *Proceedings of the 7th Annual Travel and Tourism Research Association Conference.* Lexington, KY: Travel and Tourism Research Association, pp. 211–12.

Chapter 3

Rejuvenating a Maturing Tourist Destination: The Case of the Gold Coast

Bill Faulkner

1 Introduction

In any increasingly competitive global environment, strategic planning has become a fundamental element of business survival. The lead times involved in effectively responding to market trends mean that an ongoing environmental scanning and strategic assessment process is necessary. This is no less so in the tourism industry than in any other area of economic activity. As Ritchie and Crouch (2000) have observed, while tourism has been growing over the last 50 years, it has been relatively easy for most tourist destinations to maintain a healthy rate of growth despite declining market shares. They add, however, that this is changing as growth in the total market size is slowing down and more destinations are emerging to compete within this market. Competitiveness in this setting requires the establishment of a more strategic focus at both the individual enterprise level and for the destination as a whole. Indeed, planning at these two levels needs to be an integrated process. The tourism product in any setting is a composite of services and goods, and the quality of the visitor's experience depends, to some degree, upon the extent to which the range of providers involved coordinate their efforts and have a common sense of purpose. A 'whole of destination' approach is therefore required in the development of the strategic focus and it has been the recognition of this imperative that has underpinned the creation of tourist destination marketing organisations. This development, along with the increasing commitment of financial resources for such organisations, has both been a consequence of, and added impetus to, the increasing level of competition within the global market.

In assessing the competitive position of a tourist destination and extrapolating this assessment to the consideration of future directions of development and the strategic measures necessary to ensure competitiveness within the emerging environment, consideration needs to be given to how the destination has evolved. An understanding of the sequence of events or phases that have marked the history of the destination can assist in bringing its inherent potential, and the impediments to achieving this, into sharper focus. Also, it enables comparisons with general patterns as an aid to understanding the dynamics of destination development and predicting what might happen in the future. In this latter regard, in particular, Butler's (1980) Tourist Area Life Cycle (TALC) has proven to be a useful organising framework for interpreting the stage of development of a destination and canvassing scenarios regarding its potential future. There are varying opinions on the degree to which destinations in general have adhered to the sequence of changes described by this model, with there being both non-conforming (e.g., Agarwal 1997, 1999; Choy 1991; Meyer-Arendt 1985) and conforming cases (e.g. Cohen 1982; Cooper and Jackson 1989; Pearce 1989; Strapp 1988; Weaver 1990) recognised in the literature. The TALC model has also been criticised on the grounds of it being difficult to operationalise, with it being suggested that many of the variables specified in the model are difficult to define empirically and data limitations restrict the potential to trace changes in these over the period described by the cycle (Haywood 1986). However, the model's usefulness as a heuristic device has nevertheless been amply demonstrated through its widespread utilisation within the field and, as Cooper (1994) has emphasised, its value is diminished if it is interpreted too literally.

One of the core scenarios described by Butler's model draws on insights from the product lifecycle model in marketing to suggest a sequence of stages in the evolution of a destination that leads to a point of stagnation, where the destination is confronted by a combination of challenges that threaten its performance in the market place and, therefore, its longer term viability. These challenges include:

- The possibility of the level of tourist activity approaching or exceeding the limits of acceptable change in terms of social and environmental impacts;
- The risk of aging infrastructure resulting in the destination being perceived as becoming jaded, with the quality of services and facilities also beginning to fall short of market expectations as a consequence of antiquated facilities;
- The range of product offered by the destination has not kept up with changes in consumer demand. A fixation on product options that were successful in the past creates a form of inertia that has made providers less sensitive and adaptable to emerging markets;
- The emergence of newer and more competitive destinations that are more attuned to market demands begins to erode the destination's market share.

One of the most obvious indicators of the destination's performance is the number of visitors it receives, and the trend suggested by Butler is depicted in Figure 3.1. Thus, the trend in visitor numbers reflects the passage of the destination through a series of stages that culminate in a critical turning point, at which the cumulative effect of the challenges described above precipitates a situation whereby the destination faces stagnation and decline unless there is a dramatic shift in management and planning approaches. Clearly, this shift must invariably involve the adoption of more effective methods of strategic analysis, as it is arguable that the destination would not be in such a precarious position if more effective methods had been employed in the past. Indeed, one of the underlying causes of stagnation is the inertia of entrenched management/planning practices and structures, which may have succeeded in the past but have become progressively out-of-kilter with the changing environment. This institutional inertia is reinforced by existing power relationships within the industry, and by the mindsets, comfort zones and egos of key decision-makers. One of the main challenges in the process of installing and implementing the new regime of management and planning required to rejuvenate a destination, therefore, involves convincing core stakeholders that the destination faces the prospect of stagnation. Furthermore, it needs to be emphasised that this can only be averted if it is realised that the approaches of the past will not work in the future.

This chapter looks at the specific case of Australia's Gold Coast as an example of a maturing and potentially stagnating destination to illustrate the methods being developed in that context to avert stagnation. These

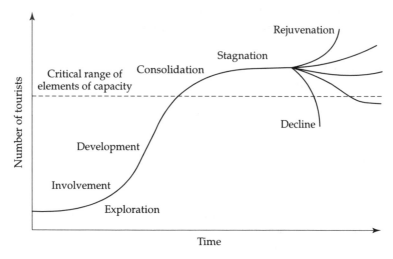

Figure 3.1 Butler's Tourist Area Lifecycle Model (1980)

methods are discussed in the context of the Gold Coast Visioning (GCV) project, the overall aim of which is to construct a vision for the future of Gold Coast tourism. More specifically, the objectives of this project are described in Table 3.1.

Given that the GCV project is essentially concerned with establishing directions for tourism development in the longer term, the principles of sustainable tourism development are adopted as a fundamental philosophical foundation for the planning process. That is, only those options for the Gold Coast's tourism future that satisfy the needs of residents and visitors alike, preserve the cultural and natural assets of the region, and are economically viable should be considered (Bramwell and Lane 1993; Twining-Ward 1999). There are two basic implications of this caveat, which are reflected in the approach described below. Firstly, the achievement of sustainable tourism objectives hinges on the adoption of a participatory model (Murphy 1985), involving the meaningful engagement of the community, along with industry stakeholders and relevant government agencies. Such engagement is necessary so that a true consensus on the preferred directions of future development, and the actions necessary to achieve this, is to be developed. Secondly, a 'whole of destination' approach referred to earlier is necessary, encompassing the

Table 3.1 Objectives of the Gold Coast Visioning Project

- To provide a systematic and comprehensive overview of the current status of Gold Coast tourism, covering such considerations as
  – market position and competitiveness, and
  – environmental, economic and social impacts;
- To develop scenarios for future global, national and local socio-economic, technological and environmental conditions, and assess the implications of these trends at the Gold Coast destination level;
- To combine insights from the above with the principles of sustainable tourism development to produce a shared vision for the Gold Coast's tourism future;
- To utilise the shared vision as a framework for generating a set of issues, core values and principles for evaluating future development options;
- To identify options for tourism development in the context of future scenarios, and evaluate these in terms of the vision and associated core values and principles;
- To arrive at a consensus on preferred tourism development options consistent with the vision and the actions/approaches necessary for this to become a reality.

integration of tourism with other sectors of the economy along with an understanding of the interrelationships and synergies between socio-cultural and environmental dimensions. A shift from a 'destination market-ing' to a 'destination management' approach is therefore advocated.

The approach developed in the GCV project is especially attuned to the inertia problem referred to above and involves a synthesis of methods that have been applied to strategic planning in the tourism field specifically and elsewhere. Among the methods in the consultative process, the construction of a shared vision of the destination's future is pivotal (Getz and Jamal 1994; Ritchie 1993, 1999). This approach is particularly relevant to the Gold Coast situation in two respects. Firstly, a properly structured visioning exercise has the potential to provide a 'circuit-breaker', in the sense that it can be instrumental in galvanizing opinion on the need for a fundamentally different approach from that which has prevailed in the past. Secondly, the visioning process can provide a catalyst for establishing a collaborative approach among the multiple stakeholders, who have both varying and common interests in the destination's future. Linkages between the development of such a vision and broader aspects of the strategic planning process are refined by referring to the learning organisation concept (Senge 1990; Senge *et al.* 1994) and van der Heijden's (1996) notion of 'strategic conversation'. These perspectives highlight the need for a transition from an individualist to a more collective orientation, within the framework of a more structured, systematic and strategically focused approach aimed at ensuring that the shared vision is informed by institutional learning and memory systems. It is argued that such an approach has the potential to produce a more creative response to the challenges of an increasingly turbulent environ-ment, while the potential for repeating past mistakes or re-inventing the wheel will be reduced.

The paper begins with an overview of the status of the Gold Coast as a tourist destination, with particular reference to the indicators of impending stagnation and the symptoms of institutional inertia. Back-ground on the methodological foundations of the GCV project is then provided, with specific attention being given to: an elaboration of sustain-able tourism development principles; the participatory model for destination management and planning; the nature and role of a vision in the strategic planning process; linkages between visioning and the learning organisation concept; and insights from van der Heijden's notion of strategic conversation. Finally, the translation of these principles into the approach to rejuvenating the Gold Coast is described.

2 The Gold Coast at a Turning Point

The Gold Coast has long been acknowledged as Australia's premier tourist destination, a position established as a consequence of a fortunate combination of natural assets and a sequence of visionary entrepreneurs whose initiatives ensured that this destination was always at the cutting edge of many innovations in Australian tourism development (Russell and Faulkner 1999). This history is reflected in the destination's international market performance in particular, as indicated in Figure 3.2, which reveals strong growth in the number of international visitors to the Gold Coast from the mid-1980s, when Australia's appeal as an international destination first began to gain momentum (Faulkner 1990), through to the late 1990s. On the other hand, the profile also reveals a strong resemblance to Butler's scenario, to the extent that the rate of growth is declining in later years and, indeed, suggests that the Gold Coast has already entered the stagnation stage. The dramatic decline in international visitors in the late 1990s, however, is a reflection of the impact of the Asian financial shock, rather than a long-term trend that might suggest the destination is already in decline. While Asian markets have generally recovered more recently (though still not to pre-1997 levels), the dramatic impact of this event highlights the destination's vulnerability arising from its heavy dependence on a narrow band of the market. In the period between 1997 and 1999, there has been a decline in international visitors to the region of 6.2 per cent, despite an overall growth of 1.5 per cent for Australia as a whole (Tideswell 2001).

As illustrated in Figure 3.3, the Gold Coast's performance in the domestic market has been somewhat erratic and less conclusive in terms of any interpretations regarding the Butler model. Over much of the period between the mid-1980s and 1997, the Gold Coast had periods where domestic tourism growth both exceeded and lagged behind

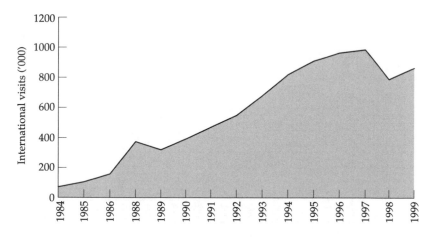

Figure 3.2 Trends in international visitor numbers to the Gold Coast

national level trends. More recently (1997–1999), growth in domestic tourism has been strong in terms of both visits (11 per cent per annum) and visitor nights (9 per cent). This contrasts with the national picture, which shows a stagnating domestic market at minus 1 per cent growth in visits and zero growth in nights. The strong position of the Gold Coast has been fuelled by increased competition in the domestic airline industry, which has seen aggressive price cutting associated with the entry of two new airlines, and similar price cutting in the Gold Coast accommodation sector. Thus, domestic holiday/leisure visitors to the Gold Coast increased by 23 per cent between 1998 and 1999, compared with a national decline of 2 per cent in this segment (Tideswell 2001). While on the surface these figures appear to reflect positively on the health of the destination, there remains a question of how sustainable a price-driven market might be.

While trends in visitor numbers have been the most commonly used indicator of the stage reached in a destination's evolution, to rely purely on this parameter is overly simplistic. A number of authors have identified a more comprehensive range of indicators of stagnation (Butler 1980; Cooper 1990; Haywood 1986; Morgan 1991). These have been outlined in Table 3.2. The Gold Coast's position with respect to each indicator is being tested empirically in a separate paper, which will be based on an examination of available data and the results of a survey of industry stakeholders. However, the preliminary analysis of the Gold Coast's position with respect to some of the indicators is possible on the basis of data

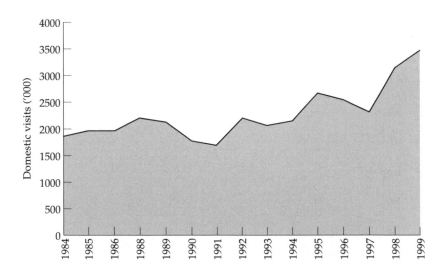

Figure 3.3 Trends in domestic visitor numbers to the Gold Coast

Table 3.2 Indicators of stagnation and their potential relevance to the Gold Coast

Area of destination performance/Indicators

1. Changing markets
   - Growth in low-status, low-spend visitors and day visitors;
   - Over dependence on long-holiday market, and lack of penetration of short-stay market;
   - **Emphasis on high-volume, low-yield inclusive tour market;**
   - **A decline in visitors length of stay;**
   - **Type of tourists increasingly organised mass tourists;**
   - A declining proportion of first time visitors, as opposed to repeat visitors;
   - **Limited or declining appeal to overseas visitors;**
   - High seasonality
2. Emerging newer destinations
   - **Competition from emerging newer destinations;**
   - **The destination is well known, but no longer fashionable;**
3. Infrastructure
   - Outdated, poorly maintained accommodation and amenities;
   - Older properties are changing hands and newer properties, if they are being built are on the periphery of the original tourist areas;
   - **Market perceptions of the destination becoming over-commercialised, crowded and 'tacky';**
   - **Tourism industry over-capacity;**
   - **Diversification into conventions and conferences to maintain numbers;**
   - **Large number of man-made attractions, which start to outnumber the more natural attractions that made the place popular in the first place;**
4. Business performance
   - **Declining profits of major tourism businesses;**
   - Lack of confidence in the tourism business community;
   - A decline in the elasticity of advertising (lower return in terms of increased visitors per advertising dollar investment) and an increase in process elasticity;
   - Lack of professional, experienced staff;
5. Social and environmental carrying capacities
   - Visitor levels approaching or exceeding social and environmental carrying capacities;
   - Local opposition to tourism as the resort's residential role increases;
6. Institutional environment
   - Local government reorganisation (amalgamation) diluting the

political power of resorts in larger authorities;
- Demands for increased operational efficiency and entrepreneurial activity in local government;
- Short-term planning horizons in local government owing to financial restrictions and a low priority given to strategic thinking;
- Shortage of research data.

[Note: Indicators in bold apply to the Gold Coast on the basis of existing data.]
(Based on Butler 1980; Cooper 1990; Haywood 1986; Morgan 1991)

already available. Those that appear to be applicable to the Gold Coast situation to some degree are highlighted in bold in Table 3.2.

An examination of data from the International Visitors' Survey (IVS) and the Domestic Tourism Monitor (DTM) reveals a consistent downward trend in the duration of stay of both international and domestic visitors to the Gold Coast over the last decade to 1997 – from 7 to 4.5 days in the former and from 5.5 to 4.5 in the latter. However, there has been a reversal of this trend for international visitors in the two years since. This is attributable partly to a market diversification strategy implemented in the wake of the Asian financial crises, which has seen an increased representation of longer staying visitors from New Zealand, USA/Canada, Europe and Other (Middle East/Africa) markets. An increase in visiting friends and relatives visitation could also explain this trend. The IVS also reveals an increased emphasis on 'organised mass tourism' within the international market, with the proportion of visitors on package, all-inclusive tours increasing from 48 to 75 per cent over the last decade. The plateauing of international visitor numbers in Figure 3.2 suggests that the destination may be losing some of its appeal in the international market, while the shift-share analysis has indicated that newer destinations, such as Tropical North Queensland, have eroded the Gold Coast's market share in both the international and domestic markets. It may be that the destination has become 'well known, but no longer fashionable'. Furthermore, even though there has been no marked or consistent decline in hotel occupancy rates, it is arguable that this is only so because of aggressive price cutting in room rates, which has produced a persistent profitless volume problem. The high volume/low yield syndrome is also a reflection of the heavy reliance of the inclusive tour market and the tight margins associated with this market.

While it cannot be claimed that the Gold Coast's tourism infrastructure is aging and in need of refurbishment generally, the Visioning Project's Infrastructure Audit study has indicated there are pockets of decay that present a real prospect of an 'infrastructure time-bomb'. Finally, also with respect to infrastructure considerations, the destination's heavy reliance on built attractions (theme parks) and the increasing emphasis on the convention sector that will follow the completion of the convention centre could be cited as symptoms of stagnation according to the literature. However, it might be equally argued that such developments are manifestations of rejuvenation strategies.

On the basis of this overview of the current status of the destination, it is reasonable to at least conclude that the Gold Coast is a mature destination showing some early signs of stagnation, paralleling the experience of coastal tourist resorts elsewhere in the world (Formica and Uysal 1996; Gomez and Rebello 1995; Ioannides 1992). Given this, it is clear that a fundamental shift in the approach to destination planning and management is necessary if the region is to rejuvenate and remain competitive in the longer term. However, regardless of the stage the destination has reached, the pressures of an increasingly competitive global environment point to the necessity of a more comprehensive approach that embraces sustainable development principles as a framework for tourism development. In short, a re-orientation from destination marketing to a more encompassing destination management approach is necessary. One of the Gold Coast's major competitors (at least, in the Japanese market) has recognised this and adjusted its approach to tourism development and marketing accordingly, as the following excerpt from an Hawaii Tourism Authority report reveals:

> Destination tourism management is increasingly becoming more sophisticated worldwide. The success of many tourism destinations has been driven by an integrated tourism management structure, including effective integration of tourism policy, long-term planning, product development and marketing. This successful tourism management approach has also led to strong and mutually supportive private/public sector partnerships that have been driven by a common tourism strategy and policy. (Hawaii Tourism Authority 1999: 9)

Apart from the tourism development and marketing considerations emphasised above, it is also arguable that the challenge confronting the region is heightened by the need to reconcile the demands of tourism with those of urban growth currently being experienced and likely to continue in the future. With a population already at around 400,000, and as a part of the Southeast Queensland urban conurbation that includes Brisbane, the Gold Coast has been one of the fastest growing urban areas in Australia over the last ten years. The same assets of the area that make it a pleasant place to visit also make it an attractive lifestyle choice for new residents. Significantly, the quality of life of these residents in the future will depend to a large extent on how effectively the potentially competing demands of tourism and urban growth are managed.

One of the first steps taken in the Gold Coast Visioning project involved the conduct of the scoping study, in which interviews with over one hundred stakeholders were carried out. Among the conclusions of this study, the following are particularly relevant to the consideration of future approaches:

- The ad hoc approach to tourism development that has prevailed to date will not work in the future. The scale and complexity of tourism development on the Gold Coast has reached a point where a fundamental rethink about the approach to tourism development is necessary. Specifically, the incremental approach of the past, where a single visionary entrepreneur's action could reinvigorate the industry and initiate a new phase of growth, will not work in the future. A more holistic approach is necessary. That is, one that takes into account economic, social and environmental considerations, and integrates the planning/policy regimes of all levels of government.
- There is a tourism policy and planning void on the Gold Coast in the sense that the actions of the various government and quasi-government agencies who have a role to play in tourism (State Government, Gold Coast City Council and Gold Coast Tourism Bureau) are not well coordinated, and the tourism implications of various policy and planning agendas are not necessarily taken into account. For example, substantial population growth on the Gold Coast is inevitable as new residents seeking a better lifestyle are attracted by the same features of the area that attract tourists. How this growth is managed in the urban planning process will impinge on the future of tourism, just as the management of tourism development will profoundly affect the quality of life of residents.
- The incremental approach alluded to previously is also flawed in the sense that it focuses on immediate contingencies and leads to a position where the options available to cope with future problems are reduced. A strategic approach is necessary, with the longer-term implications of today's decisions being considered, in conjunction with a systematic development and assessment of future scenarios.

These observations both underpin, and are reinforced by, the approach elaborated in the following section.

3 Steps Towards a Rejuvenation Strategy: Methodological Issues

Any meaningful strategic assessment of a destination's tourism development future must at least involve the basic ingredients of the traditional strategic planning approach recognised in the literature

(Inskeep 1991; Gunn 1988; Getz 1986; Heath and Wall 1992). That is, the strategic planning process should involve a series of interrelated steps including: a situation analysis; the formulation of a mission and vision statement; an environmental scanning exercise; the identification and analysis of core issues impinging on the competitive position of the destination (SWOT analysis), and derivation of strategic responses (strategies, action plans, implementation schedules, monitoring mechanisms, adjustments). For the purposes of describing the approach applied to the Gold Coast situation, therefore, it is sufficient to acknowledge this feature and focus more on elaborations of the conventional methodology developed in response to specific requirements of this destination's history and circumstances. It is envisaged, however, that similar refinements of the strategic planning model will be applicable to maturing destinations in general.

The refinements discussed below revolve around several themes:

- The adoption of sustainable tourism development principles as a guiding framework for both the planning process and the evaluation of alternative development options;
- A shift in emphasis from a destination marketing to a destination management perspective;
- The central role of a participatory model for simultaneously ensuring that, in line with the sustainable development approach, a broad spectrum of stakeholders is consulted and to provide a vehicle for exploring and building collaborative relationships;
- The up-front utilisation of an exercise focusing on the construction of a vision as a vehicle for galvanising support for a fundamental shift in the approach to destination planning and management. The visioning process also has the potential to reinforce the establishment of a collaborative approach;
- The drawing of insights from elements of the learning organisation approach as a basis for structuring the dialogue in the participatory process and building a longer-term approach to destination planning management strategy; and
- The use of a scenario-building approach based on the strategic conversation model as a basis for exploring the future.

Each theme is elaborated in turn below.

3.1 The sustainable tourism development framework

Since sustainable tourism development principles were formally recognised as a goal for modern tourism development, initially in the Manila Declaration (WTO 1980) and later in Hague Declaration (WTO 1989), this set of guidelines has become, in principle at least, the universally accepted basis for destination management and planning.

The earlier statement highlighted the importance of both natural and cultural resources to the viability of tourist destinations, and the equal importance of conserving these assets in the interest of both the community and tourism. In the later statement, particular emphasis was given to an 'unspoilt natural, cultural and human environment (being) a fundamental condition for the development of tourism' and the need to manage tourism development in a way that preserves the natural environment and cultural heritage of an area, while improving the quality of life of its residents (WTO 1989).

Drawing on these earlier prescriptions, the tourism group of the Globe '90 Conference held in Vancouver, Canada in 1990 conclude that 'sustainable tourism development is aimed at protecting and enhancing the environment, meeting basic human needs, promoting current and intergenerational equity and improving the quality of life of all people' (Inskeep 1991: 459). Accordingly, sustainable tourism development is fundamentally concerned with:

> meeting the needs of present tourists and host regions while protecting and enhancing opportunities for the future and this requires resources to be managed in such a way that we can fulfil economic, social and aesthetic needs while maintaining cultural integrity, essential ecological processes, biological diversity and life support systems. (Inskeep 1991: 461)

The emerging sustainable tourism development philosophy of the 1990s can be viewed as an extension of a broader realisation that a preoccupation with economic growth without due regard to its social and environmental consequences is self-defeating in the longer term. This perspective, in turn, had its roots in the 'limits to growth' movement of the 1970s (Meadows *et al.* 1972) and has been more recently espoused by such international organisations as the World Commission on Environment and Development (WDED 1987). Within this perspective, tourism can be construed as essentially a resource-based industry, where the integrity and continuity of the tourism product in a region is inextricably linked with the preservation of its natural, social and cultural assets (Murphy 1985). As observed by Murphy (1994: 275) in another context, the essence of the sustainable tourism agenda is encapsulated in the saying: 'we do not inherit the earth from our forefathers but borrow it from our children'. As indicated above, the relevance of this philosophy to tourism has not been lost on those directly involved in the development of this industry, although it is also arguable that the good intentions expressed in the principles have not necessarily been reflected in practical applications across the board.

The impediments to the implementation of sustainable tourism development principles go beyond simply a question of awareness levels and intentions among decision-makers at the destination level. Noting the tendency for socio-culturally and environmentally pristine locations to be degraded once they become too popular as tourist destinations, Twining-Ward (1999) asks 'why is it that despite knowledge of the risks, as well as increased understanding of conservation issues, destinations continue to make the same mistakes?' (p. 187). He offers three basic reasons:

- Ecologically and culturally sensitive areas that are most vulnerable to deterioration are also the most attractive to tourists;
- Many of the resources that are so important for tourism product are 'common pool' resources, which the private sector taps free of charge and over which no single company or authority has responsibility for management. They therefore suffer from the 'tragedy of the commons' syndrome (Hardin 1968), with over-use and a lack of investment in management ultimately degrading the resource;
- Reluctance on the part of government to regulate economic activity and thus control levels of activity within sustainable limits.

Other impediments are associated with trends in the commercial structure of tourism operations. Although he focuses on tourism development in 'peripheral destinations', where economic and political systems make the local populations more vulnerable to exploitation by external interests, many of the threats to sustainability identified by Buhalis (1999) in these settings are equally applicable to maturing destinations in developed countries, such as the Gold Coast. He refers to the following factors:

- Evolution towards mass tourism as planners fail to control development in the face of political pressure;
- Enterprises are unable to reach targets in terms of volume of business and therefore engage in heavy discounting to attract customers;
- Reliance on intermediaries, who take advantage of the situation and use their bargaining power to reduce margins (and therefore profitability of local suppliers) in order to enhance their competitiveness in the market;
- Vertical integration enables tour operators to exert price reduction and service enhancement pressure on local suppliers;
- The destination is sold on the basis of price, rather than on the basis of its intrinsic assets, and it is therefore easily substituted by cheaper destinations elsewhere;
- Lack of profits reduces capacity to renovate and upgrade facilities and invest in staff training, resulting in a decline in standards.
- A reputation as a cheap destination attracts price sensitive, less

desirable visitors, who engage in anti-social behaviour and, in turn,
discourage better quality visitors;
• Undesirable social impacts are more likely because of the above.

Buhalis adds that these trends are attributable to the prevalence of
manufacturing and retailing mindset, which assumes that profitability is
associated with increased volume of activity (and reduced unit costs),
with the consequent assumption that a destination can be developed
indefinitely without adverse effects on the quality of life of locals. Also,
as Twining-Ward (1999) emphasises, environmental and socio-cultural
resources are often regarded as zero-priced public goods, whose
vulnerability is rarely appreciated. Meanwhile, the management of this
problem by government is discouraged by short-term political cycles that
discourage adoption of a longer-term perspective.

Earlier interpretations of sustainable tourism development have been
criticised on the basis of their focus on ecological sustainability, at the
expense of socio-cultural and economic considerations, and for the
fixation on alternative tourism as the route to sustainability (Farrell 1999;
Twining-Ward 1999). Farrell (1999) has noted how the sustainable
development agenda was captured by the environmental movement and
how this has distorted policy and planning practice in a manner that
tends to overlook the social and economic dimensions of the 'three
dimensional sustainability trinity'. He has referred to this trend as a form
of 'environmental fundamentalism', which produced a tendency for
those responsible for this agenda to resist change of all kinds irrespective
of the bigger picture and longer-term sustainability issues. This agenda
also encouraged a belief that only alternative forms of tourism described
by Krippendorf (1987) (i.e. alternatives to organised mass tourism) were
consistent with sustainable tourism objectives. This assumption has since
been challenged by many authors, who have pointed out that alternative
forms of tourism can have an equally devastating effect, especially where
this involves the dispersion of tourists to environmentally and/or
culturally fragile areas (Butler 1990, 1992; Cater 1993; Jarviluoma 1992;
Wheeler 1993; Zurick 1992). Alternatively, if managed properly, mass
tourism can be instrumental in controlling tourist movements more effectively, thus enabling them to be contained within 'site hardened' areas
where their impacts can be managed.

Farrell (1999: 191) has advocated an interdisciplinary and more
encompassing approach to sustainable tourism development, involving
'a commitment to provide healthy long-term tourism thoroughly
integrated with other elements of the economy, and with the environment
and society in such a manner that a policy change in one does not unduly
interfere with the optimal functioning of any of the others'. This point is
particularly relevant to the 'whole of destination approach' referred to

earlier and revisited in more detail in the next section. Drawing on this and other insights referred to above for the purposes of the Gold Coast strategy, the objective of sustainable tourism development has thus been summarised as being:

> To develop a form of tourism that satisfies the needs and expectations of the tourist market, is economically viable and achieves a return on investment for tourism operators, safeguards and enhances the natural and cultural assets of the destination, and enhances the resident populations' quality of life and life opportunities.

This interpretation is translated to a proposed set of sustainable tourism objectives for the Gold Coast contained in Table 3.3.

In his analysis of the imperatives of destination strategic planning, Brent Ritchie (1999: 273) identified four specific implications of the sustainable tourism development agenda:

- A long-term planning horizon is essential as today's development and investment decisions have impacts beyond the lifetimes of those making the decisions, and intergenerational equity considerations demand that such impacts be taken into account;
- An 'integrated and cumulative perspective' is necessary in the consideration of environmental, social and economic impacts. The aggregate impact of a set of individual decisions may be greater or less than the simple additive effects on individual projects, depending on the synergies and cross-impacts;
- By its very nature, tourism involves a relationship between host communities and the tourism sector of such intensity that, as implied above, the integration of tourism planning and development with the broader social, economic and environmental planning agenda of the destination is absolutely essential;
- The approach to tourism planning and development must reflect

Table 3.3 Proposed sustainable tourism objectives for the Gold Coast

- To enhance visitor satisfaction and the competitiveness of the destination within the tourist market;
- To improve profitability and the return on investment of the industry;
- To maximise economic benefits to the region;
- To protect and enhance natural environmental assets;
- To provide a foundation for enhancing the host community's quality of life and life opportunities;
- To ensure that development is consistent with the local community's socio-cultural values.

broader trends and expectations with regard to the level of community consultation involved.

There are several general implications of these points that have had a particular bearing on the proposed approach to the Gold Coast. Firstly, the first two points ('long-term planning horizons' and 'integrated cumulative perspective') highlight the need for a shift from the destination marketing orientation that has dominated the approach to destination planning and development, to a more comprehensive destination management perspective. Secondly, Ritchie refers to the need for the meaningful involvement of the community, with industry stakeholders, in the development of a consensus on the directions of future development and the actions necessary for the preferred outcomes to be realised. This consensus might be expressed through 'the sharing of a common destination vision'. As mentioned previously and discussed further below, the process of constructing such a vision is pivotal in the approach developed in the Gold Coast case. Before turning to this aspect specifically, however, some of the issues associated with destination management perspective and the nexus between community participation and the building of collaborative relationships need to be addressed.

3.2 Shifting from a destination marketing to a destination management perspective

As emphasised by Ritchie's initial two points, one of the more obvious implications of the sustainable tourism development agenda is the need for a more comprehensive, integrated and holistic approach that goes beyond the traditional focus on destination marketing to take into account a broader range of environmental, social and economic issues. The fact that the necessity of such an approach is beginning to be recognised by major tourism destinations has been referred to earlier in the reference to the Hawaii Tourism Authority's (1999) latest tourism plan.

The failure of more traditional tourism development plans, with their 'top-down', market oriented approach, has been observed in several settings (e.g. Alipour 1996; Choy 1991; King *et al.* 2000). Choy (1991: 329) has suggested that, given that 'tourism plans have little probability of influencing market forces to achieve economic success, government planning efforts might be better spent on resolving issues involving ... market failure, leaving the private sector to assume the planning and financial risk of tourism projects'. Areas of market failure he referred to include: public interest in products and services which are consumed collectively (parks, beaches, historic sites, etc.); external effects (positive and negative) that affect people not directly involved in tourism activity (e.g. construction of a resort may restrict locals' access to the beach); and costs and benefits not reflected in market prices (value of open space, costs of social impacts, benefits from environmental preservation). However, while there are obvious differences in the focus of public and private sector interest, the demarcation of their involvement in this way loses sight of the interrelationships and synergies that need to be developed. A demarcated, as opposed to a truly integrated, approach will produce the sort of 'dysfunctionality' in tourism plans observed by Butler (1991). Thus, for instance, it might produce a conflict between policy mechanisms aimed at limiting environmental impacts by minimising tourist numbers, at one level, and elements of policy at a higher level that encourage increases in visitor numbers in order to improve economic benefits.

An approach that gives due consideration to the various dimensions of the sustainability agenda, while at the same time avoiding the dysfunctionality trap, hinges on a process involving participation by a broad range of stakeholders within a framework that fosters the establishment of a consensus on preferred directions of future development and the building of collaborative relationships.

3.3 Community participation and the building of collaborative relationships

One of the seminal works on community participation in tourism development planning is Murphy's (1985) book, *Tourism: A Community Approach*. Murphy proposed an ecological-systems-based model for a community involvement in tourism planning and in the process anticipated many of the elements of sustainable tourism development principles described above. In particular, he argued that:

> Residents must put up with the physical development, but have little say so in the decision-making process that will inevitably affect their community and way of life. Development and planning in isolation from the community at large cannot continue if the industry is to develop in harmony with the capacity and aspirations of destination areas. To become self renewable resource industry and agent of hospitality will require more citizen participation in the development, or non-development, of a destination. (Murphy 1985: 163)

The above rationale for community involvement is largely based on ethical considerations, in the sense that it emphasises the resident's stake in the process in terms of the potential impacts of tourism on their way of life. Emphasis is therefore placed on the need to ensure that changes associated with tourism are both within the bounds of their adaptive capabilities and consistent with the retention or enhancement of their quality of life. There is, however, another perspective, which has a more pragmatic orientation. Kotler and Armstrong's (1984) societal marketing concept has been invoked to highlight that members of the host population are simultaneously consumers of product and beneficiaries or victims of the effects of production (King *et al.* 2000; Mill 1996). Thus, if the industry can be construed as using the community itself as part of the product it sells to the market, then a planning and management regime that becomes insensitive to community interests will undermine the quality of the product, to the extent that this will precipitate a community backlash. The assets and appeal of a destination will therefore be diminished if the development of tourism product does not give due consideration to the interests and well being of the local community.

While the rationale for a community based approach to tourism planning is compelling, how extensively and effectively this approach has been adopted is another question. As Joppe (1996) has observed, despite the rhetoric about community participation in tourism planning, most instances of this are driven by government (and business) agendas, rather than community interests. She adds, 'There is a great need to evaluate the implementation of so-called community-driven tourism development plans to determine to what extent the local residents truly share in the benefits supposedly derived from increased visitation, since it is quite clear that they support the majority of the costs associated with tourism' (Joppe 1996: 475). Part of the problem arises from the difficulty of defining the community and assumptions made about the homogeneity of interests within it. While to some the notion of community implies a coherent entity with a shared identity and common sense of purpose, in reality communities generally consist of an agglomeration of special interest groups who are often antagonistic towards each other and competing for scarce resources or power (Manning 1999). Thus, for example, it is not uncommon for residents to favour options that will benefit them personally in some manner (e.g. product based on parks, outdoor recreation, restaurants) regardless of market conditions or the potential of the area (Andereck and Vogt 2000). In such circumstances, the task of building a consensus or a shared vision on the future of tourism in the destination is a major challenge that is compounded by the need to reconcile a diversity of views and interests. The implications of this are explored in more detail in the context of the following discussion on learning organisations.

To this point, discussion of the participatory model has concentrated on the rationale for providing the resident population with an opportunity to influence tourism development decisions. However, beyond residents and the tourism industry itself, there are other stakeholders who need to be involved in the process. In this context, stakeholders are defined as any individual, group of organisation who have an interest in tourism development issues and problems, and who are directly influenced or affected by the actions or inaction of others in response to these issues or problems (after Gray 1989 and Hall and McArthur 1998). Other stakeholders therefore include public sector agencies, non-government organisations (NGOs) and the business sector in general. The involvement of such a broad range of stakeholders is essential because the strategic issues associated with pursuing sustainable tourism development objectives cannot be adequately addressed if individuals act in isolation from each other (Getz and Jamal 1994). All the stakeholders need to be involved in a dynamic, flexible, evolving process, which includes elements of the learning organisation philosophy discussed later.

The need for such an approach is illustrated by Backman *et al.*'s (2001) reference to how planning in the ecotourism context involves overlapping agendas of various stakeholders. Thus it has been noted how a range of government agencies, NGOs, private sector, and community interests are involved, and how many public sector agencies and NGOs have themselves become involved in delivering ecotourism product for profit. The distinction between public and private sector involvement has therefore become blurred and, as observed by Backman *et al.* (2001), this provides the opportunity for previously unrecognised synergies to be developed:

> Whether the motivation is economic or stewardship, organisational missions and strategies are beginning to coalesce around the idea of ecotourism, capitalising on public interest in the environment. Therefore the need for collaboration, cooperation and synergy among this multitude is as obvious as it will be challenging. In the past, economics have often run counter to protection and preservation interests. But ecotourism, perhaps for the first time, provides a feasible mechanism to align economic incentives with stewardship of the environment. (Backman *et al.* 2001: 454)

While the specifics of the above argument apply to the Gold Coast situation to the extent that the natural environment is an integral part of this destination's tourism product, it also applies in a broader sense. For example, one project focused initially on the reinvigoration of a particular precinct within the Gold Coast (i.e. Surfers Paradise), but eventually recognised that a 'whole of Gold Coast' approach was necessary to achieve this. Similarly, the Gold Coast's economic development strategy identified a range of potential synergies between the tourism sector and various avenues of economic development. Significantly, many of these synergies hinge on the potential of tourism development to enhance the lifestyle of residents.

The above observations reinforce those made by Getz (1986) and Gunn (1988) some time ago, where they advocated a departure from the traditional focus of tourism planning on the development process towards one that involves a systematic integration of research, planning and evaluation on the one hand, and collaborative linkages on the other.

The circumstances under which a collaborative approach is regarded as being most appropriate are clearly applicable to the tourist development situation in general and the Gold Coast situation in particular. According to Getz and Jamal (1994), a collaborative approach is required:

- Where the solutions to the problem cannot be effectively addressed by stakeholders individually;
- Where the stakeholders have a common interest or stake in the issue or problem and the outcomes of the actions of some are influenced by those of others.
- Where there is a need to resolve potential for conflict, which can be counter-productive for all players, and advance a shared vision.
- Where there is a turbulent challenging environment.

In destination management situations, there are three primary dimensions to the value of collaboration. Firstly, there are invariably diverse and to some extent conflicting interest groups among stakeholders, who are inclined towards a counterproductive adversarial stance on issues. A properly managed collaborative approach can dilute the entrenched mindsets that would otherwise predispose participants to this approach. Secondly, collaboration fosters greater coordination in a manner that enables economic, social and environmental issues to be considered more holistically. Finally, it facilitates the sharing of knowledge and collective learning in a fashion that provides more fertile ground for innovation (Bramwell and Sharman 1999). Furthermore, collaboration is particularly necessary where problems are complex and the solutions are beyond the capacity of a single organisation to address (Gray 1989). But these benefits will not be realised unless the collaborative process is structured to achieve meaningful participation of all relevant stakeholders. Otherwise there is a danger of pre-existing power relationships having an undue bearing on the process, predisposing the outcome to a reaffirmation of the status quo (Reed 1997). Jamal and Getz (1995) suggest that one way to overcome this is to ensure all stakeholders have access to the resources and skills necessary for them to participate effectively.

Within the collaborative framework, there are four levels of stakeholder involvement in the planning process. These include: information sharing, consultation, decision making, and implementation (Paul 1987). However, to be fully effective, the structure of the consultation and decision making processes associated with the building of collaborative relationships needs to include some of the ingredients of the learning organisation dynamic described below.

3.4 Building a shared vision

The articulation of a shared vision among the stakeholders is envisaged as being the initial and most critical step in the consultative process that will lead to the development of the Gold Coast's tourism strategy. In its simplest terms, a vision can be construed as a shared view on a preferred future. Alternatively, as described by Senge *et al.* (1994: 302), a vision can be construed as '... sense of shared purpose and destiny ...' '... a picture of the future we want to create ... that gives shape and direction to the organisation's future'. Either way, it will consist of a succinct statement (core vision) of the essential ingredients of the preferred future and it will be supplemented by a series of more detailed statements, articulating benchmarks for desired outcomes in specific dimensions of tourism development. The specification of these benchmarks will be guided by the sustainable tourism objectives described earlier.

The visioning exercise is critical in two respects. Firstly, a well-designed visioning exercise has the potential to provide a 'circuit-breaker' and a 'call to action', to the extent that it can be instrumental in galvanizing opinion on the need to a fundamentally different approach from that which has prevailed in the past. This role is implied by Helling's (1998a: 336) view that '... a vision can substitute for more abstract goals, stimulating public involvement by describing specific, concrete outcomes that are important to citizens'. Senge (1990) takes this line of argument a step further by suggesting that: 'Few, if any forces in human affairs are as powerful as a shared vision.'

Secondly, a well-articulated vision that has been constructed in a manner that ensures it represents a consensus among primary stake-holders provides a focus for the strategic planning process and a vehicle for mobilising cooperative action. Here, the word 'cooperative' is used very deliberately as an alternative to 'coordinated' action. The former implies a group of equal stakeholders working together towards the same end, while the latter implies one party exerting control over others to ensure that all their activities contribute to a mutually agreed outcome. The distinction is subtle and, in reality, one cannot be achieved without the other. However, the emphasis on the equality of stakeholders in the achievement of mutually agreed outcome and the reciprocity implied by the word, 'cooperation' makes this a more meaningful concept in this context. The nexus between the visioning process and action is fundamental, as implied in the following popular quote from Joel Barker (1992):

> A vision without action is merely dream. Action without vision just passes the time. Vision with action can change the world. (Cited in Ritchie 1999: 273)

Beyond the two roles of the visioning outlined above, there are several other important contributions a vision can make to the process of shaping a destination's future. These are:

- A vision provides a framework for choosing appropriate responses and for cooperative action. External events (including changes in government policy agendas at all levels, international developments and random disasters) have the potential to profoundly affect the competitiveness of the Gold Coast as a tourism destination, and thus the direction of tourism development. While destination stakeholders may have little control over these events, a long-term shared perspective (a vision) is necessary for not only determining how they respond, but also for ensuring that we respond in a coordinated and effective way.
- Without a vision, the destination will become locked into the past. That is, an incremental approach, where decision-makers focus on responding to immediate contingencies in a piecemeal fashion, leads the destination to a position where the options available for coping with longer term eventualities are progressively reduced.
- Having a vision provides a means for ensuring that day-to-day decisions are informed by a longer term perspective. Conversely, by creating a more structured, strategically focused and shared framework for individual enterprises and organisations to operate within, a vision contributes to ensuring that decision-makers at all levels take longer-term considerations into account in their day-by-day decisions.
- A vision provides a catalyst for building a collective memory and organisational learning system at the destination level. A modest up-front investment in a visioning process, with associated planning and evaluation systems, avoids the need to think through every crisis situation from scratch. Such an approach not only creates a readiness for the unexpected, but also facilitates the transition from individual insights to collective/institutional action, and establishes an institutional learning and memory system that reduces the prospects of repeating past mistakes and/or re-inventing the wheel (van der Heijden 1996). Linkages with the organisational learning perspective are explored in more detail in the following section.
- A vision that is consistent with the sustainable tourism development principles enunciated earlier in this paper provides a vehicle for incorporating international 'best practice' models into the Gold Coast strategy.

Like most elements of strategic analysis and planning, it might be said that the route taken in constructing a vision is as important as the destination. The meaningful engagement of the community, with industry stakeholders and relevant public sector agencies, in the development of a consensus on the directions of future development and the actions necessary for the preferred outcomes to be realised is an essential ingredient in the visioning process. Such engagement of stakeholders is essential if the vision that eventuates is to provide an accurate reflection of a truly shared position of all concerned and if it is to provide a relatively stable reference point for future action. The importance of this has been emphasised by Senge *et al.* (1994: 313):

> A vision is not really shared unless it has staying power and evolving life force that lasts for years, propelling people through a continuous cycle of action, learning and reflection.

Another perspective on the reasons why a broad spectrum of stakeholder involvement is advantageous have been identified by Chalip (1996) in another context:

- More ideas are generated when more people are involved;
- More information is made available and shared;
- Alternative perspectives inform the examination of the problem;
- Fairer decisions will be made if all stakeholders are involved and their views taken into account; and
- Engagement and consensus ensures a higher level of commitment to the actions required to make the vision a reality.

Views of what constitutes a vision may vary between a statement akin to a corporate mission statement to a more detailed enunciation of some preferred future. However, the essential ingredient is that it reflects the shared values and aspirations of the relevant stakeholders. To some, the downside of this approach is that it is time-consuming and conflicts may surface. However, conflicts are healthy to the extent that they prompt the search for more information and force a more systematic evaluation of alternative views (Putnam 1986). This consideration has a bearing on the selection of people to be involved in the process. Insufficient diversity among those participating will result in the process succumbing to 'groupthink' and premature closure of many issues. To avoid these pitfalls, Putnam (1986: 88) has suggested the use of a designated devil's advocate to provide a critical perspective and inject some conflict into the process of canvassing views. While this may mean the end result may not necessarily receive unqualified support across the board, it should at least not be totally unacceptable to any stakeholders. Apart from these considerations, however, the central reason for engaging a diversity of stakeholders in the process is that a commitment to the vision from all relevant stakeholder groups is necessary if it is to have the desired effect. The shared vision thus becomes a benchmark towards which the efforts of stakeholders can be directed.

The following comment by Mintzberg (2000: 209–210) provides a useful summary of the main point regarding the role of a vision outlined above and, in particular, it alludes to linkages with the learning organisation concept, which is explored further below:

> The visionary approach is a more flexible way to deal with an uncertain world. Vision sets the broad outlines of a strategy, while leaving the specific details to be worked out. In other words, the broad perspective may be deliberate but the specific position can emerge. So when the unexpected happens, assuming the vision is sufficiently robust, the organization can adapt – it learns. Certain change is thus easily accommodated. Of course, when even vision cannot cope, then the organization may have to revert to a pure learning approach – to experiment in the hope of capturing some basic message and converging behaviors on them.

3.5 Learning organisations and organisational change

The notion of learning organisations has been developed as a tool for assisting commercial organisations to adjust to change primarily in the North American context (Senge *et al.* 1994). In one sense, a tourist destination represents a more complex situation, at least to the degree that it involves an amalgam of separate public and private sector organisations, along with a loose array of community-based interests and alliances, all pursuing separate agendas that both overlap and conflict with each other to varying degrees. However, as Senge *et al.* observe, these characteristics are not uncommon within large corporations and the art of developing a learning organisation approach involves reconciling the tensions, finding common ground for collective action and channeling rivalries into creative energy that benefits the organisation as a whole. It follows that elements of the learning organisation philosophy may be applicable to the development of a strategic approach to destination management.

As defined by Senge *et al.* (1994: 4) a learning organisation is one that is '… able to deal with the problems and opportunities of today, and invest in its capacity to embrace tomorrow, because its members are continually focused on enhancing and expanding their collective awareness and capabilities'. That this involves a combination of the systematic integration of research, planning and evaluation, along with the building of collaborative relationships, is implied by the suggestion that learning organisations are involved in a 'continuous testing of experience, and the transformation of that experience into knowledge accessible to the whole organisation, and relevant to its core purpose' (Senge *et al.* 1994: 49). At the destination level, therefore, learning would become embedded within the organisational structure. It would become integral to the planning and management process, rather than, as is too often the case, a marginal activity restricted to a few specialist researchers.

The five 'disciplines' for developing a learning organisation identified in Senge's (1990) original book on the subject and reiterated in Senge *et al.* (1994: 6–7) provide some insights into the underlying philosophy that might drive the approach to developing the Gold Coast's destination strategy:

- *Personal mastery:* learning to expand our personal capacity to create the results we most desire, and creating an organizational environment which encourages all its members to develop themselves towards the goals and purposes they choose;
- *Mental models:* reflecting upon, continually clarifying and improving our internal pictures of the world and seeing how they shape our actions and decisions;
- *Shared vision:* building a sense of commitment in a group, developing shared images of the future we seek to create, and the principles and guiding practices by which we hope to get there;
- *Team learning:* transforming conversational and collective thinking skills, so that groups of people can reliably develop intelligence and ability greater than the sum of the individual members' talents;
- *Systems thinking:* a way of thinking about, and a language for describing and understanding, the forces and interrelations that shape the behavior of systems. This perspective helps us to see how to change systems more effectively, and act more in tune with the larger processes of the natural and economic world.

A shared vision is central to the process, but without the other elements the value of the vision will be diminished. Equally important to the development of this approach is the notion of the 'primacy of the whole'. Much of the analysis and planning that has posed as a strategic approach to destination management in the past has involved a reductionist approach, whereby it is assumed that we can understand the whole in terms of an independent assessment of its parts and the whole will necessarily operate effectively so long as the parts each function well at their own level. The inter-relatedness of the parts is not taken into account in this perspective. An entity such as a tourist destination is therefore a pattern of interrelationships and fixing one problem or part of it in isolation will not guarantee the whole will survive. Indeed, the quick isolated fixes might close options for the future and compound longer term problems. In this sense, today's solution may produce a 'sting in the tail' tomorrow.

One of the more difficult conundrums associated with the holistic perspective arises from the possibility that the health of the whole destination may be dependent upon solutions that are sub-optimal for some, or even many, of the parts. This principle may be palatable for an individual organisation level if it means that the firm as a whole prospers and survives, but at the destination level it is difficult to envisage individual commercial entities tolerating reduced profits in the interests of a better outcome for the destination as a whole.

This point represents one of the main challenges of translating insights from both the sustainable tourism development agenda and the learning organisation perspective to guiding principles for destination management. The nature of this problem can be put into perspective by drawing a distinction between mutualism and competition. Traditionally, we would see mutualism (or cooperation) as dominating relationships within organisations and competition between organisations. However, Miner (1994) argues that, within the evolutionary framework she applies to her analysis, competition and mutualism should occur both between and within organisations, and an organisation's balance between the two at both levels will have a profound effect on its survival. The management of the tension between competition and mutualism among organisations is therefore equally relevant to the survival of a destination. Competition fuels vigor and variety, but can be destructive if it becomes excessive.

Aspects of the nexus between collaboration and the visioning process discussed earlier warrant revisiting at this point so that issues relating to the mutualism/competition conundrum can be explored further. Collaboration provides a means of managing the tension between co-operation and the autonomy organisations require in competitive environments to the extent that, by definition, collaboration implies a mechanism for joint decision-making among autonomous and key stakeholders of an inter-organisational domain, such as a tourism destination (Getz 1994: 155). Thus, while the process of instilling principles of collective learning and vision setting between, rather than within, organisations may represent a more complex task, it is nevertheless achievable. As mentioned earlier in references to the participatory approach and collaboration, it requires the different agendas between organisations to be reconciled, but beyond this the essence of 'cocreating' a shared vision is to find the common ground that over-rides the differences. As suggested earlier, however, in this process we need to be realistic by seeking alignments, rather than absolute agreement on every point. Indeed, as Helling's analysis of Atlanta's 2020 Vision project suggests, a consensus that is arrived at by an undue focus on the common ground will become too 'general and bland' to provide any meaningful direction, and it may result in particular interest groups gaining 'veto power over visionary reform' (Helling 1998: 345).

Against this backdrop, Bryson's (1995: 155) view of a vision as being a 'treaty negotiated among rival coalitions' would appear to apply. However, this implies an adversarial orientation that would be neither appropriate nor desirable. An interpretation that is more consistent with the learning organisation theme is provided by Gray (1989: 5), who saw collaboration (and implicitly a visioning process) as providing a means by which 'parties who see different aspects of a problem can constructively explore their differences and search for solutions that go beyond their limited vision of what is possible'. Weber (1998: 88), provided a similar perspective by suggesting that one of the benefits of a vision derived through collaboration is that 'unstable zero sum scenarios are transformed into enduring win-win outcomes as participants come to realize the benefits of thinking and acting for the whole rather than their selfish, narrow, individual interests'.

The introduction of such an approach to the Gold Coast setting will require a fundamental shift in mindsets and organisational approaches. The Gold Coast has grown and flourished in a relatively benign regulatory regime, which has fostered a combative private enterprise mentality driven by market forces and a fiercely competitive business culture. Public sector engagement in aspects of tourism development has been minimal and regarded with suspicion by the business community. One of the consequences of this has been a policy and planning void, whereby the lack of a tourism agenda within the state and local government bureaucratic structures has meant that the tourism implications of various policy and infrastructure initiatives have not been adequately addressed. Despite this, the laissez-faire environment has provided a fertile setting for a range of flamboyant entrepreneurs to introduce innovations that have rejuvenated the destination at various points in its history (Russell and Faulkner 1999). However, the scale and complexity of tourism development in the region has reached a point where it is increasingly difficult for the actions of individual entrepreneurs to initiate major shifts in the fortunes of the destination as a whole. A more collaborative and cooperative approach, involving the private, public sector agencies and other stakeholder groups within the community, is necessary if the challenges of the future are to be effectively addressed. This implies that the Gold Coast's problem is essentially one of organisational change.

Like organisations in general, the Gold Coast can be envisaged as having evolved towards a point where internal rigidities associated with hierarchical structures, specialisations and demarcations have impeded internal communication, and the inertia of established values and approaches threaten to constrain responsiveness to changing conditions (Hurst 1995). This makes the destination both less adaptive and more prone to disaster. While the constraints referred to above have the benefit of preserving successful practices/approaches, they inevitably become counterproductive when they inhibit learning and adaptation. In this context, the worst and most insidious types of constraints are those that are tacit, rather than explicit. If they are not visible and identifiable, they cannot be changed and if they cannot be changed then the organisation's ability to adapt to changing and potentially threatening external conditions will be affected. As Senge *et al.* (1994: 28) have observed, 'Changing the way we interact means redesigning not only the formal structures of the organisation, but the hard to see patterns of interaction between people and processes.'... 'Once we become conscious of how we think and interact, and begin developing capacities to think and act differently, we will have already begun to change our organisation for the better.' It is for this reason that, within the learning organisation framework, an analysis of the underlying rationale and assumptions that underpin relationships within the system is an essential early step in the development of the rejuvenation strategy.

In an observation that perhaps encapsulates the 'catch-22' predicament of many maturing destinations, Hurst (1995: 139) has suggested that many organisations are caught by the 'renewal process paradox', whereby 'the change process cannot begin until the failure of the old order is manifest, but the process is likely to be more successful if it gets underway before too much damage is done'. Given the symptoms of stagnation evident in the Gold Coast case, as demonstrated in the analysis in earlier sections of this paper, it could be argued that 'the failure of the older order' is clearly manifest. While it may be overstating the case to suggest that too much damage has already been done to make the situation retrievable, it is certainly evident that any delay in the reassessment of future directions and approaches, such as that proposed in the Visioning process, will make the eventual demise of the destination inevitable.

On the one hand, the thrust of the above discussion implies a more structured approach to destination management on the Gold Coast and most definitely this will be necessary if sustainable tourism objectives are to be achievable. On the other hand, in the establishment of a new planning and management regime, care needs to be taken to ensure procedures and practices do not become so routinised that they lose the flexibility and variety of responses required to respond to new opportunities and adapt to change (Miner 1994). Without there being scope for variety generating recombinations of organisational routines, rigidities that limit adaptability will emerge. As mentioned previously, one of the factors that has fuelled the vitality of the Gold Coast and enabled the destination to flourish in the past has been a policy and planning regime that has fostered variety through minimal restrictions on entrepreneurial activity. In the process, however, there has been a fixation on profit generation and economic objectives at the expense of other elements of the sustainable tourism agenda. As a consequence of this, there is a risk of the destination's options for the future being reduced to such an extent that its longer-term survival could be in jeopardy.

3.6 Scenarios and the art of strategic conversation

In his book, *Scenarios: The Art of Strategic Conversation*, van der Heijden
(1996) refers to three schools of thought in strategy development. At one
extreme, there are rationalists seeking to find optimal solutions, and who
are identified with Michael Porter. At the other extreme, there are the
evolutionists, who see strategies emerging and being only fully
understandable in retrospect. Between these two, are the processionalists,
whose approach 'emerges through strategic conversation' (p. vii). He
argues that in a turbulent environment, the latter approach has the most
to offer as 'uncertainty has the effect of moving the key to success from
"the optimal strategy" to "the most skilful strategy process"' (van der
Heijden 1996: vii).

According to van der Heijden's perspective, there are two 'pathologies'
in strategic decision making, with excess integration, or 'groupthink', at
one extreme and excess differentiation at the other. He adds that:

> models, to enable an organisation to come to a shared conclusion and
> move forward, and differentiation of mental models, to ensure that a
> wide range of weak signals in the environment are perceived,
> understood and brought into the system to enter the conversation
> and be acted upon. (van der Heijden 1996: viii)

In this context, the strategic vision is the counterpart of scenarios in the
process of coping with turbulence and uncertainty. Visions can thus be
construed as 'complexity reducers', which provide a common frame of
reference for organising information. They provide the signpost or signals
for navigating against a noisy background. Scenarios, on the other hand,
are 'shared and agreed upon mental models of the external world ...
created as internally consistent and challenging descriptions of possible
futures ...' (van der Heijden 1996: 5). They complement the visioning
process through their value as a basis for exploring possible futures and
the opportunity they provide for stakeholders to see the world through
different lenses. Scenario generating exercises help participants to see
things they may not have otherwise been disposed to look for, thus
dislodging them from established mindsets. The nexus between scenario
generation, visioning and learning is alluded to in Blumenfeld's (1999: 7)
comment:

> Constructive visions of the future are presented to reveal the
> abundance of potentialities ahead. Studying our future can not only
> enhance our ability to understand what is happening in a wider
> historical context but can also imbue our consequent acts with a
> greater awareness and a feeling of participation.

Scenario planning is distinct from the more traditional approaches to strategic planning by virtue of its more specific focus on ambiguity and uncertainty in the strategic issues being examined. The affinities of this approach to the learning organisation perspective are explicit in the following observation:

> The most fundamental aspect of introducing uncertainty into the strategic equation is that it turns planning for the future from a once-off episodic activity into an ongoing learning proposition. In a situation of uncertainty planning becomes learning and never stops. (van der Heijden 1996: 7)

Recognising that we operate within a turbulent environment which makes our efforts to predict the future with any degree of certainty a futile endeavour, scenario planning instead aims to identify and consider multiple, equally plausible futures. These then become the context, or 'test bed' framing the vision and identifying options for improvement (van der Heijden 1996: 53–54).

Wilkinson (1999) reflects a similar emphasis in his interpretation of the purpose of scenario planning:

> ... the purpose of scenario planning is not to pinpoint future events but to highlight large scale forces that push the future in different directions. It's about making these forces visible, so if they do happen, the planner will at least recognize them. It's about helping to make better decisions today.

Scenarios are helpful in assisting organisations to cope with future events in three ways. Firstly, they help the organisations to understand the environment, and allow many decisions to be put into perspective through them being seen not so much as isolated events, but as part of a process of 'swings and roundabouts'. Secondly, they highlight the inherent uncertainty of the environment and, in the process, foster an appreciation of exposure to 'accidents' and undue risk. Finally, they help organisations 'to become more adaptable by expanding their mental models and thereby enhancing the perceptual capabilities needed to recognize unexpected events' (van der Heijden 1996: 86). Arguably, through such an approach, individuals and organisations might not come any closer to foretelling the future, but they may place themselves in a position where they will have more control over their destiny. As Blumenfeld (1999: 8) suggests, '(it) is not possible to depict tomorrow's world with any degree of certainty, but many aspects of it can certainly be anticipated. And such prognostication may itself affect the outcome.'

To add one final clarification of the nature of scenarios, it is useful to consider the distinctions between scenarios and forecasting. Forecasting assumes that the future can be accurately predicted and is usually carried out by 'experts' who are detached from decision-makers, whereas scenario planning is process oriented and accepts that uncertainties invariably restrict the extent to which the future can be predicted. But by involving decision-makers in the process, rather than the latter abdicating responsibility to detached experts, the planning process is more attuned to the risks and variety of possibilities involved. In short, scenario-planning is more consistent with type of informed decision-making identified with learning organisations. Another distinction is that forecasting is essentially a statistical statement, whereas a scenario is a conceptual description of the future incorporating notions of cause and effect. Finally, forecasting is often based on fairly specific, mechanistic models of cause and effect that, in contrast to the scenario-planning approach, have the potential to act as a straight jacket on the way the future is explored, and gives insufficient weight to the uncertainties involved.

Many of the elements of the scenario generation based approach, and its affinities with visioning and the learning organisation concept, are succinctly encapsulated in the following excerpt from the Global Business Network (1999):

> Today, organisations and industries are facing huge structural change, uncertainty and decisions with huge opportunities and risks. Anticipating the future in this volatile environment calls for more than systematic analysis: it also demands creativity, insight and imagination. Scenarios – stories about possible futures – combine these elements into a foundation for robust strategies. The test of a good scenario is not whether it portrays the future accurately but whether it enables an organisation to learn, adapt and enrich the ongoing strategic conversation.

3.7 Synthesis

The above analysis draws on insights from a range of sources, which are synthesised into a framework for destination strategic planning and management in Figure 3.4. Thus, the philosophical foundations of the approach are encapsulated by sustainable tourism development principles, which in turn implies a perspective with two inter-related ingredients. Firstly, it is essential that a whole of destination approach be adopted, recognising that sustainability requires a balancing of social, economic and environmental considerations. From this, it follows that tourism cannot be looked at in isolation, inter-relationships and synergies with other sectors of the economy and broader equity and quality of life issues need to be taken into account. Secondly, the sustainability agenda, and the whole of destination perspective it engenders, necessitates an inclusive, community participation approach involving representatives of all relevant stakeholder groups. The effective implementation of the whole of destination approach through the participatory model, however, requires the application of techniques that take us beyond mere consultation to the meaningful engagement of stakeholders in joint decision-making. This requires a combination of the following techniques.

- *Visioning:* The engagement of stakeholders in the building of a shared vision for the future of the destination that is consistent with sustainable tourism development principles. While this exercise is of necessity an iterative process, its potential role as a vehicle for highlighting the need for change and galvanising support for the approach based on the principles and perspectives outlined above means that this technique is an important ingredient of the early stages of the process.
- *Scenario building:* As it is focused on the future, the shared vision needs to be attuned to a collective understanding of the environment and how it is changing. It is important, therefore, that the visioning stage is complemented by a scenario building process, involving an exploration of possible futures that is informed by both a strong research platform and the variety of perspectives stakeholders can contribute.
- *Learning organisation approach:* Intrinsic to both the visioning and scenario building components is the notion of stakeholders becoming engaged in a process that ensures they are continually

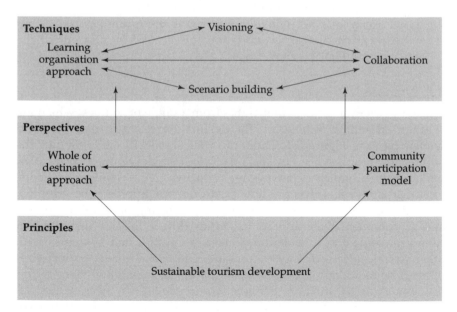

Figure 3.4 A framework for destination strategic management and planning

focused on enhancing and expanding their collective awareness and capabilities. Learning and the building of a knowledge base that is accessible to all stakeholders therefore need to become an integral part of the organisational structure at the destination level.

- *Collaboration:* The application of all of the above techniques hinges on collaboration in the sense that they require a range of stakeholders, who normally act autonomously of each other, to work together towards a mutually acceptable position on their understanding of emerging challenges, preferred futures for the destination and how these might be realised. The management of the tension between autonomy and cooperation is therefore central to both the development and implementation of the strategy.

The framework described above provides broad guidelines for the engagement of stakeholders in the Gold Coast Visioning process. The derivation of more specific guidelines has been based on insights from the literature cited above, combined with a selective adaptation of an analytical framework for assessing local collaborative arrangements developed by Bramwell and Sharman (1999). As in the case of Bramwell and Sharman's framework, the guidelines revolve around three broad areas:

- Scope of collaboration;
- Intensity of collaboration; and
- Degree to which a consensus emerges.

3.7.1 Scope of collaboration
- The range of participants should be representative of all relevant stakeholders. In this context, stakeholder are defined as individuals, groups or organisations that are affected by the issues under consideration. As mentioned previously, within a tourism destination, relevant stakeholders comprise tourism operators and other members of the business community, environmental and other special interest groups, the resident population and public sector agencies;
- The benefits of involvement by stakeholders must be clearly articulated and communicated to those invited to participate in order to encourage their commitment to the process. As emphasised by Helling (1998b: 224), 'stakeholders must see a compelling reason' for participation and 'must believe that their interests will be protected and advanced through the process'. In articulating the case for participation, however, it is essential that unrealistic expectations regarding the outcomes are not fuelled;
- Individuals and organisations that have a role to play in the implementation of the plan must be involved. As observed by Gray (1989: 64, cited in Bramwell and Sharman) 'Acceptance of any

solution is enhanced when those who must abide by it are included in designing the solution'. Hall and McArthur (1998: 19) make a similar point, but in doing so they emphasise ownership as the important link: 'an inclusive planning process by which those responsible for implementing the plan are also those who have helped to formulate it, will dramatically increase the likelihood of ownership of the plan and, hence its effective implementation'.

- Care should be taken to ensure that the specific individuals selected to represent particular groups are capable of accurately reflecting the interests of that group. This is a particular problem where efforts are made to represent the general community through particular individuals, who are invariably inclined to the view of a particular segment of the community, rather than the resident population in general. Supplementary consultative and general survey methods are clearly necessary to overcome this problem.

3.7.2 Timing and intensity of collaboration

- To ensure all stakeholders are provided with an opportunity to make a meaningful contribution to the planning process, everyone should be involved from the outset (Haywood 1988; Gunn 1998). To do otherwise runs the risk of entrenched positions becoming an inhibiting factor and stakeholder perceptions of being presented with a fait accompli;
- Stakeholders should be fully informed about every aspect of the collaborative process in order to ensure that it is fully accountable to them. Equally, relevant background information should be made available to them to ensure they can make an informed contribution to discussion;
- Opportunities for direct interaction among stakeholders is necessary to ensure that issues are effectively debated, that knowledge building occurs at a collective level, progress is made towards consensus building and the collaborative relationships required for implementation are fostered;
- In line with the principles of the learning organisation approach enunciated by Senge (1990) and Senge *et al.* (1994), the collaborative process needs to be structured in such a way that a climate of openness, honesty, tolerance and respect is fostered in the relationship among participants. The ability of participants to understand and learn from each other's arguments is central to the building of the collective knowledge base necessary to move towards a consensus.

3.7.3 The emergence of a consensus

- It is important that participants have realistic expectations regarding the potential for a consensus being achieved that receives one hundred per cent support of all involved. It needs to be understood that not everyone will agree with the final position to the same degree. As Ritchie (1993) has observed, the stakeholders represent a diverse range of often diametrically opposed value systems, and there are limits to the extent to which these can be reconciled. Where it appears an absolute consensus has been achieved, this may in fact represent a situation where the discussion has skirted around ambiguities and contentious issues and, at best, it has merely focused on the common ground;

- Along with the achievement of at least a partial consensus though a process adhering to the guidelines outlined above, a degree of ownership of the outcomes should emerge among participants. While across the board ownership is important, ownership among those upon whom implementation of the plan relies is essential.

4 The Gold Coast Tourism Visioning Project Approach

As indicated previously, the approach adopted in the Gold Coast Tourism Visioning project involves a combination of the methods employed in traditional strategic planning and some refinements informed by insights from more recent innovations involving such concepts as visioning, organisational learning and scenario-based strategic conversation. The importance of sustainable tourism development principles as the underlying philosophy of the process has also been emphasised and, as a corollary of this, a participatory approach has also been recognised as an essential element of the process. Bearing the latter point in mind, in particular, a range of methods for the engagement of stakeholders had to be considered.

The following range of potential methods for achieving community/ stakeholder involvement has been identified by Hall and McArthur (1998):

Draft documents/plans;
Discussion papers;
Information sheets and brochures;
Displays and computer simulations;
Information hotlines;
Media campaigns;
Guided tours;
Public meetings;
Small stakeholder meetings;
Surveys;
Individual interviews with stakeholders;
Focus groups;
Workshops;
Advisory committees.

Superficially, surveys would appear to maximise involvement to the extent that they enable a broad cross section of stakeholders to be given an opportunity to provide an input to the process. Surveys alone, however, are inadequate because they do not allow the degree of information sharing, collective learning and participatory decision making that is required. In their comparison of techniques listed above, Hall and McArthur (1998) identified the following as being most effective for these purposes: stakeholder interviews and meetings; focus groups; workshops; and advisory committees. The methods used to engage stakeholders in the Gold Coast Tourism Visioning process involved a combination of all of these methods apart from focus groups.

Specifically, the following methods have been, or are being, employed:

- Stakeholder interviews;
- Surveys covering the resident population and tourism industry enterprises;
- Workshops; and
- Advisory committees in the form of a steering committee driving the overall project and a series of reference groups providing a sounding board for individual research projects.

The overall approach is described in Figure 3.5, where the following ingredients are identified:

- A 'Scoping Study' was conducted involving interviews with over 100 key representatives of stakeholder groups. The main purpose of this survey was to canvas stakeholder perceptions about the status of the tourism industry on the Gold Coast, and the challenges and issues warranting attention in the consideration of its future. This exercise informed the refinement of the research agenda referred to in the next point.
- An 'audit' process involving an integrated series of research projects aimed at overviewing the current status of Gold Coast tourism in terms of social, economic (including tourism marketing) and environmental considerations has been carried out as a 'front-end' input to the visioning process. The range of research projects involved and their objects are summarised in Appendix B, where a synthesis of key findings of completed projects and associated issues is also provided. As alluded to above, each project was driven by a 'reference group' consisting of representatives of relevant stakeholder groups in order to ensure that these projects were attuned to the concerns of those stakeholders who have a legitimate interest in the focus of the research.

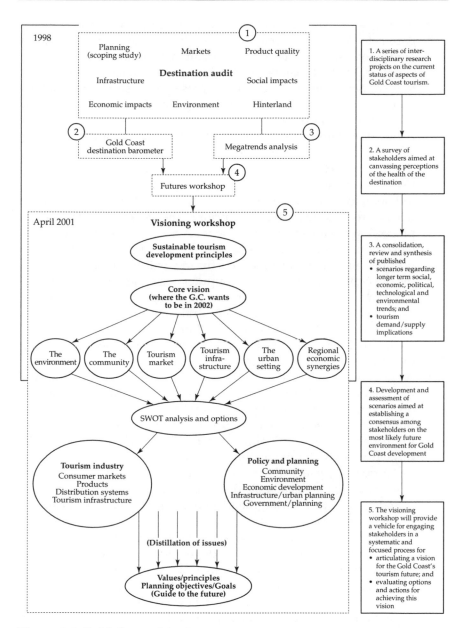

Figure 3.5 Gold Coast visioning process

- A survey of tourism industry stakeholders ('Tourism Industry Barometer') was conducted to provide an indication of industry perceptions on the status of tourism development on the Gold Coast, individual visions of the future and preferred options for tourism development. A parallel representative survey of residents ('Social Audit') was aimed at receiving similar input from the host population's perspective.
- A one-day 'Futures Workshop', involving representatives of key stakeholder groups, with the aim of producing a consensus on probable, possible and preferred future scenarios affecting the Gold Coast. A review of global and domestic social, economic, political, technological and environmental scenarios ('Megatrends Analysis' will be provided to participants prior to the workshop to inform this process), while a panel of prominent futurists will be involved in the workshop to stimulate discussion. A convergence of views on possible, probable and preferred futures will be achieved through the application of Ellyard's Grouputer technique, whereby break-out groups work at computer terminals and feed the outcomes of their deliberations directly into a central computer. Group inputs are processed so that common threads of opinion and discordant views are highlighted in feedback provided on a continuous basis during the course of group discussion.
- A one-day 'Visioning Workshop' aimed at assessing the viability of the vision derived from the first workshop in terms of sustainable development principles and a SWOT analysis based on probable future. It will also produce, in skeletal form at least, an action plan for realising the vision identified in the first workshop. Specifically, this workshop will involve the following steps:
  - An opening panel discussion involving experts who have been responsible for sustainable development agenda in other contexts and aimed at exploring the essential ingredients of a sustainable development approach.
  - As it is important that we anchor the following discussion in terms of concrete options for development (rather than basing discussion on abstractions), a range of specific options for tourism development will be introduced at this stage. These options, which are also being canvassed beyond the workshop partici-pants through separate surveys of industry and resident stake-holder groups, will be presented to workshop participants for 'short-listing', along with information on the degree of support for each option reflected in the surveys.
  - Workshop participants will be then asked to evaluate the options in terms of their consistency with the preferred future (vision) identified in the futures workshop and the sustainable tourism

development principles discussed earlier in this workshop. This process will produce a 'shortlist' of preferred options. Groups will have the opportunity to introduce additional options at this point.

- Up to this point in time, participants will be encouraged to think positively and not to allow their consideration of options to be influenced unduly by impediments that may make some options more or less achievable. However, a 'reality check' focusing on the preferred options is necessary and this will be achieved through the conduct of a SWOT analysis based on the probable future scenarios developed in the Futures Workshop.

- The SWOT analysis will be a prelude to the consideration threshold issues affecting the realisation of the vision, the action necessary to address these issues and the identification of stakeholder responsibilities in carrying these actions forward.

5 Conclusion

In any increasingly competitive global environment, strategic planning has become a fundamental element of business survival. The lead times involved in effectively responding to market trends means that an on-going environmental scanning and strategic assessment process is necessary. In the tourism sector, this is equally applicable for the individual enterprise and for the destination as a whole. Indeed, strategic planning at these two levels needs to be articulated, as the tourism product in any setting is a composite of services and goods, and the quality of the visitor's experience depends, to some degree, upon the extent to which the range of providers involved have a common sense of purpose. A critical step in the development of a destination strategic plan is therefore the formulation of a shared vision (Ritchie 1999).

Given that the host community itself is an integral element of the tourism product, an extension of the internal marketing concept to the resident population as a whole means it is equally important that this shared vision reflects the views and interests of the broader community. Apart from its relevance to the strategic marketing agenda, the latter consideration is an imperative of sustainable tourism development also in the sense that a future direction of tourism development that is inconsistent with the lifestyle and equity aspirations of the host community is neither desirable nor sustainable.

In the Gold Coast setting, the need for a more focused strategic approach to destination management and planning is accentuated by a history that has been distinctively ad hoc and piecemeal, and by the indicators that suggest the destination is entering a stagnation phase. This paper has argued that the agreement on a shared vision among stakeholders represents the first step towards developing a strategy for rejuvenating the destination. In this context, the relevant stakeholders are broadly defined to include tourism and other businesses, industry organisations, public sector agencies at the local and state government levels, and representatives of the resident community. Such a broad spectrum of involvement reflects the necessity of a holistic approach, which recognises that social and environmental considerations warrant equal consideration with the economic dimension in the mapping of a course toward a sustainable tourism future.

Bearing the above considerations in mind, the approach to the development of a vision for the Gold Coast outlined above involves two additional central caveats. Firstly, in the visioning process, as in the case of strategic planning more generally, the route taken in the development of the vision is as important as the destination. That is, the process of developing the vision should be instrumental in developing an informed and considered dialogue among stakeholders, to such an extent that the destination plan and management framework will represent not only a consensus among this group, but also it will reflect a thorough and rigorous analysis of the issues. Secondly, the visioning statement produced at the end of the process should be couched in terms that enable it provide a meaningful foundation for the strategic planning process. Beyond this, however, the visioning exercise itself should be used as a catalyst for bringing about the permanent changes in the structure of the destination planning and management process that are necessary for the Gold Coast to become a 'learning organisation' at the destination level. That is, the visioning project should be instrumental in establishing a systematic planning regime that is supported by a strong research base and a rigorous evaluation system. Such a regime will underpin the institutional learning process and memory that is so essential for creative adaptation to the challenges of the future and reducing the prospect of repeating past mistakes or re-inventing the wheel (van der Heijden 1996).

Tourist destinations generally are confronted with the dual challenges of remaining competitive in an increasingly competitive and turbulent environment, while at the same time ensuring that the management of tourism is consistent with the principles of sustainable tourism development. The magnitude of this challenge is accentuated in the specific case of the Gold Coast by the fact that this destination is at a mature stage of development, with some of the symptoms of stagnation evident. Also the rapid population growth of the region creates additional problems related to reconciling the pressures of urban expansion and tourism development in the management of impacts on the natural and social environment. This paper has argued that addressing these challenges in the Gold Coast context, specifically, requires a fundamentally different approach to destination management than that which has prevailed in the past. A holistic, all of destination approach involving a shift from a focus on destination marketing to destination management is required. Such an approach is encapsulated in the framework and suite of methods described in this chapter.

Despite the focus on the specifics of the Gold Coast situation in this chapter, the destination management framework that has been developed is essentially a generic model applicable to destinations generally. The reference to the Gold Coast situation has provided a useful backdrop for exploring some of the nuances and complications of operationalising the model. In particular, the establishment of a management regime based on the proposed model requires significant adjustments in the institutional arrangements for the planning and management of tourism in the destination. This transformation is in turn inhibited by the inertia of existing institutional structures, and the comfort zones and vested interests of individual stakeholders. Ultimately, the establishment of the more strategically focused and sustainability oriented model advocated in this paper hinges on the degree to which leading players among the stakeholder groups embrace it and champion the cause.

References

Alipour, H. (1996) Tourism development within planning paradigms: the case of Turkey, *Tourism Management*, 17, 5, 367–377.

Agarwal, S. (1997) The resort cycle and seaside tourism, *Tourism Management*, 18, 2, 65–74.

—— (1999) Restructuring and local economic development: implications for seaside resort regeneration in Southwest Britain, *Tourism Management*, 20, 4, 511–22.

Andereck, K. L. and Vogt, C. A. (2000) The relationship between residents' attitudes towards tourism and tourism development options, *Journal of Travel Research*, 39, 1, 27–36.

Backman, S., Petrick, J. and Wright, B. A. (2001) Management tools and techniques: an integrated approach to planning, in Weaver, D. (ed.) *The Encyclopedia of Ecotourism*, CAB International, 451–461.

Barker, J. A. (1992) *Discovering the Future: The Power of Vision*. Infinity Limited, Winter Park, Florida.

Baum, J. A. C. and Singh, J. V. (eds) (1994) *Evolutionary Dynamics of Organisations*, Oxford University Press, Oxford.

Blumenfeld, Y. (ed.) (1999) *Scanning the Future: 20 Eminent Thinkers on the World of Tomorrow*, Thames and Hudson, London.

Bramwell, B. and Lane, B. (1993) Sustainable tourism: an evolving global approach, *Journal of Sustainable Tourism*, 1, 1, 1–5.

Bramwell, B. and Sharman, A. (1999) Collaboration in local tourism marketing, *Annals of Tourism Research*, 26, 392–415.

Bryson, J. (1995) *Strategic Planning for Public and Non-profit Organizations: A Guide to Strengthening and Sustaining Organizational Achievement*, Josey-Bass, San Francisco.

Buhalis, D. (1999) Limits of tourism development in peripheral destinations: problems and challenges, *Tourism Management*, 20, 2, 183–185.

Butler, R. W. (1980) The concept of a tourist area life cycle of evolution: implications for management of resources, *Canadian Geographer*, 24, 1, 5–12.

—— (1990) Alternative tourism: pious hope or Trojan horse, *Journal of Travel Research*, 28, 3, 40–44.

—— (1991) Tourism, environment and sustainable development, *Environmental Conservation*, 18, 3, 201–209.

—— (1992) Alternative tourism: the thin edge of the wedge, in Smith, V. I. and Eadington, W. R. (eds) *Tourism Alternatives: Potentials and problems in the Development of Tourism*, University of Pennsylvania Press, Philadelphia, 31–46.

Cater, E. (1993) Ecotourism in the third world: problems for sustainable tourism development, *Tourism Management*, 14, 2, 85–90.

Chalip, L. (1996) Group decision making and problem solving, in Parkhouse, B. L. (ed.) *The Management of Sport: Its Foundation and Application*, Mosby-Year Book, St Louis, 84–101.

Choy, D. J. L. (1991) Tourism planning: the case for market failure, *Tourism Management*, 12, 4, 313–330.

Cohen, E. (1982) Marginal paradises: bungalow tourism on the islands of southern Thailand, *Annals of Tourism Research*, 9, 2, 189–228.

Cooper, C. (1994) The destination life cycle: an update, in Seaton, A. V., Jenkins, C. L., Wood, R. C., Deike, P., Bennett, M. M., MacLellan, L. R. and Smith, R. (eds.) *Tourism: The State of the Art*, John Wiley and Sons, Chichester, 340–346.

—— (1990) Resorts in decline – the management response, *Tourism Management*, 11, 1, 63–67.

Cooper, C. and Jackson, S. (1989) Destination life cycle: the Isle of Man case study, *Annals of Tourism Research*, 46, 377–98.

Farrell, B. H. (1999) Conventional or sustainable tourism? No room for choice, *Tourism Management*, 20, 2, 189–91.

Faulkner, H. W. (1990) Swings and roundabouts in Australian tourism, *Tourism Management*, 11, 1, 29–37.

Formica, S. and Uysal, M. (1996) The revitalization of Italy as a tourist destination, *Tourism Management*, 17, 5, 323–331.

Getz, D. (1986) Models in tourism planning, *Tourism Management*, 7, 1, 21–32.

Getz, D. and Jamal, T. B. (1994) The environment-community symbiosis: a case for collaborative tourism planning, *Journal of Sustainable Tourism*, 2, 3, 152–173.

Global Business Network (1999) GBN Scenario Planning, World Wide web: (http://www.gbn.org/scenPlan.html) 2020 SCENARIOS: Some Notes.

Gold Coast City Council (2000) Draft Gold Coast 2010: Economic Development Strategy.

Gomez, M. J. M. and Rebello, F. V. (1995) Coastal areas: processes, typologies and prospects, in Montanari, A. and Williams, A. M. (eds.) *European Tourism: Regions, Spaces and Restructuring*, John Wiley and Sons, London, 111–126.

Gray, B. (1989) *Collaborating: Finding Common Ground for Multi-Party Problems*, Josey-Bass, San Francisco.

Gunn, C. A. (1994) *Tourism Planning: Basics, Concepts and Cases*. Taylor & Francis, Washington.

Hall, C. M. and McArthur, S. (1998) *Integrated Heritage Management: Principles and Practice*. The Stationery Office, London.

Hardin, G. (1968) The tragedy of the commons, *Science*, 162, 1243–1248.

Haywood, K. M. (1988) Responsible and responsive tourism planning in the community, *Tourism Management*, 9, 105–118.

—— (1986) Can the tourism area cycle of evolution be made operational? *Tourism Management*, 7, 3, 154–167.

Hawaii Tourism Authority (1999) *Competitive Strategic Assessment of Hawaii Tourism*, Executive Summary.

Heath, E. and Wall, G. (1992) *Marketing Tourism Destinations*, John Wiley, New York.
Helling, A. (1998a) Collaborative visioning: proceed with Caution! Results from evaluating Atlanta's Vision 2020 Project, *Journal of the American Planning Association*, 64, 3, 335–347.
—— (1998b) Employer-sponsored and self-sponsored participation in collaborative visioning: Theory, evidence and implications, *Journal of Applied Behavioral Science*, 34, 2, 222–240.
Hurst, D. K. (1995) *Crisis and Renewal: Meeting the Challenge of Organizational Change*. Harvard Business School Press, Boston, Massachusetts.
Inskeep, E. (1991) *Tourism Planning: An Integrated and Sustainable Development Approach*, Van Nostrand Reinhold, New York.
Ioannides, D. (1992) Tourism development agents: the Cypriot resort cycle, *Annals of Tourism Research*, 19, 4, 711–731.
Jamal, T. and Getz, D. (1995) Collaboration theory and community tourism planning, *Annals of Tourism Research*, 22 (1), 186–204.
Jarviluoma, J. (1992) Alternative tourism and the evolution of tourist areas, *Tourism Management*, 13, 1, 118–120.
Joppe, M. (1996) Sustainable community tourism development revisited, *Tourism Management*, 17, 7, 475–479.
King, B., McVey, M. and Simmons, D. (2000) A societal marketing approach to national tourism planning: evidence from the South Pacific, *Tourism Management*, 21, 4, 407–416.
Kotler, P. and Armstrong, G. (1984) *Principles of Marketing*, 4th edition, Prentice-Hall, Englewoodcliffs.
Krippendorf, J. (1987) *The Holiday Makers*, Heinemann, London.
Manning, T. (1999) Indicators of tourism sustainability, *Tourism Management*, 20, 2, 179–81.
Meadows, D. H., Meadows, D. L., Randers, J. and Behrens, W. W. (1972) *The Limits of Growth*, Universe Books, New York.
Meyer-Arendt, K. J. (1985) The Grand Isle, Louisiana resort cycle, *Annals of Tourism Research*, 12, 449–465.
Mill, R. C. (1996) Societal marketing: implications for tourism destinations, *Journal of Vacation Marketing*, 2, 3, 215–221.
Miner, A. S. (1994) Seeking adaptive advantage: evolutionary theory and managerial action, in Baum, J. A. C. and Singh, J. V. (eds) *Evolutionary Dynamics of Organisations*, Oxford University Press, Oxford, 76–89.
Mintzberg, H. (2000) *The Rise and Fall of Strategic Planning*. Prentice Hall, London.
Morgan, M. (1991) Dressing up to survive: marketing Majorca anew, *Tourism Management*, 12, 1, 15–20.
Murphy, P. (1994) Tourism and sustainable development, in Theobald, W. (ed.) *Global Tourism: The New Decade*. Butterworth-Heinemann, Oxford, 274–290.
—— (1985) *Tourism: a Community Approach*, Methuen, New York.
Paul, S. (1987) *Community Participation in Developing Projects: The World Bank Experience*, World Bank, Washington.
Pearce, D. (1989) *Tourism Development*, Longman, U. K. and John Wiley, New York.
Prideaux, B. (2000) The resort development spectrum – a new approach to modelling resort development, *Tourism Management*, 21, 3, 225–240.
Putnam, L. L. (1986) *Conflict in Group Decision-Making*. In R. Y. Hirokawa and M. S. Poole (eds), *Communication and Group Decision-Making*. Newbury Park, California: Sage, pp. 175–196.
Reed, M.G. (1997) Power relationships and community based tourism planning, *Annals of Tourism Research*, 24, 566–591.

Ritchie, J. R. B. (1999) Crafting a value driven for a national tourism treasure, *Tourism Management*, 20, 3, 273–82.
—— (1993) Crafting a destination vision: putting the concept of resident responsive tourism into practice, *Tourism Management*, 14, 15, 29–38.
Ritchie, J. R. B. and Crouch, G. I. (2000) The competitive destination: a sustainability perspective, *Tourism Management*, 21, 1, 1–7.
Russell, R. and Faulkner, B. (1999) Movers and shakers: chaos makers in tourism development, *Tourism Management*, 20, 4, 411–423.
Senge, P. M. (1990) *The Fifth Principle: The Art and Practice of the Learning Organisation*, Doubleday, New York.
Senge P. M., Kleiner, A., Roberts, C., Ross, R. B. and Smith, B. J. (1994) *The Fifth Discipline Fieldbook: Strategies and Tools for Building a Learning Organisation*, Nicholas Brearley Publishing Ltd., London.
Strapp, J. D. (1988) The resort cycle and second homes, *Annals of Tourism Research*, 15, 504–516.
The Property Council of Australia, Gold Coast Chapter (2000) *Our Gold Coast: Refurbishing, Rejuvenating and Unifying the Gold Coast*, The Edward de Bono Workshop: Strategic Statement and Future Directions.
Tideswell, C. (2001) *Gold Coast Tourism Market Analysis (update)*, Cooperative Research Centre for Sustainable Tourism, Gold Coast Visioning Project Research Report 1.1.
Tosun, C. (1999) Towards a typology of community participation in the tourism development process, *Anatolia*, 10, 2, 113–134.
Twining-Ward, L. (1999) Towards sustainable tourism development: observations from a distance, *Tourism Management*, 20, 2, 187–88.
van der Heijden, K. (1996) *Scenarios: the Art of Strategic Conversation*. John Wiley, Chichester.
WCED (1987) *Our Common Future*, Oxford University Press, Oxford.
Weaver, D. B. (1990) Grand Cayman Island and the resort cycle concept, *Journal of Travel Research*, 29, 2, 9–15.
Weber, E. P. (1998) Collaborative leadership: how citizens can make a difference (Review of the Book by D. D. Chrislip and C. E. Larson), *Review of Public Personnel Administration*, 18, 2, 88–93.
Wheeller, B. (1993) Sustaining the ego, *Journal of Sustainable Tourism*, 1, 2, 121–129.
Wilkinson, L. (1999) How to build scenarios? Planning for 'long fuse, big bang' problems in an era of uncertainty, Hot Wired World Wide Web: http://www.wired.com/wired/scenarios/build.html
World Tourism Organisation (1980) *Manila Declaration*, WTO, Madrid
—— (1989) *The Hague Declaration*, WTO, Madrid.
Zurick, D. (1992) Adventure travel and sustainable tourism in the peripheral economy of Nepal, *Annals of the Association of American Geographers*, 83, 4, 608–628.

Appendix A: related initiatives

The outcomes of two other recent initiatives that have a bearing on the examination of strategic directions of the Gold Coast tourism industry will need to be taken into account in the approach outlined above. These initiatives include the 1999 Edward de Bono Workshop organised by the Property Council of Australia's Gold Coast Chapter (PCAGC) and the Gold Coast City Council's (GCCC) Draft Economic Development Strategy (2000).

The de Bono workshop

A workshop organised by the Property Council's Gold Coast Chapter in October 1999 engaged Edward de Bono to assist business leaders and other stakeholders to focus on issues associated with setting some strategic directions for the refurbishment and rejuvenation of the Gold Coast. Initially concerned primarily with the Surfers Paradise precinct of the Gold Coast, it was recognised that issues affecting the rejuvenation of Surfers Paradise could not be examined in isolation from the rest of the Gold Coast. A 'whole of Gold Coast' approach was therefore advocated, and it was also realised this implied that a diverse range of stakeholders (including various elements of the business sector, residents and government) needed to be engaged in the process. These two central caveats provided the rationale for the 'Our Gold Coast' badging of the exercise, which also communicates the need for the community as a whole, and especially residents, to recognise that the region faces a problem and their support is required in the solution. A clear vision with community support is paramount.

Main thrust of the 'Gold Coast City Rejuvenation Strategy':

- The primary objective should be to 'develop the Gold Coast into a unified city that celebrates and capitalises on its diversity.
- Establish a 'whole of city vision', with the allocation of resources being based on a 'whole of city benefit analysis', rather than the competitive framework that currently prevails.
- Counteract negative perceptions of the Surfers Paradise through cooperation and education, with it being recognised that the business community could play a lead role in this by 'adopting a broader all-encompassing view' and not allowing personal agendas to distract them from an approach that leads to benefits for the whole community.
- Impressing upon the resident population that there is a problem and they have a role to play in the solution. This implies an education program directed at residents and their elected representatives

highlighting the benefits of tourism to their quality of life.
- '. . . Surfers Paradise should unite under a "Champion" or "Champions" and go forward with unfettered imagination promoting the uniqueness of the asset'.
- The Gold Coast is a system, whereby the success of individual business districts relies on the success of the whole, and vice versa.

The remainder of the recommendations focused on the measures necessary to re-invigorate Surfers Paradise specifically and these generally amounted to the presentation of a case for additional local government support to strengthen the role of the public sector subsidised Surfers Paradise central management association.

Draft Gold Coast 2010: economic development strategy

This document reinforces the theme that the Gold Coast is at 'the cross-roads', with the vulnerability of the region associated with its dependence on the narrow economic base provided by tourism and construction being emphasised. It is argued that this base needs to be expanded through the development of a regional economy that is globally competitive and connected with the so-called new economy – implying a greater emphasis on knowledge based industry such as high technology, education and research (the innovation city). Globalisation means that the city/regions are increasingly dependent upon their competitiveness in international markets.

There are several implications of the draft economic strategy that are relevant to the approach adopted to the tourism visioning process. Firstly, the main theme of the strategy makes sense. It is obvious the region needs to broaden its economic base and, if it is to do so, the emphasis on the knowledge-based, so-called new economy thrust seems to be an obvious alternative. The document also seems to reflect an appreciation of the implications of globalisation and the fact that, within this environment, a region such as the Gold Coast needs to become internationally competitive in its main industries. It is already arguably so in tourism, although the spectre of stagnation highlights how difficult sustaining international competitiveness is.

Secondly, it acknowledges the inescapable – that is, whether we like it or not, tourism will have a continuing significant role in the economy (that is, notwithstanding the last point above!). However, the report seems to imply this is a liability, rather than a potential strength. That is, the dominance of tourism (and the associated sunbelt migration phenomenon) may provide some resistance to the diversification agenda to the extent, for instance, that this produces employment and demographic patterns that are not consistent with the development of 'clever', 'new-age' industries. However, this perspective obscures the potential synergies between tourism and the 'innovation city' vision. The main element of this synergy emerges from the fact that the lifestyle the Gold Coast offers to its residents is enhanced by tourism (so long as we can manage tourism development properly), and the same things that make the region a successful tourist destination also make it an attractive place to live. More emphasis could therefore be placed on the lifestyle factor as a way of attracting new residents who may have the skills required to generate wealth through the new economy, and the potential role of tourism in this process. Reference is made to the Gold Coast as a city of 'experiences', but it does not give sufficient emphasis to this theme. It is a distinctive feature of the Gold Coast that separates it from a myriad of other regions that are probably putting together similar arguments for the development of a knowledge-based focus for regional development as we speak.

Finally, following on from the previous point, there are many synergies between tourism and the key industry strategies identified in the report. Some examples are provided in Table A3.1.

Table A3.1: Tourism synergies associated with key industry strategies identified in the draft economic strategy

Key industry strategy	Tourism synergies
Communication and information	• Lifestyle implications of tourism's enhancement of leisure opportunities have the potential to play a role in locational decisions of IT firms/entre-preneurs.
Education and training	• Educational tourism: educational services attract international students who, with visiting family members, also become tourists. • Lifestyle factors in student choice: the attractiveness of the Gold Coast as a tourist destination also makes this region an attractive place to live while studying. • Alumni networks: former international students become ambassadors for Gold Coast tourism and the Gold Coast generally upon their return home. • Tourism management and planning research capabilities of the CRC and Griffith University are elements of the 'knowledge industry' development.

Environmental	• Adoption of 'Green Globe' as a framework for benchmarking tourism related environmental management on the Gold Coast, along with the identification of this concept with the CRC for Sustainable Tourism, provides an opportunity for the Gold Coast to promote both its environmental management technical capabilities abroad and its environmental tourism destination assets. • A stringent environmental management regime is essential for protecting environmental assets that are central to the region's sustainability as a tourist destination.
Film and interactive media	• Film and interactive media applications to media entertainment technology underpin the continual renewal of theme parks such as Movieworld. • Reinforcement of the leisure theme, which is central to the Gold Coast's image as a tourist destination.
Food, beverage and aquaculture	• Restaurants and fine food are essential elements of the range of services that make the Gold Coast an attractive destination. • There are potential synergies between the marketing of the Gold Coast as a tourist destination and the marketing of its food products.
Health and medical	• There are tourism sector spin-offs from the provision of medical services to international markets (families accompanying patients and patients themselves during recuperation may engage in tourist activities). • For the reasons alluded to in the previous point the Gold Coast's attractiveness as a tourist destination can give its medical providers a competitive edge in international markets.
Marine	• The marine environment constitutes a major tourism asset in the area and potential synergies exist between the

marketing of pleasure craft manufactured in the area and the recreational boating opportunities available to tourists.
- The proposed cruise shipping terminal would provide access to additional tourism marketing.

Urban development
- Urban development capabilities will support the enhancement of existing tourism infrastructure and the construction of new quality infrastructure, such as resorts, marinas, etc.

Appendix B: Gold Coast visioning

Table B3.1 Core issues generated by research projects

Research project	Issues
Issues, Policy and Planning Audit (Scoping Study)	• A tourism policy and planning void exists on the Gold Coast (G.C.): the actions of the various (state and local) government and quasi-government (G.C. Tourism Bureau) agencies that have a role to play in tourism development are not well coordinated, and the tourism implications of their policy and planning agendas are not taken into account. • The ad hoc, incremental approach to tourism development of the past will not work in the future: the scale and complexity of tourism development in the region means that a more holistic, strategic approach is necessary in the future. • The region suffers from a major image and positioning problem in the domestic market in particular: this problem is compounded by the dominance of Surfers Paradise as a visual icon, and the perception of this precinct as 'glitzy' and deteriorating. • The lack of tourism industry involvement in environmental planning needs to be remedied: the natural assets of the region, encompassing the beaches, waterways and

hinterland areas, remain as fundamental ingredients of the area's attractiveness.

- A purpose-built convention centre is essential if the G.C. is to build on its natural advantages as a MICE destination and retain its pre-eminent position.

Market Audit

- While the G.C. has consistently exceeded national average growth rates in inbound tourist numbers over the last 15–20 years, its performance in the domestic market has been patchy: there have been periods where G.C. domestic tourism growth has both exceeded and lagged behind national levels.
- The strength of the G.C. in the inbound market has been particularly attributable to its performance in Asian markets: with two-thirds of all international visitors coming from Asian countries, however, the vulnerability of the G.C. to potentially crippling impacts of external shocks was highlighted during the Asian financial crisis.
- Far North Queensland (FNQ) and Sydney are the main competitors in the inbound market, while Victoria, FNQ and, to a lesser extent, the ACT have been the main competitors in the domestic market.
- The core attractions of the G.C. revolve around four elements: beaches/relaxation; theme parks/excitement; nightlife/action; and nature and wildlife. The main market segments associated with these attractions are families, midlife and older couples and younger singles/couples.
- The G.C. has consistently performed well in the young families and younger solos markets, but its younger and older couples markets have stagnated.

Infrastructure Audit

- There is an 'infrastructure time-bomb' on the G.C., with there being a number of potential black spots arising from concentrations of high-rise accommodation of similar age:

refurbishment or replacement of buildings in these areas will be inhibited by mixed ownership and associated unrealistic expectations regarding capital appreciation.

- There is a substantial high volume, low yield ('profit-less volume') problem in G.C. accommodation infrastructure: this has emerged as a consequence of the over-reliance upon inclusive tour markets and the erosion of margins associated with this.
- An unresolved question concerns the extent to which a large holiday flat/unit rental sector exacerbates or ameliorates this problem.

Product Quality Audit

- Satisfaction levels among visitors regarding the quality of services and experiences associated with the Gold Coast's accommodation, theme parks, restaurants and beaches are generally high.
- The main negative perception among visitors concerns value for money from theme parks.
- The major danger for the G.C. regarding service quality is the prospect of high satisfaction levels encouraging complacency: regular monitoring of satisfaction levels is essential so that lapses in the quality of services can be promptly detected and remedied, while the competitiveness of the environment necessitates a more systematic approach to the continuous improvement of services in all areas.

Social Impacts Audit (preliminary)

- G.C. residents are generally positively disposed towards tourism and its impact on the community: tourism is seen to have a positive effect on the economy, job opportunities lifestyle and aspects of amenity, although costs associated with noise and congestion are also recognised.
- At the aggregate level, perceptions about

the impacts of tourism do not appear to vary among major demographic groups: older residents appear to be no more or less vulnerable to negative impacts of tourism and, indeed, appear to benefit from the same features of the G.C. that make it an appealing destination for visitors.

• Supplementary work needs to be carried out to canvas resident reactions to alternative approaches to tourism development in the future and the impacts of tourism in specific situations, such as in areas where permanent resident and visitor accommodation are integrated.

Part 2

Event Management

Introduction

Shortly after his return to academia, in 1993, Bill was requested by the members of the Research Committee of the Australian Standing Committee on Tourism, to prepare a paper on the evaluation of the tourism impacts of hallmark events. The interest in this topic was in response to the heightened awareness of large-scale events in the lead up to the announcement of Sydney's success in its bid to host the 2000 Olympic Games. There was substantial public discussion at the time on the potential benefits of hosting mega events, but also growing concern about the high costs associated with bidding for, and hosting such events.

As the first chapter in this section, a framework for the systematic monitoring of the impacts of large events is provided. Many of the issues raised in this chapter are still being debated – such as the need for a standardised and consistently applied method for evaluating the economic impacts of events; the lack of evidence supporting claims of the 'showcase effect' of major events; and the relatively superficial understanding of social impacts of events. In this paper, Bill concludes that there is a clear need to monitor all event impacts, an indication of his early recognition of what is now commonly referred to as the 'triple bottom line'. At the time that this chapter was written, the overwhelming focus of event evaluation was on economic impacts due largely to the economic imperatives of government agencies that were important providers of funds for events. Bill's argument, that the social and environmental impacts of events should also be measured and compared to the economic benefits, is a testament to his leadership in tourism academic thought.

As a result of Bill's involvement in this study, he maintained a strong research interest in the event field and went on to publish many event-related articles. His event research involved substantial collaboration and investigated many aspects of event evaluation; including economic impact assessment (Faulkner and Raybould 1995; Mules and Faulkner

1996); social impacts (Jeong and Faulkner 1996; Fredline and Faulkner 1998, 2000, 2002a, 2002b); and tourism impacts (Faulkner *et al*. 2000). Bill was instrumental in the introduction of an event research program within the CRC that has produced research outputs that lead the field. As a result of his concern that little had been done to assess the real impacts of mega-events on the host community, Bill spent considerable time trying to fund a longitudinal study examining the many dimensions of Sydney's hosting of the Olympic Games and commencing in 1997. Although this endeavour failed, Bill was successful in obtaining support from the CRC to fund a multi-faceted project on Sydney's hosting of the Olympic Games.

Much of Bill's work whilst employed by government focused to a large extent on the economic impacts of tourism. As noted above though, he was strongly of the view that this uni-dimensional perspective was too narrow. This view was apparent, even in Bill's early writing. From the early 1990s, he became particularly interested in the social impacts of tourism and by 1996, had established an innovative approach to the examination of such impacts. His approach considered both intrinsic and extrinsic factors to explain variations in community reactions to the impacts of tourism and this approach was documented in Faulkner and Tideswell (1997), which involved a case study of the Gold Coast funded by the Gold Coast City Council. As a result of the wide acceptance of this approach to assessing social impacts, Bill then worked with Liz Fredline, one of his early PhD students, to adapt the approach specifically to special events. This work focussed initially on motor sport events where communities are often divided as to the impacts of such events. The Melbourne Formula One Grand Prix and the Gold Coast Indy race were the test sites for this early work. These studies employed a theoretical framework based on social representations (Moscovici 1981), and parallels were drawn with previous literature on resident reactions observed in different communities and in response to different forms of tourism. The commonalities observed contribute to a more general theory of the interaction between communities and tourism, and the intrinsic and extrinsic characteristics of the residents, the communities, and the nature of the tourism activity likely to be associated with varying levels of support. The approach has been published widely and applied to a range of different types of events.

As indicated earlier, Bill was a vocal critic of the fact that insufficient evaluation was ever conducted on major tourism investments, and nowhere was this more evident than in the event area where state govern-ments, in particular, were making huge investments seeking to attract major events to their destinations. Bill was able to convince the Board of the CRC to fund a major study to examine in a comprehensive fashion, the tourism impacts of the Sydney 2000 Olympics. The aim of this study was to understand the role that mega events, such as the Olympic Games, play in building tourism at a destination and the actions that can be taken to leverage such opportunities. The final paper in this section (Faulkner *et al*. 2000) presents the overview of this major CRC study.

This study comprises a suite of interconnected projects that examine the broad-ranging impacts on Australia of hosting the Sydney 2000 Olympic Games. Not only was this project extremely ambitious in what it sought to achieve, but it also brought together a wide range of researchers with complementary expertise from around Australia. This demonstrates one of Bill's great skills as a tourism researcher; not only did he have great vision, but he also had the ability to enthuse others and was able to develop broadly based research teams in a way that had not happened previously in tourism research in Australia.

Key components of the Olympic research project included a study of leveraging strategies employed by public and private sector organisations around Australia, an examination of the profile, expectations and satisfaction of sponsor guests, and a longitudinal study of the impact of the games on inbound visitation. The research described in the paper is ongoing, but its contribution will be felt in three areas. Firstly, it will tangibly document in an analytical fashion, the tourism outcomes of what is generally considered to be a very successful games. Secondly, it will provide a benchmark for destinations bidding for and hosting similar events, by documenting the strategies that proved most effective in delivering tourism benefits from the Sydney 2000 Olympics. Finally, the studies will demonstrate a range of methods appropriate for investigating tourism impacts, which can be employed for future events.

Special events play a very important role in the tourism plans of all states and territories in Australia. As a result of Bill Faulkner's influence in this field, tourism research now underpins much of the development and evaluation of event product around the country and Australia is widely regarded as a leader in event research. One of Bill's legacies in this area is the CRC's national event tourism research program that he initiated, and which has acted as a catalyst for advanced national and international collaborative research.

References

Faulkner, B. and Raybould, M. (1995) Monitoring visitor expenditure associated with attendance at sporting events: an experimental assessment of the diary and recall methods. *Festival Management and Event Tourism* 3, 73–81.

Faulkner, B., Chalip, L., Brown, G., Jago, L., March, R. and Woodside, A. (2000) Monitoring the tourism impacts of the Sydney 2000 Olympics. *Event Management* 6 (4), 231–246.

Faulkner, B. and Tideswell, C. (1997) A framework for monitoring community impacts of tourism. *Journal of Sustainable Tourism* 5 (1), 3–28.

Fredline, E. and Faulkner, B. (1998) Resident reactions to a major tourist event: the

Gold Coast Indy car race. *Festival Management and Event Tourism* 5 (4), 185–205.
—— (2000) Host community reactions: a cluster analysis. *Annals of Tourism Research* 27 (3), 763–784.
—— (2002a) Residents' reactions to the staging of major motorsport events within their communities: a cluster analysis. *Event Management* 7 (2), 103–114.
—— (2002b) Variations in residents' reactions to major motorsport events: why residents perceive the impacts of event differently. *Event Management* 7 (2), 115–126.
Jeong, G.-H. and Faulkner, B. (1996) Resident perceptions of mega-event impacts: the Taejon international exposition case. *Festival Management and Event Tourism* 1 (2), 3–11.
Moscovici, S. (1981) On social representations. In J.P. Forgas (ed.) *Social Cognition: Perspectives on Everyday Understanding* (pp. 181–209). London: Academic Press.
Mules, T. and Faulkner, B. (1996) An economic perspective on special events. *Tourism Economics* 2 (2), 107–117.

Chapter 4
Evaluating the Tourism Impacts of Hallmark Events

Bill Faulkner

1 Introduction

Major events have tended to be organised with sporting, cultural and other non-tourism objectives in mind. Increasingly, however, these events are seen as an instrument for tourism development. Indeed, one of the most frequently quoted definitions of hallmark events, offered by Ritchie (1984: 2), explicitly emphasises this role by describing them as 'major one-time or recurring events of limited duration, developed primarily to enhance the awareness, appeal and profitability of a tourism destination in the short or long term'.

Hall (1991: 198) has identified a range of events in Australia that can be regarded as hallmark events in terms of this definition. These include world fairs or expositions (Brisbane Expo 1988), major sporting events (such as the 1956 Melbourne Olympic Games, the 1982 Brisbane Commonwealth Games, the Adelaide Grand Prix), carnivals and festivals (Melbourne's Moomba), significant cultural events (Festival of Sydney), historical milestones (Australian Bicentennial celebrations in 1988), major commercial and agricultural shows (Royal Agricultural Shows in most state capitals) and major State events (such as Royal visits).

Other authors have referred to tourism development as a rationale for the staging of hallmark events (Getz 1989; Hall 1987; Mazitelli 1987; Pyo *et al.* 1988; Van der Lee and Williams 1986) and Ritchie (1984: 2) adds that the capacity of a particular event to achieve tourism promotional objectives depends on its uniqueness, status, ability to attract attention and, ultimately, on how successfully it is marketed in tourist generating areas.

Reflecting the links between hallmark events and tourism, such events are becoming an important part of tourism marketing strategies. Just as national and state tourism agencies have been placed under increasing pressure to justify the community's investment by substantiating the effectiveness of their promotional and marketing programs through the conduct of more rigorous evaluations (Faulkner and Shaw 1992), it is now equally important that the effectiveness of hallmark events as extensions of promotional programs be demonstrated.

In this paper an overview is given of work carried out to date on assessing the impacts of hallmark events. The insights from this analysis are used to outline a framework for the development of a more systematic approach to monitoring, and therefore planning and evaluating, the promotional outcomes of these events.

2 Towards a Framework

Analyses of the role of hallmark events commonly distinguish between short-term cost recovery and longer-term promotional objectives. This is illustrated in the following reference to the Olympic Games by Pyo *et al.* (1988: 144):

> The short term objective of the tourism sector during the Olympic Games is to attract a large number of tourists to offset part of the financial burdens of the host country's tax payers. The long term goal should be to upgrade the popularity of the host city as a desirable tourist destination. . . Above all, the Olympic Games should be recognised as an investment for the future and an image building event rather than a profit generating opportunity.

The last sentence, in particular, highlights an evasiveness among the proponents of hallmark events to the extent that their subsidisation from public funding sources is being justified on the basis of presumed downstream benefits that have not been demonstrated. While it is plausible that, in many instances, short-term costs may be offset by longer-term promotional effects, the magnitude and distribution of these costs still need to be identified so that they can be compared with benefits arising from the promotional effects. More importantly, this requires the promotional effects to be monitored and quantified on an ongoing basis so that the effectiveness of the hallmark event oriented tourism strategy can be properly evaluated.

Some progress has been made towards the development of methodologies for identifying and comparing the more immediate costs and benefits associated with hallmark events. However, the challenge to establish the systems for monitoring and evaluating longer-term promotional effects remains to be addressed.

In the Australian context, emphasis has been placed on major sporting events such as the Adelaide Grand Prix, the America's Cup defence, the World Cup Athletics and the Eleventh Commonwealth Games. This emphasis has partly been because of the international profile of such events, but also because they have generally been dependent upon substantial funding support from government sources (Burns *et al.* 1986; Centre for Applied and Business Research 1986, 1987; Department of Sport, Recreation and Tourism 1986; Lynch and Jensen 1984). The emphasis in most analyses has been largely on economic and tourism impacts, while relatively little attention has been given to other dimensions such as environmental, sociocultural and psychological impacts. A series of studies published in Burns *et al.* (1986), however, represented a significant departure from this trend by providing a relatively comprehensive analysis of the full range of impacts of a single event – in this case, the Adelaide Grand Prix.

Two works have added to this contribution. Getz (1992) provides an overview of the relationships between hallmark events and tourism. However, Hall's (1992) analysis complements the theme of this paper more specifically in that it focuses on the impacts of hallmark events and their management and planning implications, with greater emphasis being placed on Australasian examples.

The impacts of an event can be summarised in terms of a range of dimensions identified by Ritchie (1984: 4). These are:

- economic;
- tourism and commercial;
- physical;
- sociocultural;
- psychological; and
- political.

While this schema is adopted in a broad sense for the purposes of this paper, the categories of impacts have been condensed into just three key dimensions (Economic, Tourism/ Commercial and Social/Environmental). What Ritchie regards as positive manifestations of physical impacts, such as construction of new facilities and improvements in local infrastructure, are treated as economic impacts in the following analysis because such benefits can largely be measured in economic terms. Meanwhile, Ritchie's negative manifestations of physical impacts, such as environmental damage and crowding, overlap with socio-cultural and psychological impacts, although they warrant special reference in their own right if they impinge upon environmental and conservation issues. Socio-cultural, psychological and political impacts are combined because, from the perspective adopted in this paper, they coalesce to a degree that makes them less distinctive from each other.

The main dimensions of these impacts of hallmark events are identified in the left hand column of Figure 4.1. The associated systems required to monitor these impacts are shown in the right hand column. This framework is elaborated in the following sections.

Impacts   Monitoring systems

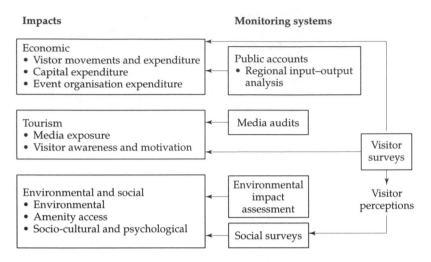

Figure 4.1 A framework for monitoring the impact of tourism events

3 Economic Impacts

Historically, predictions and estimates of the economic impacts of hallmark events have been plagued by two possibly related problems. First, as Lynch and Jensen (1984: 11) have noted, 'opinions on the economic desirability of major events seem to be based more on personal conviction or political stance than on sound economic logic'. Before an event, predictions of its positive economic impacts tend to be exaggerated by its proponents partly because of their enthusiasm for the event, but also because in so doing they bolster the case for government funding and general community support. In this context the benefits of increased visitor expenditure and associated employment generation tend to be emphasised while downside effects such as increased local prices and real estate speculation tend to be ignored.

Second, analyses of economic impacts have tended to lack the rigour required to properly identify the net economic impacts. However, recent economic analyses of such events as the Adelaide Grand Prix, the America's Cup in Perth, the World Cup Athletics in Canberra and the Brisbane Commonwealth Games have contributed to the development of a more rigorous framework for analysing the economic impacts of such events (Burns and Mules 1986; Thomson 1986; Centre for Applied and Business Research 1986; Burns 1987; McCloud and Syme 1987; Rey 1987; Lynch and Jensen 1984). An examination of the methodologies applied in these studies suggests a number of fundamental guidelines for the analysis of the economic impacts of special events.

In general, the economic effects of hallmark events are derived from three sources, in terms of which the following guidelines are structured (Burns and Mules 1986; Burns 1987; Lynch and Jensen 1984):

- expenditure by visitors from outside the region;
- capital expenditure on facilities required for the conduct of the event; and
- expenditure incurred by event organisers associated with the staging of the event.

3.1 Visitor expenditure

As noted above, the rationale for the staging of a hallmark event hinges largely on the role the event can play in attracting visitors to the venue. The expenditure of these visitors within the region on goods and services such as accommodation, food transport and souvenirs is injected into the local economy and provides a stimulus to the region's income and employment. In attributing visitor expenditure to the local economy, however, a number of factors need to be taken into account.

Geographical frame of reference
As Burns and Mules (1986) emphasise, the 'viewpoint' or geographical frame of reference within which costs and benefits are being assessed is critical. The smaller the area of reference (nation, state, region, city and so on) the greater the range of those attending who can be classified as visitors – and, thus, the greater the number of attendees whose expenditure can be regarded as an injection of funds from outside. Similarly, the smaller the region, the greater the potential for public funds from higher levels of government to be regarded as income rather than costs. On the other hand the smaller the region, the greater is the potential for leakages associated with imported goods and services.

For example, in the case of the analysis of the economic impacts of the 1985 Adelaide Grand Prix, the state of South Australia was adopted as the level of analysis. The expenditure of visitors to Adelaide from within the state was not taken into account. This expenditure did not constitute a gain to the state's economy as a whole, but simply involved a redistribution of income within the state. On the other hand, expenditure by interstate and international visitors was taken into account as the servicing of their needs in effect constituted export income at the state level.

Switching
Switching phenomena can occur in connection with both the timing and the geographical distribution of visits. It is necessary to establish the extent to which the event has actually generated an increase in visitor numbers over the number who would have visited the region in any case. Often the impact of an event is to influence the timing of a visit rather

than to stimulate an extra visit. Where this occurs, the increase in visits during the event is offset by a decrease over a longer period and the net gain to the regional economy is reduced accordingly. The effect of the event in these situations may even be negative if the peaking of visits causes congestion and strains local facilities to such an extent that the quality of services suffers and repeat visits are jeopardised.

A particular effort was made to take time switching into account in the Adelaide Grand Prix impact assessment. A survey conducted by the then South Australian Department of Tourism revealed that 21 per cent of visitors had rearranged the timing of a visit to Adelaide they had already intended to make (Burns and Mules 1986).

Switches can also occur in the destinations visitors choose, resulting in visits being concentrated in one location at the expense of others without there being a net increase overall. The possibility that this may have been the case for Australians as a whole is evidenced by the fact that, according to the Domestic Tourism Monitor (Bureau of Tourism Research 1992) there has been no increase in the level of domestic travel by Australians over recent years. Large influxes of domestic visitors to particular regions during the staging of particular hallmark events have, therefore, largely been at the expense of visits to other areas.

The Brisbane Expo provides an example of this phenomenon at the state level. Expo attracted 1 057 000 international visitors (Bureau of Tourism Research 1988), of whom over 170 000 indicated that they would not have visited Australia otherwise. An additional 306 000 intrastate and 894 000 interstate domestic trips also were generated by the event (Bureau of Tourism Research 1989: 2). However, while Queensland's share of both inbound and domestic trips increased because of Expo, Domestic Tourism Monitor data suggest that there was a diversion of tourists away from areas of the state outside the environs of Brisbane, resulting in these parts of Queensland being disadvantaged by the event.

This switching effect of the Expo is illustrated in Table 4.1, where the change in domestic visitor numbers and visitor nights over the period of the event (April to October), relative to the corresponding period in the previous year, is indicated for different regions of Queensland. While the state as a whole experienced increases in visitors and visitor nights of 15.1 per cent and 22.3 per cent respectively, to some extent Brisbane and the Gold Coast benefited at the expense of other regions. The Far North, in particular, suffered from a decline in both visits and nights of 17 per cent and 5.7 per respectively, compared with Brisbane's increases of 57.1 per cent and 112.2 per cent.

Leakages and indirect expenditure impacts
Expenditure by visitors is directly beneficial to the suppliers of the goods and services consumed by visitors, but it also has spin-off effects for

secondary suppliers of goods and services. For example, when visitors purchase a meal at a restaurant, their expenditure is immediately beneficial to the restaurant owner and a proportion of this expenditure filters through to other businesses such as local suppliers of food products and beverages who provide goods and services necessary for the restaurant to operate. These transactions stimulate economic activity and generate jobs within the reference region.

A distinction can be drawn between direct and indirect impacts of tourist expenditure. Direct impacts arise from expenditure on goods and services by tourists during their visit, while indirect impacts arise from money remaining in the area because of successive rounds of business transactions associated with the provision of these goods and services. Reference is also sometimes made to induced effects, which relate to the increased consumer expenditure arising from increased personal incomes associated with the stimulus to economic activity provided by tourist expenditure.

These impacts can be quantified by the calculation of multipliers, which provide an expression of the total effect (direct, indirect and induced) as a function of incremental tourist expenditure. A review of the range of multiplier ratios used in tourism is provided by Archer (1982), while Burns and Mules (1986) comment specifically on their use in the events context. In particular, Burns and Mules (1986: 13) note that estimates of the economic impacts of events are often exaggerated by the incorrect use of output, rather than value added, multipliers. Value added multipliers cannot exceed 1, because it is impossible for the sum of profits, wages, salaries and overheads in the chain of producers to exceed the initial expenditure of visitors. Indeed, as some of the goods and services consumed are usually imported from outside the reference region,

Table 4.1 Change in domestic visits and nights in Queensland regions during EXPO 88

Region	Change (April to October 1988 compared with April to October 1987)	
	Visits %	Nights %
Gold Coast	+18.9	+14.3
Brisbane	+57.1	+112.2
Far North	−17.0	−5.7
Other	−2.8	−3.3
Total	+15.1	+22.3

Source: Bureau of Tourism Research, Domestic Tourism Monitor.

leakages of visitor expenditure inevitably occur and the value added multiplier is inevitably less than 1.

Employment impacts

With the stimulation of economic activity implied by the direct and indirect impacts referred to above, employment opportunities will be created. The identification of direct and indirect income generating effects of visitor expenditure, and the associated derivation of multipliers, is generally based on the construction of input–output models of the region's economy. Estimates of employment generating effects are usually derived from a proportional allocation based on the income accruing to different sectors of the economy. As noted by Adams and Parmenter (1991), however, the input–output based approach is limited as a basis for analysing impacts at the macro level because it does not take into account offsetting effects such as the crowding out of investment capital, labour market pressures and exchange rate effects.

Furthermore, in the case of hallmark events, where impacts are relatively short term, it is likely that employment impacts will be overstated. Studies of the impact of the Adelaide Grand Prix on businesses in Adelaide revealed that most business adjusted to increased demand by increasing the hours worked by existing staff rather than by hiring new staff (Arnold 1986; Bishop and Hayles 1986; Hatch 1986). Thus, while the America's Cup defence in Perth, for example, was expected to generate employment equivalent to 14 400 person years (McCloud and Syme 1987), less than this number of new jobs would have been created because much of the employment involved would have been in additional hours worked by people who are already employed.

On the other hand, there is evidence to suggest that by providing an opportunity for goods and services produced by South Australian firms to receive greater exposure, and by facilitating the establishment of more positive business links, the Adelaide Grand Prix acted as a catalyst for expanding the interstate market for these firms (Bentick 1986). In the longer term, therefore, the Grand Prix may be instrumental in creating more permanent job opportunities within the state.

3.2 Capital expenditure

The staging of a major event often requires either new facilities to be constructed or established facilities to be upgraded. Especially in the case of one-off events, the contribution they make to the regional, state or national economy can often hinge on the extent to which new facilities are required. This point is illustrated in the distinction drawn by Taylor and Gratton (1988) between the 'commercial model', upon which the organisation of the Los Angeles Olympics was based, and the 'high public investment' model that has characterised most other Olympic Games since World War Two. The Los Angeles Games involved a limited outlay of public funds and the maximum utilisation of existing facilities – an approach that contributed to a claimed $250 million surplus. By contrast, the Munich Olympics in 1972 incurred a public debt of $178 million, while the Seoul Olympics involved an injection of public funds (largely for infrastructure development) amounting to an estimated $3 billion. The surplus from the Los Angeles Games was not only attributed to the containment of expenditure on facilities, as a feature of this event was also a commercially oriented approach that attracted large contributions of private funds through sponsorships and licensing arrangements ($481 million) and for the sale of television rights ($268 million).

Opportunity costs and incremental expenditure
In considering the implications of facility development associated with major events, it commonly has been recognised that the benefits of such developments go beyond the immediate requirements of the event itself. In the longer term, the community gains from access to improved facilities. The hosting of a major sporting event can thereby act as a catalyst for the development of the sport or sports concerned. Facilities other than those directly required for the event (roads, communications systems, visitor accommodation and so on) are also often involved. During the construction phase, the community also gains from the increased economic activity and employment that is generated. Again, however, leakages associated with imported construction materials, equipment and technology need to be taken into account. Construction associated with the staging of the America's Cup defence in Perth in 1986–87 was estimated to be a minimum of $60 million by the University of Western Australia's Centre for Applied and Business Research (1986). This expenditure resulted in a further output in supplying industries of $42 million and was estimated to have generated employment equivalent to 1350 persons a year.

As in the case of assessing the impact of visitor expenditure, however, the extent to which expenditures related to infrastructure development are advantageous depends upon the level of geographical disaggregation at which the analysis is carried out. Where the funds required for the capital works come from outside the region in question, then the advantage to the community concerned is obviously accentuated. In the America's Cup example referred to above, $30 million was provided by the Commonwealth Government for construction purposes. Similarly, $5 million was received from Commonwealth sources for the staging of the Adelaide Grand Prix. However, whether these contributions an be regarded as incremental expenditures from each state's point of view may be debatable. In the case of the Adelaide Grand Prix, Thomson (1986) notes that opportunity costs were involved to the extent that the $5 million provided by the Commonwealth was offset in the allocation of general revenue to South Australia.

In their analysis of the economic impact of the 1982 Commonwealth Games in Brisbane, Lynch and Jensen (1984) highlighted the importance of the impact of capital expenditure in determining the overall impacts of that event. They also highlighted the importance of identifying the source of funds used for capital works:

> ... The Brisbane region gained the additional impact of capital expenditure associated with the games only to the extent that the funds were diverted from use in other parts of the country. (Lynch and Jensen 1984: 14)

On the other hand, if the upgrading of facilities is funded by the state government, the question of whether there is net advantage to that state is problematic because the construction activity represents a diversion of expenditure from one area (school facilities, road improvements, health services and so on) to another. In other words, there is an opportunity cost that offsets any benefits derived from the facility development associated with the event. There will be a net loss to the state if a diversion of funds from potentially more productive areas is involved.

Switching
Another consideration relating to construction activity is analogous to the time switching factor referred to in the analysis of visitor expenditure. Often, the effect of an event is simply to bring planned construction programs forward rather than being the reason for the construction. The staging of the Fourth World Cup Athletics competition in Canberra in 1985 required infrastructure improvements at the Australian Institute of Sport's complex. However, as these improvements were already on the drawing board and would have been carried out irrespective of the World Cup, the effect of the event was mainly to accelerate the construction program. For this reason capital works costs were excluded from the economic impact assessments of the then Department of Sport, Recreation and Tourism (1986). Nor could it be legitimately claimed that this event benefited the Canberra community by being instrumental in upgrading their athletics facilities.

3.2 Event organisation expenditure

The conduct of a major event requires an elaborate organisational infra-structure to plan and co-ordinate the many facets of the event. Substantial lead times and resources are required to plan and organise such items as:

- marketing activities (including promotions, media coverage, communications and public relations);

- sponsorships and funding;
- ticketing and spectator services and control;
- transport and accommodation arrangements for spectators, competitors and officials;
- security and emergency services; and
- preparation of facilities and the conduct of the event itself.

The establishment of the organisation required to carry out these tasks creates jobs and provides a stimulus to economic activities within the region. Again, however, the extent to which expenditure associated with the organisation of the event constitutes a net gain to the community depends upon the degree to which the funds involved come from sources outside the region. If the organisation is totally funded from within the region, then opportunity costs are involved whereby resources are simply being transferred from one sector of the regional economy to another. Thus, for example, in their analysis of the Brisbane Commonwealth Games, Lynch and Jensen (1984) note that the organisation responsible for the games (the Commonwealth Games Foundation) had a budget of $23.2 million. Once funds and resources transferred from other sectors within the Brisbane region are deleted, the estimation of event expenditure for the purposes of establishing the direct impact on the Brisbane region was half this amount ($12.4 million).

The narrow application of a balance sheet approach to the analysis of event funding usually reveals a deficit in the operations of the event organisation. As these organisations are normally underwritten by funds from government sources, the cost of the operating loss is borne by the community. The question that then needs to be addressed is whether the benefits derived from staging the event justify this and other costs.

The books of the organisation responsible for staging an event do not always identify all the direct costs involved, as some costs are often absorbed by other organisations. For example, as Hall (1991: 200) observes, the staging of the Fourth World Cup of Athletics in Canberra required a commitment of 12 565 police person hours, while the America's Cup defence required a 250 member police task force to be deployed for the duration of the event. Yet, in neither of the evaluations of these events (Department of Sport, Recreation and Tourism 1986; Centre for Applied and Business Research 1987) were these costs taken into account.

4 Tourism Impacts

There is little doubt that, apart from the sporting, cultural or other objectives at which they are aimed, the rationale for staging hallmark events hinges largely on their tourism development potential. In drawing attention to the significance of sporting events as an instrument for tourism development in Australia, Mazitelli (1987) noted that 400 major sporting events were conducted by sporting organisations each year. Most of these would only be significant for tourism at a regional or inter-state level, but 15 of the events held in 1986–87 were world champion-ships. Mazitelli's analysis of the profile of visitors associated with such events revealed that in general they have a greater propensity to stay longer and spend more then the average visitor. In other words, visitors associated with sporting events were found to provide a higher yield of visitor expenditure.

However, observations elsewhere suggest that sports related travellers have a lower level of expenditure than the average for all tourists. For example, on the basis of their analysis of several Olympic Games, Pyo *et al.* (1988) claim that sports related travellers are on average less affluent than international travellers in general and this is reflected in expenditure patterns. These contradictions, however, may reflect differences in the scope of the studies involved, with the studies referred to by Mazitelli encompassing a large domestic component compared with those referred to by Pyo *et al.* Whatever the pattern in this regard, these expenditures need to be viewed in the light of offsetting factors such as switching, import leakages and so on noted earlier in this paper.

In their examination of the tourism implications of the Adelaide Grand Prix, Van der Lee and Williams (1986) identified a number of beneficial effects of that event.

- A large proportion of visitors (82 per cent) indicated they would definitely or probably return to subsequent grand prix events in Adelaide.
- The high level of satisfaction with Adelaide as a tourist destination among visitors associated with the Grand Prix would ensure that Adelaide would be promoted as a credible tourist destination by word of mouth.
- Electronic and print media exposure of the event would increase the awareness of Adelaide in overseas and interstate markets, and thereby promote Adelaide as a tourist destination and, ultimately, generate additional visitation.
- The success of the event was instrumental in increasing pride in their city and greater self confidence among Adelaide residents. This improvement in the general attitude of residents translated into a more receptive and helpful attitude towards visitors, which in turn significantly enhanced the quality of the local tourism product.
- The staging of the event acted as a catalyst for increasing investment in tourism infrastructure by local operators and the influx of additional investment from outside the state. The increased investment activity was stimulated not only by increased demand

associated with the event, but also from the heightened tourism profile.

On the basis of their assessment of the tourism development impacts of the Adelaide Grand Prix, Van der Lee and Williams concluded that for an event to have real tourism potential it must:

- Be of international standard, involving an internationally recognised sporting, cultural or similar body with international participants;
- Be a visitor generator, with the ability to generate international and interstate visitors as competitors and spectators;
- Be capable of providing significant international exposure and promotional value to the state. In order to achieve this, electronic media exposure is particularly important, although coverage in high profile print media is also necessary;
- Have an established organisational structure and demonstrate sufficient up front financial capability;
- Have a marketing plan which outlines key marketing strategies to ensure the event maximises its potential;
- Demonstrate ongoing tourism benefits which build up after several years of operation, in the case of annual or biennial events, or demonstrate that, as a one-off event, it can still provide maximum exposure benefits which are likely to generate future tourism in the state.

It should be emphasised, however, that all these tourism development benefits will only arise if the staging of the event is a success. There is always a risk of the event being counter productive from a tourism development point of view. A range of factors may intervene to turn a potentially beneficial event into a tourism disaster. Many of these are beyond the control of the organisers and tourism planners involved, such as natural disasters, adverse weather, terrorist activity or competition boycotts. Others are clearly within the control of the organisers, such as event failure owing to organisational deficiencies; while others are clearly the responsibility of the tourism industry itself, such as deficiencies in the quality of service or profiteering.

At another level, if event organisers and the tourism industry are not sensitive to community attitudes and concerns, and if they do not take appropriate remedial action where there is a need to do so, a hostile community reaction could undermine their efforts. If, for instance, the staging of an event involves a high incidence of negative social impacts, then a significant portion of the community could become alienated and openly hostile. This would ultimately affect relations between visitors and locals, and leave some visitors with a negative impression of the local tourism product.

Event planners and the tourism industry in general, therefore, take a grave risk in ignoring such impacts of an event. If these impacts are not anticipated and understood then effective remedial action cannot be taken. Hall (1991) implies that the most effective remedial action should take the form of a consultative or community based approach to planning, which may ultimately lead to a consensus within the community. Other types of remedial action might take the form of compensatory payments to individuals who are disadvantaged by the event, provision of social programs targeting particular sectors of the community who are adversely affected and mounting community awareness and education programs aimed at gaining acceptance and co-operation.

It is obvious that the tourism marketing benefits attributed to the Adelaide Grand Prix by Van der Lee and Williams cannot necessarily be applied to all events. Nor can it be assumed that these benefits will be sustained even by that event in successive years. The media profile of the event, and thus the destination, may change over time, changes in the market place may affect the response to the exposure, and other changes (for example, in community attitudes) may impact on the quality of the product sufficiently to influence the response of the market.

In the case of recurring events, therefore, the dynamics of the situation demand an on-going assessment of media exposure and market response if the promotional benefits are to be verified. Meanwhile, in one-off events, systems need to be put in place to measure media and market reactions not only before and during the event, but also over a period after the event if longer term promotional effects are to be measured. As the organisers of such events often have little interest in what happens after it has been staged, and associated organisational infrastructure is usually dismantled at this point in any case, interest in monitoring longer term effects usually lapses. However, if tourism promotional benefits are part of the rationale for public funding, an effort needs to be made to ensure that appropriate systems are put in place. Because the event is, implicitly or explicitly, an element of the destination's tourism marketing strategy, the tourism authority could reasonably be expected to assume this responsibility.

Apart from establishing whether the media coverage was positive or negative, there are two aspects of the promotional effects that need to be monitored. First, the coverage of the event in electronic and print media, both domestically and overseas, should be recorded and costed as a surrogate for paid advertising. Second, the number of visitors whose decision to visit the destination in question was in some way influenced by the staging of the event, or the media coverage associated with it, needs to be ascertained through visitor surveys.

In Australia, one strategy for achieving this, at least for major events, could be through extensions of existing national surveys such as the

International Visitor Survey (IVS) and Domestic Tourism Monitor (DTM) conducted by the Bureau of Tourism Research. However, it needs to be taken into account that these surveys are origin, as opposed to destination, based. Respondents are intercepted at their point of origin: at their home in the case of domestic tourists, and at international airports, in the case of international visitors. As origin-based surveys, these instruments can only yield adequate sample sizes for events of international significance, such as the Brisbane Expo or an Olympic or Commonwealth Games. Special purpose local visitor surveys would therefore be necessary in most cases.

As a minimum requirement, visitor surveys should be structured to enable the following items of information to be collected:

- For those visiting during the period of the event, the extent to which they are visiting specifically or partly because of the event, whether as a spectator, participant or official, or for other reasons;
- The extent to which those identified above have visited the destination at the time of the event in place of a visit at some other time (the time switching effect) and whether, as a consequence of this visit, they intend to make a return trip either to witness the event again (in the case of recurring events) or for some other reason;
- The extent to which visitors to the event, and visitors in general over the period prior to, during and after the event, have been influenced by media exposure of the destination associated with the event;
- The degree of satisfaction associated with the trip, and the extent to which the event itself and the reactions of the local community affected the quality of the experience; and
- Visitor expenditure by item of expenditure during the visit (required as input to the estimation of economic impacts of the event).

5 Environmental and Social Impacts

Some hallmark events have the potential to do irreversible environmental damage when, as is sometimes the case, they are conducted in sensitive natural environments. This potential obviously requires a full assessment of environmental impacts before the event, to ensure that adequate planning and management measures aimed at ameliorating or minimising negative impacts are put in place. Alternatively, if environmental damage cannot be avoided there may be grounds for reconsidering the venue. Such measures are integral to tourism development needs because the tourism potential of many areas is ultimately dependent upon their environmental assets.

The risk of detrimental environmental and associated social impacts not being given due consideration in the planning process is highlighted by Hall (1987), who has noted the tendency for 'fast track' planning procedures to be introduced where government and industry are required to organise local resources and infrastructure for an event within a short time. He refers to the America's Cup in Perth and the Darling Harbour Bicentennial redevelopment to illustrate this point.

Apart from the obvious direct impact some events have on the environment, many also have social impacts because of their effect on the physical environment. The impact of the Grand Prix on residents of inner suburbs of Adelaide has been examined by Dunstan (1986) who drew attention to the noise generated by the event and the parking problems and congestion of roads that resulted from the redirection of traffic around the race course. The disruption to the lives of residents in both the inner and outer suburbs was measured in terms of the extra time required to travel to and from work. On this basis the social cost of the event was valued at $6.2 million. However, as Dunstan (1986: 105) notes, the implications of such externality or spill-over effects are not always readily quantifiable:

> Some of them (for example, damage to property) are readily measured in money terms. Others (for example, an exciting atmosphere or a dislike of driving in the heavy traffic generated by the Grand Prix) are not. But the importance of any given spill-over effect does not depend on the ease with which one can attach a dollar value to it. And it must be remembered that the ultimate purpose of economic activity is not to produce goods or profits, but to produce human welfare.

Other negative social impacts of hallmark events are not so directly related to their environmental impacts. Fischer *et al.* (1986), for instance, draw attention to a bizarre manifestation of the demonstration effect in the case of the Adelaide Grand Prix. In what they refer to as the 'hoon effect', an increase in the incidence of road accidents in the Adelaide region was attributed to an increased tendency among motorists to drive recklessly and irresponsibly because of their efforts to emulate the Grand Prix competitors. The cost of the increased accidents was estimated at $7.6 million.

Another example of negative social impacts associated with a hallmark event is provided by the America's Cup defence, where a 36 per cent increase in arrests for anti-social behaviour was recorded during the period of the event (Hall 1988: 8).

In another context, while events such as the Brisbane Expo and the Darling Harbour Bicentennial redevelopment provided a stimulus for the rejuvenation of areas suffering from the effects of urban blight, these developments also have the potential to displace low income groups through the escalation of real estate prices and the reduction of low cost rental accommodation. Similarly, pressure on rental accommodation caused by the increased demand associated with an event can result in low income tenants being displaced from areas that are particularly important as focuses of social support systems.

These examples highlight the fact that the external costs and benefits associated with an event are seldom spread evenly throughout the community. As Dunstan (1986: 123) observes:

> while for most people the benefits outweighed the costs, for some the costs outweighed the benefits. In this sense some members of the community 'paid' for the enjoyment of others, and problems of inter-personal comparisons and considerations of equity may therefore temper the view that the positive spill-overs were more than sufficient to offset the negative spill-overs.

Inequities in the distribution of costs and benefits associated with an event may also arise from the way in which the event is funded. When the staging of an event, for instance, involves a redirection of public funds from schools and hospitals, then it can be argued that those who are directly advantaged by the event are gaining at the expense of those sectors of the community most dependent upon these facilities.

There is a tendency for both economic and social impacts of events to be considered mainly in terms of their implications for the community as a whole, rather than in terms of who gains and who loses. Not only is the downside of events often underestimated as a consequence, but also certain tourism development implications are overlooked. As mentioned in the previous section, hallmark events can act as a catalyst for tourism development by improving the attitude of residents to visitors and thereby enhancing the quality of the local product. In cases where inequities generated by events are not identified and remedied, the potential of a community backlash is increased. Where this occurs, the event could easily become counter productive in a tourism sense.

As mentioned previously, the impacts referred to in this section, along with some of the social impacts alluded to in the previous section, encompass the physical, socio-cultural and psychological impacts referred to by Ritchie (1984). For the purposes of delineating the systems for monitoring these impacts, however, it is more convenient to reclassify them in terms of the following dimensions:

- Environmental impacts: impacts that affect the ecological balance of the local environment and that need to be assessed through environmental impact assessment mechanisms;
- Amenity and access impacts: impacts that affect the aesthetics and convenience of the environment as a place for locals to live in, and their access to services, facilities and social support systems. The

assessment of these impacts requires a combination of social surveys and methodologies for assessing the equity implications of changes induced by the event;

- Socio-cultural and psychological impacts: this category combines impacts previously identified separately under these two headings by Ritchie. They include such phenomena as demonstration effects, social pathologies, changes in local pride and community spirit, and attitudes to visitors. While attitudinal surveys of both locals and visitors will provide some insights into these effects, other sources of information such as newspaper reports, health and crime statistics need to also be tapped.

6 Conclusion

Few, if any, hallmark events occur without some degree of public funding support at some stage. To the extent that the rationale for this use of public funds hinges on the tourism promotional effects of such events, tourism authorities should have an interest in evaluating this aspect of the event. As these agencies have been required by government to justify the allocation of public funds by demonstrating the effectiveness of their tourism promotional programs (Faulkner and Shaw 1992), it is appropriate that they include the impacts of events as an adjunct to the evaluation process. This is necessary to the extent that events have become an integral part of their programs or impinge upon their other activities, although responsibility for events may be carried by a separate agency. Also it needs to be established whether the events represent a more effective instrument of tourism promotion than programs aimed more directly at this objective. Self interest, alone, should be enough to motivate tourism agencies to take action in this area, because it is conceivable that the funding of events represents a diversion of funds from programs explicitly designed for tourism promotional purposes.

While the need to respond to externally imposed requirements associated with the justification of public funding has provided the immediate impetus for more rigorous evaluations of the effectiveness of events in achieving organisational and community objectives, such evaluations should in any case be carried out as a routine element of the on-going management process. There is a strong argument, therefore, for tourism agencies to include a consideration of event impacts irrespective of whether responsibility for events resides within the organisation.

Research cited in this paper reveals that there are many facets of an event's impacts, all of which must be taken into account if the promotional and other benefits are to be put into their proper perspective. This requires the battery of instruments for monitoring impacts outlined in previous sections of this paper and summarised in Figure 4.1. On the basis of this overview, a number of observations can be made about the status of hallmark event evaluations:

- While visitor surveys have been fairly standard elements of evaluations carried out to date, their tendency to focus on visitors during the event, rather than over a longer period, has meant that claims regarding longer term promotional effects have not been substantiated;
- Attempts to systematically monitor media coverage arising from the event have been rare and, as a consequence, the reach and frequency of the exposure achieved have not been properly measured and evaluated. Nor has it been possible, therefore, to establish the most effective means of maximising the promotional benefits of the event; and
- The monitoring and evaluation of environmental and social impacts of events has generally been perfunctory or non-existent, resulting in many so-called evaluations being little more than a superficial justification aimed simply at securing continued funding.

As indicated in Figure 4.1, elaborate monitoring systems need to be put into place if the impacts of events are to be comprehensively and effectively monitored. Given the costs involved in establishing and maintaining such systems, it may be difficult to justify doing so in the case of many smaller one-off events. However, the scale of investment of public funds in major one-off and recurrent events, which often involve substantial outlays over a number of years, necessitates a commensurate allocation of resources to the evaluation process. In particular, it would be prudent for tourism authorities to consider this point seriously given that the staging of events has become an integral part of tourism promotional strategies, and public investment in events could, in some cases, be at the expense of more direct and conventional approaches adopted by these agencies.

Acknowledgments

The author wishes to acknowledge the contributions of Mr Barry Jones (Director, Bureau of Tourism Research) and Professor Robin Shaw (Griffith University) to the preparation of this paper. Their comments and advice have been greatly appreciated.

References

Adams, P. D. and Parmenter, B. R. (1991) *The Medium Term Significance of International Tourism for the Australian Economy: Part 1*, Bureau of Tourism Research, Canberra.

Archer, B. H. (1982) The Value of Multipliers and their Policy Implications, *Tourism Management*, 3, 4, pp. 236–41.

Arnold, A. (1986) The Impacts of the Grand Prix on the Transport Sector, in Burns, J. P. A., Hatch, J. H. and Mules, T. J. (eds), *The Adelaide Grand Prix: The Impact of a Special Event*, The Centre for South Australian Economic Studies, Adelaide, pp. 58–81.

Bentick, B. L. (1986) The Role of the Grand Prix in Promoting South Australian Entrepreneurship: Exports and the Terms of Trade, in Burns J. P. A., Hatch, J. H. and Mules, T. J. (eds), *The Adelaide Grand Prix. The Impacts of a Special Event*, The Centre for South Australian Economic Studies, Adelaide, pp. 169–185.

Bishop, G. and Hayles, J. (1986) The Impact of the Grand Prix on the Accommodation Sector, in Burns, J. P. A., Hatch, J. H. and Mules, T. J. (eds), *The Adelaide Grand Prix: The Impact of a Special Event*, The Centre for South Australian Economic Studies, Adelaide, pp. 82–94.

Bureau of Tourism Research (1988) *International Visitors Survey: Annual Summary*, Bureau of Tourism Research, Canberra.

—— (1989) *Tourism Update*, 4, 2, Bureau of Tourism Research, Canberra.

—— (1992) *Domestic Tourism Monitor 1990–91: Annual Summary*, Bureau of Tourism Research, Canberra (and previous issues).

Burns, J. P. A., Hatch, J. H. and Mules, T. J. (eds) (1986) *The Adelaide Grand Prix: The Impact of a Special Event*, The Centre for South Australian Economic Studies, Adelaide.

Burns, J. P. A. and Mules, T. J. (1986) A Framework for the Analysis of Major Special Events, in Burns, J. P. A., Hatch, J. H. and Mules, T. J. (eds) *The Adelaide Grand Prix: The Impact of a Special Event*, The Centre for South Australian Economic Studies, Adelaide, pp. 5–38.

—— (1987) *Analysing Special Events, with Illustrations from the 1985 Adelaide Grand Prix*, Papers of the Australian Travel Research Workshop: The Impact and Marketing of Special Events, Australian Standing Committee on Tourism, Mount Buffalo, pp. 1–14.

Centre for Applied and Business Research (1986) *America's Cup: Economic Impact*, CABR, Perth.

—— (1987) *America's Cup Reference Series. 1986–87: Impact on the Community*, CABR, Perth.

Department of Sport, Recreation and Tourism (1986) *Economic Impact of the World Cup of Athletics Held in Canberra in October 1985*, Commonwealth of Australia, Canberra.

Dunstan, G. (1986) Living with the Grand Prix: Good or Bad?, in Burns, J. P. A., Hatch, J. H. and Mules, T. J. (eds) *The Adelaide Grand Prix. The Impact of a Special Event*, The Centre for South Australia Economic Studies, Adelaide, pp. 105–123.

Faulkner, H. W. and Shaw, R. H. (eds) (1992) *Evaluation of Tourism Marketing*, Occasional Paper No. 13, Bureau of Tourism Research, Canberra.

Fischer, A., Hatch, J. and Paix, B. (1986) Road Accidents and the Grand Prix, in Burns, J. P, A., Hatch, J. H. and Mules, T. J. (eds), *The Adelaide Grand Prix: The Impact of a Special Event*, The Centre for South Australian Economic Studies, Adelaide, pp. 151–168.

Getz, D. (1989) Special Events: Defining the Product, *Tourism Management*, 10, 2, pp. 125–137

—— (1992) *Festivals, Special Events and Tourism*, Van Nostrand Reinhold, New York.

Hall, C. M. (1987) The Effects of Hallmark Events on Cities, *Journal of Travel Research*, 26, 2, pp. 44–45.

Hall, C. M. (1988) The Future of Tourism in Australia: Counting Pennies Without Counting the Costs, *Recreation Australia*, 7, 4, pp. 2–11, 20.

Hall, C. M. (1991) *Introduction to Tourism in Australia: Impacts, Planning and Development*, Longman Cheshire, Melbourne.

Hall, C. M. (1992) *Hallmark Tourist Events: Impacts Management and Planning*, Belhaven Press, London.

Hatch, J. A. (1986) The Impact of the Grand Prix on the Restaurant Industry, in Burns, J. P. A., Hatch, J. H. and Mules, T. J. (eds), *The Adelaide Grand Prix: The Impact of a Special Event*, The Centre for South Australian Economic Studies, Adelaide, pp. 95–104.

Lynch, P. G. and Jensen, R. C. (1984) The Economic Impact of the X11 Commonwealth Games on the Brisbane Region, *Urban Policy and Research*, 2, 3, pp 11–14.

Mazitelli, D. (1987) *The Benefits of Hosting Major Sporting Events*. Paper presented to the Royal Institute of Parks and Recreation 60th Conference, Canberra.

McCloud, P. and Syme, J. (1987) Forecasting the Economic Impact of the America's Cup, in Australian Standing Committee on Tourism, *The Impact and Marketing of Special Events: Papers of the Australian Travel Research Workshop*, Mount Buffalo, pp. 44–74.

Pyo, S., Cook, R. and Howell, R.L. (1988) Summer Olympic Tourist Market: Learning From the Past, *Tourism Management*, 9, 2, pp. 32–34.

Rey, P. (1987) Economic Impacts of Special Events Using the Example of the World Cup Athletics, Canberra, in Australian Standing Committee on Tourism, *The Impact and Marketing of Special Events: Papers of the Australian Travel Research Workshop*, Mount Buffalo, pp. 35–43.

Ritchie, J. R. B. (1984) Assessing the Impact of Hallmark Events: Conceptual and Research Issues, *Journal of Travel Research*, 23, 1, pp. 2–11.

Taylor, P. and Gratton, C. (1988) The Olympic Games: An Economic Analysis, *Leisure Management*, March, pp. 32–34.

Thomson, N. J. (1986) Financial Impacts Upon the Public Sector, in Burns, J. P. A., Hatch, J. H. and Mules, T. J. (eds) *The Adelaide Grand Prix: The Impact of a Special Event*, The Centre for South Australian Economic Studies, Adelaide, pp. 186–198.

Van der Lee, P. and Williams, J. (1986) The Grand Prix and Tourism, in Burns, J. P. A., Hatch, J. H. and Mules, T. J. (eds) *The Adelaide Grand Prix: The Impact of a Special Event*, The Centre for South Australian Economic Studies, Adelaide, pp. 39–57.

Chapter 5

Host Community Reactions: A Cluster Analysis

Elizabeth Fredline and Bill Faulkner

Introduction

The staging of major events has become an integral part of tourism destination marketing (Mules and Faulkner 1996; Ritchie and Smith 1991; Thorne and Munro-Clark 1989). Although they are transitory, events may be construed as additions to a region's inventory of attractions and, accordingly, they are instrumental in augmenting both the range of markets relevant to the destination and its critical mass of attractions. Apart from this, however, high profile events produce significant promotional benefits by virtue of the exposure they receive in the media beyond the destination. Indeed, it has been suggested that the latter effect is as important, if not more, than the event itself in terms of roles in destination marketing (Pyo *et al.* 1988).

As with other elements of the destination mix, events may have positive or negative impacts on residents. Sound management of the event (and other elements of the destination associated with it) hinges on the ability of those responsible to avoid, or at least ameliorate, the negative impacts and accentuate the positive ones. These objectives are driven as much by ethical concerns, encompassing equity and quality of life issues, as they are by more pragmatic destination marketing considerations emphasized in the literature. In considering the destination marketing implications of host community reactions, Madrigal (1995) has alluded to Kotler's (1988) internal marketing concept. The internal culture of a firm is seen to be a factor affecting the receptiveness of its staff to customers and thus, the quality of service it provides. Similarly, it is argued that a host community that is positively disposed will enhance the tourists' experience and contribute to the destination's attractiveness. Given that the quality of life and equity outcomes within a community will have a significant bearing on resident perceptions, a planning/management regime sensitive to community needs is an essential ingredient of sustain-

114

able tourism development. The feasibility of such an approach ultimately depends upon how effectively the impacts of tourism and events on communities are monitored and understood.

When compared with the considerable body of research on the social impacts of tourism, relatively little progress has been made on social impacts specifically associated with events. While some authors have highlighted the tourism/events nexus and the similarities between the two in order to draw insights about the impacts of events from the tourism literature, no comparative studies on their respective impacts have been carried out. The purpose of this paper is to investigate host community reactions to the Gold Coast Indy event in Australia and to explore similarities in the clustering tendencies of residents based on their perceptions of tourism in general and reactions to a major event.

The methodological approach adopted in most studies has generally involved an emphasis on measuring resident perceptions, attitudes, and behavioural adjustments at the individual level, and identifying predominant patterns in these responses and how they are related to various independent variables. The point of departure of the research described here is that, while it also has a foundation involving measurement at the individual resident level, it is more concerned with how such information can be utilized to identify groups of residents. These groups or "nested communities" (Madrigal 1995: 87) vary in terms of their reaction to tourism. This approach relies on the use of cluster analysis and the rationale for its application is that it provides more generalized information on community reactions. This information enables those responsible for planning and managing tourism activities to more effectively target remedial action aimed at avoiding or counteracting negative impacts (Davis *et al.* 1988; Madrigal 1995). An equally important justification for the examination of clustering tendencies within communities is it provides an insight into the structure of community reactions to tourism (and events), and thus provides a powerful tool for investigating the generality of these responses.

Resident Responses to Tourism and Events

As noted earlier, there is a large and growing volume of studies concerned with the social impacts of tourism on resident communities. Pearce *et al.* (1996), for instance, refer to over 30 studies in this area. It is beyond the scope of this paper to provide a thorough review and, in any case, comprehensive reviews have been provided elsewhere by the latter authors. However, the relevant findings are briefly outlined below.

Broadly speaking, the bulk of previous research into host community perceptions can be summarized in terms of the "intrinsic"/"extrinsic" dichotomy described by Faulkner and Tideswell (1997). Here, the extrinsic: dimension refers to variables that affect resident reactions at the macro level in the sense that they have a common impact on the community as a whole. The intrinsic dimension recognizes that the host community is heterogeneous and perceptions of impacts may vary according to variations in the characteristics and circumstances of individuals.

Extrinsic and intrinsic dichotomy

In the tourism context, it has been argued that resident reactions are affected by extrinsic factors such as the stage of development (Butler 1980; Doxey 1975), seasonality in patterns of activity (Belisle and Hoy 1980; Sheldon and Var 1984), and cultural differences between tourists and residents (Butler 1975). Such variables in general have little bearing on the current study because it is looking at one event only. Therefore, there is no basis for carrying out the comparisons necessary to draw conclusions regarding their implications. However, it can be speculated that the stage of tourism and event development might be relevant in two respects. First, the development stage in the host region will have an underlying influence on the impact of the event, because the residents' perceptions of tourism in general will influence their reactions to tourists generated by the event. Second, the stage of an event's development needs to also be taken into account. It could be suggested that, in contrast with the tourism situation, resident reactions to recurring events become less negative over time largely because organizers become more experienced at minimizing disruptive effects of the event and marketing it to the local public. Longitudinal research on resident reactions to one-off events has demonstrated growing support over time (Ritchie and Aitken 1984, 1985; Ritchie and Lyons 1987, 1990; Ritchie and Smith 1991; Soutar and McLeod 1989). In the case of recurring situations, successive exposures may result in locals becoming more adapted, either through the development of effective coping strategies or passively by becoming desensitized to its effects.

The seasonality factor is relevant to the event context to the extent that events might ameliorate or exacerbate peaks and troughs in the level of general tourism activity. Major events have often been utilized specifically to moderate fluctuations in demand by being scheduled during off-peak seasons (Ritchie and Beliveau 1974) and this has been a major consideration in the planning of the Gold Coast Indy. Again, however, this variable is not being investigated in the present study because it is concerned with the impact of a single event in a single year. Similarly, the cultural difference factor is not being examined specifically because attendees to the Indy generally resemble residents of the Gold Coast in this respect. The 1995 attendees comprised 25% Gold Coast residents, 35% other Queenslanders, 25% tourists from elsewhere in Australia, and only 14% from overseas (Ernst and Young 1995).

The main intrinsic variables that have been observed to influence variations in the response to tourism within a community include geographical proximity to activity concentrations (Brougham and Butler 1981; Pizam 1978; Teo 1994) and involvement in tourism (Ap 1992; Brougham and Butler 1981; Milman and Pizam 1988; Pizam 1978; Pizam *et al*. 1994). Drawing on social exchange theory, Ap (1992) suggested that members of the host community who have business or employment interests in the tourism industry will be generally more positively disposed to it because they trade off resulting costs with benefits. Conversely, those who are not involved in tourism derive no substantial direct benefits, yet may still experience some costs and are more inclined to hold negative perceptions. In the Indy study context, involvement implies a business or employment interest that is positively affected by the event or tourism.

Demographic characteristics provide another set of intrinsic variables which, in Western developed countries, has generally had no bearing on variations in perceptions of tourism (Belisle and Hoy 1980; Liu and Var 1986; Ryan and Montgomery 1994). However, a survey of spectators at the 1995 Gold Coast Indy race has revealed that this event appeals to a relatively narrow demographic group, with 83% of spectators being males and 68% under the age of 40 (Ernst and Young 1995). Therefore, it might be expected that demographic characteristics would have a bearing on resident reactions, with those who have similar characteristics being more positively disposed towards the event. These variables have had mixed success in explaining variation in residents' perceptions. While most studies have found a positive relationship between involvement in tourism and favorable perceptions of it, a closer inspection of the results reveals that the relationship is more complex in many instances.

Pearce *et al*. (1996) suggest that the use of social exchange theory to explain resident perceptions has three problems. First it is based on an assumption that humans are "systematic information processors" whereas psychological research suggests that in some cases it is more likely that they are "cognitive misers" (Taylor 1981, cited in Pearce *et al*. 1996). Second, much of an individual's knowledge is socially derived, rather than the result of direct experience. Third, peoples' perceptions are formed within a societal and historical context. Thus, Pearce *et al*. propose an alternative theoretical framework based on social representations theory.

Social representations

Originally used by Durkheim, the concept of social representations was adopted and expanded upon by Moscovici (1981, 1983, 1984, 1988), who defined them as " 'systems' of preconceptions, images and values which have their own cultural meaning and persist independently of individual experience" (1983: 122). Representations are the mechanisms people use to try and understand objects and events in the world around them. They tend to turn the unfamiliar into the familiar, as objects and events are recognized on the basis of past experiences, and prior knowledge serves as the reference point for new encounters. Moscovici stresses that this process is not simply analogy, but "socially meaningful fusion, with a shift in values and feelings" (1981: 189). These preconceptions are often reinforced, even when disparity between the representation and the actual phenomenon exists. Echabe and Rovira (1989) found that people had more accurate recall of facts that were consistent with their representations, and tended to "modify" the facts that were inconsistent.

The "social" element refers to the fact that these representations are shared by groups within a society and help facilitate communication. However, not all groups are uniformly cohesive and, as a consequence of this, Moscovici (1988) has proposed three levels of consensus of social representations. "Hegemonic" representations are described as stable and homogeneously accepted by the whole community, "emancipated" representations exist when subgroups have somewhat differentiated opinions and ideas, and "polemical" representations exist in the context of group conflict, with subgroups having opposing outlooks. These social representations are afforded a degree of stability because of their prescriptive power, as well as the fact that they are reinforced socially. However, it would be misleading to suggest that they are the sole determinants of individual perceptions. They determine how people see the world, but are simultaneously determined by their interactions and communications within society (Purkhardt 1993). Sources of social representations can be divided into three groups. The first group is direct experience. Existing representations have strong prescriptive powers, but direct experience of an event provides residents with more information on which to base their perceptions, and this information is more directly under the control of the individual than other sources. Therefore, it may be a catalyst for change, as people question inconsistencies between prevailing social representations and actual observations (Pearce *et al.* 1996). When direct experience with a phenomenon is limited, other sources of social representations become more important.

Social interaction constitutes the second group. This includes interaction with family, friends, colleagues, casual acquaintances, and strangers. This is a powerful means of transmission of social representations and is probably closely related to group membership. People are likely to be affiliated with groups that have similar social identities to themselves, and they are inclined to adopt representations comparable with other group members (Breakwell 1993). However, people are likely to be members of more than one reference group, and where such collectivities have different representations, individuals may be forced to reconcile contradictory positions (Dougherty *et al.* 1992). Significantly, not all members of a community have the same exposure or contact with the object or event that is the basis of the representation. Therefore, it has been suggested that where direct experience is limited, groups will "borrow" a social representation from some other source. In this regard the media, political figures, and other important individuals and groups are likely to be important references.

The media, as the third group, has the potential to influence perceptions through the actual content of stories, as well as through their decision either to report or not report particular issues. In addition, it is common for the media to present some issues in the context of a conflict between various subgroups, which enables observers to identify with a particular group's perspective (Gamson *et al.* 1992).

The key to identifying social representations within a community is to identify commonality or consensus of residents' perceptions (Pearce *et al.* 1996). Two studies, by Davis *et al.* (1988) and Madrigal (1995), have identified groups with common perception by analyzing cluster patterns in community reactions to tourism. The first one involved the segmentation of Florida residents in terms of their attitudes and opinions regarding tourism development in that state. Apart from the immediate aim of classifying residents on the basis of their attitude towards tourism, the primary purpose of the study was to provide a foundation for public education initiatives. The method employed involved four basic steps. A self completion/mail-back survey of Florida residents was carried out, utilizing a battery of questions designed to measure their knowledge of tourism, perceptions of its impacts, and demographic background of respondents. A cluster analysis based on Euclidean distance was then applied to the perceptions data with a view to identifying "distinct, mutually exclusive and exhaustive empirical clusters" (1988: 4). Irrespective of the particular approach that is adopted, the fundamental objective of cluster analysis is to derive a cluster solution in which between-group variations are maximized and within-group variations minimized (Fife-Shaw 1993). A comparison of response profiles of the five groups produced by the previous step was then carried out to identify their distinctive characteristic and to enable each group to be appropriately labelled. Finally, the profiles of individual groups were then investigated to ascertain whether or not particular demographic categories were more inclined to be members of one group or another.

Madrigal's (1995) study adopted a cluster analysis approach to examine community reactions in two different types of cities in the United States and the United Kingdom. The US city (Sedona, Arizona) was a rural city of 7,720 people with extensive tourism development based on natural attractions and an active artisan community, while the UK city (York), with a population of 100,000, had a long history of urban-based tourism. An important objective of the study was to establish the extent that common dimensions in the clusters are identifiable in the two contrasting settings. A methodology similar to that developed by Davis *et al.* (1988) was used, although principal, components factor analysis was applied to condense the data and individuals were clustered on the basis of factor scores on each dimension. With regard to the focus of the present study, Madrigal's most important conclusion was that "clusters of residents with similar perceptions of the positive and negative impacts of tourism do coexist within and across the two cities" and interestingly, "cluster membership accounted for a far greater percentage of variance than city of residence" (1995: 98–99). In other words, residents in the two cities exhibit similar clustering tendencies despite their differences in terms of size, level of tourism development, and national context.

In order to further develop this theme, the clusters derived from these two studies were compared. Even though they were driven by different objectives and measurement instruments, there are some common themes in the clusters identified. This suggests some general patterns in community responses to tourism, which may also be applicable to the event situation. The study by Davis *et al.* identified five groups. "Haters" (16% of the sample) exhibited strong sentiments against tourism and growth and were strongly in favor of activities aimed at limiting the industry. "Lovers" (20%) expressed opposite opinions, being pro-tourism and growth and expressing support for initiatives designed to increase it. "Cautious romantics" (21%) appear to be in favor of tourism but not pro-growth. The authors use the modifier "cautious" because these respondents tended to have more moderate opinions. They seem to appreciate many of the benefits derived from tourism but are more cautious with respect to allowing further growth. "In betweeners" (18%) can be characterized as having middle of the road opinions, and "love 'em for a reason" (26%) had similar responses to those of lovers, but not as strong. They were also less likely to dismiss the negative impacts. In Madrigal's study, three clusters were described. "Haters" (31%) agreed with negative impacts but disagreed with positive impacts, "lovers" (13%) agreed with positive impacts and disagreed with the negative impacts, and "realists" (56%) agreed with both positive and negative impacts.

As specified in the introduction, the purpose of this study is to explore clusters evident among resident reactions to a major event, and investigate the similarities that can be observed between them and those identified in the Davis *et al.* and Madrigal studies. As already noted, relatively little research has been undertaken that looks specifically at host community reactions to events. However, given the fact that in many respects hallmark events resemble general tourism in terms of their potential impacts on host communities, the general tourism literature provides an adequate theoretical background. Furthermore, while the event itself may be concentrated in both time and space, their impacts are neither limited to the short time frame in which they take place nor confined to their immediate geographical vicinity (Hall 1992). Short term benefits include resulting expenditure and its multiplier effects (Mules and Faulkner 1996), while one of the major longer term benefits can be the "showcase effect" which magnifies the region's profile and improves its future tourism and investment potential (Hiller 1989: 129). Similarly, costs associated with such impacts as crowding, noise, and disruption may be limited to the actual duration of the event, but the financial burden, environmental damage, and other impacts may be felt over a prolonged period of time. Some impacts, such as changes in community values, may be permanent (Hall 1992).

The literature on the impacts of hallmark events is dominated by studies that have primarily focused on the economic dimension (Burns and Mules 1986; Commonwealth Deptartment of Sport, Recreation and Tourism 1986; McDonald 1990; Rey 1987). A number of studies have examined social impacts using secondary data such as court records and newspaper reports (Hall and Selwood 1989; Hall *et al.* 1996), but this approach is limited in terms of the insights produced into quality of life effects and variations in the impacts on various sectors of the community. Relatively few studies have involved the direct measurement of residents' perceptions as an indicator of the impacts of events (Jeong 1992; Jeong and Faulkner 1996; Soutar and McLeod 1989, 1993), even though it is arguable that this method provides a more meaningful foundation for assessing quality of life implications. The approach is more attuned to the population's frame of reference, provides a gauge of the relative import-ance of various impacts, and enables variables affecting the impacts within the resident population to be detected (Jeong and Faulkner 1996).

The Gold Coast IndyCar Race

The Gold Coast, located in Southeast Queensland (Australia), is Australia's premier tourism resort. In 1996, the area attracted 976,600 overseas tourists, making it the second most important international destination after Sydney, while 2.7 million domestic tourists also visit the area annually (Bureau of Tourism Research 1997). With a population of 369,550 and an annual population growth of 3.7 % (ABS 1998), the Gold Coast is also one of the fastest growing urban areas in the country (Stimpson *et al.* 1996).

Since 1991 the Gold Coast Indy has been a prominent feature of the region's events calendar, and its value as a vehicle for tourism promotion was a major reason for its public sector support from the outset (Massey 1991). The spectacular backdrop to the street circuit used for the race, featuring surf beaches and high-rise buildings, was seen as providing the ideal visual imagery for promoting the Gold Coast through the international and domestic television coverage of the contest. The four-day event is focused in Surfers Paradise, the tourism heart of the Gold Coast, and is centered around the IndyCar race held on the final afternoon. However, a number of support events from Australian motor racing codes are also included, and a multitude of both official and unofficial social activities take place in the days leading up to and including the IndyCar race.

However, the event became the subject of considerable controversy immediately after it was first proposed in 1990. Prior to its first occurrence, local papers reported a number of objections raised by residents, including concerns over the lack of any consultation with them about it (Weston 1990a). The Gold Coast Rate Payers Association feared that residents would suffer alienation during the event, owing to the disruption caused by preparation of the facilities (Gold Coast Bulletin 1990). One resident even prepared a submission to the United Nations to overturn the IndyCar Grand Prix Bill, citing an infringement of civil liberties (Weston 1990b). A rally in August 1990 attracted about 1,000 protesters anxious about environmental damage to a park within the vicinity of the racetrack and the surrounding beaches (Gold Coast Bulletin 1990). Immediately prior to the inaugural event in 1991, residents complained of a "nightmare" weekend, reporting that "hammering and drilling" continued throughout the night. Concern was also raised for security, with some minor crimes cited as evidence of the "influx of a different element"(Gold Coast Bulletin 1991).

More recently, the focus of debate concerning the costs and benefits of the event has shifted to questions regarding its value to Queensland as a whole and the equity implications of diverting tax payers' money into an event that creates disproportionate benefits for one region (Black and Pape 1995; Deiley 1995; Smith 1996; Stolz 1996; Wright 1996). While such issues are obviously relevant to its overall evaluation, this paper concentrates on its impact on the Gold Coast community itself, and, more specifically, whether or not certain sectors of the community are unduly disadvantaged.

Study methods and data analysis

The approach adopted in the Indy study broadly mirrors that used by Davis *et al.* (1988), with a face to face survey of 350 residents within the contiguous urban area of the Gold Coast being the primary source of data. The affinities between events and tourism, along with the more substantial history of social impact research in the area, meant that the theoretical frameworks and methods developed in the latter field could be readily adapted as a framework for the design of the survey. This can be elaborated in terms of several core sets of assumptions, which have been summarized in terms of the intrinsic/extrinsic dichotomy (Faulkner and Tideswell 1997).

The survey instrument comprised three main parts. First, a battery of 36 statements referred to positive and negative economic, social, and environmental impacts of the Indy, in relation to which respondents were asked to indicate the degree of their agreement or disagreement on a five point Likert scale. The second part included questions concerned with demographic background and the involvement of respondents in the event and/or tourism. There was also a question regarding activities undertaken by residents during the period of the event. Here, residents were asked which of the following best describes the activities engaged in during the weekend of the Indy in 1996: attended Indy, watched it on television, worked, usual weekend activities, went away for the weekend, and other.

In the Gold Coast Indy context, proximity is clearly a relevant variable given that disruptive effects associated with the event are concentrated in a small area around the track. In particular, the street circuit characteristic of the race means that those living in the vicinity of the track are disrupted by street closures, while noise levels and crowding generated by the influx of spectators are most pronounced in these areas. Therefore, a disproportionate stratified sample was necessary, with those living closest to the Indy zone being over represented. The non-Indy zone, which was very large when compared with the Indy zone, was then further stratified into ten zones to ensure representation of all sectors of the relevant population. A coordinate system defined each zone, and random numbers were used to establish a map reference of clusters comprising three adjacent households. The cluster procedure was used to reduce travel time per interview and thus reduce the overall cost of the survey. Given that the clusters used were small and randomly selected, it is unlikely that any significant bias would have been introduced as a consequence of this approach. Next, personal interviews were conducted and a stringent three-phased call back procedure was adopted to minimize any non-response biases that might be introduced owing to residents not being home at the time interviewers called. A 79% response rate was obtained giving a sample size of 353 households. Of these, 16 responses were rejected due to missing data, leaving 337 valid cases.

Cluster analysis was performed on the 36 impact statements in an effort to identify groups of residents with similar response patterns. The use of factor scores as cluster variables (as in Madrigal 1995) is debated in some research areas, as there is some evidence to suggest the variables which truly discriminate among underlying groups are not well represented in many factor solutions (Rohlf 1970, cited in Hair *et al.* 1995). The application of factor analysis prior to the cluster analysis involves a premature loss of information that might distort the outcome. Initially, a hierarchical technique was applied using Ward's method with squared Euclidean distances. Three and five cluster solutions were examined, based on the previous work by Davis *et al.* (1988) and Madrigal (1995), with the five cluster solution seeming to provide a more interpretable result. The means for each variable established in this analysis were then used to seed a non-hierarchical analysis. This resulted in the reassignment of some respondents but made little difference to the means of each cluster.

Study results

In order to simplify the description of clusters, resident responses to the 36 impact statements were summarized into six factors using a Principal Components Analysis that explained 55.5% of the variance. Factor one, labeled Community Benefits, comprised mainly the benefits accruing to the whole community, such as increased pride, community spirit, business and trade opportunities, and higher levels of service. The second factor, described as Short Term Negative Impacts, included mostly physical problems such as noise, encouragement of "hoons", overcrowding, traffic congestion, and disruption to lifestyle. International Profile and Economic Benefits was the description given to factor three, which included a range of statements similar to those that loaded onto factor one, such as tourism promotion and social and economic benefits. What differentiated these statements is that a high level of consensus was registered with regard to these impacts, whereas those in factor one exhibited a polarization of opinion. Factor four was called Negative Economic Impacts, and dealt with issues such as demand driven price increases, but the overall response to these statements was largely ambivalent. The fifth factor, Negative Physical Impacts, included litter, noise levels, and parking congestion, and the final factor dealt with Amenity and Facility Development Benefits such as maintenance and development of facilities, and improvements in the appearance of the area.

Comparison of the between-group variability as evidenced by the distance among cluster centroids, and the within-group variability as evidenced by the mean distances of each resident from their cluster centroid, are provided in Table 5.1, which shows that in some cases within-group variability did exceed between-group variability.

However, the closest clusters, one and three, are clearly distinguishable in their responses to factors two, four, and five. Therefore, it was decided to use the solution which acknowledged these differences.

Cluster one: ambivalent supporter (cautious romantics)
This cluster contained 99 residents. Their response patterns could be described as fairly ambivalent, as they tended toward moderate responses and their mean was generally the middle response. They agreed slightly with the community benefits factor and with some short term negative impacts though not with others, agreed with the international profile and economic benefits, but were largely ambivalent to negative economic and

Table 5.1 Between and within group variability[a]

Clusters	1	2	3	4	5
1	*4.66*				
2	6.12	*5.13*			
3	3.26	5.15	*4.76*		
4	3.69	9.47	5.68	*4.68*	
5	4.82	4.62	5.01	7.58	*4.29*

[a] The means of the distances between each resident and their cluster are shown in italics on the diagonal (within group variability), and the distances between cluster centroids are shown in the lower part of the table (between group variability).

physical impacts and amenity and facility development benefits. The statements that attracted the most extreme responses for cluster one were examined. There were only four that had means of two or lower, indicating that overall the cluster agreed with them. Three of these are related to positive impacts while one involves a negative consequence (shown in bold in Table 5.2). There were no statements that attracted high levels of disagreement.

The vast majority of residents in cluster one were in favor of the continuation of Indy (97%), and many of these were in favor of the current location (60%). They were more likely to live in the non-Indy zone (62%).

Cluster two: haters
This cluster contained 50 residents and the group can quite clearly be labeled as haters of the event. They exhibited a higher level of disagreement with the community benefit items and agreed strongly with the short-term negative impacts. They were largely ambivalent toward the international profile and economic benefits, agreed with the negative economic and physical impacts, and disagreed with the amenity and facility development benefits. The statements with which this cluster agreed most strongly are displayed in Table 5.2, where the predominance of references to negative impacts is apparent. Conversely, statements with which this cluster generally disagrees refer to positive impacts.

Cluster two was predominantly made up of older residents with 66% over 50 years and 44% over 60 years of age. Of this group, 65% were not in favor of the continuation of the Indy, and only two residents in this cluster were in favor of the event remaining in its current location. The preferred options were "not on the Gold Coast" and "Dreamworld", an alternative site on the northern outskirts of the city. Of this group, 65% were not in the demographic group that is similar to spectators and very

Table 5.2 Mean responses of clusters to the 36 Statements

Statements	Clusters				
	1	2	3	4	5
The Indy increases employment opportunities on the Gold Coast	2.30	3.36	1.99	1.78	2.61
The Indy diverts public funds from more worthwhile projects	3.25	1.94	2.78	3.51	1.97
The Indy increases trade for local businesses	2.01	3.26	1.91	1.65	3.35
The demand for accommodation during Indy leads to higher rents for local residents	2.95	2.46	2.40	3.43	3.48
Prices in shops increase because of Indy	3.23	2.64	2.61	3.61	3.94
There are increased business opportunities because of Indy	2.27	3.44	2.16	1.92	3.00
The Indy promotes the Gold Coast as a tourism destination	1.71	2.48	1.71	1.39	1.65
Real estate prices are inflated because of Indy	3.34	3.22	2.94	3.62	3.77
The Indy causes damage to the environment	3.27	1.66	2.36	3.92	2.00
The Indy creates noise levels which annoy local residents	2.09	1.28	1.64	2.99	1.13
Because of the Indy roads in the area are well maintained	3.03	3.70	2.64	2.39	3.13
The Indy leads to increased litter in the area	2.90	1.70	2.15	3.62	3.39
The appearance of the area is improved because of Indy	3.07	4.18	3.06	2.26	3.90
The Indy has made the Gold Coast a more interesting place to live	2.90	4.34	2.86	1.97	3.65
Visitors to Indy are inconsiderate of local residents	3.42	2.12	2.55	3.82	3.87
The Indy has increased the pride of local residents in their city	3.00	4.02	2.51	2.12	3.58
The Indy greatly inconveniences residents through traffic congestion	1.95	1.22	1.44	3.00	1.06
The Indy has led to the development of new facilities which can be used by local residents	3.69	4.40	3.16	2.73	3.94
The Indy causes overcrowding and makes it difficult to use local facilities	2.44	1.56	1.96	3.64	2.35

Table 5.2 (continued)

Showing the Indy around the world gives the Gold Coast an international identity	**1.82**	2.50	1.75	**1.48**	2.06
The Indy brings too many tourists to the area	3.91	3.06	3.29	**4.22**	**4.35**
There is a wider range of goods available in the shops because of Indy	3.31	3.96	2.93	2.90	**4.00**
The Indy encourages "hoons" to drive in a dangerous manner	3.16	**1.82**	**1.99**	3.42	**1.16**
Holding the Indy on the Gold Coast gives local residents an opportunity to attend an international event	**1.94**	2.66	2.00	**1.57**	**1.90**
During the Indy it is difficult to find a parking space	2.44	**1.48**	**1.60**	2.68	2.55
The Indy promotes Australian motor sport and gives young drivers new opportunities	2.78	3.20	2.50	**1.92**	3.61
The Indy encourages the wrong type of people to the area	3.96	2.56	3.16	**4.14**	3.97
The night life is more exciting because of Indy	2.54	3.28	2.23	2.06	2.19
The Indy causes higher crime levels in the area	3.40	2.46	2.42	3.73	3.26
The Indy gives the Gold Coast a chance to show the world what we can do	2.02	2.74	2.09	**1.74**	2.13
The Indy brings the community together	2.89	**4.12**	2.80	2.32	3.94
The Indy has led to higher levels of service offered by local businesses	3.00	3.94	3.00	2.43	3.90
The Indy disrupts the lives of local residents	2.43	**1.36**	**1.74**	3.36	**1.19**
The Indy enhances local residents' spirit of hospitality	2.88	3.96	2.76	2.16	3.55
The Indy has disrupted the peace and tranquility of the Gold Coast	3.38	**1.68**	2.38	**4.00**	**1.65**
The Indy gives residents an opportunity to meet new people	2.47	3.44	2.46	2.04	2.94

few attended Indy (2%) or watched it on TV (4%). The majority went about their usual activities (50%) or went away for the weekend (40%). A relatively large proportion of these residents had lived on the Gold Coast for more than 20 years (36%).

Cluster three: realists

Cluster three has been tentatively labeled as realists. This is not intended to imply that these residents are more correct in their opinions than those in the other clusters. It merely reflects the fact that this group acknowledges that the event has both positive and negative impacts, which is intuitively realistic. The cluster contains 80 residents who could be described as having mixed opinions about the event, tending to agree with both the positive and negative impacts. They are mostly ambivalent to the community benefits in factor one, but moderately agree with the short term negative impacts in factor two. They also agree with the international profile and economic benefits, negative economic and physical impacts, but are ambivalent about the amenity and facility development benefits. The statements that attract the highest levels of agreement are a mixture of positive and negative impacts as shown in Table 5.2. No statements attracted high levels of disagreement. Of the residents in cluster three who were employed, 51% worked in tourism, with an additional 32% working in industries whose volume of business is affected by tourism. A relatively large percentage of these residents were low income earners, with 48% earning less than US $12,600 per annum.

Cluster four: lovers

Cluster four is made up of 77 residents and this group could be described as lovers of the Indy. They agreed most highly with the community benefits in factor one, the international profile and economic benefits of factor three, and the amenity and facility development benefits of factor six. They were the only group to disagree with the short-term negative impacts in factor two, and they also disagreed with all of the negative economic and physical impacts except for "during the Indy it is difficult to find a parking space". The statements that elicited the highest levels of agreement and disagreement for this cluster are shown in Table 5.2. As might be expected in the case of enthusiastic supporters of the event, statements that attracted the most agreement are all positive, while those that attracted disagreement all suggest negative impacts. All of the residents in this cluster were in favor of continuation of the Indy, with 76% favoring the current location, and 18% selecting the Broadwater as a preferred option. Residents in this cluster were more likely to fit the demographic profile of spectators, but less likely to be involved in tourism. 38% of this group attended the Indy, and a further 35% watched it on TV.

Cluster five: concerned for a reason

The final group, cluster five, contained 31 residents who appeared to be deeply concerned about specific impacts of the Indy, but did not have completely negative perceptions of the event. They disagreed with most of the community benefits in factor one, but did agree that the Indy had made the nightlife more exciting. They very strongly agreed with the short term negative impacts except they disagreed that the Indy had led to increased crime. With regard to these two factors, the responses of cluster five were similar to those of cluster two. However, these groups differed in their perceptions of the remaining impacts. This cluster agreed with most of the international profile and economic benefits in factor three, and were largely ambivalent to the negative economic and physical impacts of factor four and five. They disagreed slightly with the amenity and facility development benefits of factor six. The statements that attracted the strongest responses from this group were mostly about negative impacts, but some positive impacts were also agreed with, as shown in Table 5.2. This cluster also disagreed with two statements, one positive and one negative. The residents in this cluster were largely supportive of the continuation of Indy (97%) despite their concern about some impacts, but many of them favored its continuation at another location, with 39% favoring the Broadwater option and 26% favoring the Dreamworld option. They mostly did not fit the demographic profile of spectators, and the majority of these residents lived in the Indy zone (90%). They also tended to be higher income earners, with 63% having annual incomes of over US $25,200.

Parallels in comunity clusters

While it is obviously relatively easy to identify corresponding groups among those who have the most extreme views (lovers and haters), the complexity of views among the remainder undermines the precision of this process. This is compounded by variations in the instruments used in each study, which limit the degree to which direct comparisons can be made. The first difficulty for comparison is the difference between the clustering variables. The Davis *et al.* study used 31 statements measuring activities, interests and opinions, while the Madrigal study used eight impact statements, four positive and four negative. The Indy research utilized 36 impact statements that attempted to exhaustively cover all possible impacts of the event. The next difficulty lay in the fact that different descriptive statistics were reported in each case. Madrigal reported mean responses to the statements for each cluster, while Davis *et al.* reported only percentages in agreement for each cluster. A direct

Table 5.3 Parallels between Indy clusters and those identified by others

Davis et al. (1988)	Madrigal (1995)	Indy study
Haters (16%)	Haters (31%)	Haters (15%)
Lovers (20%)	Lovers (13%)	Lovers (23%)
Cautious romantics (21%)		Ambivalent supporters (29%)
In-betweeners (18%)	Realists (56%)	Realists (24%)
Love'em for a reason (26%)		Concerned for a reason (9%)

comparison between the three studies was thus impossible. However, it can be said that, in general, in all studies, clusters of residents who either loved or hated tourism/the Indy were clearly identifiable, and among the remainder of the population there is a diversity of views ranging from conditional support/concern to ambivalence. Parallels between the clusters identified in this study and those previously identified by Madrigal (1995) and Davis *et al.* (1988) are described in Table 5.3.

In order to take this comparison a step further, the results of Madrigal's study are aligned with those of the Indy study in Figure 5.1. Here, the mean scores of the different clusters identified in the two studies have been calculated in terms of aggregated positive and negative statements and plotted. As the scales of the two studies were originally in opposite directions, responses to the Indy statements were recoded for the purposes of this part of the analysis. The figure suggests a strong correspondence between the lovers and haters identified in the two studies and a relatively close relationship between the realists. The "ambivalent supporters" and "concerned for a reason" groups in the Indy study are both more ambivalent than Madrigal's realists. Unfortunately, by summing the impact statements into only two groups, positive and negative, a lot of the interesting detail has been lost, and some of the important impacts which are of particular interest to specific clusters cannot be discerned.

Conclusion

In their study of community reactions to tourism, Pearce *et al.* (1996) drew a distinction between etic and emic paradigms. The former approach is based on the researcher's *a priori* assumptions and constructs regarding the dimensions of the community's response, which are then imposed upon the community through the measurement process. Drawing on social representations theory, the latter (emic) approach recognizes the complexities of community representations of phenomena and the role of social networks in their development, and thus relies more on the community itself to spontaneously generate its own constructs. They advocated the adoption of the latter on the grounds that, in the etic approach, the researcher's conceptualization of the problem acts as a filter that may result in important aspects of individual community's reactions being obscured.

This study, along with the earlier work by Davis *et al.* (1988) and Madrigal (1995), has involved an essentially etic approach in the sense that the framework for the analysis was imposed upon the community through a pre-determined battery of statements which was used to elicit individual responses. On the other hand, it can also be argued that there is an element of the emic approach, at least to the extent that the cluster analysis in effect allows respondents to "choose" which group they belong to and the underlying patterns of community reactions are defined in the process. This differs from previous studies of residents' perceptions of tourism, which attempt to place residents in a priori defined groups. As such, the cluster analysis approach has utility as a tool for investigating the underlying structure of community reactions to tourism and events, and exploring the profiles of the various clusters.

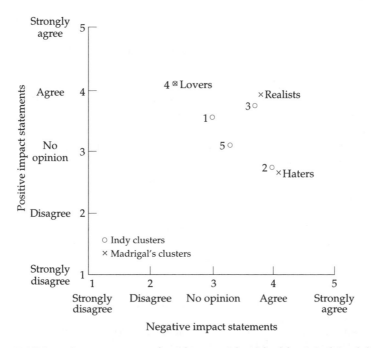

Figure 5.1 Mean impact scores for clusters identified by Madrigal (1995) and Indy Study

By identifying coherent groups of individuals who share a common set of views which distinguishes them from other groups, cluster analysis can provide the basis for a more targeted approach to the planning and management of tourism and events. Thus, for instance, in the case of the Gold Coast Indy, it is necessary to examine the "haters" and the "concerned for a reason" groups to establish whether or not specific management measures might be implemented to alleviate the causes of their concerns. Meanwhile, research on these groups might be instrumental in uncovering misconceptions or blind spots regarding perceptions of the event's impacts, which may need to be counteracted in marketing the event to the community. A closer examination of the lovers group might provide the insights necessary for accentuating the positive aspects of the event in marketing programs both within and beyond the host community.

The clarity and conclusiveness of the analysis contained in this paper has undoubtedly been limited by the fact that the attempt was made to compare results derived from three different studies which have been based on different data collection instruments. Given this, a valuable extension of this study might be to carry out a similar analysis of community reactions with the same instrument being utilized across several communities. However, the fact that similarities are apparent in the pattern of responses within the communities concerned, despite the differences in the instruments used, highlights the durability of these patterns and the potential utility of cluster analysis as a tool for comparative studies based on the emic approach.

The identification of similar response patterns across different communities may bring researchers closer to developing more general theory concerning the interface between communities and tourism/events. Real progress in this area, however, depends upon a better understanding of the factors underlying these patterns. This requires a more thorough investigation of variables such as sociopolitical values which may influence residents' perceptions, and also exploration of perception development and transmission via direct contact, social interaction, and the media as suggested by social representations theory. A study of this nature is currently being undertaken by the authors, including a comparative component examining two similar events in different locations to investigate the influence of extrinsic variables.

References

Ap, J. (1992) Residents' Perceptions on Tourism Impacts. *Annals of Tourism Research* 19: 665–690.

Australian Bureau of Statistics (1998) *Population Queensland, Catalogue No. 3234.3.* Canberra: Australia's Bureau of Statistics.

Belisle, F., and D. Hoy (1980) The Perceived Impact of Tourism by Residents. *Annals of Tourism Research* 11: 83–101.

Black, T., and A. Pape (1995) The IndyCar Grand Prix: Costs and Benefits. *Australian Accountant* 65(8): 25–28.

Breakwell, G. M. (1993) Integrating Paradigms, Methodological Implications. In *Empirical Approaches to Social Representations*, G. M. Breakwell and D. V. Canter, eds., pp. 180–199. Oxford: Clarendon Press.

Brougham, J. E., and R. W. Butler (1981) A Segmentation Analysis of Resident Attitudes. *Annals of Tourism Research* 8: 569–590.

Bureau of Tourism Research (1997) *International Visitors Survey: Summary Report*. Canberra: Bureau of Tourism Research.

Burns, J. P. A., and T. J. Mules (1986) A Framework for the Analysis of Major Special Events. In *The Adelaide Grand Prix: The Impact of a Special Event*, J. P. A. Burns, J. H. Hatch and T. J. Mules, eds., pp. 5–38. Adelaide: The Center for South Australian Economic Studies.

Butler, R. W. (1975) Tourism as an Agent of Social Change. In *Proceedings of the International Geographical Union's Working Group on the Geography of Tourism and Recreation*, Trent University, Peterborough, Ontario, pp. 85–90.

—— (1980) The Concept of a Tourist Area Cycle of Evolution: Implications for Management of Resources. *Canadian Geographer* 24(1): 5–12.

Commonwealth Department of Sport Recreation and Tourism (1986) *Economic Impact of the World Cup Athletics held in Canberra in October 1985*. Canberra: Commonwealth of Australia.

Davis, D., J. Allen, and R. M. Cosenza (1988) Segmenting Local Residents by their Attitudes, Interests and Opinions toward Tourism. *Journal of Travel Research* 27(2): 2–8.

Deiley, R. (1995) The Grand Spree: Row Over Indy Funding Revived. *The Gold Coast Bulletin* (November 1): 9.

Dougherty, K. C., M. Eisenhart, and P. Webley (1992) The Role of Social Representations and National Identities in the Development of Territorial Knowledge: A Study of Political Socialization in Argentina and England. *American Educational Research Journal* 29: 809–835.

Doxey, G. V. (1975) A Causation Theory of Visitor Resident Irritants: Methodology and Research Inferences. In *Travel and Tourism Research Association Sixth Annual Conference Proceedings*, San Diego, pp. 195–198.

Echabe, A. E., and D. P. Rovira (1989) Social Representations and Memory. *European Journal of Social Psychology* 19: 543–551.

Ernst, and Young (1995) Economic Impact of the 1995 IndyCar Event. In *Economic Impact Study: Final Report*. Brisbane: Ernst and Young.

Faulkner, B., and C. Tideswell (1997) A Framework for Monitoring Community Impacts of Tourism. *Journal of Sustainable Tourism* 5(1): 3–28.

Fife-Shaw, C. R. (1993) Finding Social Representations in Attribute Check lists: How Will We Know When We Have Found One? In *Empirical Approaches to Social Representations*, G. M. Breakwell and D. V. Canter, eds. Oxford: Clarendon Press.

Gamson, W. A., D. Croteau, W. Hoynes, and T. Sasson (1992) Media Images and the Social Construction of Reality. *Annual Review of Sociology* 18: 373–393.

Gold Coast Bulletin (1990) Injunction Bid to Save "Indy" Park. *The Gold Coast Bulletin* (August 6): 6.

—— (1991) For Residents, a Noisy Nightmare. *The Gold Coast Bulletin* (March 15): 4.

Hair, J. F., R. E. Anderson, R. L. Tatham, and W. C. Black (1995) *Multivariate Data Analysis* (4th ed.). Englewood Cliffs NJ: Prentice-Hall.

Hall, C. M. (1992) *Hallmark Tourist Events: Impacts, Management and Planning*. London: Belhaven Press.

Hall, C. M., and H. J. Selwood (1989) America's Cup Lost: Paradise Retained? The Dynamics of a Hallmark Tourist Event. In *The Planning and Evaluation of Hallmark Events*, G. J. Syme, B. J. Shaw, D. M. Fenton and W. S. Mueller, eds., pp. 103–118. Aldershot: Avebury.

Hall, C. M., J. Selwood, and E. McKewon (1996) Hedonists, Ladies and Larrikins: Crime, Prostitution and the 1987 America's Cup. *Visions in Leisure and Business* 14(3): 28–51.

Hiller, H. (1989) Impact and Image: The Convergence of Urban Factors in Preparing for the 1988 Calgary Winter Olympics. In *The Planning and Evaluation of Hallmark Events*, G. J. Syme, B. J. Shaw, D. M. Fenton and W. S. Mueller, eds., pp. 119–131. Aldershot: Avebury.

Jeong, G. (1992) *Perceived Post-Olympic Sociocultural Impacts by Residents from a Tourism Perspective: A Case Study in Charmail, Seoul, Korea.* Minnesota: University of Minnesota.

Jeong, G., and B. Faulkner (1996) Resident Perceptions of Mega-Event Impacts: The Tajeon International Exposition Case. *Festival Management and Event Tourism* 4: 3–11.

Kotler, P. (1988) *Marketing Management: Analysis, Planning, Implementation, and Control* (6th ed.). Englewood Cliffs NJ: Prentice-Hall.

Liu, J., and T. Var (1986) Resident Attitudes Toward Tourism Impacts in Hawaii. *Annals of Tourism Research* 13: 193–214.

Madrigal, R. (1995) Residents' Perceptions and the Role of Government. *Annals of Tourism Research* 22: 86–102.

Massey, M. (1991) Gold Coast Challenges Adelaide. *Financial Review* (19 March): 26.

McDonald, S. (1990) *The 1990 Adelaide Festival: The Economic Impact. Volume II: Methodology and Results: Details.* Adelaide: The Center for South Australian Economic Studies.

Milman, A., and A. Pizam (1988) Social Impacts of Tourism on Central Florida. *Annals of Tourism Research* 15: 208–220.

Moscovici, S. (1981) On Social Representations. In *Social Cognition: Perspectives on Everyday Understanding*, J. P. Forgas, ed., pp. 181–209. London: Academic Press.

—— (1983) The Coming Era of Social Representations. In *Cognitive Approaches to Social Behaviour*, J. P. Codol and J. P. Leyens, eds. The Hague: Nijhoff.

—— (1984) The Phenomenon of Social Representations. In *Social Representation*, R. M. Farr and S. Moscovici, eds., pp. 3–69. Cambridge: Cambridge University Press.

—— (1988) Notes Toward a Description of Social Representations. *European Journal of Social Psychology* 18: 211–250.

Mules, T., and B. Faulkner (1996) An Economic Perspective on Special Events. *Tourism Economics* 2: 107–117.

Pearce, P. L., G. Moscardo, and G. F. Ross (1996) *Tourism Community Relationships.* Oxford: Pergamon Press.

Pizam, A. (1978) Tourism's Impacts: The Social Costs to the Destination Community as Perceived by its Residents. *Journal of Travel Research* 16(4): 8–12.

Pizam, A., A. Milman, and B. King (1994) The Perceptions of Tourism Employees and their Families toward Tourism. *Tourism Management* 15: 53–61.

Purkhardt, S. C. (1993) *Transforming Social Representations: A Social Psychology of Common Sense and Science.* London: Routledge.

Pyo, S., R. Cook, and R. L. Howell (1988) Summer Olympic Tourism Marketing: Learning from the Past. *Tourism Marketing* 9: 137–144.

Rey, P. (1987) Economic Impacts of Special Events using Examples of World Cup

Athletics, Canberra. In *The Impact and Marketing of Special Events*. Canberra: Australian Standing Committee on Tourism Canberra: Australian Standing Committee on Tourism.

Ritchie, J. R. B., and C. E. Aitken (1984) Assessing the Impacts of the 1988 Olympic Winter Games: The Research Program and Initial Results. *Journal of Travel Research* 22(3): 17–25.

—— (1985) OLYMPULSE I/II: Evolving Resident Attitudes Towards the 1988 Olympic Winter Games. *Journal of Travel Research* 23(3): 28–33.

Ritchie, J. R. B., and D. Beliveau (1974) Hallmark Events: An Evaluation of a Strategic Response to Seasonality in the Travel Market. *Journal of Travel Research* 14(2): 14–20.

Ritchie, J. R. B., and M. M. Lyons (1987) OLYMPULSE III/IV: A Midterm Report on Resident Attitudes Concerning the 1988 Olympic Winter Games. *Journal of Travel Research* 26(1): 18–26.

—— (1990) OLYMPULSE VI: A Post Event Assessment of Resident Reaction to the XV Olympic Winter Games. *Journal of Travel Research* 28(3): 14–23.

Ritchie, J. R. B., and B. H. Smith (1991) The Impact of a Mega-Event on Host Region Awareness: A Longitudinal Study. *Journal of Travel Research* 29(1): 3–10.

Ryan, C., and D. Montgomery (1994) The Attitudes of Bakewell Residents to Tourism and Issues in Community Responsive Tourism. *Tourism Management* 15: 358–369.

Sheldon, P. J., and T. Var (1984) Resident Attitudes to Tourism in North Wales. *Tourism Management* 15: 40–47.

Smith, D. (1996) Indy Boasts $2.2m Profit. *The Gold Coast Bulletin* (April 23): 1.

Soutar, G. N., and P. B. McLeod (1989) The Impacts of the America's Cup on Fremantle Residents: Some Empirical Evidence. In *The Planning and Evaluation of Hallmark Events*, G. J. Syme, B. J. Shaw, D. M. Fenton and W. S. Mueller, eds., pp. 92–102. Aldershot: Avebury.

—— (1993) Residents' Perceptions on Impacts of the America's Cup. *Annals of Tourism Research* 20: 571–582.

Stimpson, R. J., J. R. Minnery, A. Kabamba and B. Moon (1996) *"Sun-belt" Migration Decisions: A Study of the Gold Coast*. Canberra: Australian Government Publishing Services.

Stolz, G. (1996) IndyCar Future on Track: Premier. *The Gold Coast Bulletin* (April 25): 6.

Teo, P. (1994) Assessing Socio-Cultural Impacts: The Case of Singapore. *Tourism Management* 15: 126–136.

Thorne, R., and M. Munro-Clark (1989) Hallmark Events as an Excuse for Autocracy in Urban Planning. In *The Planning and Evaluation of Hallmark Events*, G. J. Syme, B. J. Shaw, D. M. Fenton and W. S. Mueller, eds., pp. 154–171. Aldershot: Avebury.

Weston, P. (1990a) Indy Silence Alarms Trackside Residents. *The Gold Coast Bulletin* (June 26): 6.

—— (1990b) UN to be Asked to Stop Surfers Race. *The Gold Coast Bulletin* (October 20): 11.

Wright, J (1996) Fast Cash. *The Courier Mail* (April 23): 13.

Chapter 6

Monitoring the Tourism Impacts of the Sydney 2000 Olympics

Bill Faulkner, Laurence Chalip, Graham Brown, Leo Jago, Roger March and Arch Woodside

The potential for events to play a central role in tourism destination development and marketing has been widely recognized (Getz 1997; Mules and Faulkner 1996; Ritchie 1984; Ritchie and Smith 1991). In general, it has been argued that events not only contribute to increased visitation by adding to the critical mass of a destination's attractions, but also they have the capacity to enhance visitation levels beyond the duration of the event itself by virtue of the longer term marketing effects produced by media and related promotional benefits (Hall 1987; Hiller 1989; Kang and Perdue 1994; Pyo *et al.* 1988; Ritchie 1984; Ritchie and Smith 1991; Socher 1987). The range and magnitude of an event's tourism impacts are, to a considerable extent, dependent upon its scale and significance. Indeed, it is possible that some larger events will have additional impacts, such as providing a stimulus for the expansion of tourism-related infrastructure, the refurbishment of existing infrastructure, or the enhancement of destination marketing capabilities through increased resources or organizational change. The term "mega-event" has been used to describe the largest category of events, whose distinguishing feature has been their international profile (Law 1993). While there may be some ambiguities concerning the precise definition of mega-events and the criteria used for assigning events to this category (Jafari 1988; Jago and Shaw 1998; Witt 1988), there is little doubt that the Summer Olympic Games stands out as the ultimate benchmark.

If the Summer Olympic Games is, in fact, the epitome of mega-events then, in theory at least, this event should maximize the range and magnitude of potential tourism benefits. Despite this, research on successive Olympic Games has been both limited and insufficiently systematic to enable their tourism impacts to be effectively identified and quantified. Therefore, there has been little development of the cumulative knowledge required for destination planners to learn how to maximize the tourism benefits that can be derived from such events, and many of the claims that are made about positive tourism spin-offs are assertions that are not supported by rigorous measurement and analysis. Fundamental research questions remain to be addressed. These include:

- To what extent do mega-events such as the Olympics actually produce tourism benefits?
- What is the nature of these benefits?
- How can tourism benefits be more effectively leveraged from such events in order to increase their economic and social value to the community?

The Sydney 2000 Olympics has provided an opportunity for these questions to be examined in a more comprehensive and systematic way than has been previously attempted. In one respect, Sydney may provide the ideal case for such a study because it has been suggested that there has been a more deliberate and coordinated approach to leveraging tourism opportunities off this Olympics than has been attempted previously. Indeed, this has been acknowledged by the International Olympic Committee's (IOC) Director of Marketing, who has observed that the Australian approach may provide a model for other countries to follow and, perhaps, this should be facilitated through the inclusion of the tourism factor as a new dimension of the Olympic movement's legacy (Brown 2000: 88). This article describes an integrated suite of research projects that comprise the (Australian) Cooperative Research Centre for Sustainable Tourism's Sydney Olympics Tourism Impacts Study. This project is aimed at addressing the research questions described above and, ultimately, at providing insights into how marketing and management strategies might be developed to ensure that the maximum tourism potential of events might be realized. An overview of previous research on tourism impacts of earlier Summer Olympics is provided to put the Sydney case study into context, and this is followed by an outline of each component of the study.

Research on the Impacts of the Olympic Games

When one considers the history, magnitude, and the global profile of the Olympic Games, it is surprising that so little systematic research has been carried out on the tourism impacts of this event. An examination of the research that has been carried out, however, reveals several broad themes: impacts on visitor numbers directly associated with the event; longer term promotional and associated visitor impacts; and organizational change implications.

Visitor numbers associated with the event

The attention that is given to increased levels of visitation to the host city or country as a direct consequence of the Games is, perhaps, understandable given the visibility and immediacy of this impact. However, if anything, the research carried out on previous Olympics has highlighted how limited and uncertain this impact actually is.

Expectations of number of visitors generated by the event have generally exceeded the actual numbers and in some cases the Games have actually reduced the number of visitors below the levels that would be normally received. As Pyo *et al.* (1988) observed, the latter phenomenon was particularly evident in the case of the Los Angeles 1984 Olympics, which experienced significant diversion effects as a consequence of adverse publicity concerning capacity constraints, prices, and ticketing confusion. In their study of the 1988 Seoul Olympics, Kang and Perdue (1994) also observed that the net effect of the Games on visitor numbers is modest once the combined influence of diversion and time switching effects are taken into account. Also, as Hiller (1989) suggested in the case of the Calgary Winter Olympics, the relatively short duration of the event limits its overall impact. Thus, even the most optimistic forecasts of visitors attending the Sydney 2000 Olympics involves only a marginal increase when compared with normal levels of visitation to this city (Faulkner and Tideswell 1999). However, the tourism impact of the Olympic Games is not limited to visitors to the event itself. When the effect is forecast over a 10-year period – from the time the bid was won until the start of the summer Olympic Games in Sydney and several years beyond – the aggregate tourism impact is projected to be substantial, accounting for better than half the projected economic impact of the Games (Spurr 1999).

Longer-term effects

Given the above observations, it is plausible that the longer term promotional effects of the Olympic Games might be more significant for the host city than the direct impacts (Brunet 1992). One of the most detailed studies of promotional spin-offs associated with an Olympic Games involved a longitudinal study of the impacts of the 1988 Calgary Winter Olympics on awareness and interest in Calgary as a tourist destination in the US and European markets (Ritchie and Smith 1991). This revealed that there were significant, but transitory, promotional benefits of the Games. A related study revealed a high propensity for repeat visitation among visitors to the same event. Similar observations were made by Iton (1988) with regard to the impacts of the Montreal Olympics. While these observations suggest there are tangible effects on awareness and interest within the market, there remains some uncertainty concerning the extent to which this might be translated into additional visitors.

Alternative approaches to examining the tourism promotional effects of the Olympics, specifically designed to isolate the incremental effect on visitor numbers, have been applied to the 1988 Seoul Olympics. Hyun (1990) estimated the long-term impact of the Games on inbound travel to Korea at around 640,000 by using univariate regression as a benchmark for the trend in the absence of the event. In their analysis of the same event, Kang and Perdue (1994) emphasized that, whatever effects the Olympics may have, these take place against a background of other factors that affect fluctuations in inbound travel (global economic cycles, changes in the competitive environment, etc.), and this invariably complicates any attempt to isolate the impacts of the event. After applying a multi-regression modelling approach encompassing some of these variables to a range of competing destinations, they estimated the increase in visitors to Korea attributable to the games was just below 1 million between 1988 and 1990.

On the basis of an econometric modelling approach in which other environmental factors (income levels, relative prices, etc.) were held constant, Witt and Martin (1987) concluded that mega-events had no discernible impact on international tourism flows. At the aggregate level, therefore, it would appear that the so-called showcase effect of mega-events is marginal because they generally take place in large cities that are already well known (Hiller 1989) and any positive effects on emerging destinations such as Korea are outweighed by the more general negligible impact elsewhere (Jeong *et al.* 1990; Kang and Perdue 1994). From this it might be concluded that the magnitude of any promotional effect associated with the Sydney Olympics might depend on where Sydney and Australia are situated along the profile spectrum. However, it might be equally argued that the tourism dividend derived from the event is significantly influenced by the organizational arrangements that are put in place to realize these impacts. This is an aspect of the tourism implications of mega-events that has been given little attention in the past.

Organizational responses

One of the main observations regarding organizational responses associated with previous Olympics concerns the event's potential role as, a catalyst for a more concerted and coordinated approach to tourism planning and marketing in the host city or country. In Calgary's case, for instance, Ritchie and Lyons (1990) noted that, "At a minimum the Games have greatly enhanced the status of the local industry and have led to substantial increases in the budgets for tourism development and promotion at both the municipal and provincial level" (p. 23). Meanwhile,

Simon (1988) observed how the 1984 LA Olympics served as a catalyst for greater cooperation among government agencies in a manner that had lasting effects. However, these conclusions are little more than incidental observations of the researchers, rather than the product of systematic analyses of organizational responses. One of the few instances where organizational responses to the challenge of leveraging tourism opportunities off a mega-event has been the focus of research was the study of the 1991 Sheffield World Student Games by Bramwell (1997). Bramwell recognized that, as the organizational and strategic planning implications of such an event would be neither immediate nor confined to the year it was staged, a long-term perspective spanning more than 5 years before, during, and after the event was necessary. However, the depth of the study was compromised by its reliance on the examination of documents and newspaper articles over the period, with the involvement of key people in the management of tourism initiatives being limited to a series of interviews conducted in 1995. Despite this limitation, the study produced some useful insights into the lessons that can be drawn from the Sheffield experience. In particular, it demonstrated how strategies developed to foster sports-tourism linkages involved a blend of "classical," "processual," and "systemic" elements.

The complication of multiple agendas

The examination of the organizational responses associated with the staging of mega-events such as the Olympics is complicated by the multiple agendas associated with such events, the diversity of stakeholders driving these agendas, and the inevitable maze of tradeoffs in the decision-making and planning processes. Thus, for example, apart from the more obvious sporting and tourism benefits that motivate public sector underwriting of the event, there are other considerations such as: enhancing national prestige; generation of new industry activity; rejuvenation, renewal, and revitalization of depressed urban areas; development of new infrastructure; employment generation associated with event organization and other flow-on effects; additional recreational opportunities for residents (both during the event and afterwards through the use of facilities); improved community pride and morale; promotion of interest in sport and more healthy lifestyle (Getz 1997, 1998; Hall 1992a; Hall and Hodges 1996; Ritchie 1984). Some commentators have argued that the sport–tourism linkage can provide the momentum required for the economic regeneration of many cities (Gratton and Kokolakakis 1997). As in the case of the Barcelona Olympics (Ajuntament de Barcelona 1992; Wilkinson 1989), the rejuvenation of blighted urban areas and the development of new infrastructure are significant elements of the benefits derived from the Sydney Olympics. The promotional advantages of major events such as the Olympic Games are, therefore, not confined to the tourism sector. It has been suggested that they are being increasingly construed as an instrument for reimaging cities, with the event being used as a mechanism for attracting investment capital at a time when there is intense competition between cities (Hall 1994, 1995; Hall and Jenkins 1995; Harvey 1989).

This feature of mega-events in general, and the Olympic Games in particular, has not gone uncriticized. Critics question the value of mega-events for civic redevelopment. They emphasize that the opportunity costs associated with event investments are substantial, and that the benefits accrue to economic (and political) elite, whereas the costs are borne by all taxpayers (Boyle 1997; Mules 1998a; Putsis 1998). Whitson and Macintosh (1996) take this argument a step further, contending that claims of economic benefits from mega-events, including the Olympic Games, are intended to mask a more sinister purpose, namely, to legitimize public subsidy for the purpose of promoting the status of local elite. Sack and Johnson (1996) demonstrate precisely that outcome in the case of the Volvo International Tennis Tournament in New Haven, Connecticut. Rosentraub *et al.* (1994) found no significant change in the Indianapolis economy despite substantial public investment in international sport events.

What distinguishes the Olympic Games in Sydney is that there has been a substantial public effort to leverage the Games for tourism development. This is a subtle but important shift in thinking about the potential of mega-events for tourism development. The emphasis is not on the impact of the Games; it is on what can be done to optimize the impact of the Games. Perhaps as a consequence of the sheer size of the Olympics, tourism policymakers have taken a more assertively instrumental approach to the Games in Sydney than is typically the case with other sport events. The event is no longer merely an economic development tactic; it has become an opportunity through which to put new strategies and an array of associated tactics into place. There is an opportunity, then, to learn something about event leveraging.

The policy and evaluation conundrum

As emphasized at the outset of this section, the quantity of research on the tourism implications of the Olympic Games appears to be out of proportion with the size and significance of this event. On the basis of the above review, it is also apparent that the piecemeal nature of the research carried out to date has contributed little to the development of a cumulative knowledge about the event. This situation is perhaps doubly surprising when it is viewed in the context of the increasingly explicit recognition of events-based tourism destination development strategies referred to in the introduction. However, it is more surprising when one considers the fact that the staging of the Olympic games usually involves a significant

investment of public funds, which is at least partially justified in terms of
tourism promotional and development objectives. The explanation for
this conundrum may have something to do with ambiguities associated
with the multiple agendas referred to above. That is, given the varied
agendas of the many stakeholders in an Olympic Games, it may be easier
for public officials if they do not know precisely which public investments
obtained (or did not obtain) what outcomes. If claims about outcomes can
be phrased in terms of aggregate impacts and piecemeal impressions,
claims that the specific objectives of particular stakeholders were attained
would be difficult to refute. In any case, the interrelatedness of agendas
complicates the isolations of specific outcomes. Nevertheless, in the
process, the opportunity to learn from the Games has been lost.

From the Olympic Movement's perspective, such objectives as the
provision of opportunities for elite sporting contest, the stimulation of
athletic development through the provision of state-of-the-art facilities,
and the general promotion of sport are paramount, and these objectives
also feature in the host city/country's rationale (Hiller 1989). However, as
observed in the review of research on the Olympic Games and mega-
events generally, there are much broader agendas. This is explicitly
acknowledged in the following statement relating to the Sydney Olympic
Games:

> An Olympic Games that is successfully staged and financially
> managed leaves a positive legacy for the host city in terms of new
> and upgraded sporting facilities and venues; new and improved
> infrastructure; enhanced international recognition; enhanced
> international reputation; increased tourism; new trade, investment
> and marketing opportunities; and increased participation in sport.
> (Sydney Olympic Games Review Committee 1990: 3)

While this statement indicates that tourism benefits represent just one of
many dimensions associated with the Games, it also alludes to less
tangible considerations that may nevertheless be more significant in
terms of the priorities that drive the decisions of government. As Hall
(1992b) has emphasized, international politics have played an important
role in shaping the history of the Olympic Games, while at the domestic
level such events have been utilized as an instrument for enhancing and
legitimizing local power elite. Within the context of these other considerations, tourism impacts represent just one of many dimensions for evaluating the return on public sector investment in the event and, despite
claims to the contrary, it may well be that the tourism factor has not been
a key consideration within the government policy framework. Indeed, on
the basis of the commitment of funds to researching these impacts in the
past, there appears to have been at least disdain for, if not a resistance to,
any effort to measure tourism effects.

Alternatively, or perhaps in addition to this explanation, the lack of a commitment to monitoring the tourism impacts of the Olympics may reflect a form of "policy fatalism." That is, having committed public resources to the event on such a large scale, the responsible politicians and their advisors regard any evaluation of the outcomes of this investment as being superfluous or, more importantly, potentially embarrassing. Bramwell (1997) has alluded to this in the case of the Sheffield City administration's attitude to research in the context of the 1991 World Student Games by noting that the reluctance to commit funds to research might have been affected by a fear of unfavorable findings.

The outcome of the apparent dearth of evaluative research on the tourism impacts of past Olympics Games is that there has been no systematic and cumulative development of knowledge about the Olympics/ tourism nexus. The opportunity for lessons about the most effective means for maximizing the tourism benefits of such events being drawn from past experience has therefore been lost.

Learning from experience

The loss is significant because public investment in sport events has become such an integral component of tourism destination marketing strategies. The very size and scope of an Olympic Games provide a unique opportunity to examine the many dimensions of potential tourism benefits from sport events, and to do so more thoroughly and more comprehensively than would be possible with an event of smaller size or duration.

The lessons to be obtained should provide insights that can inform the bidding for, and hosting of, events in the future – not merely the Olympic Games, but other large sport events as well.

When assessing the tourism impacts of the Olympic Games, the challenge is to identify particular effects, and then to attribute those effects to particular leveraging activities. In other words, one first needs to know what was done by tourism marketers, and then one needs to know how the market responded. The objective is to move beyond aggregate impact statements or piecemeal evaluations. Rather, the objective is to identify the range of strategies and tactics that were (and were not) used to leverage the Games, and then to link those to specific outcomes (or a lack of outcomes) in particular market segments.

In order to obtain the necessary breadth of focus, three studies have been put into place to examine the tourism impacts of the Sydney Olympic Games. The first study maps the leveraging strategies and organizational responses that have been put into place by tourism organizations (both public and private) at national, state, regional, and local levels. The second study looks at a specific aspect of leveraging by focusing on one of the core stakeholders – the sponsors – in order to identify the potential for tourism leveraging through sponsorship linkages. The third study maps international market responses to the Sydney Olympics. Two additional studies, focusing on domestic market responses and tourism-related economic impacts, are being developed, but these are not described in this article. As reflected in Figure 6.1, this suite of studies comprises integrated components of a single project designed to identify the tourism development potential of the Olympic Games, and to draw lessons for the tourism leveraging of sport events in the future. Each of the three existing studies is described below.

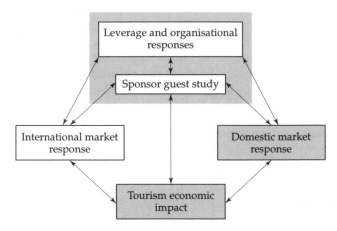

Figure 6.1 Sydney Olympics tourism impacts study

The Leveraging Study

A close look at the economic impact forecasts for the Sydney Olympics reveals that tourist visits to the Games represent only a very small portion of the expected number of tourist visits that will be generated as a result of the Games (Arthur Anderson Consulting and University of Tasmania Centre for Regional Economic Analysis 1999; Tourism Forecasting Council 1998b). The more important effect will be visitation in the lead up to the Games and in the years immediately following the Games. The core issue, then, is to determine what tourism organizations are doing to optimize the tourism impact of the Games.

The leveraging study seeks to extend earlier work carried out by Faulkner and Tideswell (1999), by identifying the strategies and tactics that have been put into place by tourism organizations throughout Australia in order to leverage the Games. It maps the strategies that have been formulated to optimize tourism benefits from the Games, and it locates the tactics that have been devised to constitute those strategies. The study examines strategies and tactics at national, state, regional, and local levels. It encompasses public and private organizations, and it has involved interviews with key informants and the collection and analysis of marketing collateral and planning documents. Surveys and some media analyses are also being undertaken.

Strategies and tactics

Although there has been substantial study of event management and event impacts, very little has been done to explore the techniques of event leveraging. However, a close analysis of the relevant literature suggests at least four key components of event leveraging:

- Using the event to build or enhance the destination's position in the market (Kotler *et al*. 1993; van den Berg *et al*. 2000).
- Employing tactics to enhance visitor spending while at the event (cf. Frechtling 1987; Mules and Faulkner 1996).
- Fostering longer stays and flow-on tourism from visitors (cf. Frechtling 1987; Mules 1998b).
- Building new relationships through the event (Brenner 1997; Gillam 1996; Jensen 1994). The leveraging study examines how these have been developed and applied by tourism organizations in Australia. Because each of these components poses particular challenges, it is useful to consider each in turn.

Positioning

Although the Olympic Games focus the world's attention on the Olympic host, much of that attention is on matters surrounding the event itself (e.g., politics, competition, athletes). From a tourism perspective, the challenge is to piggyback on that interest by finding ways to showcase the host city and the host nation as destinations. A marketing communications strategy needs to be developed that directs the attention of journalists to the destination, and that does so in a manner consistent with the position that the destination seeks to attain in the market.

The publicity enjoyed by an Olympic host will build as the Games approach, and will peak while the Games take place. As a result, international awareness and interest can be expected to peak just as the Games come to an end, but may wane as time passes (Ritchie and Smith 1991). Consequently, the marketing communications strategy needs to incorporate plans to capitalize on Games interest, and then to exploit the enhanced destination awareness and interest that the Games may have rendered.

Stimulating visitor spending

The economic impact of any event depends on the spending of visitors while at the event (Mules and Faulkner 1996). This includes spending for souvenirs and socializing as well as spending on room, board, and event admissions. For many event visitors, the festival atmosphere at an event can be conducive to free spending and impulse buying (Godbey and Graefe 1991; Hausman 2000; Rook and Fisher 1995). So, the challenge is to provide an appropriate festival atmosphere in the areas that event visitors will stay or frequent – an atmosphere that is congenial to a multicultural assemblage. This may foster repeat visitation, as well as visitor spending (Green and Chalip 1998).

The standard means for developing an appropriate festival atmosphere are theming (Gottdiener 1997; Pine and Gilmore 1999) and/or special promotions by local businesses (Blattberg and Neslin 1990). In order to theme an area, local businesses must work together collectively. Special promotions require strategic market planning to implement effectively. However, it is sometimes difficult to get local businesses to work together collectively – either because cooperation seems antithetical to normal business practice (Herrigel 1993) or because the businesses that must cooperate have an established tradition of competing against one another (Levin 1993). Further, small business owners and managers typically lack the skills (Davis 1997; Robinson and Pearce 1984) or the inclination (Malone and Jenster 1991) to develop promotions designed to capitalize on a unique strategic opportunity. Consequently, the leveraging challenge is to help local businesses to recognize and then capitalize upon the opportunities that an event like the Olympics affords.

Flow-on tourism
Visitors to the Games will have traveled to Australia to see Olympic events, but not necessarily to see Australia (cf. Chalip *et al.* 1998). For destinations beyond Sydney, the challenge is to get Olympic visitors to extend their stay in order to travel elsewhere in Australia. There are two essential elements. First, the destination must make itself attractive to Olympic visitors. Second, it must create opportunities for Olympic visitors to extend their travel. The first element is a marketing communications task. The second is a task of bundling or packaging, and the building of relationships associated with this. The consequent challenge is to bring the destination into brochures and travel packages offering pre-Games and/or post-Games itineraries for Olympic visitors.

Building relationships
Large events, particularly the Olympic Games, provide an opportunity to create useful relationships. Journalists who attend the event can become contacts for placement of stories in the future, or to put a desired spin on stories as they break. Sports officials and athletes might be sold on the opportunity to visit again to train or to compete. Business people may

discover the benefits of a particular location for future conventions or for incentive travel. The challenge for tourism organizations is to use the interest and visitors that the event brings in order to build relationships that can become the engines of future tourism business.

Formulating and implementing strategy
The four components of event leveraging sound deceptively straight-forward. In practice, the effort required to formulate appropriate strategies, to devise the necessary tactics, and to implement those strategies and tactics is enormous. This is due, in part, to the large number of stake-holders that must be coordinated. There are national, state, regional, and local tourism organizations, each of which may have different notions about what constitutes an appropriate strategic focus. There are private tour companies with their own needs and interests. There are sport organizations at national, state, regional, and local levels that have necessary expertise about sport, but that know very little about tourism (and may care even less). There are local businesses that seek to benefit from the Games, but that lack fundamental skills or resources.

Each of the components of strategy described above requires that a number of different organizations work together, some of which may come from sectors that have not previously worked on tourism policies. For example, a coordinated positioning strategy requires that national, state, regional, and local tourism organizations work in harmony. On the other hand, efforts to generate flow-on tourism may bring destinations (and destination positioning strategies) into competition with one another as they pursue the same Olympic visitors. Efforts to stimulate visitor spending require local businesses to coordinate their efforts. But if theming or specialized promotions are applied, then they need to be compatible with the position that the destination is trying to convey. Finally, relationships can be compromised as different stakeholders seek separate or even incompatible advantages from particular partners.

The strategic opportunities that business partnerships can provide have been well demonstrated (e.g., Lorenzoni and Lipparini 1999; Murphy 1992). However, strategies that require collaboration among an array of organizations are notoriously difficult to formulate and to implement. As the number of organizations required to formulate and implement a strategy increases, the probability that it can be formulated or implemented successfully converges toward zero. Free riding, social loafing, and defec-tion become probable (Sandler 1992), and the likelihood of a breakdown in the chain of implementation increases (Pressman and Wildavsky 1984). In order to overcome these barriers, strong coordination mechanisms need to be put into place, and each tactic needs to be designed so that it requires only a small number of organizations to cooperate.

As a result, leveraging an event like the Olympic Games is more than a creative marketing exercise; it is a task of stakeholder coordination and commitment. The challenges of stakeholder coordination can have profound impacts on policy choice as well as policy implementation. For example, at the level of choice, leveraging strategies for which stakeholder agreement may be relatively easy to reach may emerge as the focus of leveraging efforts – perhaps to the exclusion of strategies that might bring stakeholders into competition. Thus, a national positioning strategy designed to capitalize upon the attention focused on the Games might take precedence over a coordinated strategy to induce flow-on tourism. It is easier to build a consensus around a shared positioning effort than it is to build one around the itineraries for pre-Games and post-Games tours.

The capacity of key stakeholders to contribute to a leveraging tactic may also affect the choice or the implementation of particular strategies. If, for example, particular industry sectors, such as small retailers, have few resources or minimal strategic expertise, then the tactics developed may make minimal use of those industry sectors. In other words, what is done will depend to a degree on what it is that existing institutional structures and resources make most doable.

Towards a foundation for the learning organization

There has been a substantial amount of interest in the ways that organiz-ations do (and do not) learn from experience (e.g., Crossan *et al.* 1999; Edwards 1999). Learning organizations are thought to be more adaptive and, therefore, more successful. The complexity of strategic leveraging of the Olympic Games complicates the learning task. It is important to know more than what was done; it is necessary to know how various stake-holders did (and did not) coordinate with one another. It is useful to know what new relationships were established and when potential relationships failed to materialize. It is essential to consider what oppor-tunities were present but never capitalized upon. Each of these facets can inform future tourism leveraging efforts, not merely for the Olympic Games, but for large sport events more generally.

In the case of a mega-event like the Olympic Games, these tasks are made all the more challenging by the fact that the Games are a one-time event. They come, and then they are gone. The organizations that are created to produce the Games are dismantled shortly after the Games are over. There is no institutionalized memory – no resource that collects what has been learned about leveraging those Games, that ponders the implications of that learning, or that disseminates the resulting insights. The project described here is designed to fill that void.

The Sponsor Guest Study

Some tourism organizations become involved in Olympic planning up to 10 years before the event is staged. Those that support the bid and then work in close collaboration with the organizing committee will be introduced to many new organizations including Olympic sponsors. Some of the sponsors of the Sydney Olympics, particularly Visa and Kodak, have worked closely with the Australian Tourist Commission (ATC) to produce promotional campaigns that feature Australia as an attractive tourist destination. The impact of these co-branded promotions may be felt in future years if they help to increase tourist demand for Australia in overseas markets. However, a more immediate tourism impact of sponsor activity is created by the number of guests sponsors bring to the Games, and it was expected that approximately 50,000 people would take part in the hospitality programs offered by the 25 Team Millennium partners. It was also expected that 40% of these guests would be from overseas and, for many, the Olympics trip would be their first visit to Australia. Two features of particular note concern the opportunity for product testing and the impact of subsequent word-of-mouth communication. The invitations may be regarded as an opportunity to sample Australia as a tourism destination by people who may not have otherwise considered visiting the country. In addition, the status of the positions occupied by some of the guests may mean that they have the potential to be disproportionately influential when they return to their home and work environments. Such considerations helped shape the objectives of this study.

Sponsorship study objectives

Although reference has been made to the role of event hospitality in marketing (Howard and Crompton 1995) and how it may be used to achieve corporate objectives (Delpy *et al.* 1998), very little information exists about the characteristics of the people who are invited to attend the events. No research has attempted to examine guest perceptions and the impact of their experience on their attitudes toward the host city as a tourist destination. The Sydney Olympics provided an opportunity to explore these issues by addressing the following objectives:

- To determine the characteristics of the sponsor guest market (country of origin, socioeconomic background, and previous involvement in corporate hospitality at major sports events).
- To evaluate the experience of sponsor guests (guest satisfaction with different elements of the program provided by the sponsor, the extent to which business opportunities were presented during their visit, attitudes toward Australia as a tourist destination).

- To evaluate the market potential for tourism through the examination of guest expectations regarding return trips to Australia for leisure or business purposes and whether they were likely to influence the attitudes of others in their home environment about Australia as a tourist destination.

Method

The research design was shaped by a recognition of the role played by gatekeepers who have the ability to restrict access to the population of the study. In addition to the need to gain the approval of the International Olympic Committee (IOC) and the Sydney Organizing Committee for the Olympic Games (SOCOG), many of the sponsors imposed constraints due to concerns about the confidentiality of their guest list and a desire to control the experience of guests during their stay. Fortunately, the value of the information that would be generated by the study was recognized, at an early stage, by the ATC. The support of the ATC provided access to the Sponsor Hospitality section of SOCOG and to senior representatives of the sponsors. Negotiations with these representatives resulted in agreements with 11 sponsors to allow the distribution of a questionnaire to their guests during their visit to attend the Olympic Games in Sydney. Approval was gained following assurances that the findings of each program would be treated confidentially. Sponsors were also persuaded that the results would give valuable feedback about the success of their programs and would assist in the planning and management of hospitality programs offered at other events in the future.

Considerable attention was devoted to the design of the questionnaire. This was important to ensure that relevant variables were measured and, to this end, a series of satisfaction scales was developed. It was considered particularly important to gain an immediate and favorable reaction from respondents by providing an attractive, non-threatening layout. This was achieved by restricting the length to three A5 pages, presented as a booklet, with a covering page comprising an introduction from the Managing Director of the ATC. This page also contained color logos of the ATC and the relevant sponsor. It was necessary for the size and appearance to afford flexibility due to the range of settings in which it would be completed. Each sponsor accepted responsibility for the distribution of questionnaires to their guests. Most chose to place them in welcome packs or in guest rooms with one sponsor handing out them out on a bus, an approach that made it possible to ensure that they were completed at the end of their visit.

Outcomes

This study will make a valuable contribution to our understanding of the role of corporate hospitality from the guest's perspective. It will provide insights about the effectiveness of the Olympics as an incentive to the development of business relationships and the importance of the setting in shaping favorable outcomes. This is of particular significance when analyzing the impact of the Sydney Games due to the emphasis that has been placed on the tourism benefits that may accrue to the host country from staging the Games. It is hoped that recommendations may stem from the findings that will make it possible to influence practices to the advantage of tourism in Australia. This includes opportunities to increase the number of pre- and post-event tours taken by guests and to encourage repeat visitation. The study complements the two other research projects by generating data about the pre- and post-Games travel patterns of one specific tourist market: the guests of Olympic sponsors.

International Market Responses

This component of the project involves a longitudinal study that seeks to measure the influence of the 2000 Sydney Olympic Games upon international travelers' awareness, attitudes, and behaviors regarding visiting Australia before, during, and after the Games. Strong expectations are often expressed about the positive impact of the Olympics on visitor levels to the host country, and host city in particular, yet the research undertaken after previous Olympic Games suggests that where positive effects do occur, they may only be short term at best (e.g., see Kang and Perdue's study 1994, of the Seoul Olympics).

In this study on the Sydney Olympics, funding from the Cooperative Research Centre in Sustainable Tourism (CRC) has provided the opportunity to add a number of questions to the International Visitor Survey (IVS) that is conducted by Australia's government-funded tourism research organization, the Bureau of Tourism Research (BTR). The IVS is a comprehensive survey of international visitor travel behavior within Australia and is administered to approximately 20,000 departing international tourists at airports around Australia each year. Data from the IVS are collated and reported on a quarterly basis. Other data sources will also be used in conjunction with the IVS data.

Objectives

The additional questions relating to the Sydney Olympics that have been added to the IVS relate to addressing the following issues:

- What has been the impact of the Olympics on awareness of Australia within international markets?

- What has been the impact of the Olympics on intention to visit or revisit Australia?
- What sources of information have been used in relation to Australia in general and the Olympics in particular, and how has this affected the above?

Although it would have been useful to commence this project some years prior to staging the Olympics in Sydney in order to assess the impacts over a longer period, this has not been possible. The supplementary questions relating to the Sydney Olympics were added to the IVS in the final quarter of 1999 and will continue in each quarter until at least the first quarter of 2002, thereby providing information on the period leading up to the games, during the games, and in the years immediately after the games.

International visitor awareness of Australia and visitor arrivals to Australia

There are many reasons for staging a major special event, such as the Olympic Games. However, two of the more important reasons are improvement of a destination's image or awareness (Backman *et al.* 1995; Burns *et al.* 1986; Faulkner 1993; Hall 1992b; Mules and Faulkner 1996) and, as a consequence of this, increased visitation to the region (Getz 1997; Hall 1992b; Faulkner 1993; Kang and Perdue 1994; Light 1996; Mules and Faulkner 1996). Seeking to understand the impact that hosting the Sydney Olympics has on the awareness of Australia as a travel destination for international visitors and on prompting international travel to Australia are important aspects of this part of the Olympic Impacts study.

As observed earlier in this article, the study conducted by Ritchie and Smith (1991) on the impact that hosting the Winter Olympics in Calgary in 1988 had on international awareness of Calgary is the only substantial study that has been found in this area. Ritchie and Smith (1991) demonstrated that the level of awareness of Calgary as a destination increased dramatically compared with other Canadian cities as a result of hosting the Winter Olympics, but that the awareness decreased quite quickly afterwards. Unfortunately, the Ritchie and Smith study did not continue beyond the year after the games. The Sydney Olympics study will enable the impact of hosting the Olympics in Sydney on awareness of Australia for international tourists to be monitored over time, particularly in the period after the games. Similarly, the impact of the games on the intention to visit or revisit Australia will be monitored for international visitors to Australia.

The primary focus of this research is whether the staging of the Olympic Games in Sydney influenced individuals to travel to Australia. Research already undertaken in Australia suggests that the Sydney Olympics will generate an extra 1.5 million visitors to Australia in the period 1997–2004. The two principal causes of this increase in visitors are suggested to be: first, direct promotional impacts and, second, some 130,000 visitors through so-called direct impacts (specific visits to Australia by athletes, officials, administrators, media and related service providers) (Tourism Forecasting Council 1998a).

According to Kang and Perdue (1994), little is known about the long-term impacts on international tourism as a result of hosting a mega-event. Although there is some debate about the size of the impact on international tourism as a result of hosting a mega-event such as an Olympic Games, there is general agreement that visitation does increase. For some, however, increases in international visitor flows may only be short term, coinciding with the year of the event itself. In contrast, Witt and Martin (1987) suggest that there is no such increase on international tourism flows. There is also general consensus in the literature that predicted attendance figures to such events that are generally used to obtain government funding and community support are overstated (Faulkner 1993; Getz 1997). In this study, data collected via the IVS as well as other sources will be used to estimate more accurately the impact on international visitation to Australia as a consequence of hosting the Olympics in Sydney. The results will be broken down into various nationalities, as it is likely that such impacts will not be constant across different countries of origin.

There is an argument to suggest that international visitation will not increase substantially until at least a year after hosting a mega-event (Kang and Perdue 1994). This view is based on the premise that it takes time to convert the increased awareness that results from hosting the Olympic Games into travel bookings and finally actual visitation. The current study will allow this thesis to be tested.

Olympic tourist expenditure

Tourists attending special events are often termed big spenders (Getz 1997) or high-yield tourists (Prosser 1993). According to Getz (1994a), event tourists have a higher than average daily expenditure, although the expenditure profile varies with the type of event. The events, which are the most attractive in an economic sense, are "those which attract older and more affluent visitors, such as the World Masters Games" (Mules and Faulkner 1996: 112). Event tourists have the potential to be classed as high "quality tourists" (Getz 1994b) as they not only increase the yield of the industry, but they are concerned also about the social and environmental impacts of their travels. This is one of the key reasons that governments in many regions have established major event agencies to actively increase the number of major events that are attracted to the region (Jago and Shaw 1994). Hughes (1993), however, suggests that it is still not clear that special event tourists are in fact more beneficial than other categories of tourists. One should be careful, therefore, in ascribing too much importance to the aforementioned assertions.

The current study will enable a more accurate assessment of the expenditure profile of international visitors attending the Olympic Games in Sydney compared with non-Games visitors. The comprehensive nature of the IVS will enable the researchers to assess the impact on Games-related expenditure of a range of variables including nationality, age, and travel party.

Travel behavior of Olympic visitors

Related to tourist expenditure is the more general issue of tourist travel behavior. This includes duration of stay, activities undertaken, and destinations visited. Clearly, there is value from a tourism management perspective in understanding the duration of stay in Australia of international visitors coming specifically for the Olympics. Comparisons, by nationality, can be made between Olympic visitors and non-Olympic visitors, which will help identify whether the "crowding out" effect of the Games was positive or negative. The value of Olympic visitors to Australia will be greatly reduced if most international visitors are simply here for the duration of the Games. As in the conference and convention market, pre- and post-event touring opportunities are of fundamental importance, and this study should enable some assessment of this to be made.

A number of State Tourism Authorities have been active in seeking to encourage international visitors to the Sydney Olympic Games to extend their stays and visit other states within Australia (Victoria and Queensland in particular). Tourism NSW has also been keen to encourage international visitors to spend time in other parts of NSW during their visits to attend the Games in Sydney. Analysis of the IVS results for respondents attending the Olympics will be valuable in assessing the success of such endeavors.

Similarly, the IVS results will be useful for identifying whether there are patterns in the types of activities that are undertaken by international visitors to the Olympic Games compared with international visitors coming to Australia for purposes other than the Olympics. This analysis should provide some information as to whether such visitors can be categorized according to activity or whether they are diverse in terms of the activities that they choose.

Switching behavior as a result of the Olympics

For a number of years now, "switching" has been recognized as a factor that must be assessed in evaluations of the performance of events. Results of the IVS will help identify visitors who rescheduled their visit to

Australia to coincide with the Olympic Games. Because the supplementary questions on the Olympics will be included in the IVS for 2 years after the close of the games, it will be possible to obtain some indication of visitors who actually delayed their visit so as not to coincide with the staging of the Olympics. Clearly, this approach only identifies people who delayed their visit and does not identify those who elected not to come at all as a result of the Olympics.

Information sources used to inform visit decision

With the increasing use of the Internet, there is now much interest in understanding the relationship between the type and method of collecting travel information with the international travel behavior that follows. A range of questions on this topic has been included in the supplementary questions appended to the IVS, which will enhance understanding of this issue.

Outcomes

There are many claims about the substantial benefits that can be derived from hosting a mega-event such as the Olympic Games. The results of this study will enable many of these claims to be tested. As importantly, increased understanding of international tourist flows resulting from hosting an Olympic Games will provide a basis for developing more effective marketing strategies to capitalize on mega-events. Such strategies will be of great value for Australian cities hosting, or seeking to host, mega-events in the future. For instance, Melbourne will host the Commonwealth Games in 2006 and the same city has announced its intention to bid for the 2020 Olympic Games. A heightened understanding of consumer decision-making processes is likely to translate into the development of improved marketing strategies for managers of subsequent, similar events, with economic benefits for Australian tourism. Although there is no suggestion that the results of this study will be conclusive, the systematic and longitudinal nature of the study will certainly advance our understanding of the impact of mega-events on international tourist flows and behavior.

Conclusion

The research project described in this article is important from two perspectives. First, the staging of the Sydney 2000 Olympics has involved a substantial investment of State and Federal Government funds, partly on the grounds of anticipated tourism benefits. An evaluation of tourism impacts is therefore essential not only for accountability reasons, but also to guide public sector policy on support for major events in the future. If a substantial tourism dividend is demonstrated, then government might be in a position to support an events-based strategy to economic development more confidently in the future. Alternatively, if the tourism impacts are demonstrated as being limited, then the tourism rationale for the commitment of resources to mega-events in the future should be questioned or, at the very least, made conditional upon remedial action being directed at ensuring potential benefits are realized in the future.

The latter point brings us to the second perspective on the importance of the study. That is, by examining leveraging strategies more closely and evaluating their effectiveness, we will be in a position to identify approaches that may enable the potential tourism benefits of events to be exploited more effectively in the future. Far from being simply a retrospective examination of a single example of the Olympics, therefore, the outcomes of the Sydney project will provide valuable insights for other cities/countries in the process of, or contemplating, bidding for future Olympic Games. Of particular importance will be the value of the study in facilitating the learning of lessons from the Sydney experience regarding approaches maximizing the tourism benefits of this event. It is important to bear in mind, however, that the outcomes of this study have broader relevance than the Olympics in the sense that insights generated by the examination of this case will apply to other mega-events and, to some degree, to events in general. The value of examining an event of this scale is that it provides an opportunity for the many dimensions of potential tourism benefits to be more thoroughly and comprehensively examined.

Given the above discussion, the rationale for a cohesive research program such as that described in this paper can be summarized in terms of three essential considerations.

First, hallmark events in general, and major events associated with sport in particular, have become an integral component of tourism destination marketing strategies at the national, state/territory, and regional levels. However, while the tourism benefits of such events are often emphasized in the justification for public sector financial support, the evidence used to support this argument is generally very limited.

Second, bidding for, and hosting, major events has become an increasingly expensive undertaking for host cities/countries. As noted above, the process of justifying government underwriting of such initiatives is increasingly dependent upon the provision of convincing evidence of the ultimate benefits to the community. This project will not only provide a more rigorous assessment of the extent of tourism benefits associated with the Sydney Olympics (which may or may not support events-based strategies in the future), but it will also provide insights into how organizers of future events, the tourism industry, and relevant public sector agencies might work together more effectively to maximize the tourism benefits of such events.

Finally, this study will be the first of its kind involving a mega-event such as the Olympics. Given the points outlined above and the widespread international interest in staging high-profile events, the research outcomes will be of interest to government and major sporting organizations in other countries. It is also expected that international sporting organizations who control major sporting events (e.g., the International Olympic Committee, the Commonwealth Games Federation, World Cup Soccer [FIFA]), and who have a fundamental interest in maintaining government support for the staging of their events, will benefit from the study.

References

Ajuntament de Barcelona. (1992) *The Economic Impact of the Barcelona 1992 Olympics*. Barcelona: Gabinet Tecnic de Programaciv.

Arthur Anderson Consulting, and University of Tasmania Centre for Regional Economic Analysis. (1999) *Economic Impact Study of the Sydney 2000 Olympic Games*. Sydney and Launceston: Author.

Backman, K., Backman, S., Uysal, M. and Mohr Sunshine, K. (1995) Event tourism: An examination of motivations and activities. *Festival Management and Event Tourism*, 3(1), 1524.

Blattberg, R. C. and Neslin, S. A. (1990) *Sales Promotion: Concept, Methods and Strategies*. Englewood Cliffs, NJ: Prentice-Hall.

Boyle, M. (1997) Civic boosterism in the politics of local economic development: Institutional positions and "strategic orientations" in the consumption of hallmark events. *Environment and Planning*, 29, 1957–1997.

Bramwell, B. (1997) Strategic planning before and after a megaevent. *Tourism Management*, 18(3), 167–176.

Brenner, S. (1997) Pursuing relationships in professional sport. *Sport Marketing Quarterly*, 6(2), 33–34.

Brown, G. (2000) Emerging issues in Olympic sponsorship: Implications for host cities. *Sport Management Review*, 3(1), 71–92.

Brunet, R (1992) *Economy of the 1992 Barcelona Olympic Games*. Barcelona: Centre d' Estudis Olympics, Universitat Autonoma de Barcelona.

Burns, J., Hatch, J. and Mules, T. (1986) *The Adelaide Grand Prix: The Impact of a Special Event*. Adelaide: The Centre for South Australian Economic Studies.

Chalip, L., Green, B. C. and Vander Velden, L. (1998) Sources of interest in travel to the Olympic Games. *Journal of Vacation Marketing*, 4, 7–22.

Crossan, M. M., Lane, H. W. and White, R. E. (1999). An organizational learning framework: From intuition to institution. *Academy of Management Review*, 24, 522–537.

Davis, J. R (1997) Determining promotional effectiveness in small retail firms: An empirical analysis. *Mid-American Journal of Business*, 12(2), 21–28.

Delpy, L., Grabijas, M. and Stefanovich, A. (1998) Sport tourism and corporate sponsorship: A winning combination. *Journal of Vacation Marketing*, 4, 91–10.

Edwards, A. (1999). Reflective practice in sport management. *Sport Management Review*, 2, 67–81.

Faulkner, B. and Tideswell, C. (1999) Leveraging tourism benefits from the Sydney 2000 Olympics. *Pacific Tourism Review*, 3(3–4), 227–238.

Faulkner, B. (1993) *Evaluating the Tourism Impact of Hallmark Events* (Occasional Paper No. 16). Canberra: Bureau of Tourism Research.

Frechtling, D. C. (1987) Assessing the impacts of travel and tourism: Measuring economic benefits. In J. R. B. Ritchie and C. Goeldner (eds), *Travel, Tourism, and Hospitality Research* (pp. 325–331). New York: John Wiley and Sons.

Getz, D. (1994a) Event tourism: Evaluating the impacts. In J. Ritchie and C. Goeldner (eds), *Travel, Tourism, and Hospitality Research* (pp. 437–450). New York: John Wiley and Sons.

—— (1994b) In pursuit of the quality tourist. Paper presented at Tourism Downunder Conference, Massey University, Palmerston North, December.

—— (1997) *Event Management and Event Tourism*. New York: Cognizant Communication Corporation.

—— (1998) Trends, strategies and issues in sport-event tourism. *Sport Marketing Quarterly*, 7(2), 8–13.

Gillam, C. (1996) Delivering the dream. *Sales and Marketing Management*, 148(6), 74–78.

Godbey, G. and Graefe, A. (1991) Repeat tourism, play, and monetary spending. *Annals of Tourism Research*, 18, 213–225.

Gottdiener, M. (1997) *The Theming of America: Dreams, Visions, and Commercial Spaces*. Boulder, CO: Westview Press.

Gratton, C. and Kokolakakis, T. (1997) Financial games. *Leisure Management*, 17(7), 13–15.

Green, B. C. and Chalip, L. (1998) Sport tourism as the celebration of subculture. *Annals of Tourism Research*, 25, 275–291.

Hall, C. M. (1987) The effects of hallmark events on cities. *Journal of Travel Research*, 26, 44–45.

—— (1992a) Adventure, sport and health tourism. In B. Weiler and C. M. Hall (eds), *Special Interest Tourism* (pp. 141–158). London: Belhaven Press.

—— (1992b) *Hallmark Tourist Events: Impacts, Management and Planning*. Chichester: John Wiley.

—— (1994) *Tourism and Politics: Policy, Power and Place*. London: John Wiley.

—— (1995) Urban redevelopment policy and imaging strategies: The Sydney 2000 Olympics and the Melbourne Formula One Grand Prix. Paper presented at the Public Policy network Conference, February 2–3, Australian National University, Canberra.

Hall, C. M. and Hodges, J. (1996) The party's great, but what about the hangover?: The housing and social impacts of mega-events with special reference to the 2000 Sydney Olympics. *Festival Management and Event Tourism*, 4(1/2),13–20.

Hall, C. M. and Jenkins, J. (1995) *Tourism and Public Policy*. London/New York: Routledge.

Harvey, D. (1989) *The Condition of Postmodernity and Equity into the Origins of Cultural Change*. Oxford: Basil Blackwell.

Hausman, A. (2000) A multi-method investigation of consumer motivations in impulse buying behavior. *Journal of Consumer Marketing*, 17, 403–419.

Herrigel, G. (1993) Power and the redefinition of industrial districts: The case of Baden-Wurttemberg. In G. Grabner (ed.), *The Embedded Firm: On the Socioeconomics of Industrial Networks* (pp. 227–251). London: Routledge.

Hiller, H. H. (1989) Impact and image: The convergence of urban factors in preparing for the 1988 Calgary Winter Olympics. In G. J. Syme, B. J. Shaw, D. M. Fenton, and W S. Mueller (eds), *The Planning and Evaluation of Hallmark Events* (pp. 119–131). Aldershot: Avebury.

Howard, D. and Crompton, J. L. (1995) *Financing Sport*. Morgantown, WV: Fitness Information Technology.

Hughes, H. (1993) Olympic tourism and urban regeneration. *Festival Management and Event Tourism*, 1(4), 157–162.

Hyun, J. (1990) The impact of 1988 Seoul Olympics on inbound tourism to Korea. In *Study on Tourism* (14, pp. 235–245). Seoul: The Korean Academic Society of Tourism.

Iton, J. (1988) The longer term impact of Montreal's 1976 Olympic Games. In *1988 Seoul International Conference, Hosting the Olympics: The Long Term Impact* (pp. 195–239). Seoul: East Asian Architecture and Planning Program, Massachusetts Institute of Technology and Graduate School of Environmental Studies, Seoul National University.

Jafari, J. (1988) Tourism mega-events. *Annals of Tourism Research*, 15(2), 272–273.

Jago, L., and Shaw, R. (1994) Categorisation of special events: A market perspective. In *Tourism Down Under: Perceptions, Problems and Proposals, Conference Proceedings* (pp. 682–708). Palmerston North: Massey University.

—— (1998) Special events: A conceptual and differential framework. *Festival Management and Event Tourism*, 5(1/2), 21–32.

Jensen, J. (1994, March 28) Sports marketing links need nurturing. *Advertising Age*, S30.

Jeong, G-H., Jafari, J. and Gartner, W. (1990) Expectations of the 1988 Seoul Olympics: A Korean perspective. *Tourism Recreation Research*, 15(1), 26–33.

Kang, Y S. and Perdue, R. (1994) Long term impacts of a megaevent on international tourism to the host country: A conceptual model and the case of the 1988 Seoul Olympics. In M. Uysal (ed.), *Global Tourism Behaviour* (pp. 205–225). New York: International Business Press.

Kotler, P., Haider, D. H. and Rein, I. (1993) *Marketing Places: Attracting Investment, Industry, and Tourism to Cities, States, and Nations*. New York: Free Press.

Law, C. M. (1993). *Urban Tourism: Attracting Visitors to Large Cities*. London: Mansell.

Levin, M. (1993) Creating networks for rural economic development in Norway. *Human Relations*, 46, 193–218.

Light, D. (1996). Characteristics of the audience for events at a heritage site. *Tourism Management*, 17(3), 183–190.

Lorenzoni, G. and Lipparini, A. (1999) The leveraging of interfirm relationships as a distinctive organizational capability: A longitudinal study. *Strategic Management Journal*, 20, 317–338.

Malone, S. and Jenster, P. (1991) Resting on your laurels: The plateauing of the owner-manager. *European Management Journal*, 9, 412–418.

Mules, T. (1998a) Tax-payer subsidies for major sporting events. *Sport Management Review*, 1, 25–43.

—— (1998b) Decomposition of Australian tourism expenditure. *Tourism Management* 19, 267–271.

Mules, T. and Faulkner, B. (1996) An economic perspective on special events. *Tourism Economics*, 2(2), 107–117.

Murphy, P. E. (1992) Urban tourism and visitor behavior. *American Behavioral Scientist*, 36, 200–211.

Pine, B. J. and Gilmore, J. H. (1999) *The Experience Economy: Work is Theatre and Every Business a Stage*. Boston: Harvard Business School Press.

Pressman, J. L., and Wildavsky, A. (1984) *Implementation* (3rd ed.). Berkeley, CA: University of California Press.

Prosser, G. (1993) Mansell meets Mozart: Event tourism in Adelaide, South Australia. *Festival Management and Event Tourism*, 1(3), 125–130.

Putsis, W. P. (1998) Winners and losers: Redistribution and use of economic impact analysis in marketing. *Journal of Macromarketing*, 18, 24–33.

Pyo, S., Cook, R. and Howell, R. L. (1988) Summer Olympic tourist market: Learning from the past. *Tourism Management*, 9(2), 137–144.

Ritchie, J. R. B. (1984) Assessing the impact of hallmark events; conceptual and measurement issues. *Journal of Travel Research*, 23(1), 2–11.

Ritchie, J. R. B. and Lyons, M. (1990) Olympulse VI: A postevent assessment of resident reaction to the XV Olympic Winter Games. *Journal of Travel Research*, 28(3), 14–23.

Ritchie, J. R. B. and Smith, B. H. (1991) The impact of a megaevent on host region awareness: A longitudinal study. *Journal of Travel Research*, 30(1), 3–10.

Robinson, R. and Pearce, J. (1984) Research thrusts in small firm strategic planning. *Academy of Management Review*, 9, 128–137.

Rook, D. W., and Fisher, R. J. (1995) Normative influences on impulsive buying behavior. *Journal of Consumer Research*, 22, 305–313.

Rosentraub, M. S., Swindell, D., Przybylski, M. and Mullins, D. R. (1994) Sport and downtown development strategy: If you build it, will jobs come? *Journal of Urban Affairs*, 16, 221–239.

Sack, A. L. and Johnson, A. T. (1996) Politics, economic development and the Volvo International Tennis Tournament. *Journal of Sport Management*, 10, 1–14.

Sandler, T. (1992) *Collective Action: Theory and Applications*. Ann Arbor, MI: University of Michigan Press.

Simon, D. (1988) *Long-term Impact of the Olympic Games in Los Angeles*. In 1988 Seoul International Conference, Hosting the Olympics: The Long Term Impact (pp. 41–53). Seoul: East Asian Architecture and Planning Program, Massachusetts Institute of technology and Graduate School of Environmental Studies, Seoul National University.

Socher, K. (1987) Economic impacts of the Olympic Winter Games. *Revue de Tourism*, 2.

Spurr, R. (1999) Tourism. In R. Cashman and A. Hughed (eds), *Staging the Olympics: The Event and its Impact* (pp. 148–156). Sydney: University of New south Wales Press.

Sydney Olympic Games Review Committee (1990) *Report to the Premier of New South Wales*, Sydney Olympic Games Review Committee, Sydney.

Tourism Forecasting Council (1998a) *The Olympic Effect: A Report on the Potential Tourism Impacts of the Sydney 2000 Games*. Canberra: Commonwealth of Australia.

—— (1998b) Tourism impacts of the "Athletes Games" *Forecast*, 4(2), 14–15.

van den Berg, L., Braun, E. and Otgaar, A. H. J. (2000) *Sports and City Marketing in European Cities*. Rotterdam, The Netherlands: euricur.

Whitson, D. and Macintosh, D. (1996) The global crisis: International sport, tourism and the marketing of cities. *Journal of Sport and Social Issues*, 20, 278–279.

Wilkinson, J. (1989) Sport regenerated cities: Worldwide opportunities. Paper presented at the Council of Europe International Conference, Lilleshol, Great Britain.

Witt, S. F (1988) Mega-events and mega-attractions. *Tourism Management*, 9(1), 76–77.

Witt, S. F. and Martin, C. A. (1987) Measuring the impact of mega-events on tourism flows. In AIEST (ed.), *The Role and Impact of Mega-Events and Attractions on Regional and National Tourism Development* (Vol. 28, pp. 213–219). St-Gall, Switzerland: AIEST.

Part 3
Tourism Research Methods

Introduction

Bill was particularly gifted as a lateral thinker. He was always trying to identify new and innovative solutions to problems and thus his contribution to methods in the field has been substantial. One of the reasons that Bill returned to academia after many years employed as a senior bureaucrat, was that he craved the opportunity that academe provided to develop and test innovative approaches to tourism research. This section has been divided into three sub-sections looking at tourism forecasting, chaos theory as an alternative framework for investigating tourism phenomena, and planning for disaster management. Although at first glance, these areas may appear disparate, there is a strong connection between them in the way in which Bill examined them. In particular, Bill was fascinated by chaos and complexity theory, as he felt that it represented a way to augment the knowledge that could be generated through the primarily positivistic methods that dominate tourism research.

Tourism Forecasting

In his role as director of the BTR, Bill was responsible for overseeing the generation of tourism forecasts, which were based on quantitative modelling techniques. However, in 1993, he was invited to Canberra to present a keynote paper at a conference on tourism forecasting, and his brief on this occasion was to take a sceptical approach to existing forecasting practices in an effort to shake practitioners out of their comfort zones. He reports that 'this proved to be an easier task than I originally anticipated and it was one that launched me onto the path towards the exploration of chaos and turbulence' (Faulkner 2000: 4).

Bill was concerned that 'experts' in the field had elevated forecasting techniques to a level of complexity that made it impossible for them to be understood by those whose needed to use them. He argued that forecasting had become an end in itself rather than a tool to be used in the strategic planning process and that many forecasters did little to link their forecasts back to the real world. The first paper in this section presents a series of cogent arguments for integrative tourism demand forecasting. Bill uses the term integrative in two ways. Firstly, to imply that a combination of methods should be used, but also, that forecasting should be a consultative process. Bill often made the point that the aim of forecasting should not necessarily be accuracy, and that an accurate forecast is not necessarily a good one. He made this point with reference to a forecast he had made in 1990 (while at the BTR) about visitation levels in the year 2000. His prediction was 5 million visitors, and this was criticised at the time as being ridiculously optimistic. However, the forecast was remarkably accurate (actual visitation in the year 2000 was 4,946,200 (ABS 2001)), but Bill was quick to point out that this was serendipitous, and that the premises on which the forecast was based were not the grounds on which these visitation levels were achieved.

The second chapter in this section retrospectively evaluates the precision of a forecast undertaken for the South Australian Tourism Commission in 1996. The chapter documents the methods used in developing the forecast (a combination of quantitative approaches followed by a quasi-delphi process) and demonstrates the value of employing an integrative approach to forecasting.

Chaos Theory

In Bill's Professorial Lecture at Griffith University in 2000, entitled 'The Future ain't what it used to be: Coping with Change, Turbulence and Disasters in Tourism Research and Destination Management', he argues strongly in support of the role that chaos theory and complexity theory can play in tourism research. He suggests that they 'provide the basis for an alternative conceptual framework, which has the potential to help tourism researchers to develop an understanding of the dynamics of change more effectively' (p. 38). The next two chapters in this section demonstrate the applicability of chaos and complexity theory to the study of tourism phenomena, the first providing a series of examples, and the second focussing more specifically on the examination of the role played by entrepreneurs in tourism destination development. The point is made that traditional mechanistic models, driven by the Cartesian–Newtonian paradigm, have been valuable for investigation of the relatively stable aspects of tourism. However, these approaches have been unable to explain situations in tourism where disorder is more evident, such as the influence of entrepreneurs in the development of a destination. As the authors suggest, entrepreneurs are in fact the outliers that quantitative methodologists seek to avoid, as they unduly influence the models, and they cannot be examined as a population in their own right because, by definition, entrepreneurs are rare.

Tourism Disaster Management

Flowing directly from Bill's interest in chaos theory was his increasing interest in the consequences of tourism disasters, which are a predicted outcome using chaos theory. There is evidence in the literature to suggest that tourism destinations and tourists themselves are more vulnerable to natural and man-made disasters due to the high-risk exotic locations of some destinations and the fact that tourists are less familiar with the location than are locals. Despite this, Bill argued, relatively few destinations seem to have well considered tourism disaster plans.

The final two chapters in this section consider tourism disaster management. The first chapter presents a model for analysing and developing tourism disaster management strategies, whilst the second chapter applies this framework for tourism disaster management to an actual tourism disaster, namely, the 1998 Australia Day Flood in Katherine.

References

Australian Bureau of Statistics (2001) *Overseas Arrivals and Departures: December 2000* (3401.0). Canberra: ABS.

Faulkner, B. (2000) The Future Ain't What it Used to Be. Unpublished Professorial Lecture, Griffith University, Gold Coast.

Chapter 7

An Integrative Approach to Tourism Demand Forecasting

Bill Faulkner and Peter Valerio

Progress has been made in the development of tourism forecasting techniques in Australia over the last few years to the extent that we have moved beyond a reliance on guesswork and gut feelings to more rigorous approaches involving, for instance, the use of econometric models. Yet, by viewing forecasting as simply an attempt to anticipate the future, we have tended to lose sight of the fact that the forecasting process itself is an integral part of strategic management. An appreciation of this aspect of forecasting, and the limitations of the methodologies currently being applied, highlights the need for a reorientation towards an integrative approach.

However, in addition to employing a combination of existing approaches, we need to explore also innovations that may help us cope with what appears to be an increasingly volatile and unpredictable environment. This point is pursued below in three stages. First, the background to the problem is outlined by referring briefly to the role of forecasting and some of the observations that have been made about the limitations of existing approaches. Second, some insights are drawn from the emerging field of chaos theory to provide a different perspective on forecasting, which is in turn used as a basis for elaborating on elements of the integrative approach being advocated. Finally, a methodology being developed by the Australian Tourist Commission (ATC) is described to illustrate how an integrative approach might be applied. The recency of this technique's introduction in the ATC context precludes any meaningful comparison between forecast and actual trends at this stage. However, its potential has been demonstrated by immediate beneficial effects on the involvement of management and stakeholders in the organization's goal-setting process.

On the Need for an Integrative Approach

In any context, forecasting is an essential step in the minimization of disparities between the demand for, and supply of, services and facilities. Given the lead times usually involved in the development of the infrastructure required to service markets, future demand must often be anticipated up to several years in advance if we are to avoid missed opportunities through insufficient and inappropriate capacity on the one hand, or wasteful and counter-productive under-utilized capacity on the other. This applies equally to situations where elaborate physical structures have to be put in place or where skills have to be developed in the workforce through training programmes.

As considerable lead times are involved in both these aspects of tourism product development, the above observation regarding the central role of forecasting in the management process is certainly no less applicable to this industry. Indeed, there are two distinctive (but not necessarily unique) features of tourism which accentuate this point. First, the necessity of matching supply and demand is heightened by the perishability of the tourism product (Greenley and Matcham 1971; Middleton 1990). Unused capacity at a particular point in time cannot be stored or stockpiled for later use and, as a consequence, represents a loss of revenue which cannot be recovered. Second, the inherent volatility of tourism demand, stemming from its predominantly discretionary nature, underscores both the need for, and difficulty of, forecasting in this field. If, as Poon (1993) suggests, we are witnessing a transformation to a predominance of so-called 'new tourists' whose behaviour is increasingly unpredictable, then this volatility is likely to become even more pronounced in the future (Poon 1993).

Forecasting has therefore become an important element of tourism management in both the private and public sectors. However, its potential contribution to this process has not always been realized because of the general failure to adopt an integrative approach. In this context, the term 'integrative' has a double meaning. First, it refers to the application of a combination of methodologies to a particular forecasting problem. Second, it is concerned with the relationship between these methodologies and the decision-making process itself.

Integration by the combination of methodologies

Descriptions of the various techniques employed in the forecasting of tourism demand have been documented in some detail by several authors (Archer 1987; Armstrong 1985; Calantone *et al*. 1987; Bar On 1984; Uysal and Crompton 1985; Van Doorn 1984). The main general conclusion one can draw from these contributions is that each approach has specific strengths and weaknesses and, accordingly, it would be prudent to apply a combination of such approaches to a given situation. Specifically, approaches that complement each other in terms of their respective strengths and weaknesses might be considered.

However, there are several specific observations that can be drawn from this literature, which have a particular bearing on the following discussion:

- Over the past 30 years there has been a considerable emphasis on econometric approaches concentrating on income and price factors as determinants of demand (Crouch and Shaw 1990).
- The emphasis placed on modelling is a matter of concern if, as some authors have noted, data limitations result in an over-reliance on a limited range of variables (Armstrong 1985; Calantone *et al.* 1987).
- As Witt and Witt (1992) observe, complex econometric modelling approaches do not necessarily produce more accurate forecasts than simpler time-series approaches and, as a consequence, the benefits derived from such approaches may not be commensurate with the additional time and cost involved (Witt and Witt 1992).
- These approaches nevertheless provide a systematic basis for understanding relationships among variables and exploring the effects of alternative scenarios for the future (Makridakis 1986).
- Approaches such as the Delphi technique offer the dual advantage of enabling a broader range of quantifiable and non-quantifiable variables to be taken into account, while at the same time providing a framework for consultation. More specifically, these techniques provide a vehicle for integrating a range of approaches.

Integration with the decision-making process

As emphasized at the outset of this paper, the ultimate purpose of tourism demand forecasting is to assist in management decision making. Yet, forecasting has, to a large extent, become an end in itself, resulting in its alienation from the planning process and, in association with this, naive perceptions of the nature and role of forecasting prevail among users.

This point is highlighted in a more general commentary on forecasting by Schaffer (1993):

> Experts need their own private world where ignorant outsiders cannot penetrate. The very obscurity of the sums in which cost benefit analysts or astrologers engage helps give them impressive authority. But the expert predictors also need outsiders' trust: They need to show that the terms they use are, in some way, connected to what matters to the customers. (p. 54)

Forecasting often becomes an end in itself, rather than an integral part of the strategic management process, because of the complexity of the methodologies used and the consequent need for specialist analysts to be involved. The analysts, however, have become isolated and detached, and forecasting has become a black box as far as most users are concerned. With the decision makers becoming mesmerized by the 'science' of forecasting, much of the debate about the outcome has focused on the bottom-line numbers, rather than the methodologies and assumptions on which they are based.

Under these circumstances, the role of the forecasting process in strategic planning has become very limited. The technicians need to make forecasting a transparent and iterative process through the installation of consultative mechanisms that give users an opportunity to challenge the assumptions made and explore the implications of their own scenarios.

As a consequence of the alienation process described above, there is a general naivety in attitudes towards forecasting which is reflected in, for instance, the frequent acceptance of forecasts at face value without questioning underlying assumptions. Another symptom of naivety is the tendency to regard those forecasts that turn out to be accurate as necessarily superior (Archer 1987; Carbone and Armstrong 1982).

There are several reasons that can be put forward to suggest that this may not necessarily be the case:

- The accurate forecast might be right for the wrong reasons. While this situation may not have negative planning implications in the short term, it will in the longer term if it results in too much faith being placed in an ostensibly 'proven' but potentially flawed approach.
- Under certain circumstances a good forecast may be one which does not eventuate. That is, if a forecast foreshadows the prospect of negative developments, and thereby triggers remedial action to prevent these from occurring, it will have served its purposes without being accurate in the long run. It is easy in retrospect, for instance, to condemn the Club of Rome's predictions about the resource implications of global population growth as being unrealistically alarmist (Meadows *et al.* 1972). However, these predictions were instrumental in the initiation of programmes which alleviated some of the problems in advance.
- There are occasions when forecasts have such an influence on planning targets that they become self-fulfilling prophecies. This has a positive effect if it results in the infrastructure required to take up growth opportunities being put in place. On the other hand, unduly conservative forecasts can also become self-fulfilling prophecies if they discourage the development of capacity and, as a consequence, restrict growth in demand. The fear of the latter has resulted in the promotion of unrealistically high growth scenarios by some tourism industry commentators in the Australian context.

Effective integration of tourism demand forecasting with management decision making implies the establishment of a meaningful dialogue between technicians and users. Such a dialogue would arrest the alienation process referred to above and lead to a more informed view of the nature and role of forecasting across the board. Furthermore, through the use of Delphi and similar techniques, there will be more scope for bringing a range of alternative approaches to bear on the problem and the over-reliance on modelling techniques will be reduced. There are, however, more fundamental reasons for diversifying the range of approaches we rely on. These are explored in the following section.

Chaos and Uncertainty

The development of methodologies for understanding the underlying causal relationships affecting changes in tourism demand is fundamental to the development of better forecasting systems. While the modelling approaches referred to in the previous section have provided valuable frameworks for assembling available data, exploring relationships between variables and (on the basis of this) considering the implications of possible future developments, insights from the physical sciences in particular highlight limitations in the ability of such approaches to further our understanding of causal relationships. On the one hand, such limitations might be construed as signalling the need for a 'paradigm shift' in accord with Thomas Kuhn's (1962) interpretation of scientific revolutions. However, on the other hand, the utility of existing approaches and the lack of fully operational alternatives suggests that it would be more appropriate to supplement, rather than actually displace, existing methodologies.

In the physical sciences, the probing of sub-atomic phenomena at one extreme and of the outer reaches of the cosmos at the other has highlighted the limitations of the mechanistic Newtonian-Cartesian paradigm as a basis for understanding the mysteries of the universe. It is being increasingly recognized that our physical environment does not operate like a gigantic clockwork machine, with its various parts fitting neatly together and acting in unison in a manner which can be both measured and predicted with mathematical precision. A new wave of thought has grown out of Einstein's theory of relativity, quantum mechanics, Heisenberg's uncertainty principle and, more recently, chaos theory to challenge the mechanistic world-view (Capra 1982). The linear, machine vocabulary of classical physics is thus being displaced by concepts which depict a confusing world of non-linearity, spontaneity and surprise juxtaposed with attributes normally associated with living organisms, such as adaptation, coherence and organization (Davies and Gribbin 1992).

In their analysis of the implications of these developments, Davies and Gribbin (1992) offer the following interpretation:

Physicist Joseph Ford has described the materialistic, mechanistic paradigm as one of the 'Founding myths' of classical science. Myths of course are not literal expressions of truth. Are we to suppose, then, that the immense progress made in science during the past three hundred years is rooted in a complete misconception about the nature of nature? No, this would be to misunderstand the role of scientific paradigms. A particular paradigm is neither right nor wrong, but merely reflects a perspective, an aspect of reality that may prove more or less fruitful depending on circumstance – just as a myth, although not literally true, may contain allegorical insights that prove more or less fruitful depending on circumstances. In the event, the mechanistic paradigm proved so successful that there has been an almost universal tendency to identify it with reality, to see it not as a facet of truth but as the whole truth. Now, increasing numbers of scientists are coming to recognise the limitations of the materialistic view of nature, and to appreciate that there is more to the world than cogs in a gigantic machine. (p. 3)

If the reservations are being expressed about the ability of the mechanistic framework to explain the behaviour of inanimate objects, then its applicability to the explanation of human behaviour, as reflected in tourism demand, must also be questioned.

The neo-classical economic theory, on which the modelling approach referred to in the previous section is largely based, is analogous to Newtonian physics in several respects. First, it is based on the application of the 'materialistic, mechanistic' paradigm to socio-economic phenomena. Second, it has so dominated the field of tourism demand analysis and forecasting that, despite its limited success in explaining this aspect of human behaviour, there has also been a tendency to 'see it not as a facet of truth but as the whole truth'. Finally, in a broader context, there is a growing body of opinion which sees conventional economic theory as being demonstrably incapable of understanding modern economic events and, as a consequence, increasingly irrelevant as a framework for guiding policy development towards the solution of current economic problems. Indeed, some commentators have suggested that it is the moribund status of economic theory which is responsible for modern economic problems and that this is symptomatic of the need for a paradigm shift (Waldrop 1992).

One of the basic assumptions of the prevailing methodologies, and the reason they are generally only suitable for relatively short-term forecasts, is that relationships between variables remain constant. The possibility, indeed likelihood, of these relationships changing over time tends to be overlooked. Meanwhile, social commentators such as Toffler (1970) have emphasized the accelerating pace of change in modern society and the associated destabilization of social relations, which have resulted in increasing levels of uncertainty and greater pressure on adaptive capabilities at both the institutional and individual level. This process is undoubtedly reflected in factors which have a bearing on tourism demand and will have a compounding effect on forecasting efforts in this field.

The limitations of the mechanistic orientation of orthodox economics and the simpler mathematical time-series approach to forecasting stand out in the context of this dynamic setting. Both these approaches are analogous to Newtonian physics in that they assume constancy and linearity (or quasi linearity) in relationships and, implicitly, a tendency towards an equilibrium state owing to the dominance of negative feedback mechanisms. Drawing on insights from the new wave in physics, Waldrop argues that socio-economic systems are: open rather than closed; organic as opposed to mechanistic; dynamic rather than static; and driven by positive feedback rather than negative feedback (Waldrop 1992). It is ironic that, whereas the imitation of the physical sciences by the social sciences has resulted in mechanistic qualities being attributed to socio-economic systems, we could perhaps be witnessing over the next few years a situation where lessons from the physical sciences may result in the recognition of lifelike characteristics in such systems.

The notion of socio-economic systems driven by positive feedback mechanisms points to the possible relevance of chaos theory to the forecasting process. Positive feedback refers to the progressive accentuation of small changes or deviations and contrasts with negative feedback, where the effects of such shifts are ameliorated with the system being restored to equilibrium. Chaos theory focuses on the non-linearity of phenomena and the tendency for initially small changes eventually to produce large cumulative effects which precipitate fundamental changes in the system.

Obvious examples of non-linearity in tourism include the slow-down in the growth of a maturing market as demand approaches saturation (Mazanie 1981) and the passage of a destination through the product life cycle as described by Butler (1980). The opposite process, whereby an initial small perturbation cascades upwards through a system to produce eventually an event or shift of considerable magnitude, has been referred to by chaos theorists as the 'butterfly effect' (Gleick 1987). Examples of the butterfly effect in tourism would include instances where an exponential growth in visitor numbers arises from the compounding effect of a single event, such as the extension of jet airline services to a previously isolated destination or the development of an innovative holiday package which taps a particularly significant emerging market.

It is not yet clear how a realignment in the theoretical foundations of our analysis might be translated into new forecasting methodologies. If we take Davies and Gribbin's (1992) reference to different paradigms reflecting different facets of the truth literally, then we should accept that conventional econometric techniques may have a continuing role to the extent that they may be useful in broadly defining constraints on tourism demand. It is obvious, however, that this approach needs to be used in conjunction with other methodologies which are less limited in terms of assumptions made about the underlying dynamics of change. Accordingly, an approach which permits the integration of conventional methodologies with others that incorporate the new perspective described in this section may lead to more innovative and effective forecasting in the future.

The Certainty of the Unexpected

While, at this stage, it may not be clear where chaos theory might lead us, this perspective at least helps to highlight our general naivety regarding the capabilities of existing methodology to actually predict the future. Chaos theory and numerous instances of recent events have demonstrated that, if anything, the only certainty about the future is that the unexpected will happen. Who in 1974 predicted the 1975 oil crisis? Yet this single event precipitated a global recession and an associated slump in world travel. Nobody could predict the Chernobyl and Lockerbie disasters, which impacted dramatically on travel patterns owing to heightened concerns over the safety of travel in Europe. Did anyone predict the dismemberment of the Soviet bloc more than a few months or even weeks in advance? Closer to home in Australia, no one predicted the 1989 domestic pilots' dispute and its devastating impact on tourism more than a few days before it actually happened.

If forecasting tourism demand is so difficult, and if it is virtually impossible to predict the future with any certainty in any case, why bother?

There are two rejoinders to the question. First, whatever the limitations of our forecasting capabilities, management outcomes based on partially correct visions of the future will be superior to those based on no vision at all. Second, and more importantly, if it is done properly, forecasting involves a structured analysis of recent and possible future developments. As noted above, such analyses should be an integral part of the management routine of all enterprises and organizations. Yet this has not generally been the case among decision makers in both industry and government, where there has been a tendency to accept or reject forecasts produced by the 'experts' at face value without any serious attempt being made to become involved in the forecasting process itself. As argued previously, a dialogue between the technicians who produce the forecasts and the decision makers who use them is essential if underlying assumptions are to be questioned and debated, and if insights generated by the analysis of trends are to be utilized in the management process.

A step towards the development of a more open consultative approach to tourism forecasting has been taken in Australia with the establishment of the Federal Government's Tourism Forecasting Council. The Council will provide a consultative framework which will have the potential not only to facilitate an industry input to the forecasting process, but also it will enable the development of a broader understanding of the assumptions on which the forecasts are based and the insights produced by associated analyses. A similar approach needs to be developed at the enterprise level, with forecasting exercises becoming an integral part of the ongoing management process.

No matter how far we go in this direction, we still cannot alter the fact that the future is intrinsically unpredictable and, accordingly, we will inevitably be surprised by events no matter how sophisticated our forecasting technology becomes. An important adjunct to the integration of the forecasting and management processes should therefore be the development of contingency planning capabilities. This involves the development of a relatively free-wheeling approach to the generation of alternative scenarios, the assignment of notional probabilities to these scenarios and the planning of specific strategies for coping with each one. The value of this approach is that, by considering potential developments and responses in advance, the organization will not be forced to make quick, ill-considered decisions when the unexpected occurs.

Given the unavoidable uncertainties of the future, the tourism management process should involve not only a sceptical consideration of various forecasts, but also an examination of alternative extreme scenarios. For example:

- What if the OPEC countries suddenly doubled the price of oil?
- What if there is a global financial crisis of the same magnitude as the 1930s Wall Street crash?
- What if domestic air services are again disrupted by another pilots' dispute?
- What if the ozone layer precipitously disintegrates, resulting in severe constraints on outdoor activities?
- What if a major military conflict erupts in Asia or Europe?

Some of these scenarios may appear to be outlandish. But are they any more improbable than some of the actual events referred to earlier? To become overly concerned by such possibilities is a recipe for personal and corporate neuroses. In our personal lives we should not fuel anxieties by worrying about future developments that may never eventuate. However, it is sensible for organizations periodically to assess the potential impacts of extreme events, and consider alternative coping strategies so that these can be mobilized quickly in response to events if and when they occur.

The Australian Tourist Commission Approach

The Australian Tourist Commission (ATC) promotes Australia internationally as a tourist destination. As part of its ongoing management process, the Commission sets targets which are expressed in terms of the expected number of visitors from respective overseas markets in future years. These targets provide a basis for planning the organization's marketing strategies and allocating resources within its marketing programme. They also serve as benchmarks for evaluating the ATC's overall performance. The targets are published to provide the industry with an indication of the market potential of various international markets and, in this respect, they are instrumental in the development of a coordinated approach to the international marketing of the Australian tourism product.

Targets are distinct from forecasts in that, in effect, they define a set of aspirations for the ATC and the Australian tourism industry to aim at, and in this sense provide a focus for action. On the other hand, forecasts provide an assessment of what is likely to happen, given certain assumptions about the conditions affecting demand. However, the ATC's process of setting targets is intrinsically a forecasting exercise to the extent that the determination of targets must ultimately take into account background conditions affecting demand and an assessment of what is likely to happen in the absence of the ATC's intervention. While targets must therefore inevitably exceed forecasts, they need to be considered in the context of existing forecasts in order to ensure that they remain in touch with reality.

The approach to target setting which has evolved within the ATC reflects an appreciation of several observations that can be drawn from previous discussion. First, as all techniques currently employed for tourism forecasting have limitations, a combination of these techniques needs to be applied so that their respective strengths and weaknesses complement each other. In particular, it has been noted that, by limiting analyses to the impact of quantifiable economic factors, conventional methodologies overlook the numerous other factors involved in a potential tourist's decision-making process. Second, a systematic approach to forecasting should be an integral part of the planning process, as this provides the basis for assessing emerging opportunities and threats. Third, as a consequence of the previous point, forecasting (and target setting) should be a consultative process and the approaches adopted should be 'transparent' from the point of view of all parties involved. Furthermore, participants should be encouraged not to accept forecasts produced by the technicians at face value. The assumptions on which forecasts are based should be scrutinized and challenged, while the implications of methodological limitations should be understood and taken into account. While this approach demands that managers and decision makers become more sophisticated, it also demands that the technicians involved become more effective in communicating with, and educating, users.

Key features of the ATC's forecasting and target setting methodology applied in the recent past include:

- structured and unstructured consultation with the tourism industry and ATC staff, both in Australia and overseas;
- consideration of a wide range of demand factors, in addition to quantifiable economic variables;
- an assessment of the competitive environment through the conduct of market share analysis; and
- travel propensity and outbound trend analysis.

The integration of these components into the overall approach is depicted in Figure 7.1.

The Australian Bureau of Tourism Research's (BTR) forecasts, which are based on econometric models, provide a benchmark for the analysis of individual markets. This is supplemented by an analysis of such factors as GDP growth projections, existing and projected future travel propensities, aviation market trends and political/trade considerations such as agreements on the establishment of closer economic relations.

A key feature of the ATC approach is market share analysis. Market share analysis is rarely incorporated in tourism demand estimation, possibly because of the difficulties associated with the collation of meaningful outbound data. For example, certain countries may only record outbound travel en masse, capturing short and long haul together. In a market such as the UK, this could mean including all trips to Continental Europe. Some countries do not produce any outbound data at all, in which case it is necessary to capture arrivals from that country as reported at several destinations and combine these figures.

Despite these limitations, ATC considers that market share estimates provide useful input to the target-setting process, particularly as they have not previously been used in demand estimation work in Australia and are rarely used (if at all) by other countries. Using market share trend analysis gives us a snap-shot of how Australia is performing in relation to its competitors. Relying on trends in gross visitor arrivals obscures the gains to be made from exploiting competitive advantage in a market. By looking at market share trends, the overall prospect for the origin market can be related to Australia's likely performance. In some cases, where market share has been increasing, this may override a downfall in general travel prospects from a market. In this scenario, relying on income projections for a market will indicate a decline in travel whereas the opposite may occur.

Predictably, some measures of market share are better than others but using the same method to measure market share over time is relevant from a trend analysis perspective. For example, only total outbound figures are available for Malaysia with no distinction made between short-haul travel to neighbouring countries and more relevant long-haul travel. Despite this limitation, a useful measure of Australia's relative performance in this market can be derived.

Market share trends are calculated over a period of approximately 10 years. This analysis is then used, in combination with outbound projections, to produce two scenarios: a 'trend' scenario and a 'static' scenario. The trend scenario assumes that the market share trend which exists will apply in the future, whereas the 'static' scenario assumes that market share remains constant.

In combination with outbound projections, these scenarios form 'working' or draft targets. The outbound projections used are themselves

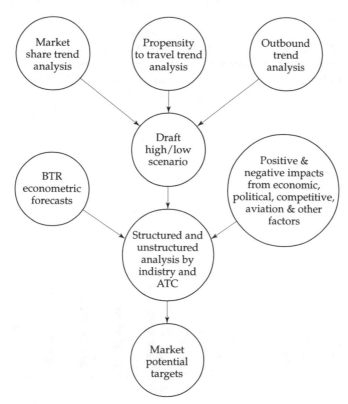

Figure 7.1 Overview of ATC target-setting methodology

given considerable consideration. A number of outbound estimates are reviewed including actual forecasts, simple outbound trend analysis and travel propensity trend analysis in conjunction with population projections. The final outbound figure used is opened to debate.

The consultative phase is largely based on the workshop format with participants drawn from airlines, hotels, attractions, inbound operators and the Bureau of Tourism Research. Representatives of the latter body provide technical input on forecasts based on econometric models. Some emphasis is placed on the presentation of data and analytical material in a format which can readily be interpreted by participants from a range of backgrounds and critical comment is invited on the proposed targets for each country. An example of the style of presentation is provided in Figure 7.2. In addition to the data provided by ATC, participants involved in the review process were requested to combine these data with their knowledge of each market when commenting on individual country targets. A more structured written feedback form is also provided to enable participants to record their assessment of the targets after further consideration. An extract from this pro forma is shown as Figure 7.3. Meanwhile, ATC overseas offices organize industry involvement in the target revision process within individual origin countries. Briefings on the output of ATC research (segmentation studies, satisfaction surveys, internal marketing evaluation research such as tracking studies and barriers to travel studies) are given as an integral part of this process.

When viewed in the light of the analysis contained in earlier sections of this paper, the approach to forecasting and target setting being

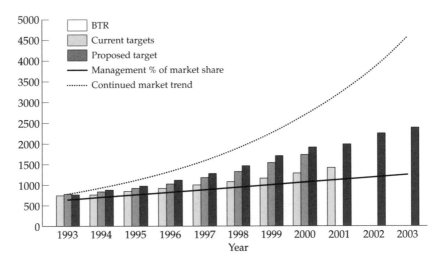

Figure 7.2 Example of workshop data presentation style

NEW ZEALAND	1993	1994	1995	1996	1997
Draft target (000)	475	505	537	560	580
% growth	6%	6%	6%	5%	4%
Growth assessment (H/L/OK)					
Suggested growth (optional)					

Figure 7.3 Example of industry feedback pro forma (actual form extended to year 2003)

developed by the ATC represents a significant step forward. In particular, the previous dependence upon econometric modelling has been reduced, with this approach being supplemented by others that take into account factors which are less amenable to quantitative analysis. In addition, more emphasis is being placed on a consultative approach which not only permits a more diverse range of factors to be taken into account, but also facilitates the integration of forecasting with the management decision process.

However, at this stage, the ATC's approach does not adequately take into account the implications of the chaos theory perspective. This requires the inclusion of a stage in the target-setting process where extreme scenarios are canvassed so that the need to consider contingency plans for coping with these potential eventualities can be signalled to the industry. It also requires background analysis to be carried out in an effort to identify positive feedback-driven phenomena that may precipitate dramatic shifts in the dynamics of tourism demand in the near or distant future.

Conclusion

Forecasting is a fundamental element of strategic planning. Without a systematic and rigorous assessment of emerging market trends, the tourism industry at individual destinations will have difficulty positioning itself in order to take advantage of opportunities as they arise, or to counteract potentially threatening developments. Where forecasting has been embraced as a tool for planning, however, there has been a tendency to rely on a limited range of methodologies, while the technical sophistication of popular approaches has hindered the establishment of an effective dialogue between specialist analysts and decision makers.

Reliance on a limited range of approaches denies planners access to the varied perspectives other approaches can bring to bear on the problem. More importantly, it means that the deficiencies of one approach are not compensated by the strengths of another. The emphasis placed on econometric methods, in particular, could contribute to significant blind spots in our vision of the future because of the mechanistic orientation of this approach. Specifically, the incidence of non-linear phenomena highlighted by chaos theory (such as the butterfly effect and saturation cycles) may have more significant tourism marketing implications than the linear relationships highlighted by conventional methodologies based on economic theory. Whatever approach is adopted, however, we have no option but to accept the fact that we cannot predict the future with any degree of certainty. The inclusion of a contingency planning phase within the planning cycle is therefore a useful adjunct to the planning process.

The establishment of a dialogue between specialist forecasters and decision markers is essential for the effective integration of forecasting and the planning process. Forecasters therefore need to develop more user-friendly approaches to presenting information to, and educating, users. They also need to devise a format of presentation which facilitates more meaningful two-way discussion not only to ensure that the underlying assumptions and logic of their forecasts are scrutinized, questioned and debated, but also to make the forecasting process open to alternative perspectives.

The system being developed by the ATC has been presented as an example of the move towards a more open, consultative approach to forecasting which epitomizes the integrative approach advocated in this paper. Even in this instance, however, there is scope for further development to take into account limitations of the forecasting methodologies described above.

References

Archer, B. (1987) Demand forecasting and estimation, in Brent Ritche, J. R. and Goeldner, C. R. (eds) *Travel Tourism and Hospitality Research: A Handbook for Managers and Researchers*, Wiley, New York, pp. 77–85.

Armstrong, J. S. (1985) *Long Range Forecasting*, 2nd edn, Wiley, New York.

Bar On, R. V. (1984) Forecasting tourism and travel series, in Van Doorn, J. W. M. (ed.) *Problems of Tourism* 3, 24–39.

Butler, R. W. (1980) The concept of a tourist area cycle of evolution: implications for management of resources, *Canadian Geographer* 24 (1), 5–12.

Calantone, R. J., Benedito, A. and Bojanic, D. (1987) A comprehensive review of tourism forecasting literature, *Journal Travel Research* (Fall), 28–39.

Capra, F. (1982) *The Turning Point: Science, Society and the Rising Culture*, Flamingo, London.

Carbone, R. and Armstrong, J. S. (1982) Note. Evaluation of extrapolative forecasting methods: results of a survey of academicians and practitioners, *Journal Forecasting* 1, 215–217.

Crouch, G. I. and Shaw, R. H (1990) Determinants of international tourist flows: findings from 30 years of empirical research, Monash University Graduate School of Management, *Management Papers* No. 29.

Davies, P. and Gribbin, J. (1992) *The Matter Myth: Beyond Chaos and Complexity*, Penguin, London.

Gleick, J. (1987) *Chaos: Making a New Science*, Heinemann, London.

Greenley, G. E. and Matcham, A. S. (1971) Problems in marketing services: the case of incoming tourism, *European Journal of Marketing* 17 (6), 57–64.

Kuhn, T. S. (1962) *The Structure of Scientific Revolutions*, 2nd edn, University of Chicago Press, Chicago.

Makridakis, S. (1986) The art and science of forecasting: an assessment of future directions. *International Journal of Forecasting* 2, 15–39.

Mazanie, I. (1981) The tourism/leisure ratio: anticipating the limits of growth, *Tourist Review* 36 (4), 2–12.

Meadows, D. H., Meadows, D. L., Randers, J. and Behrens, W. W. III (1972) *The Limits of Growth*, Universe Books, New York.

Middleton, V. T. C. (1990) *Marketing in Travel and Tourism*, Heinemann, Oxford.

Poon, A. (1993) *Tourism Technology and Competitive Strategies*, CAB International, Wallingford 115.

Schaffer, S. (1993) Comets and the world's end, in Howe, L. and Wain, A. *Predicting the Future*, Cambridge University Press, Cambridge, pp. 52–76.

Toffler, A. (1970) *Future Shock*, Bodley Head, London.

Uysal, M. and Crompton, J. L. (1985) An overview of approaches used to forecast tourism demand, *Journal of Travel Research* (Spring), 7–15.

Van Doorn, J. W. M. (1984) Tourism forecasting techniques: a brief overview, in Van Doom, J. W. M. (ed.) *Problems of Tourism* 3, 7–15.

Waldrop, M. (1992) *Complexity: The Emerging Science and the Edge of Order and Chaos*, Simon and Schuster, London.

Witt, S. F. and Witt, C. A. (1992) *Modelling and Forecasting Demand in Tourism*, Academic Press, London.

Chapter 8

An Integrative Approach to Tourism Forecasting: A Glance in the Rearview Mirror

Carmen Tideswell, Trevor Mules and Bill Faulkner

The application reported here is for forecasts of tourism to 2005 in the Australian state of South Australia. South Australia is not a mass tourism destination. As Faulkner *et al.* (1999) reported, the state relies heavily on its wine regions (e.g., Barossa Valley, Clare Valley, and McLaren Vale regions) and the "big river" theme associated with the Murray River in attracting tourists. The state accounts for only 4% of visitor nights by international visitors to Australia and 7% of domestic Australian visitor nights. However, the state tourism authority (South Australian Tourism Commission, or SATC) regards tourism as a growth industry and is keen to capitalize on the economic potential of growth in tourism to destinations within the state, hence the value placed on the forecasting process.

Forecasting is an attempt to anticipate the future, and in many business endeavors, its value lies in enabling operators to minimize losses due to disparities between demand and supply. In tourism, it is necessary to anticipate future demand for transport, accommodation, skilled labor, retail, and entertainment facilities. Given the lead time usually involved in the development of the infrastructure required to service markets, future demand must be anticipated several years in advance.

Should a tourism destination underestimate future demand, the result will be lack of amenity, congestion, poor service, missed market opportunities, and ultimately, loss of market share as a result of visitors seeking alternative destinations. Overestimation of future demand will result in excess supply of infrastructure, inefficient use of resources, and low returns on investment. If provision of tourism infrastructure is left to market forces, it is likely that the lead time involved will result in a cycle of excess demand followed by excess supply, resulting in considerable damage to visitor perceptions and investor confidence.

It is unlikely that any approach to tourism forecasting will provide accurate forecasts for all times and all destinations. Witt and Witt (1992) provided a review of many statistical approaches to tourism forecasting, including detailed econometric modeling and time-series modeling. Specifically excluded from their study was the use of qualitative forecasting methods, such as the Delphi or expert opinion technique. Other research studies have, however, included coverage of this qualitative forecasting method (Calantone *et al.* 1987; Uysal and Crompton 1985).

In this study, we report on a case study of tourism forecasting that combined statistical techniques with expert opinion in a quasi-Delphi process that enabled tourism industry practitioners to respond to the opinions of their peers. They were encouraged to form and review their own opinions about the future in light of both their peer group opinion and the mechanistic forecasts based on statistical methods.

Tourism Forecasting

There is a large quantity of academic and other literature on tourism demand forecasting (e.g., Uysal and Crompton 1985; Calantone *et al.* 1987; Martin and Witt 1987; Witt and Martin 1987; Witt and Witt 1991; Turner *et al.* 1997). Some of this forecasting work is based on time-series methods, whereby intrinsic qualities of the past behavior of the data are used to drive projections regarding visitor numbers into the future. For example, Turner *et al.* (1997) compared forecast accuracy using Autoregressive Integrated Moving Average (ARIMA) models, autoregressive models, exponential smoothing models, and econometric models (demand-based models).

Econometric models concentrate on the demand relationship and the statistical relationship between visitor numbers and economic variables such as air fares, income of tourists, exchange rates, and tourism promotion expenditure being estimated. Crouch (1995) consolidated 30 studies of this type, covering tourism demand in all of the world's major destinations. In the Australian context, Poole (1988) used this approach to produce regression equations for each of seven of Australia's major tourism foreign-origin markets, while Hamal (1996) has applied a similar approach to domestic Australian holiday tourism.

This economic approach is often referred to as "structural demand modeling," relying as it does on the structure of demand for household consumption items of which tourism and travel is but one. Lim (1997) surveyed this field, finding more than 100 published articles of the genre. She was highly critical of the statistical robustness of most of the articles surveyed, many of them relying on proxies for missing variables.

Witt and Witt (1992) found that quite naive forecasting methods, such as the assumption of no change, performed generally better than structural demand models using various tests of forecast accuracy such as Mean Absolute Percentage Error (MAPE). Turner *et al.* (1997) also found that simple models tended to outperform more complex time-series models using similar measures of forecast accuracy. Elsewhere, Faulkner and Valerio (1995) have questioned the value of highly technical statistical approaches, which have the effect of alienating the users of the forecasts from the forecasting process. It is suggested that in the strategic planning context, many practitioners have lost sight of the suggestion that the process of forecasting is as important as the outcome. Accordingly, a method that actively engages decision makers in the forecasting exercise can contribute more to the broader strategic planning process than one that does not.

As will be discussed subsequently, this study incorporated a qualitative component using expert opinions in developing the forecasts. In considering the quantitative approaches that would provide the foundation of this expert opinion phase, it was decided not to employ economic-demand modeling techniques, partly because of the statistical problems alluded by Lim (1997). In addition, when using such models for forecasting, it is necessary to first forecast the values of the independent variables, such as air fares, exchange rates, and gross domestic product in originating markets. This requirement means that regardless of the virtue of the structural equations, the accuracy of forecast tourism numbers depends critically on the accuracy of the forecasts of the independent variables. The forecaster is therefore faced with an unavoidable error compounding effect.

In the area of event tourism, neither time-series nor structural equation approaches are of much use because special events are, in a sense, statistical outliers. Mules and McDonald (1994) therefore relied on an approach to forecasting the visitor impact of the Sydney 2000 Olympic Games using data from a brace of special events, including other Olympic events.

Bearing these considerations in mind, the South Australian study used time-series approaches to generating statistical forecasts, rather than structural equation approaches because of the impracticality of developing credible forecasts out to 2005 of originating country exchange rates and GDP. These quantitative techniques were complemented by a qualitative quasi-Delphi method, a forecasting approach that is discussed in the following section.

The Delphi and Consultation Process

As noted by Frechtling (1996), "The Delphi method is designed to produce a group consensus on forecasts while avoiding some of the problems of other group forecasting methods, such as the jury of executive opinion" (p. 185). The problems that it is specifically intended to overcome include the undue influence of "recognised experts" and respondent unwillingness to go against the "popular view" of panel respondents (Frechtling 1996).

The Delphi method, which evolved in the 1950s in the area of U.S. defence research, involves a panel of respondents with recognized expertise in the subject area, who are invited to respond to a series of questionnaires covering a similar range of questions. After each round of the questionnaire, respondents receive feedback on the group's response and are invited to adjust their responses to the questionnaire in light of this information. The anonymity and confidentiality of individual responses is preserved through this process (Faulkner 1987). The ultimate aim of the exercise is to guide panel members toward an informed assessment of the issues in question and to arrive at some degree of consensus (Faulkner 1987). The basic premise of the Delphi approach is to involve the panel in several iterations of the survey, with feedback on each occasion designed to drive the group toward a consensus or at least toward a clearly recognizable polarization of views that enables alternative scenarios to be identified.

Overview of the Integrative Approach

To put the overall approach adopted in this study into perspective, a combination of quantitative and qualitative forecasting methods have been used as advocated by Frechtling (1996). In particular a combination of naive forecasts, single exponential smoothing forecasts, and a Delphi panel were used in the study.

The South Australian Forecasting Approach

Tourism into South Australia was segmented according to origin as shown in Table 8.1. For each international segment, six different time-series forecasting methods were applied to past data to generate six different forecasts of visitor numbers for each year up to 2005. As at the time of carrying out this exercise, the latest available data were for 1995; all years beyond 1995 are treated as forecasts.

For international visitors to the state, annual data on visitor numbers from 1984 to 1995 were used. Three simple time-series approaches, and one "top-down" approach, were applied to each of the originating segments shown in Table 8.1. The time-series approaches were the following:

1. Holt's exponential smoothing. This time-series method incorporates average changes in the long-run trend (Pindyck and Rubinfeld 1991). With this model, greater emphasis is placed on the more recent trends within the data, and hence the resulting forecasts are most reflective of the latest trends.
2. A form of "naive" method based on the assumption that the average

Table 8.1 Average proportion of visitor nights from each market into
South Australia, 1985–1995

International Market Origin	%	Domestic Market Origin	%
United Kingdom/Ireland	27	South Australia	58
Other Europe	25	Victoria	18
United States/Canada	16	New South Wales/	
Other Asia	15	Australian Capital	
New Zealand	10	Territory	12
Japan	4	Queensland	4
Other	3	Western Australia	4
		Northern Territory	3
		Tasmania	1
Total	100	Total	100

    annual rate of change from the past 11 years would continue in the
future.
3. A simple linear trend fitted to the annual data using regression
analysis. Here, the forecasting model assumes that the series will
increase by a constant absolute amount in each time period. The
amount of such an increase is based on the average change from the
first to the last point in the actual data set.

The top-down approach consisted of using forecast numbers of tourist
arrivals for Australia as a whole, generated by the Australian Tourism
Forecasting Council (TFC), and applying a percentage for South
Australia's share of visitors from each originating market. The TFC
publishes forecasts of international inbound tourism to Australia for each
of our originating segments using a process whereby forecasts derived
from an economic-demand model are modified by industry practitioners.
While an 11–year series (1985 to 1995) of historical data to South Australia
was available for use in the study, the forecasting methods, which relied
on South Australia's market share of national forecasts, were based on
median shares of visitation during more recent times (i.e. 1989 to 1995).
This time frame was chosen as it was considered to more accurately
reflect more recent trends, providing a sounder basis for the forecasts. For
South Australia's share of the national total, three different percentages
based on the highest, the lowest, and the median share of the past 7 years
of data were used.
    Table 8.2 provides an example of the type of information that resulted
from the forecasts. Tables such as this for each of the originating international segments were included in the Delphi instrument. The top half

Table 8.2 Forecasts for United States/Canada visitors to South Australia (in thousands)

	Forecast method					
	State Share of Tourism Forecast Council's National Forecasts					
Year	Low	Median	High	Holt	Naive	Trend
1984	28.0	28.0	28.0	28.0	28.0	28.0
1985	30.9	30.9	30.9	30.9	30.9	30.9
1986	36.2	36.2	36.2	36.2	36.2	36.2
1988	54.4	54.4	54.4	54.4	54.4	54.4
1989	48.6	48.6	48.6	48.6	48.6	48.6
1990	43.1	43.1	43.1	43.1	43.1	43.1
1991	36.2	36.2	36.2	36.2	36.2	36.2
1992	40.8	40.8	40.8	40.8	40.8	40.8
1993	38.2	38.2	38.2	38.2	38.2	38.2
1994	42.2	42.2	42.2	42.2	42.2	42.2
1995	41.7	41.7	41.7	41.7	41.7	41.7
1996	*42.5*	*48.4*	*58.9*	*42.9*	*43.2*	*44.4*
1997	*44.6*	*50.7*	*61.7*	*43.9*	*44.8*	*45.1*
1998	*46.8*	*53.2*	*64.8*	*45.0*	*46.5*	*45.9*
1999	*49.2*	*56.0*	*68.2*	*46.0*	*48.2*	*46.6*
2000	*53.7*	*61.1*	*74.4*	*47.0*	*50.0*	*47.3*
2001	*58.6*	*66.7*	*81.2*	*48.0*	*51.8*	*48.0*
2002	*62.7*	*71.3*	*86.9*	*49.0*	*53.7*	*48.8*
2003	*65.7*	*74.8*	*91.0*	*50.0*	*55.7*	*49.5*
2004	*67.1*	*76.3*	*92.9*	*51.1*	*57.8*	*50.2*
2005	*68.7*	*78.2*	*95.2*	*52.1*	*59.9*	*51.0*

Note: Figures for 1984–1995 are actual historical data (not generated forecasts); hence no difference exists across the alternative methods. Note that there was no data collection for 1987. The figures in italics are the forecasts.

of the table shows the actual tourism numbers for the segment from 1984 to 1995, while the numbers in italics are the forecasts. Note that there was no data collection for 1987.

For the domestic market segments shown in Table 8.1, there were no available TFC forecasts on the required state-of-origin basis, so it was not possible to use the top-down approach. The same three time-series methods used for the international market (i.e., last three columns of Table 8.2) were used for the domestic market, and tables similar to Table 8.2 for each domestic market segment were distributed to the panel.

For all forecasts, visitor numbers were used rather than visitor nights as it was felt that tourism industry people would be better able to relate to numbers of visitors. Extensions of this work to produce estimates of future economic impacts of tourism growth would require the conversion of the forecasts to visitor nights so that the expenditure parameter can be more readily devised (Mules 1998). Details of the statistical methods used to generate each set of forecasts are given in the next section.

The South Australian Delphi Process

The complete set of statistical forecasts were mailed out in July 1996 to a Delphi panel of 45 people involved in the local South Australian tourism industry, ranging from airline management, inbound tour businesses, hospitality sector management, and tourism marketers and planners from the SATC. The mail out included a non-technical (i.e., layman's terms) explanation of how the alternative forecasts were derived and an invitation to participate in the study. The panel was asked to choose the forecasts they considered to be the most plausible from the sets mailed out to them and to return their responses to the researchers. For each segment, the responses were averaged, or in a small number of cases where responses were skewed, the mode was used to represent the group view.

Of the 45 tourism industry practitioners invited to participate in the Delphi process, 26 responded. Their preferred forecast for each segment and forecast method are shown in Table 8.3 for international tourists and in Table 8.4 for domestic tourists. There was a clear modal dominance in preference in most cases. The exceptions were Other Europe, where both TFC median and Holt's method were equally popular, and perhaps Other Asia and Other, where in both cases the dominant opinion was "don't know."

As time constraints associated with the SATC's strategic planning agenda did not allow for more than two iterations of the Delphi process, a workshop involving panel participants was convened. In essence, as a result of these actions, the nature of the qualitative component of the forecasting process moved more toward an expert opinion-type method rather than a pure Delphi approach. As two of the key principles of Delphi, according to Frechtling (1996), were not strictly adhered to from this point onward (i.e., ensuring respondent anonymity and conducting several rounds of the survey), it must be acknowledged that the resulting process was a variation on the true Delphi approach. As described below, the final workshop was used to supplement the qualitative process by providing the tourism forecast team with an opportunity to discuss the Delphi results in person with the expert panel. To this extent, therefore, the anonymity of the panel was sacrificed, but only to the extent that each knew who else had submitted questionnaire responses. No confidential details regarding individual responses prior to the workshop were divulged by the forecasting team. Obviously, however, the problem of biases with unwanted group discussion effects was encountered during the workshop, but it was felt that the previous Delphi rounds had allowed all respondents to indicate their views in an unaffected manner that then fed into the workshop discussion.

The most important international market to South Australia, in terms of visitor nights, is the United Kingdom/Ireland, followed by other European countries. For the first of these, there was a solid weight of opinion supporting the forecasts produced by the Holt method (Table 8.3). However, there was some division of views regarding Other Europe, which possibly reflects the diversity of nationalities that are embraced under this heading.

The second stage of the Delphi process involved the full-day workshop with a subgroup of 18 of the original Delphi panel of 26. This workshop consisted of some introductory discussion of the factors affecting growth in tourism in South Australia. This included a review of supply of accommodation, a consideration of attractions and price competitiveness, and a discussion of tourism promotion initiatives.

With this background information fresh in their minds, the participants were then presented with the results of the Delphi survey, which showed what their peers' opinions were of the various forecasts. This process was employed to enable participants to modify their earlier opinions in light of their peers' revealed opinions and, ultimately, to move toward a group view regarding the forecasts for each market segment.

The information contained in Tables 8.3 and 8.4 provoked discussion at the workshop, with various participants debating with each other about likely future scenarios for tourism in South Australia. The workshop moderator's task was to attempt to steer the group toward a consensus about the preferred forecasts for each segment. This was achieved for all segments except United Kingdom/Ireland, where the workshop partici-pants were polarized between the Holt and "naive" forecasts, eventually agreeing that their preference was for a forecast midway between two sets of forecasts.

Forecasts for each segment were discussed in turn until a consensus was reached. This process enabled industry participants to see where their views were placed in relation to their peer group and also enabled the researchers to add "on the ground knowledge" to the forecasting exercise. An added attribute was the sense of involvement in, and under-standing and ownership of, the forecasting process that members of the tourism industry in the state took away with them from the workshop. This contrasts with the feeling of alienation and "black box" impression

Table 8.3 Delphi panel's preferred tourism forecasts for international visitor numbers to South Australia, 2005: workshop responses

Origin of Visitors to South Australia	Australian Tourism Forecasting Council-Median	Frequency of Responses (%)				Number of Usable Responses
		Holt	Naive	Linear Trend	No Opinion	
USA/Canada	52	4	9	—	35	23
United Kingdom/Ireland	9	48	17	9	17	23
Other Europe	35	35	—	4	26	23
Japan	18	9	50	5	18	22
Other Asia	15	27	4	15	38	26
New Zealand	15	27	4	15	38	26
Other	41	—	18	—	41	22

Table 8.4 Delphi panel's preferred tourism forecasts for domestic trips to South Australia, 2005: workshop responses

Origin of Trips to South Australia	Frequency of Responses (%)					Number of Usable Responses
	Holt	Naive	Linear Trend	No Opinion		
New South Wales	63	13	13	11		24
Victoria	4	—	71	25		24
Queensland	17	13	67	4		24
South Australia	13	—	67	20		24
Western Australia	5	27	50	18		22
Tasmania	5	5	84	5		19
Northern Territory	6	39	28	28		18

that industry participants often have about tourism forecasting being carried out by government agencies.

A comparison of the before and after preferences of the group is shown in Table 8.5. The workshop discussion caused a change in the most preferred forecast for every international market segment, except New Zealand. Conversely, the participants did not alter any of their preferred forecasts for domestic tourism segments.

One possible explanation for this difference between the domestic and international outcomes is that participants generally felt that they had a better understanding of the factors that affect domestic tourism and were therefore in a better position to assess future scenarios in this area from the outset. On the other hand, they are less familiar with more distant international markets, which are exposed to more volatile, and therefore less predictable, influences. Another possible explanation is that some of the original 26 respondents were not present at the workshop. The missing respondents may have been key people in international rather than domestic tourism, and this may have led to more instability in the group's responses at the workshop.

Assessment of South Australian Visitor Forecast Accuracy 1996–1998

In general, there are three types of papers produced in the tourism forecasting arena. The first type of work aims to report the results and draw conclusions as to what the future holds for the tourism industry in a given region in light of these forecasts (Evans 1996). The second group contains technical forecasting papers written with the aim to discuss the relative merits of different forecasting approaches in terms of their potential forecasting accuracy (Uysal and Crompton 1985; Calantone *et al.* 1987; Martin and Witt 1987; Witt and Martin 1987). The third type of study aims to provide a retrospective assessment of the accuracy of forecasts produced in previous studies. Several studies have included some form of retrospective evaluation of the methodologies used to forecast tourist visitation (e.g., Athiyaman and Robertson 1992; Choy 1984; Martin and Witt 1989; Witt *et al.* 1992). Of note, however, is the exclusion of the use of the qualitative Delphi methods in deriving the final forecasts reviewed in any these studies.

Undoubtedly, part of the "integrative approach" to tourism forecasting should involve a means for systematically updating past forecasts on a regular basis to ensure that more recent changes in the marketplace are considered as time goes by. One approach to achieving this is to simply update the original forecasts using the most recent data available via the same methods conducted in the original studies. However, to do so without reference to the performance of previous forecasts using similar

Table 8.5 A comparison of panel members' preferred forecasting method, pre- and postworkshop discussion

Market Segment	Most Popular Mail Response	Most Popular in Workshop
International market		
United States/Canada	Australian Tourism Forecasting Council (TFC)-median	Holt
United Kingdom/Ireland	Holt	Holt/naive
Other Europe	TFC-median/Holt	TFC-low
Japan	Naive	Holt
Other Asia	Holt	TFC-low
New Zealand	TFC-median	TFC-median
Other	TFC-median	TFC-low
Domestic market		
New South Wales/Australian Capital Territory	Holt	Holt
Victoria (VIC)	Linear trend	Linear trend
Queensland (QLD)	Linear trend	Linear trend
South Australia (SA)	Linear trend	Linear trend
Western Australia (WA)	Linear trend	Linear trend
Tasmania	Linear trend	Linear trend
Northern Territory (NT)	Naive	Average (naive and linear)

methods is inadvisable. The remainder of this article will focus on the assessment of the forecast accuracy of the original South Australian visitor forecasts, followed by an assessment of the approach to forecast updating as just described.

Forecasting model assessment

The accuracy of tourism demand forecasts (i.e., to what extent they predict reality) has been found to be the most important evaluation criterion required by the users and producers of tourism forecasts (Witt and Witt 1992). A series of measures that can be used to evaluate the accuracy of forecasts is discussed by Frechtling (1996), who noted that "one of the most useful ... due to its simplicity and intuitive clarity, is the mean absolute percentage error, or MAPE." MAPE is defined by Frechtling as "the sum of the absolute errors for each time period divided by the actual value for the period this sum is divided by the number of periods to obtain a mean value" (and multiplied by 100 to arrive at a percentage figure). The relative MAPEs of alternative forecast models can then be assessed to determine how accurate various models are. A suggested interpretation of the resulting MAPE values has been given as follows:

- Less than 10% (highly accurate forecasts)
- 10%–20% (good forecasting)
- 20%-50% (reasonable forecasting)
- 50% or more (inaccurate forecasting). (Lewis 1982, quoted in Witt and Witt 1992: 40)

The remainder of this article assesses the accuracy of the South Australian tourism demand forecasts using MAPE as the assessment criterion in most instances.

What really happened to South Australian tourism 1996–1998?
With 3 years having lapsed since the initial South Australian forecasts were produced in 1996, it is possible to assess the forecast accuracy against actual visitation achieved by the state between 1996 and 1998. The Bureau of Tourism Research's International Visitor Survey and Domestic Tourism Monitor results for these years are presented in Tables 8.6 and 8.7, respectively, along with forecast visitation levels for these periods.

International forecast assessment

As Table 8.6 reveals, total international visitor forecasts for each of the 3 years forecast by the research were within 5% of the actual level of visitation achieved by South Australia in these years. While the forecasts underestimated (–4.6%) visitation in 1996, the more recent years have been over-forecast by just more than 2%, suggesting that the forecast

Table 8.6 Actual versus forecast international visitors to South Australia, 1996–1998

	Visitors (in thousands)									
	1996			1997			1998			MAPE
Market	Actual	Forecast	Error (%)	Actual	Forecast	Error (%)	Actual	Forecast	Error (%)	1996–1998
Other Europe	98.2	90.2	–8.1	93.5	90.2	–3.5	97	104.7	7.9	6.5
United Kingdom/Ireland	47.2	48.8	3.4	54.6	50.4	–7.7	69.1	52.2	–24.5	11.9
United States/Canada	44.0	42.9	–2.5	42.7	44.6	4.4	46.5	46.8	0.6	2.5
Other Asia	32.4	35.8	10.5	33.1	41.3	24.8	34.2	47.3	38.3	24.5
New Zealand	30.7	31.5	2.6	24.6	34.4	39.8	27.7	34.8	25.6	22.7
Japan	24.0	14.8	–38.3	16.9	16.7	–1.2	16.7	18.8	12.6	17.4
Other	7.2	6.6	–8.3	12.5	6.5	–48.0	13.4	6.4	–52.2	36.2
Total	283.7	270.6	–4.6	277.9	284.1	2.2	304.6	311.0	2.1	3.0

Source: Based on data from the Bureau of Tourism Research, International Visitor Survey (1996–1998) and Mules et al. (1996).
Note: MAPS = Mean Absolute Percentage Error.

Table 8.7 Actual versus forecast domestic trips to South Australia, 1996–1997

	Trips (in thousands)									
	1996			1997			1998[a]			MAPE
Market %	Actual	Forecast	Error (%)	Actual	Forecast	Error (%)	Actual	Forecast	Error (%)	1996–1997
South Australia	3,444	3,069	-10.9	3,388	3,095	-8.6	3,638	3,121	-14.2	9.8
Victoria	602	544	-9.6	542	551	1.7	899	558	-37.9	5.7
New South Wales	262	261	-0.4	311	268	-13.8	512	276	-46.1	7.1
Queensland	111	63	-43.2	73	65	-11.0	142	67	-52.8	27.1
Western Australia	93	47	-49.5	74	47	-36.5	149	46	-69.1	43.0
Northern Territory	31	31	0.0	51	32	-37.3	72	31.5	-56.3	18.7
Tasmania	11	17	54.5	17	18	5.9	25	19	-24.0	30.2
Total	4,554	4,032	-11.5	4,456	4,076	-8.5	5,437	4,119	-24.2	10.0

Source: Based on data from the Bureau of Tourism Research, Domestic Tourism Monitor (1996–97) and National Visitor Survey (1998); Mules et al. (1996).
Note: MAPE = Mean Absolute Percentage Error.
a. Forecast accuracy for 1998 is not assessed due to change in survey method.

methods used, at the overall level, have been considerably accurate. MAPE (3.0%) suggests that the overall international forecasts were "highly accurate" according to the criteria established by Lewis (1982).

When the forecasts of specific origin markets are considered, however, assessment of the level of accuracy becomes less clear. In general, the accuracy of the forecasts fluctuate in each market from year to year. For example, in the Other European market (South Australia's main source of international visitors), the 1996 forecast underestimated visitation achieved by 8.1%. The accuracy of the forecasts for 1997 improved slightly, but the forecasts were still underestimated (–3.5%). By 1998, preliminary data from the Bureau of Tourism Research suggest that the forecasts exceeded actual figures by 7.9%. At 6.5%, the MAPE for this key market suggests that the forecasts for Other Europe were "highly accurate." Forecasts for the next largest market, the United Kingdom/ Ireland were also within an acceptable margin (i.e., less than 10%) for 1996–1997, although by 1998, they were underestimating reported visitation levels by almost 25%. However, with an overall MAPE of 11.9%, a good forecast result was obtained overall. Forecasts for the third major market, the United States and Canada, were within an acceptable error range (less than 5%) for all years, with an impressive MAPE of 2.5%.

With the exception of the Japanese market (which was forecast using the Holt exponential smoothing method and resulted in a MAPE of 17.4%), all of the remaining markets were estimated by some form of top-down forecasting method (i.e., pro rata share of national forecasts) and accounted for just 30% of South Australia's international visitation in 1998 (Bureau of Tourism Research 1999). In general, the accuracy of the forecasts produced via this method is more questionable given the resulting errors shown in Table 8.6. In the Other Asian market, for instance, forecasts were consistently overestimated by between 10% and 40%, despite a "reasonable" MAPE of 24.5%. This is perhaps not surprising considering the Asian economic crisis, which was not predicted at the time the forecasts were developed. The application of the TFC's methodology therefore significantly overestimates South Australia's potential in this market. A similar situation is reported for the New Zealand market (MAPE of 22.7%). What this suggests is that where a market is not as dominant in South Australia as it is to Australia as a whole, the application of the TFC's methodology, in fact, may not be the best option, and time-series modeling of the state's historical performance should be considered more suitable.

Domestic forecast assessment

Table 8.7 summarizes the accuracy of the domestic visitor forecasts, all of which were derived using time-series methods as previously outlined. It must be emphasized that the break in series associated with the replacement of the Domestic Tourism Monitor by the National Visitor Survey in 1998, complicates the assessment of the visitor forecasts accuracy in this year.

Overall domestic trips were underestimated by the forecasts by as much as 11.5% in 1996 (8.5% in 1997). The total MAPE for domestic trips between 1996 and 1997 was 10%, suggesting that the forecasts in overall terms were highly accurate. Although these forecasts were based on historical data reported for South Australia, it is clear that the forecast methods used should be reconsidered in light of more recent trends. For instance, the more aggressive domestic marketing campaigns now being pursued by the South Australian Tourism Commission should ensure that a new, increased level of domestic travel to the state is witnessed, hereby altering past trends less likely to continue as new strategies are adopted. One possible explanation of the general trend across all origin markets is that the time series used in deriving the original forecasts took into account too much of history and failed to detect the more recent trends of higher growth rates in South Australia's domestic tourism. This would certainly explain the poor performance of these forecasts, the majority of which were based on a linear trend function of past visitation from 1984 to 1995. An alternative time-series method, such as the "naive" method, which is based on the average annual growth rate, appears to be more appropriate. As indicated in Table 8.8, it is clear that the MAPE (2.5%) is minimized under this method. This finding should not be surprising, given that previous studies described by Frechtling (1996: 59) show that the naive forecast models are often more accurate than more complex forecast models.

Given the poor performance of forecasts produced for the smaller domestic markets (i.e., Queensland, Western Australia, Northern Territory, and Tasmania) under the methods chosen in the original study following industry consultation, it seems a logical step to reconsider the most

Table 8.8 A retrospective assessment of alternative intrastate forecasts – comparison of forecast to actual trips undertaken by South Australians within South Australia

	Error (%)		
	1996	*1997*	*MAPE 1996–1997 (%)*
Difference between			
Linear and actual	−11	−9	10.0
Holt and actual	−6	−2	4.0
Naive and actual	−2	3	2.5

Note: MAPE = Mean Absolute Percentage Error.

appropriate forecast method for each domestic market by taking into account the overall accuracy of the 1996–1997 forecasts. Table 8.9 presents a retrospective list of most appropriate forecast methods based on a review of the alternative forecasts vis-à-vis actual visitation in these years.

As illustrated in Table 8.9, only two of the forecasts (Western Australia and Northern Territory), originally chosen by the Delphi panel in conjunction with the forecasting team, appear to be considered the most appropriate forecast in light of actual visitation levels. In fact, in the case of New South Wales and Australian Capital Territory (ACT), Queensland, and South Australia, the naive forecast method produced the forecasts with the lowest overall error in 1996–1997, with New South Wales and ACT and South Australia falling within the highly accurate range (i.e., less than 10%), while the Queensland forecasts are considered to be reasonable (i.e., MAPE = 23.1 %). Although it is tempting to suggest that future tourism forecasts for the domestic market in South Australia should use the methods shown in Table 8.9, applying the wisdom of hindsight could be hazardous in this context. The dynamics of markets are continually changing, and consequently, the forecasting method that is most effective in a period may not necessarily be so in another.

An alternative strategy was employed in this study to determine if, in fact, the original forecast methods were simply not suitable for the South Australian context, or rather, if they were merely based on data that were not up-to-date enough to reflect more recent changes in the marketplace. For example, at the time of reporting the original forecasts, the most recent domestic data available were for 1995. As the study was finalized

Table 8.9 A retrospective assessment of the most accurate forecast methods for South Australia's domestic tourism

Visitor's State of Origin	Most Accurate Method Based on 1996–1997 Performance	MAPE 1996–1997 (%)	Agree or Disagree with Chosen Method
New South Wales	Naive	6.5	Disagree
Victoria	Holt	5.4	Disagree
Queensland	Naive	23.1	Disagree
South Australia	Naive	2.5	Disagree
Western Australia	Linear	43.0	Agree
Tasmania	Holt	25.7	Disagree
Northern Territory	Average (naive and linear)	18.9	Agree

Note: MAPE = Mean Absolute Percentage Error.

at the end of 1996, it is quite clear that the most recent changes in the
South Australian tourism industry were not incorporated into the initial
forecasts.

South Australia tourism forecast update: 1998–2005

In recognizing that the tourism forecasts originally produced were clearly
out-of-date, the South Australian Tourism Commission commissioned an
update of the original forecasts at the end of 1998. The process of updating the forecasts was done, subject to project time and budget constraints, via merely updating the original forecast methods advocated
(see Table 8.5) using the most recent data available (i.e., up to 1997). With
the change in the domestic survey occurring in 1998, it is not feasible to
report on the accuracy of the updated domestic forecasts in comparison
to the new survey results. This section is therefore focused on detecting if
there has been any improvement in the accuracy of the updated
international tourism forecasts using actual visitation to South Australia
in 1998. Table 8.10 summarizes the original study's accuracy with that of
the updated forecasts in forecasting international visitation in 1998.

It is evident from Table 8.10 that the updating exercise has improved
considerably the forecast accuracy for 1998 for the two major international
markets for South Australia, namely, the United Kingdom/Ireland and
Other Europe, where the errors dropped from 24.5% and 7.9% to 12.7%
and 1.5%, respectively. A similar improvement is evident for Japan,
although this is not a major market for South Australia.

Interestingly, the updated forecast was far too pessimistic about the
Other Asian market. Clearly, the Asian financial crisis has not had as big
an impact as expected. This may be due to the particular weightings of
different Asian countries in this category for South Australia. For
example, Singapore is a relatively important component of this segment
but was less affected by the crisis than other Asian countries.

Overall, however, the updated forecast did not outperform the original
for 1998 (6% error compared with 2.1%). The main reason for this was the
substantial overestimation for New Zealand and the United States, which
are two moderately significant segments for South Australia. Further
research is needed into the reasons for this.

Clearly, no forecasting method should be evaluated on one year's
results. The tourist numbers for any particular market for any particular
year will always be subject to influences that are unique to the particular
situation. Frechtling (1996) suggested that forecasting methods should be
evaluated on the basis of accuracy across a number of years and that the
evaluation should include the ability to predict turning points. This
research for the South Australian data awaits the passage of time and the
accumulation of data.

Table 8.10 Comparing the accuracy of original versus updated international forecasts, 1998

Visitors' Country of Origin	Original Forecast	Updated Forecast	1998 Visitors		
			Actual	Original Error (%)	Updated Error (%)
Other Europe	104.7	98.5	97	7.9	1.5
United Kingdom/Ireland	52.2	60.3	69.1	−24.5	−12.7
United States/Canada	46.8	49.7	46.5	0.6	6.9
Other Asia	47.3	24.5	34.2	38.3	−28.4
New Zealand	34.8	35.9	27.7	25.6	29.6
Japan	18.8	17.7	16.7	12.6	6.0
Other	6.4	6.2	13.4	−52.2	−53.7
Total	311.0	322.8	304.6	2.1	6.0

Conclusion

This article has reported on an innovative approach to tourism forecasting that moderates forecasts obtained using statistical methods by consultation with tourism industry participants. The moderation process was a combination of the Delphi and expert opinion method.

The forecasts of tourism numbers for the major markets for the state of South Australia were evaluated during a 3-year period post-forecast. The forecast accuracy for international visitors was found to be quite high overall (MAPE of 3.0%). However, this apparent accuracy disguised some significant inaccuracy for particular segments, such as New Zealand and Other Asia.

This result illustrates the difficulty of using time-series-type approaches to tourism forecasting in situations where the numbers are quite small and subject to significant variability. In the Australian context, this study has specifically highlighted the difficulty associated with adopting the top-down approach to tourism forecasting, whereby an individual state's historical share of a given market is applied to national tourism forecasts to derive a state-based forecast. With South Australia accounting for only 4% of international visitor nights to Australia, particular segments will always be subject to variation due to specific circumstances. The inaccuracy of the forecasts produced by the top-down approach highlights the need to avoid simply accepting national forecast trends as being indicative of what individual states can expect to achieve. In cases where such markets do not dominate a state's tourism market to the extent to which they do the country as a whole, the time-series modeling approach to tourism based on state-specific historical data is preferred. In the case of some markets, however, the moderation process appears to have worked well in allowing for technical forecasting and market-specific issues to be ascertained in some market segments prior to the finalization of the forecasts.

Despite the highly acceptable performance of overall domestic market forecasts in this study (MAPE of 10%), forecasts for the smaller individual segments were characterized by highly inaccurate forecasts.

References

Athiyaman, A., and R W. Robertson (1992) Time Series Forecasting Techniques: Short-Term Planning in Tourism. *International Journal of Contemporary Hospitality Management*, 4 (4): 8–11.

Bureau of Tourism Research (1996) *1996 Domestic Tourism Monitor*. Canberra: BTR.

—— (1997) *1997 Domestic Tourism Monitor*. Canberra: BTR.

—— (1998) *1998 National Visitor Survey*. Canberra: BTR.

—— (1997) *1996 International Visitor Survey*. Canberra: BTR.

—— (1998) *1997 International Visitor Survey*. Canberra: BTR.

—— (1999) *1998 International Visitor Survey*. Canberra: BTR.

Calantone, R. J., C. A. di Benedetto, and D. Bojanic (1987) A Comprehensive Review of the Tourism Forecasting Literature. *Journal of Travel Research*, 26 (2): 28–39.

Choy, D.J.L. (1984) Forecasting Tourism Revisited. *Tourism Management*, 5: 171–76.

Crouch, G. (1995) A Meta-Analytic Study of International Tourism Demand. *Annals of Tourism Research*, 22: 103–18.

Evans, G. (1996) Planning for the British Millennium Festival: Establishing the Visitor Baseline and a Framework for Forecasting. *Festival Management & Event Tourism*, 3: 183–96.

Faulkner, B. (1987) The Delphi Technique: A Tool for Forecasting and Strategic Planning. In *Strategic Planning for Tourism: Papers of the 1987 Australian Travel Research Workshop*. Perth: Australian Tourism Research Committee, pp. 44–81.

Faulkner, B., M. Oppermann, and E. Fredline (1999) Destination Competitiveness: An Exploratory Examination of South Australia's Core Attractions. *Journal of Vacation Marketing*, 5 (2): 125–39.

Faulkner, B. and P. Valerio (1995) Towards an Integrative Approach to Tourism Demand Forecasting. *Tourism Management*, 16 (1): 29–37.

Frechtling, D. C. (1996) *Practical Tourism Forecasting*. Oxford, UK: Butterworth-Heinemann.

Hamal, K. (1996) Modelling Domestic Holiday Tourism Demand in Australia: Problems and Solutions. Paper presented at the conference of the Asia Pacific Tourism Association, Townsville, Australia.

Lewis, C. D. (1982) *Industrial and Business Forecasting Methods*. London: Butterworths.

Lim, C. (1997) An Econometric Classification and Review of International Tourism Models. *Tourism Economics*, 3 (2): 69–82.

Martin, C. A., and S. F. Witt (1987) Tourism Demand Forecasting Models: Choice of Appropriate Variable to Represent Tourists' Cost of Living. *Tourism Management*, 8: 233–46.

Martin, C. A., and S. F. Witt (1989) Accuracy of Econometric Forecasts of Tourism. *Annals of Tourism Research*, 16: 407–28.

Mules, T. (1998) Decomposition of Australian Tourist Expenditure. *Tourism Management*, 19 (3): 267–72.

Mules, T., B. Faulkner, and C. Tideswell (1996) *South Australian Tourism Forecasts, 1996–2005*. Research Report. Centre for Tourism & Hotel Management Research, Griffith University, Gold Coast, Australia.

Mules, T. and S. McDonald (1994) The Economic Impact of Special Events: The Use of Forecasts. *Festival Management and Event Tourism*, 2 (1): 45–54.

Pindyck, R. S, and D. L. Rubinfeld (1991) *Econometric Models and Economic Forecasts*. New York: McGraw-Hill.

Poole, M. (1988) *Forecasting Methodology*. BTR Occasional Paper No. 3, Bureau of Tourism Research, Canberra, Australia.

Turner, L., N. Kulendran, and H. Fernando (1997) Univariate Modelling Using Periodic and Non-Periodic Analysis: Inbound Tourism to Japan, Australia and New Zealand Compared. *Tourism Economics*, 3 (2):39–56.

Uysal, M., and J. L. Crompton (1985) An Overview of Approaches Used to Forecast Tourism Demand. *Journal of Travel Research*, 23 (Spring): 7–15.

Witt, S. F. and C. A. Martin (1987) Econometric Models for Forecasting International Tourism Demand. *Journal of Travel Research*, 25: 23–30.

Witt, S. F., G. D. Newbould and A. J. Watkins (1992) Forecasting Domestic Tourism Demand: Application to Las Vegas Arrivals Data. *Journal of Travel Research*, 31 (1): 36–41.

Witt, S. F. and C. A. Witt (1991) Tourism Forecasting: Error Magnitude, Direction of Change Error, and Trend Change Error. *Journal of Travel Research*, 30 (2): 26–33.

—— (1992) *Modeling and Forecasting Demand in Tourism*. London: Academic Press.

Chapter 9

Chaos and Complexity in Tourism: In Search of a New Perspective

Bill Faulkner and Roslyn Russell

The multifaceted nature of tourism and the relative recency of its emergence as a distinct field of study has meant that research in this area has been essentially multidisciplinary (Gunn 1994; Graburn and Jafari 1991). Historically, therefore, established social sciences disciplines, such as sociology, psychology, anthropology, economics, and geography, have provided the theoretical and methodological foundation for much of the tourism research that has been carried out. With the research traditions of these disciplines, we have inherited an overriding paradigm that has, arguably, been both functional and productive in terms of enhancing our understanding of tourism phenomena. On the other hand, however, it can also be argued that the prevailing paradigm is limited and alternative perspectives are necessary if new insights into the nature of tourism are to be generated.

The aim of this article is to initiate discussion on the development of alternative frameworks for explaining tourism phenomena. We set the scene by focusing on the limitations of the so-called Newtonian (or Cartesian) model of scientific inquiry, which has dominated the social sciences and, therefore, our approach to tourism research. These limitations have been highlighted most cogently by authors such as Capra (1975, 1982), who has emphasized the deficiencies of seeking to understand systems by dissecting them into their component parts and assuming that the relationships between these parts resemble a static clockwork mechanism. Building on this argument, there has been a range of authors who have drawn attention to the relevance of chaos and complexity to our understanding of both natural and social phenomena (Davies and Gribbin 1992; Gleick 1987; Prigogine and Stengers 1985; Waldrop 1992). The implications of this body of research with regard to our understanding of tourism phenomena are explored by identifying parallels between patterns of tourism development and various elements of chaos

205

and complexity, and by reinterpreting Butler's destination life cycle model in terms of this perspective.

Alternative Paradigms: Newton and "New Physics"

Analogy has the potential to play a central role as a tool for scientific theory building to the extent that it helps us to visualize systems and thus comprehend relationships. The utility of such an approach is that it enables phenomena in one domain of investigation to be interpreted in terms of another, which is more readily understood, or in relation to which we have an established "calculus" for interpretation (Bunge 1964: 5, 1970; Caws 1965: 127; Hempel 1965: 440; Harvey 1969: 153). Given this, it is not surprising that the certain parallels between physical and human systems have been exploited in the development of theory in the social sciences. In the tourism field, the use of gravity models in forecasting tourism demand stands as one of the more obvious examples of this (Ellis and Van Doren 1996; Freund and Wilson 1974; Van Doorn 1984; Wolfe 1972). However, the physical sciences have influenced the progress of social research in a more profound way than examples such as this suggest.

The physical sciences in general, and physics in particular, have been looked upon by social scientists as epitomizing the standards of rigor and precision that they should emulate. Conventional (neoclassical) economics has carried this to such an extreme that Toohey (1994) accuses the discipline of "physics envy," which he describes as an apparent assumption that what the precision physics has achieved in the study of inanimate objects can be achieved in the study of human economic behavior. He notes that "[the] enthusiasm of early neoclassical economists for cloaking themselves in the authority of physics has not waned among their 20th century successors, even if the enormous changes in physics since the 19th century have gone largely unnoticed" (Toohey 1994: 18). Ironically, as alluded to in these comments, the paradigm of physics adopted by economics and other social sciences in the early 20th century has been substantially displaced, and the failure of social scientists to appreciate this shift has meant that important insights arising from the "new" physics have not yet filtered through to produce new perspectives in their respective fields. To elaborate on this point, and appreciate its implications for tourism research, it is necessary for us to first examine the changes that have occurred in physics.

The Cartesian-Newtonian world view upon which classical physics and other branches of both the natural and social sciences have been based was derived from the 17th century philosopher, Descartes, who saw nature as a perfect machine that is governed by precise mathematical laws. This vision was realized by Newton, who developed a complete mathematical formulation of the mechanistic view of nature, and thus accomplished a grand synthesis of the works of Copernicus and Kepler, Bacon, Galileo, and Descartes (Capra 1982: 48–49). Newton's success encouraged a reductionist view of the world, where objects and events could be understood in terms of their constituent parts and where these parts fit together like cogs in a cosmic machine. Thus, according to this view, every event is determined by initial conditions that are, at least in principle, predictable with precision.

Although the technological advances that have driven the emergence of modern industrial (and post-industrial) society would appear to have vindicated the Cartesian-Newtonian paradigm, the limitations of this paradigm became more apparent as physicists have strived to unravel the mysteries of subatomic phenomena at one extreme and the outer reaches of the cosmos at the other. Thus, a new wave of thought has grown out of Einstein's theory of relativity, quantum mechanics, Heisenberg's uncertainty principle, and, more recently, chaos theory (Capra 1982) to challenge the mechanistic world view. The linear, machine vocabulary of classical physics is being challenged by concepts that depict a confusing world of non-linearity, spontaneity, and surprise, juxtaposed with attributes normally associated with living organisms, such as adaptation, coherence, and organization (Davies and Gribbin 1992). In their analysis of the implications of these developments, Davies and Gribbin (1992) offer the following interpretation:

> Physicist Joseph Ford has described the materialistic, mechanistic paradigm as one of the "founding myths" of classical science. Myths of course are not literal expressions of truth. Are we to suppose, then, that the immense progress made in science during the past three hundred years is rooted in a complete misconception about the nature of nature? No, this would be to misunderstand the role of scientific paradigms. A particular paradigm is neither right nor wrong, but merely reflects a perspective, an aspect of reality that may prove more or less fruitful depending on circumstance-just as a myth, although not literally true, may contain allegorical insights that prove more or less fruitful depending on circumstances. In the event, the mechanistic paradigm proved so successful that there has been an almost universal tendency to identify it with reality, to see it not as a facet of truth but as the whole truth. Now, increasing numbers of scientists are coming to recognise the limitations of the materialistic view of nature, and to appreciate that there is more to the world than cogs in a gigantic machine. (p. 3)

With regard to the progress of tourism research, there are two fundamentally important implications of this interpretation of developments in physics. First, if these reservations are being expressed about the ability of the mechanistic framework to explain the behavior of inanimate objects, then its applicability to the explanation of human behavior that provides the basis for tourism phenomena must also be questioned. Second, just as the Cartesian-Newtonian model has proven to be inappropriate for certain domains of physical phenomena, there may be certain domains of tourism where this approach is less effective and where, as a consequence, the applicability of the alternative perspective ought to be explored.

Prigogine and Stengers (1985) have argued that traditional science in "the age of the machine" tended to emphasize stability, order, uniformity, and equilibrium. It concerned itself mostly with closed systems and linear relationships in which small inputs uniformly yield small results. This preoccupation has meant that aspects of reality that exemplify tendencies towards instability, disorder, disequilibrium, and non-linearity have received less attention and are, in effect, assumed away. Thus, in his critique of modern Economics, Toohey (1994: 4) has observed that something had to be excluded to create the elegance so often admired in the equations used to describe these types of closed, steady-state systems. In the neoclassical sense, some of the most interesting questions to confront modern society are excluded from consideration. In the jargon, they are regarded as exogenous or external to the system.

Toohey's comments have a particular poignancy when the fixation of modern economists and other social scientists on stability, equilibrium, and linearity is viewed in the context of concerns raised by social commentators such as Toffler (1970). By highlighting the accelerating pace of (technology-driven) change in modern society, the associated destabilization of social relationships and increasing levels of uncertainty, Toffler (1970) has drawn attention to the mounting pressure on adaptive capabilities at both the institutional and individual level. Clearly, in such an environment, we can expect instability, disorder, disequilibrium, and non-linearity to be more prevalent. An alternative framework that is more attuned to these phenomena is, therefore, necessary and it is in this context that the Chaos and Complexity perspective has emerged.

A number of authors (most notably, Gleick 1987; Peat 1991; Prigogine and Stengers 1985) have drawn parallels between physical and living systems in terms of their chaos tendencies. According to Peat (1991), chaos is not just an absence or apparent lack of order, but rather "a new order so rich and subtle that it lies beyond any pattern of periodicity" (p. 196). He adds that "chaos is an order of infinite complexity" and in order to properly describe and explain it we need an infinite amount of information. Just as analogies drawn from apparently simpler systems were instrumental in the extension of the Cartesian-Newtonian model to the social sciences, the following description of chaos phenomena in social systems relies on a metaphorical approach.

Chaos and Complexity: Towards a New Perspective

To recap, and elaborate on, points regarding the chaos perspective raised above, there are several key propositions regarding the fundamental properties of complex systems. These are summarized in Table 9.1, where the corresponding position of the Cartesian-Newtonian model is also represented. As emphasized in this table, the living systems metaphor is central to the chaos perspective.

Proponents of the alternative perspective have argued that the Cartesian-Newtonian paradigm is moribund because its dissection (analysis) of systems into their component parts results in us seeing the world in terms of static clockwork mechanisms. Conventional, "top-down" analysis (as opposed to bottom-up synthesis) results in individual parts being examined in isolation with mechanistic clock-like relationships being assumed. We, therefore, tend to lose sight of the fact that "the whole is greater than the sum of its parts" and there is a dynamic life-like, emergent complexity in many systems (Capra 1982).

The notion of "bottom-up synthesis" provides the key to appreciating the processes that drive the immense variety of forms among lifelike systems, and hence the seemingly contradictory juxtaposition of order and chaos alluded to by Prigogine and Stengers (1985). Life has often been viewed as involving an energy, force, or spirit that transcends mere matter. However, as Waldrop (1992) observes, living systems transcend matter not so much because they "are animated by some vital essence outside the laws of physics and chemistry, but because a population of small things following simple rules of interaction can behave in eternally surprising ways" (p. 280). Thus, the essence of complex, life-like systems lies in their bottom-up organization, whereby individual agents driven by simple rules provide the basis of the emergence of a complex dynamic system. The classic example used by Waldrop to illustrate this point is Reynold's "boids" experiment, in which the complex behavior of flocking birds was simulated using a series of agents ("boids") whose individual behavior was governed by three simple rules (Waldrop 1992: 242). However, the outstanding manifestation of this phenomenon is the huge diversity of individual human differences (phenotypes) generated by a process that hinges on a simple set of rules governing the interactions between genes.

This feature of life-like or self-organizing systems partly explains the paradox of the Second Law of Thermodynamics. According to this law, there is an inexorable increase in entropy, whereby the universe is supposed to run down as atoms try to randomize. Yet, as observed by Waldrop (1992: 2860), if we have increasing levels of randomness and disorder at the atomic scale, why is matter constantly becoming more and more organized on a large scale? Clearly, if simple rules of behavior

Table 9.1 The Cartesian – Newtonian versus chaos – complexity models

Cartesian – Newtonian Model	Chaos – Complexity Model
Based on 19th century Newtonian physics (deterministic, reductionist, clockwork model).	Based on biological model of living systems (structure, patterns, self-organization).
Systems seen as structurally simple, with a tendency towards linear or quasi-linear relationships between variables.	Systems viewed as inherently complex, with a tendency towards nonlinear relationships being more prevalent.
Systems tend towards equilibrium and are driven by negative feedback.	Systems are inherently unstable and positive feedback-driven processes are more common.
Individual differences, externalities, and exogenous influences that create deviations from the norm are exceptional, noise-generating factors.	Individual differences and random externalities provide the driving force for variety, adaptation, and complexity.

Adapted from Toohey (1994: 286) and Waldrop (1992: 37–38).

governing individual particles (agents) can give rise to astonishingly complicated and highly structured arrangements at the macro-level, the random perturbations of individual particles simply become initiators of the constant flux of structures (emergence, coalescence, decay) that can be observed at this level. The dynamics of these processes have been described in terms of the so-called "butterfly effect" (Gleick 1987) and "edge of chaos" phenomena (Waldrop 1992).

The butterfly effect describes a situation where a small change or perturbation in the condition of an individual particle can precipitate a chain reaction that culminates in a fundamental shift in the structure of a system or a dramatic event. Thus, a butterfly flapping its wings in Beijing is said to be capable of initiating a series of events that produces a cyclone in Florida (Gleick 1987: 20–23). We therefore have a contrast between systems of this sort and those emphasized in the Cartesian-Newtonian paradigm, where the effects of such disturbances are ameliorated by negative feedback processes and equilibrium is eventually restored. In life-like or self-organizing systems, on the other hand, positive feedback and nonlinear relationships are more prevalent. The effects of even minor random disturbances are accentuated and magnified by mutually re-inforcing positive feedback loops as agents within the system adjust to changing configurations and linkages, and find new niches in the emerging structure.

Although the positive feedback-driven, self-organizing tendencies described above imply systems in a constant state of flux, these tend-encies can also be, paradoxically, responsible for inertial effects. Thus, Waldrop (1992: 38–39) refers to "lock-in" phenomena to describe situations where accidents of history have certain lasting effects long after their initial impact was felt. He uses the example of the QWERTY keyboard to demonstrate this effect. The QWERTY keyboard continues to be universally used even though the reasons for its original adoption (i.e., to prevent the keys of the most frequently used letters of the alphabet from locking together in mechanical typewriters) have been superseded by modern technology. Alternatively, therefore, "lock-in" also describes a situation where an innovation of the past has a lasting effect despite changes in the conditions that originally made it necessary.

The final concept associated with the alternative perspective that we are considering for the purposes of this article concerns the condition of dynamic systems Waldrop refers to as "edge of chaos" phenomena. Edge of chaos is a situation (analogous to phase shifts in physics) where a system is in a state of tenuous equilibrium, on the verge of "collapsing" into a rapidly changing state of dynamic evolution. Drawing on a metaphor originated by Per Bak for the purposes of elaboration, Waldrop (1992: 304) asks the reader to imagine a pile of sand on a tabletop with a steady trickle of new grains being poured from above. As the pile grows higher and higher, it eventually reaches a point where it can't grow any more and "old sand is cascading down the sides and off the edge of the table as fast as the new sand dribbles down." The result is a "self-organizing" system that reaches a steady state of its own accord, and it has reached a point of "criticality" in the sense that sand grains on the surface are just barely stable. The point of criticality is described in the following way by Per Bak:

> So when a falling grain hits there's no telling what might happen. Maybe nothing. Maybe just a tiny shift in a few grains. Or maybe, if one tiny collision leads to another in just the right chain reaction, a catastrophic landslide will take off one whole face of the sand pile. (Quoted in Waldrop 1992: 305)

The implications of this metaphor are summed up in the following way:

> The sand pile metaphor suggests an answer, he [Per Bak] says. Just as a steady trickle of sand drives a sand pile to organize itself into a critical state, a steady input of energy, water or electrons drives a great many systems in nature to organise themselves in the same way. They become a mass of interlocking subsystems just barely on the edge of criticality – with breakdowns of all sizes ripping through and rearranging things just often enough to keep them poised on the edge. (Waldrop 1992: 305)

Extending this further, Waldrop explains how the principle of criticality described in the sand metaphor might apply more widely by referring to a stable ecosystem or a mature industrial sector in which all the component agents have adapted to each other. He points out that, whereas in such systems there may be little or no evolutionary pressure to change, agents within it can nevertheless not stay as they are forever. If just one agent experiences a mutation large enough to knock it out of equilibrium, this is enough to create the necessity for neighbours to change and adjust, which in turn might induce an avalanche of changes until some new equilibrium is reached. But the essential message is that no such equilibrium is permanent. There is a punctuated equilibrium, with long periods of stasis being interrupted by bursts of evolutionary change, which may be triggered by a single event that precipitates the extinction of unsustainable or unfit "organisms." As Kauffman (in Waldrop 1992) observes, "the maximum fitness is occurring right at the phase transition. So the crux is, as if by an invisible hand, all the players change their landscape, each to its own advantage, and the whole system coevolves to the edge of chaos" (p. 313).

Technological innovation is potentially a common initiator of phase shifts in many domains of human activity, including tourism. Thus, with the invention of the internal combustion engine and the widespread individual mobility this eventually permitted, a complex web of facilities evolved to service car-based tourists (highway networks, service stations, motels, etc.). These webs are inherently dynamic and unstable because technological webs can experience bursts of evolutionary creativity that result in whole sub-networks collapsing or becoming extinct as they are superseded by new ones. The car-oriented web, for instance, displaced railway systems that included tourist accommodation in close proximity to railway stations and feeder transport services, just as information technology is precipitating new configurations in the tourism industry today (Poon 1993). With the introduction of new technology new niches for the provision of goods and services emerge and, as these niches are consolidated, inertia sets in to resist change and thus encourage lock-in phenomena. However, as innovation feeds on itself and is in part a consequence of finding new combinations of old technologies, we can expect the threshold necessary to precipitate phase transition to be achieved with increasing frequency in the future.

Manifestations of Chaos and Complexity in Tourism

In the discussion so far, we have identified four concepts that encapsulate fundamental aspects of the chaos-complexity perspective. These are described in summary form in Table 9.2, where examples of their manifestations in the tourism domain are also indicated.

Among the examples used in the table, we can distinguish between those that refer to macro-level events and others that are essentially concerned with impacts at the micro-level. Thus, the reference to the Las Vegas example is clearly a micro-level effect because it concerns a single destination, whereas the phase transition initiated by the introduction of the automobile is clearly a more generalized, macro-level event. It may be that the use of the chaos-complexity perspective to explore the linkages between events at these two levels may provide the basis of a new and potentially insightful area of tourism research. To expand on this point, we have referred to Butler's Destination Life Cycle Model (Butler 1980), which is reinterpreted in terms of the chaos-complexity perspective below.

Butler's model draws upon the product life cycle (PLC) concept originating from the discipline of marketing to describe the evolution of tourist destinations. The PLC is based on the proposition that a product's sales follow an asymptotic S-shaped curve, reflecting its passage through different stages of market performance-introduction, growth, maturity, and decline. Similarly, Butler envisages tourist destinations experiencing a series of developmental stages, beginning with exploration and progressing to involvement, development, consolidation, and culminating in stagnation and decline when the carrying capacity has been exceeded

Table 9.2 Basic concepts of chaos and complexity and corresponding examples in tourism

Concept	Tourism Elements/Examples
Bottom-up synthesis: individual agents driven by simple rules of transaction give rise to complex, dynamic systems.	• Host – guest relationship between visitors and residents. • Client – service provider relationship between tourist and tourism industry. • Competitive relationships between providers of similar services/products. • Cooperative relationships between vertically integrated providers or coalitions of providers at a single destination. • Regulator-regulatee relationship between public and private sector agents.
Butterfly effect: initial small random change or perturbation induces a chain reaction that precipitates a dramatic event or shift of considerable magnitude.	• Relaxation of legal restrictions on gambling in Nevada initiates development of Las Vegas as major tourist destination. • Terrorist activities in Europe in the 1980s boost international arrivals in safe destinations such as Australia (Faulkner 1990).
Lock-in effect: where accidents of history have a lasting effect long after the conditions that influenced their initial impact have subsided or where innovations have a lasting effect despite being superseded by new technology.	• The Las Vegas example (i.e, in the sense that this destination has maintained and enhanced its position in spite of Nevada no longer being the only state in the US to have legalized gambling).
Edge of chaos (phase shift): a state of tenuous equilibrium whereby small changes ("mutations") involving individual agents may be enough to precipitate evolutionary change in the system through mutual adaptation of its constituents.	• Displacement of a railway-based system of tourist services by a car-based network. • Phase shifts in the life cycle of destinations.

and/or the destination's assets are degraded. However, Butler also recognizes the possibility of a turning point along the curve, at which decline and demise can be averted by rejuvenation and vitalization.

Since its inception, Butler's model has proven to be a valuable heuristic tool in analyzing and understanding the evolution of tourist destinations. While many case studies (Choy 1992; Cohen 1982; Hovinen 1981) have highlighted deviations from Butler's model, few have disputed its value to tourism management. By using such a framework for analyzing the development of a destination, we can identify the many variables and "turning points" that have influenced the evolution of tourism in a region (Russell 1995). In terms of the chaos-complexity perspective, we can envisage the successive phases of the Butler cycle as being driven by essentially random events, each of which triggers a positive feedback process culminating in a new plane of tourist activity. Thus, for instance, at the involvement stage, random encounters between a trickle of visitors and local residents induces the latter to begin offering services on a commercial basis. The provision of services by a few opens up new opportunities for others and before long there is a complex web of tourism-oriented service providers and the market responds by arriving in greater numbers as the attractiveness of the area is enhanced. Each stage of the cycle represents a period of instability, which is being driven by fundamental shifts in relationships between the various parties involved. An intense process of mutual adaptation among individual agents occurs as old niches become redundant, new opportunities emerge, markets shift, and competitive relationships change. Meanwhile, specific manifestations of the butterfly effect and lock-in phenomenon at individual destinations will either impede or facilitate the growth of tourism, and add to the varying patterns of tourism development at this level.

In one respect, Butler's stagnation stage epitomizes the point of criticality referred to in the description of "edge of chaos" or phase shift phenomenon, as this stage represents a point of tenuous equilibrium at which the system (tourist destination) is at the edge of a dramatic transformation that could have distinctly different outcomes (i.e., ranging from rejuvenation to absolute decline). However, it might be that destinations are at the edge of chaos at all stages of their evolution. That is, there is an ever present prospect of events precipitating dramatic transformations at individual destinations, irrespective of the stage reached according to Butler's model. In other words, tourist destinations are perpetually in a state that resembles Per Bak's pile of sand. The sequence depicted in the model is therefore not inevitable and, accordingly, cases where the cycle is truncated might be just as numerous as those that conform with the expected pattern. Destinations that undergo a precipitous decline immediately after reaching the involvement stage owing to some random political or natural event, for instance, are hardly likely to attract much research attention.

Although the factors that influence the evolution of tourism at an individual destination are often unique to that destination, transformations at this level are nevertheless often initiated by broader level shifts at the macro-level. Thus, the transition from railway- to automobile-based mass tourism may have been simultaneously instrumental in precipitating a phase shift towards decline in some destinations (i.e., those where tourism development hinged on an advantageous position vis à vis railway systems) and accelerated growth in others that could capitalize on the increased mobility of tourists.

Given these observations, a potentially fruitful approach to the further development of the chaos-complexity perspective in tourism might be to explore the incidence, interrelationships and underlying dynamics of phase shift phenomena at the macro- and micro-levels. In this context, as illustrated in Figure 9.1, the macro- and micro-levels represent poles in the spectrum of the geographical scales of investigation. At one extreme, we have systems, events, and phenomena that are global in scope, whereas at the other we have individual destinations or even individual consumers as the focus of attention. At either level, a phase shift might be triggered by a social, political, economic, technological, or natural event that necessitates adjustments in the configuration of relationships between individual agents, and this process is driven by positive feedback mechanisms that might be manifest in instances of the butterfly or lock-in effects. Although we might expect that phase shifts at the macro-level will often provide the source of changes that initiates a chain reaction of shifts at lower levels, the bottom-up synthesis factor serves to remind us of the fact that "mutations" can be initiated at any level.

Conclusion

As tourism research is largely a multidisciplinary field of study, there is no identifiable pre-eminent general theory in this area, as is the case in many of the sciences and traditional social sciences such as economics. However, tourism research in general can be described as adhering to the Cartesian-Newtonian paradigm to the extent that the theory and methodologies we have applied are derived from disciplines that have been modeled on this approach. The analysis of the nature of chaos and complexity contained in this article identifies fundamental limitations of this paradigm, which suggest an alternative perspective is necessary. This does not necessarily imply that a paradigm shift in the Kuhnian sense is required (Kuhn 1962), but rather that room should be made for a diversification of perspectives. As Davies and Gribbin (1992) have emphasized, an approach to scientific investigation involving the adoption of

paradigms according to their utility in specific situations is more pragmatic and potentially more productive. Thus, rather than assuming that
the alternative paradigms are mutually exclusive, each should be applied
to certain domains of phenomenon within a field, depending on where
they prove to be more or less useful.

The potential utility of the chaos-complexity perspective to generate
new insights into the nature and dynamics of tourism has been explored;

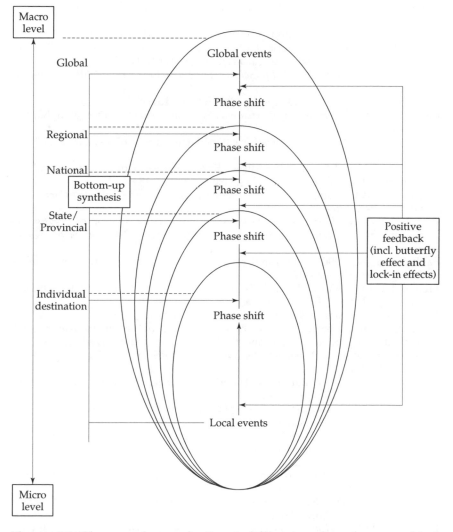

Figure 9.1 Chaos and complexity at different scales of geographical
resolution

first, by observing examples of tourism phenomena that illustrate butterfly and lock-in effects and, second, by reinterpreting the destination life cycle in terms of Waldrop's (1992) edge of chaos (phase shift) metaphor. This latter exercise revealed that, whereas Butler's destination Life Cycle Model implicitly recognized the life-like characteristics of social phenomenon emphasized by the chaos-complexity perspective, this perspective has the potential to enrich our analysis of tourism.

References

Bunge, M. (1964) *The Critical Approach to Science and Philosophy*. London: The Free Press of Glencoe.
—— (1970) Analogy, simulation, representation. *General Systems*, 15, 27–34.
Butler, R. W. (1980) The concept of a tourist area cycle of evolution: Implications for management of resources. *Canadian Geographer*, 24(1), 5–12.
Capra, F. (1982) *The Turning Point: Science, Society and the Rising Culture*. London: Flamingo.
—— (1975) *The Tao of Physics*. London: Wildwood House.
Caws, P. (1965) *The Philosophy of Science: A Systematic Account*. Princeton, NJ: Van Nostrand.
Choy, D. (1992) Life cycle models for Pacific Island destinations. *Journal of Travel Research*, 30(3), 26–31.
Cohen, E. (1982) Marginal paradises: Bungalow tourism on the islands of Southern Thailand. *Annals of Tourism Research*, 9(2), 189–228.
Davies, P. and Gribbin, J. (1992) *The Matter Myth: Beyond Chaos and Complexity*. London: Penguin.
Ellis, B. J. and Van Doren, C. S. (1996) A comparative evaluation of gravity and systems theory models for statewide recreational traffic flow. *Journal of Regional Sciences*, 6, 57–70.
Faulkner, H. W. (1990) Swings and roundabouts in Australian tourism. *Tourism Management*, 11(1), 29–37.
Freund, J. R., and Wilson, R. R. (1974) An example of a gravity model to estimate recreational travel. *Journal of Leisure Research*, 6, 241–256.
Gleick, J. (1987) *Chaos: Making a New Science*. London: Heinemann.
Gunn, C. (1994) A perspective on the purpose and nature of tourism research methods. In J. R. B. Ritchie and C. R. Goeldner (eds), *Travel, Tourism and Hospitality Research: A Handbook for Managers and Researchers* (2nd ed., pp. 3–11). New York: John Wiley.
Graburn, N. H. H., and Jafari, J. (eds) (1991) Tourism social science [Special issue]. *Annals of Tourism Research*, 18(1).
Harvey, D. (1969) *Explanation in Geography*. London: Edward Arnold.
Hempel, C. G. (1965) *Aspects of Scientific Explanation and Other Essays in the Philosophy of Science*. New York: The Free Press.
Hovinen, G. R. (1981) A tourist cycle in Lancaster County, Pennsylvania. *Canadian Geographer*, 25 (3), 283–286.
Kuhn, T. S. (1962) *The Structure of Scientific Revolutions* (2nd ed.). Chicane: University of Chicane Press.
Peat, F. D. (1991) *The Philosopher's Stone: Chaos, Synchronicity and the Hidden Order of the World*. New York: Bantam.
Poon, A. (1993) *Tourism, Technology and Competitive Strategies*. Wallingford: CAB International.

Prigogine, I., and Stengers, I. (1985) *Order Out of Chaos: Man's New Dialogue with Nature*. Hammersmith: Flamingo.

Russell, R. (1995) *Tourism Development in Coolangatta: An Historical Perspective*. Honours thesis, Griffith University, Gold Coast.

Toffler, A. (1970) *Future Shock*. London: Bodley Head.

Toohey, B. (1994) *Tumbling Dice*. Melbourne: Heinemann.

Van Doorn, J. W. (1984) Tourism forecasting techniques: A brief overview. In J. W. Van Doorn (ed.), *Problems of Tourism* (Vol. 23, pp. 7–15).

Waldrop, M. (1992) *Complexity: The Emerging Science and the Edge of Order and Chaos*. London: Simon and Schuster/Penguin.

Wolfe, R. L. (1972) The inertia model. *Journal of Leisure Research*, 4, 73–76.

Chapter 10

Movers and Shakers: Chaos Makers in Tourism Development

Roslyn Russell and Bill Faulkner

1 Introduction

Tourist behaviour and tourism development patterns have generally been viewed in terms of the Cartesian or Newtonian paradigm of scientific inquiry, with attention being focused on aspects of these phenomena that display a tendency towards linear relationships, equilibrium and structural simplicity. This approach is founded on a reductionist position, which sees small changes in the initial conditions of a system being invariably reflected in small changes in the final state. Through the lens provided by the traditional approach, individual differences that deviate from the norm are too frequently dismissed as exceptions, and events or actions that add to the diversity of responses are assumed away as noise generating factors. As a consequence of this filtering process, researchers in the tourism field have often overlooked the key events (and individuals) which are ultimately responsible for triggering major shifts in the configuration of tourist behaviour and development. Our understanding of the dynamics of change in tourism has suffered as a consequence.

Chaos/Complexity Theory provides an alternative perspective, which enables us to gain a deeper understanding of the change process. In contrast to the traditional paradigm described above, chaos theory sees systems as being inherently complex and unstable. Small changes, individual differences and random externalities are therefore recognised as having the potential to precipitate major realignments in systems through disequilibriating positive feedback processes. Non-linear relationships therefore prevail in such systems, which are driven by self-organising and adaptive tendencies to produce new complex ('emergent') configurations.

The Chaos perspective has provided a useful framework for analysing the history of tourism development on the Gold Coast, one of Australia's major seaside resorts. Here, specific phases in tourism development can be associated with the actions of individual entrepreneurs, who were each responsible for an innovation that initiated a sequence of changes culminating in a major shift in the structure of tourism activities. The sequence of changes that the Gold Coast has experienced can therefore be interpreted in terms of the tension between the entrepreneurs (the chaos makers) and planners and regulators (the dampeners), whose actions are generally focused on moderating and controlling change. Periods of rapid change, which are characterised by the chaos perspective, occur when the chaos-makers prevail over the dampeners.

In the investigation of the entrepreneurial activity and its impact on the development of tourism on the Gold Coast, an historiographic approach was utilised, including the use of oral histories, archival documents (newspapers and Gold Coast City Council records), and photographic evidence. Although historical data is inherently fragmentary and subjective, verification of the information was achieved by adopting a triangulation method using a combination of various sources (Janesick 1994).

In developing the theme of linking entrepreneurship and Chaos Theory, with the practical application of the Gold Coast case study, the paper begins with an overview of recent research on the role of entrepreneurs in tourism development. Principles of the chaos/complexity perspective are then outlined to provide a framework for the analysis of the entrepreneurial process that follows. The Gold Coast case study, and particularly the role of two entrepreneurs in the development of this destination, is then examined for illustrative purposes.

2 Entrepreneurship in Tourism

The study of entrepreneurship is reasonably well established, with several journals specifically focusing on this subject (e.g. *Entrepreneurship Theory and Practice*; *Journal of Business Venturing*; *Journal of Business and Entrepreneurship*; *Frontiers of Entrepreneurship Research*) and a number of significant contributions over the last decade (e.g. Stevenson and Harmeling 1990; Bygrave 1993; Smilor and Feeser 1991; Stacey 1992; Storey 1994). However, the context of much of the research in this area has been manufacturing and technology based industries, rather than the service sector and tourism. While several authors have referred to aspects of entrepreneurial behaviour in tourism development (Barr 1990; Echtner 1995; Kaspar 1989; Kibedi 1979; Koh 1996; Lewis and Green 1998; Snepenger *et al.* 1995; Sofield 1993), this area of analysis has not, in general, been informed by the insights that can be provided by the chaos theory/complexity perspective. Nor has the anatomy of the entrepreneurial process been sufficiently investigated. A brief examination of research carried out in this area so far helps to put the current study into perspective.

One thrust of research on entrepreneurial aspects of tourism has highlighted the linkage between entrepreneurial decisions and the evolution of tourist destinations, as described in Butler's Destination Life Cycle (DLC) model (Butler 1980). In their examination of travel induced business migration to parts of the Greater Yellowstone Ecosystem of Montana, Snepenger *et al.* (1995) observed how this phenomenon has contributed to the diversification of the local economy. They suggest this involves an extension of the Butler's model in the sense that such migration, and the economic growth it engenders, may have ameliorated impacts of the stagnation phase of the destination life cycle. Unlike the entrepreneurial activities analysed in the Gold Coast study described below, however, few of the business migrants referred to in Snepenger *et al.* are actually engaged directly in the tourism industry. Barr's (1990) study of entrepreneurial activities in the transition of the Whitsundays has a similar emphasis as the current study, however, to the extent that he focuses on their direct involvement in tourism development. In particular, he emphasises how small-scale local entrepreneurial initiatives contributed to tourism development during the 'involvement' phase and many larger scale tourism investments in later phases were attributable to the actions of entrepreneurial migrants to the area. As in the case of some Gold Coast entrepreneurs referred to below, these migrants moved to the Whitsundays for life style reasons and their entrepreneurial inclinations meant that they could not resist responding to the tourism business opportunities the area presented.

Both of the studies referred to above concentrate on the outcomes of entrepreneurial actions, rather than the structure of the entrepreneurial process itself. Koh (1996) takes this area of research a step further by drawing on the broader literature to explore the anatomy of entrepreneurship in tourism development. He identifies several stages in the entrepreneurial process – i.e., cognitive (predisposing) orientation, opportunity search, opportunity assessment, consideration, opportunity pursuit, birth, operation, evaluation. In doing so, however, a degree of structure and logic is assumed which is unrealistic and certainly not consistent with the behaviour of tourism entrepreneurs observed below. In particular, Koh's suggestion that entrepreneurs research tourism industry statistics and rigorously seek out all available relevant information in the 'opportunity search' phase is at odds with the disdain for research many successful entrepreneurs have exhibited. Admittedly, this paper deals specifically with the few 'larger than life' entrepreneurs whose innovations initiated significant turning points in the evolution of tourism at a destination, and who therefore, might not be comparable with the 'average' entrepreneurs observed by Koh. The elements of chaos/complexity that are intrinsic to the entrepreneurial process involving the movers and shakers are therefore overlooked in most analyses, including Koh's.

The study of entrepreneurial behaviour among developers and operators in the European Alpine ski resorts by Lewis and Green (1998) emphasises the relevance of the chaos/complexity perspective in this context and is, as a consequence, more closely related to the approach adopted in the current paper. Lewis and Green distinguish between the modus operandi of entrepreneurs and managers (planners and regulators) by drawing on the chaos/steady-state dichotomy. Entrepreneurs thrive on chaos as their creative response to new opportunities which predisposes them to an approach that endeavours to circumvent constraints imposed by the managers, who aim to maintain a steady state through regulations designed to control change. In his study of indigenous tourism development in the Solomon Islands, Sofield (1993) draws attention to a situation where antiquated landuse regulations inherited from the colonial administration have stifled tourism development initiatives. Here the regulators have neutralised both indigenous and expatriate entrepreneurs. These two examples highlight the ongoing tension between the generators and the moderators of change. This theme is carried a step further in the following section, where the Chaos perspective and the contrasting orientations of entrepreneurial and planning behaviour are elaborated.

Insights into linkages between entrepreneurship and tourism provided by the literature are consolidated in Figure 10.1, where each form of entrepreneurial activity is depicted in terms of their potential bearing on the progress of Butler's (1980) Destination Life Cycle model. Thus, the local entrepreneur described by Barr (1990) is, theoretically, more prevalent at the involvement stage, migrant entrepreneurs who invest in tourism might be expected to have a more profound impact at the consolidation stage, while those described by Snepenger *et al.* (1995) have a more significant impact at the decline or rejuvenation stage. Echtner's (1995) examination of educational aspects of promoting entrepreneurship in developing countries is, implicitly, more relevant to the involvement stage. Entrepreneurial behaviour such as that described by Lewis and Green (1998) might induce turning points in the evolution of tourism at any stage throughout the cycle.

3 Chaos and Complexity

As a field of research, tourism is generally regarded as a multi-disciplinary field of study rather than a discipline in its own right (Graburn and Jafari 1991; Gunn 1994). This is largely attributable to the complex, multi-faceted nature of tourism phenomena and the relative recency of its emergence as a distinct field of study. While this feature of tourism studies has meant that research in this area has been enriched by a variety of theoretical perspectives, it has also meant that tourism research has inherited the Newtonian or Cartesian research tradition

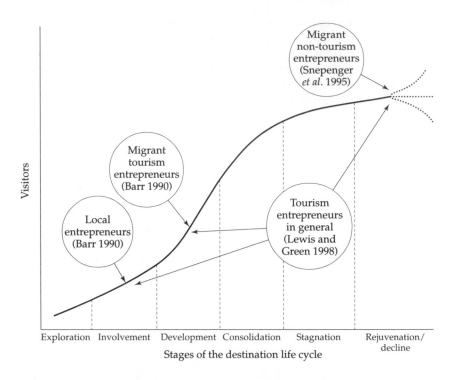

Figure 10.1 Entrepreneurs and Butler's (1980) Destination Life Cycle.

which has dominated most of the social sciences (Faulkner and Russell 1997). Although it is arguable that this approach has served us well in terms of advancing knowledge in tourism, it has also created some blind spots which have resulted in certain aspects of tourism being poorly understood. In particular, conventional approaches to tourism research are more attuned to the analysis of relatively stable systems, resulting in large gaps in the understanding of turbulent phases in tourism development and the underlying dynamics of change (Hall 1995; Faulkner 1998). While entrepreneurial behaviour is often an integral part of the change process in the sense it may either be a response to, or an initiator of change, the understanding of this type of activity in the tourism context, and its relationship with turbulence and change, has been inhibited by the limitations of the Newtonian paradigm. To expand on this point, it is necessary for us to examine the distinction between the conventional Newtonian paradigm and the alternative presented by Chaos Theory. A more detailed comparison of these two perspectives, and their implications for the interpretation of tourism issues is provided in Faulkner and Russell (1997).

The conventional, Newtonian/Cartesian paradigm is derived from classical physics and has encouraged a reductionist view of the world, whereby objects and events are understood in terms of their constituent parts which are assumed to fit together like cogs in a clockwork machine. Every event is therefore determined by initial conditions that are, at least in principle, predictable with some degree of precision owing to the predominance of linear or quasi-linear relationships. Small changes at the outset yield correspondingly small shifts in the final state of the system (Capra 1982). As Prigogine and Stengers (1985) have emphasised, this approach has tended to concentrate on those aspects of systems where stability, order, uniformity and equilibrium are accentuated. Meanwhile, situations where instability, disorder, non-linearity and disequilibrium are more prevalent tend to be construed as aberrations and are therefore ignored, and variations from the 'norm' that offend the elegance of conventional explanatory frameworks are often assumed away as being attributable to 'noise' or 'exogenous factors' (Toohey 1994). The fact that such variations have the potential to signal an underlying turbulence which may precipitate fundamental shifts in the system means that our understanding of the dynamics of change is limited.

Chaos Theory and the associated complexity perspective offers a more meaningful framework for examining and understanding change by virtue of its appreciation of turbulence as a feature of most systems. Many closed systems which normally exhibit the steady-state characteristics characterised by the Newtonian model are periodically disturbed by changes in their environment or internal structural changes, which precipitate a period of turbulence until a new steady-state configuration is established. In this context, chaos should not be seen as simply a lack of order or a condition reflecting the degeneration of a system, but rather as a creative phase leading to a new, more complex order (Peat 1991). There is therefore a linkage between chaos and the notion of complexity.

A key distinction between the key propositions of the Chaos/Complexity perspective that distinguishes it from the Newtonian/Cartesian view draws on the living systems metaphor (Gleick 1987; Peat 1991; Prigogine and Stengers 1985), which in turn highlights the complexity factor. The reductionist approach of the Newtonian paradigm dissects systems into their component parts and interprets the behaviour of the system additively in terms of the static relationships between these parts. Individual parts are examined in isolation, with mechanistic, clock-like relationships being assumed. We therefore lose sight of the potential for situations to arise where synergies result in 'the whole being greater than the sum of its parts' and where the system exhibits a dynamic, life-like emergent complexity (Capra 1982). The Chaos perspective captures the life-like, self-organising characteristics of systems. It appreciates that systems are inherently complex and unstable, and focuses attention on the prevalence of non-linear relationships. Of particular relevance to this paper's interest in the role of entrepreneurs is the proposition that individual differences and random externalities provide the driving force for variety, adaptation and complexity.

Several concepts associated with the Chaos/Complexity perspective have particular relevance to our interpretation of the role of entrepreneurs in tourism development. The first of these concerns the 'butterfly effect' described by Gleick (1987), whereby a small and apparently insignificant change or perturbation can precipitate a chain reaction that culminates in a fundamental shift in the structure of the system or a dramatic large-scale event. Through such an effect, reflecting the inherent non-linearity of many systems, it is feasible for a butterfly flapping its wings in Beijing to initiate a series of effects that will result in a cyclone in Florida (Gleick 1987: 20–23). In the steady-state systems assumed by the Newtonian paradigm, such small changes in the initial state are reflected in equally small shifts overall as any disturbances are ameliorated by a negative feedback process that restores equilibrium within the system. On the other hand, in life-like systems where positive feedback and non-linear relationships are more prevalent, the effects of even minor random disturbances are accentuated and magnified by mutually reinforcing positive feedback loops. In the tourism context, therefore, it is feasible for an initiative of a single entrepreneur to precipitate a major shift in the evolution of a tourist destination. The changes they introduce can reverberate throughout the destination in question as other enterprises within the system adjust and find new niches, resulting in a new configuration of linkages.

Paradoxically, while the positive feedback driven, self-organising tendencies described above imply a system in a constant state of flux, these tendencies can also be responsible for creating inertia within the system. Thus, it is possible that an accident of history or an initiative of an entrepreneur can be responsible for the establishment of such a strong network of mutually reinforcing relationships that these endure long after the initiating conditions have been superseded. Through this 'lock-in effect' (Waldrop 1992), it is possible for an innovation introduced by an entrepreneur in the past to have a lasting effect despite changes in the conditions that would otherwise make the original response redundant. At a tourist destination, the lock-in effect might be evident in the continuing concentration of tourist accommodation capacity and attractions around a location, which was originally advantaged by access to rail transport. With the passage of time, rail transport might have become less relevant as a means of access for tourists, but the original location might retain its dominance owing to agglomeration effects.

The final concept, which is relevant to the interpretation of entrepreneurial activity in tourism destination development, concerns the dual notions of 'edge of chaos' and 'phase shift'. Edge of chaos is a situation where a system is in a state of tenuous equilibrium, on the verge of collapsing into a rapidly changing state of dynamic evolution (Waldrop 1992). The interlocking relationships between the components of a system means that, in accord with the butterfly effect, if just one agent experiences a shock or mutation large enough to knock it out of equilibrium, this may be enough to create the necessity of other agents to change and adjust. In turn, this may induce an avalanche of changes until a new equilibrium is reached. Crucially, no such equilibrium is permanent. The equilibrium of the system is punctuated, with long periods of relative stasis (phases) interrupted by bursts of evolutionary change (phase shifts). Each phase shift may be associated with changes that precipitate the extinction of unsustainable or 'unfit' enterprises, while creating new opportunities for those enterprises capable of adapting. Entrepreneurs are at the forefront of phase shifts in individual destinations as they respond creatively to new opportunities or threats arising from changes in the external environment and, in the process, generate changes within the destination which demands adaptive responses on the part of other enterprises within (and beyond) the destination. Phases in a destination's evolution are periods when a relatively stable profile of tourism activities exists and this is reflected in a corresponding stability in the profile of visitors. A phase shift might be induced by factors such as: changes in the socio-economic environment that affect market demand patterns; gradual or sudden changes in the natural environment that impinge on the sustainability of tourism development; technological innovations that create new opportunities in the market place; and initiatives elsewhere that affect the competitiveness of the destination.

4 The Anatomy of the Entrepreneurial Process

As suggested by Lewis and Green (1998), the evolution of tourism at a destination can be construed in terms of an on-going tension between entrepreneurs, who are the agents of change, and planners whose role is to moderate change or at least control change within certain parameters. The modus operandi of these two sets of actors respectively parallels the Chaos and Newtonian perspectives outlined above. In order to develop this theme further, it is necessary to first elaborate on the characteristics and structure of entrepreneurial activity and then contrast this with corresponding attributes of planning and regulatory processes.

Bygrave (1993) describes an entrepreneur as "someone who perceives an opportunity and creates an organisation to pursue it" (p. 257). However, this description of the entrepreneur may understate the proactive inclinations of entrepreneurs in the sense that it implies they passively wait for opportunities to emerge. Arguably, many entrepreneurs go beyond this by actually creating their opportunities. In terms of the contrasting chaos and Newtonian perspectives referred to above, therefore, they disturb the equilibrium of business systems with a 'perennial gale of creative destruction' (Schumpeter 1949).

One approach to studying entrepreneurial behaviour has involved an examination of the personal characteristics of entrepreneurs themselves. While the outcome of this research has been far from conclusive, a meta-analysis carried out by Storey (1994) encapsulates some of the key observations by identifying the following dimensions of entrepreneurial personality:

- *Motivation.* A distinction has been drawn between 'positive' and 'negative' motivations, with the former involving an inclination to recognise opportunities and a strong desire to create wealth, whereas the latter stems from dissatisfaction with present employment or the threat of unemployment. Overall, positive motivation has been identified as a key characteristic of an entrepreneur.
- *Education.* There appears to be two schools of thought regarding the importance of education in entrepreneurship. On the one hand, it is argued that human capital is essential for a successful new venture and education provides the means for developing the required skills. On the other hand, it has been suggested that entrepreneurship is not dependent on formal education. Indeed, the opposite may be the case, to the extent that education can stifle creativity by imposing frameworks for decision-making that suppress lateral thinking. Entrepreneurs with degrees often talk of having to 'unlearn' business school gospel to make firms work (Drucker 1985). Conversely, as some of the examples described in the next section illustrate, some successful entrepreneurs have succeeded despite a limited formal education and have a disdain for education and academia.
- *Family history.* Although the empirical evidence for this particular factor has not been sufficiently addressed for conclusions to be drawn, Storey (1994) maintains that the potential of success for an entrepreneurial venture is greater if there is a history of business involvement in the family. He argues that the necessary financing is more readily available in such cases, while business expertise is associated with family traditions.
- *Social marginality.* On the basis of work carried out by Stanworth and Curran (1976), it has been found that entrepreneurial tendencies are prevalent among individuals who are disassociated from mainstream society in some way. While the results of studies examining this aspect of entrepreneurial behaviour are inconclusive, there is anecdotal evidence, which suggests social marginality plays a significant motivational role in such behaviour.

- Prior business failure. Storey expresses surprise that none of the studies examined in his analysis did not address this factor in their surveys, even though it had been established in popular business literature that 'highly successful entrepreneurs are individuals who have previously failed in business' (Storey 1994: 134). These failures are apparently construed as valuable learning experiences by entrepreneurs, rather than as a demonstration of personal limitations or a source of shame (Timmons 1989).

The most important insight derived from research on the attributes of entrepreneurs, however, is that the personal characteristics of entrepreneurs are highly variable and, at this stage, there appears to be no simple recipe for entrepreneurial success (Stevenson *et al.* 1985). The focus of entrepreneurial research has therefore shifted from the entrepreneur as a person to the entrepreneurial process (Bygrave 1993). Thus, by developing a theoretical model that better explains entrepreneurial events, it is believed that the mysteries of the entrepreneur can be unravelled.

More importantly, however, it has been realised that traditional models and methods used in the management field to date are inadequate for dealing with the complex nature of entrepreneurship and, indeed, most management issues (Stevenson and Harmeling 1990; Bygrave 1993; Smilor and Feeser 1991). Stacey (1992) implicitly recognises the potential utility of the chaos perspective in this context by proposing that the whole world of business needs to be approached with a new perspective, one which recognises instability, turbulence and complexity not as unavoidable environmental factors to be endured, but as integral and vital ingredients for the creativity and innovation which are so essential for adaptation and long-term survival of economic systems. Through its preoccupation with stability and linear change, the conventional approach is oblivious to the entrepreneur induced discontinuities and dramatic shifts that are illuminated by the chaos perspective. Change processes are therefore poorly understood, and the most interesting and dynamic aspects of socio-economic phenomena are relegated to the fringe of the research agenda.

The relevance of the Chaos perspective is reflected in Bygrave's (1993: 257) interpretation of entrepreneurial events, in which he listed the fundamental ingredients of such events as being:

- initiated by an act of human volition;
- at the level of the individual firm;
- a change of state;
- a discontinuity;
- a holistic process;
- a dynamic process;
- involvement of numerous antecedent variables;

- outcomes that are extremely sensitive to initial conditions; and
- unique.

By drawing attention to the 'human volition' element, Bygrave emphasises the individual's role in the entrepreneurial process and the fact that conscious action is involved. Traditional models are thus limited in this context to the degree that 'there is an essential non-algorithmic aspect to the role of conscious action' (Penrose 1989). The entrepreneurial process involves a change of state from being without to having the venture, and this involves a discontinuity in the sense that the new situation is not a natural progression from what existed in the past. Entrepreneurial episodes are holistic in that they cannot be understood using reductionist approaches, where the components are disassembled and examined in isolation from each other. As emphasised in the previous section, there are synergies between the components, which means that the whole is greater than the sum of its parts. The description of the process as being extremely sensitive to initial conditions suggests that, in accord with the butterfly effect, small changes in some variables can have a disproportionate impact on the outcomes. As suggested by Bygrave (1993: 258), therefore, the entrepreneurial process is incredibly sensitive to a multiplicity of antecedent variables, with tiny changes in any one of a myriad of input variables being capable of producing huge changes in the outcome. Prediction of outcomes with the mathematical precision of the Newtonian approach is therefore impossible.

Finally, the reference to uniqueness of entrepreneurial events high-lights the tendency of traditional approaches' focus on larger numbers of cases and averages and, as a consequence, ignores outliers. Yet, as Stevenson and Harmeling (1990: 8) emphasise, the study of entre-preneurship is concerned with 'the few who have made a difference or who desire to'. They add that 'those who succeed in accomplishing that which normal analysis deems to be impossible do so by exploiting small advantages, recognising the importance of timing, recruiting allies, and exercising creativity that goes well beyond the norm' (p. 8). The 'butterfly effect', and the related notion of sensitivity to initial conditions, are partially explained in terms of the leverage entrepreneurs achieve from small advantages through their ability to identify opportunities and create the organisations and alliances required to maximise the benefits derived from these opportunities. Wherever there is a fundamental interest in a change process and turning points in socio-economic phenomena, therefore, it is the outliers who make the difference and warrant attention, rather than the averages.

Stevenson *et al.* (1994) refer to the spectrum of decision-makers ranging from 'promoters' or entrepreneurs at one extreme to 'trustees' or administrators at the other. The latter can be equated with planners and regulators in terms of their mindset and mode of behaviour. They note that firms may themselves become dominated by administrators and, as a consequence, entrepreneurial behaviour may be stifled internally. Where this happens, the vitality and adaptability of the firm will eventually be compromised by its own inertia. One style of decision-making (entrepreneurs) focuses on creating and exploiting new opportunities, while the other is more concerned with fulfilling their responsibilities within the constraints of the parameters of past practices and the resources under their control. Karl Weick's discussion of self-designing systems highlights how aspects of entrepreneurial behaviour can be built into organisations in order to increase their adaptability. In the process, elements of the contrast between entrepreneurial and regulator behaviour can be seen when he refers to moribund organisations (incapable of self design) as:

- valuing 'forecasts rather than improvisation';
- dwelling 'on constraints rather than opportunities';
- borrowing solutions rather than inventing new ones;
- removing doubt rather than encouraging it;
- being content with final solutions rather than continuously experimenting; and
- discouraging contradictions rather than seeking them (Weick 1977: 37).

The contrasting styles of entrepreneurs (chaos-makers) and planners (regulators) are summarised in Figure 10.2. Here, the risk-taking inclinations of the entrepreneur are contrasted with the tendency of planners to avoid risks and establish greater certainty and predictability within their domain of responsibility. Similarly, the intuitive, experimental and innovative characteristics of the entrepreneur is diametrically opposed to the more calculated approach of the planner, who is more intent upon providing conventional solutions that have been thoroughly tested elsewhere. The planners' brief is to provide rigid parameters for development in order to produce a degree of continuity that is consistent with some consensus within the community regarding preferred outcomes. On the other hand, entrepreneurs seek the flexibility that is required for them to respond to new threats and opportunities within their environment, while their innovative and individualistic pursuit of their own ends means that they produce discontinuities in the direction of development. The effect of the planners/regulators, therefore, is to establish a 'Newtonian' regime of equilibrium and linear change, whereas the entrepreneurs/chaos-makers are associated with the disequilibrium, non-linearity and spontaneity described by the chaos/complexity model. Through their actions, the chaos-makers are responsible for the 'life-like' characteristics of the tourism system, whereby new coherent configurations of supply and demand are constantly emerging in response to changing conditions.

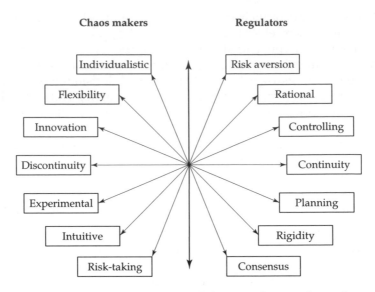

Figure 10.2 Contrasting inclinations of chaos-makers and regulators

5 The Gold Coast as a Setting for Entrepreneurial Activity

The Gold Coast is situated in southeastern Queensland, 70 km south of
the State's capital city, Brisbane (see Figure 10.3). As a tourist destination,
this area has a history that spans over 100 years. In the earlier part of this
century it consisted of a chain of small business centres that provided
services to both the local population of agricultural producers and
visitors from Brisbane seeking to enjoy the area's rich natural endow-
ments of expansive beaches, fish-rich estuaries and rivers, and a hinterland of scenic mountains and rainforest. Tourists initially met their own
accommodation needs by camping or constructing primitive holiday
dwellings. With the increasing volume of visitors that accompanied the
extension of railway linkages to the area, however, local involvement in
tourism intensified as resident entrepreneurs established guesthouses to
meet the accommodation needs of the growing market. While tourism
development proceeded through a series of surges and lurches over much
of this century, the scale of this activity reached new levels in the last 30
years as improvements in inter-regional transport systems (especially
airlines) allowed burgeoning broader domestic markets to be tapped
initially, with international markets following in more recent years. The
central position of the Gold Coast, relative to the major population
concentrations on Australia's eastern seaboard has contributed to its
strength within the domestic market. By 1996, the Gold Coast was
receiving 2.5 million domestic and 1 million international visitors per

year (Domestic Tourism Monitor and International Visitors Survey, Bureau of Tourism Research 1997).

What brings these hordes? Mullins (1991) attributes the attraction of the Gold Coast to its being developed purely for pleasure. He sees it as a

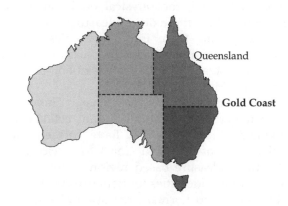

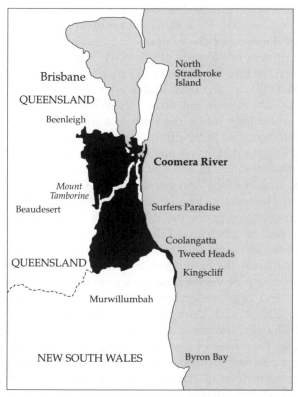

Figure 10.3 The location of Australia's Gold Coast

'city of consumption', a phenomena of recent times (Bauman 1988) where pleasure-related services have become the main component of mass consumption in a society. Mullins (1991) claims that tourism urbanisation is a fundamental ingredient shaping these 'cities of consumption' with the specialised 'mix' of natural and social characteristics making the city a pleasure zone. 'Indeed, the physical environment seems to be the packaging around which these other pleasures are wrapped; it acts as a lure to tourists, pulling them into these cities and, once there, the ambience seduces them into buying the pleasures for sale. Under these circumstances, the spreading of these cities ribbon-fashion along the coast is understandable' (Mullins 1991: 332).

Mullins' argument reinforces the Chaos Theory principle of the importance of 'underlying conditions' for any action to be effective. What are the distinctive factors which have formed the basis for this phenomonal growth of the Gold Coast as a 'city of pleasure'? What differentiates these pleasure based regions from cities with traditional urban growth? Mullins identifies tourism urbanisation as being: spatially and socially different to normal urbanisation; symbolically distinctive with most urban symbols aimed at tourists; experiencing rapid growth in population; characterised by a state government which takes a strong interest in development of the region – a 'boosterist' attitude; mass but unique consumption of pleasure (1991: 331). Surely this unique mix of factors has been the lure for not only the pleasure consuming tourist but also for the pleasure creating individuals who recognised the potential of the Gold Coast, saw visions and turned them into reality.

From its earliest beginnings, the path of tourism development on the Gold Coast is linked with individuals who have had a significant impact, through innovations that have precipitated fundamental shifts in the direction of development. In the earlier days such innovators included Paddy Fagan, who built the first guesthouse at Coolangatta (Russell and Faulkner 1998). However, as implied above, the region's coming-of-age as a tourist destination was in the 1960s 1970s and 1980s, when a procession of remarkable individuals focused their attention largely on the northern (Surfers Paradise) end of the coastal strip. The men (feminism was still an infant) responsible for the emergence of Surfers Paradise as the focus of tourist activity were in varying degrees colourful, flamboyant, innovative, driven, and often reflecting in their personal relationships the attributes of Chaos and Complexity described earlier. They were constantly challenging the norm, shaking the rules and making waves on the Gold Coast. They were chaos makers, shattering the status quo, and then creating a new order out of the apparent disorder. Several of these entrepreneurs were sons of families of long residence who seized the opportunities and ran with them. That is, they were local innovators, who contributed to involvement in the fashion described by Barr (1990). However, most were late arrivals or entrepreneurial migrants, several of whom retired on the Gold Coast bringing with them wealth generated elsewhere in Australia. Once they had been seduced by the charm of the place, they were unable to sit still amid such opportunity and were still unretired in their 80s. Others were internationalists on the prowl and quick to pounce on such world-class potential.

What made the Gold Coast such an entrepreneurial haven? Apart from the specific nature of tourism urbanisation which dominates the region, there are also more general environmental factors that were conducive to the success of these entrepreneurs. Smilor and Feeser (1991) in their study of the entrepreneurial process within the technology field of business note that successful entrepreneurship is dependent on a certain 'climate' or environment conducive to nurturing the spirit of entrepreneurs.

In retrospect, the changes which occurred on the Gold Coast in the first half of the century were just miniscule ripples, compared with what has happened in the last 30 years. Although firm foundations for a thriving tourism industry were established earlier, it was the second half of the century which saw 'fundamental shifts in the system', the 'great leaps' and 'discontinuity with the past'. By the 1950s there was a ripeness for change, an ambience of readiness akin to the 'edge of chaos' referred to in the Chaos Theory literature (Waldrop 1992). In such an original state, in Chaos/Complexity terms, small, even remote changes can trigger tumultuous adaptations.

Globally, the restraints and insecurities of war had diminished. There was a boom period with longer vacations, higher earnings and an explorer attitude consistent with changing concepts of leisure. Rapid advances in communication and air and land travel were facilitating lower fares, greater security and global perspectives.

Nationally, post-war migration and the Melbourne Olympics publicised Australia. With the waning of the hitherto prosperous wool industry, Australia wanted its slice of a lucrative tourism pie. Governments began to recognise the potential of tourism and upgraded promotional and infrastructure development activities accordingly, although it was not until much later (i.e., the 1980s) that significant public resources were channelled into the tourism sector.

Locally, the Gold Coast was richly endowed with the qualities that would appeal to both national and international tourists as well as retirees seeking the quality of life the area had to offer. The availability of local technical skill to plan and build the required infrastructure combined with an optimistic pro-development climate and ready availability of finance to facilitate development. Meanwhile, Queensland's long-standing National Party government, particularly under Premier Joh Bjelke Peterson and Lands Minister Russ Hinze, themselves self-made men from lowly beginnings, was particularly accommodating to

free enterprise and favourably disposed towards the Coast's development. Jones (1986) identifies some key characteristics which have made
the Gold Coast the perfect place for entrepreneurial activity:

- close relationship between the government and the entrepreneurs;
- Queensland government underwrites the private sector;
- Queensland government is keen to provide public infrastructure
  such as roads and bridges;
- rapid legislative changes allowed for private development, even in
  flood-prone land, and facilitated timesharing, a rapid growth
  scheme in Gold Coast real estate;
- change of tax laws – abolishment of death duties; and
- ability of developers to become members of government and
  council.

Perhaps even more importantly, the Gold Coast attracted these
entrepreneurs because it was 'about Australian hopes and dreams and
expectations' (Jones 1986: 6). It was a place which seemed to reward the
'capitalist values of hard work, thrift and optimism and freedom from
Government control' (ibid). It was more than just being about money, it
was about the new, the modern and the exciting. Unlike the southern,
more established areas, the Gold Coast did not distinguish between 'old'
and 'new' money – all capital was welcome. The opposition of chaos-
makers and regulators described earlier in this paper was therefore
diluted in the Gold Coast situation, and the regulators role had been
compromised.

6 Movers and shakers on the Gold Coast

In using the term 'movers and shakers', we are referring to a particular
type of entrepreneur who, through their innovative flair, is responsible for
major changes in the direction of tourism development at a destination.
In one respect, entrepreneurs of this kind defy description in terms of
simple generalisations because they are exceptional individuals, who do
not readily fit into a single mould. However, by combining aspects of
Storey's (1994) profile of entrepreneurs and the elements of Chaos/
Complexity described earlier, a profile of entrepreneurial traits can be
produced. According to this profile, entrepreneurs tend to:

- be outspoken non-conformists unbound by traditional wisdom;
- be creatively unorthodox lateral thinkers;
- would do things in their own non-linear ways;
- be flexible, not locked into a single means of achieving goals;
- be confident in themselves, their goals and their right to uninhibited
  pursuit of their goals;
- cause disquiet if not alarm among regulators;

- live comfortably with disequilibrium, uncertainty, tension and dissonance;
- have strong motivation, possibly stimulated by previous success or failure;
- have had minimal exposure to the 'normalising' conformism of school and church enculturation;
- be broadly approved, even popular, at least ostensibly, but have few close, permanent relationships; and
- be impatient with anyone unwilling or unable to move at their pace.

Two entrepreneurs have been selected as representative of the movers and shakers genre, who were active in initiating innovations in tourism development on the Gold Coast during the 1960s 1970s and 1980s. The individuals concerned are Bernard Elsey and Keith Williams.

6.1 Bernard Elsey

Bernard Elsey was an English migrant of lowly origins, who had little formal education, and whose distinguishing feature was his chronic stuttering. He worked in the mundane trade of plumbing in the Queensland regional city of Toowoomba until he was 40. His motto was 'To succeed in this life, you have to sell yourself and believe in what you are doing' (GCB, 20.12.83 p. 4). He did succeed in spite of apparent impediments.

He was unorthodox as well as grossly confident. After quitting the plumbing trade, he embarked on a new career by gambling on his sales-manship and offering himself to a Brisbane food wholesaler without pay for a month's trial. Again he succeeded and after a successful interlude with his own food distribution business arrived on the Gold Coast in 1949 to build the reputation as the 'self-made millionaire whose colourful character helped paint the Gold Coast bright' (ibid).

Elsey was a visionary who worked hard to sell and achieve his dreams. While consolidating his day-cruises to Tipplers Passage on Stradbroke Island, he hawked Singer sewing machines door to door. Quick to recognise the potential of the Broadwater, he successfully sold to Ansett Airlines the vision of a Sandringham flying boat service to Southport. Seeing passengers arriving from Sydney in lots of 44, ferrying them to their accommodation, he recognised that there was a deficiency in appropriate accommodation, a need which he set about filling.

He saw entertainment as an adjunct of accommodation and set himself with a salesman's discernment to get the best for the least for the greatest profit. When he found that the Beatles whom he had engaged to appear at his Coolangatta Beachcomber, expected free food as well as pay, he, cancelled the arrangement and substituted an unknown Brisbane group, the Bee Gees.

After deciding that Coolangatta was too conservative for his style of development, Elsey concentrated his energy on Surfers Paradise where restraints were few and opportunities many. He built the Surfrider Hotel, the Surfers Paradise Beachcomber and Tiki Village. His in-house entertainments were legendary. The pyjama parties and Hawaiian nights pushed the edges of the law, filling national newspapers with copy and his establishments with patrons. Nor was his creative boldness limited to in-house activity. After an acrimonious struggle with rivals, he became chairman of the Surfers Paradise Chamber of Commerce and proceeded to promote the region with considerable emphasis on sex. In a classic example of the mover and shaker tilting at the regulators, he introduced the metermaids, clad in minimal, gold bikinis and armed with sixpences employed to rescue motorists from expired parking meters. They were an Elsey creation.

Elsey also nudged regulators towards a relaxation of regulations that restricted his commercial activities. Although he did not drink or smoke, Elsey campaigned vigorously for relaxed liquor laws and ultimately succeeded. With an eye to attracting international tourists, he initiated a push for a casino, basing his case on investigative visits to 22 countries with casinos.

Unfortunately in his post-Surfers Paradise enterprise on Daydream Island, Elsey was not so advantaged by pliant regulators or accommodating banks. As is often the case with those who back their judgement to the limit, he lost. That he married four times and fathered a son at 75, may indicate his persistence, his energy or his inability to form close permanent relationships or all of those, but without doubt, he moved and shook Surfers Paradise vigorously.

6.2 Keith Williams

Williams, grew up in a workers cottage on the Brisbane River during the great depression. Because his father was unemployed for eight years, he knew poverty and determined to escape it. At 13, he left school not staying to do the scholarship examination, then regarded as the basic measure of scholastic respectability. However although he was anti-establishment, he was not anti-education. 'I can't stand a sloppy attitude,' he commented with characteristic impatience. 'I taught myself grammar and spelling' (GCB, 31.3.88: 26).

While still in his mid teens, and with money borrowed from his sister, he got his first Velocette and his love of all things fast moving. Ultimately he accumulated the world's largest collection of restored motor bikes. Beginning by making leather motor bike accessories under the house, his initial enterprises were associated with speed.

In 1956, he developed the Surfers Paradise Ski Gardens on a reach of the Nerang River where he and his troupe polished routines unique in

Australia and an imperative for tourist viewing. In 1959, he won both the Queensland go-karting championship and the Australian Water-ski championship. His success in attracting the World Water-ski Championship to his centre in 1965 gave him enormous press coverage and provided impetus for the promotion of his attraction. It was the first international event on the Gold Coast. The Surfers Paradise Speedway, which he opened in 1966 on leased land, became a leading motor sport venue giving him another arena for his flamboyance and speed-lust.

Williams has been described as 'abrasive, tough, wheel-dealing' (GCB, 30.1.87: 26) as having 'bloody minded tenacity', refusing 'to let little things stand in his way' (Sunday Mail, 11.10.87). He is a man of charm but scathing in his rebukes of staff who lag behind his expectations. And equally disrespectful of functionaries who would modify his plans or delay the progress of his plans.

In quick succession, he bought and sold the Porpoise Pool at Tweed Heads, built Fisherman's Wharf at Main Beach, established a Brisbane-Gold Coast plane and helicopter service, and acquired Marine Land on the spit. He expanded this last acquisition over 50 acres of leased crown land transferring some of the water skiing routines to this new location. In this, he showed little regard for his competitors or for officialdom. Much of the excavation work for the pools at Sea World (the upgraded Marineland) was done on a do-first-ask-later basis. Former mayor, Denis Pie, recalls that no progress inspections were done during the building of the whole new structure (interview 1998). It was presented for inspection only in its completed state, claiming that, 'its no different from Woolies and Coles' (GCB, 30.1.87). To the surprise of competing themeparks such as Dreamworld, he was also quite candid about the regular spy flights he flew over their territory in order to obtain intelligence on the 'enemy's movements'. To the disgust of the enemy.

Always one to skate on the thinnest of financial ice, Williams found the ice dangerously thin during the high-interest, high inflation crisis of the late 1980s. He sold SeaWorld for $35million and like Elsey shifted his focus to the Whitsunday Passage. His Hamilton Island luxury resort went through a similar cycle, with his dream frustrated by the pilot's strike, continuing high interest rates and the Gulf War. Not one to abandon the struggle, he has again drawn swords, this time at Hinchinbrook Channel and this time against a consortium of government authorities, conservationists and academics who are opposed to his resort development on the basis of its potential impact on adjacent World Heritage listed areas. In this case, however, the traditional boundary between regulators and the mover and shaker has become blurred as government agencies at the State and local level have been co-opted by political supporters of Williams' plans.

6.3 Summary

Individually, Bernard Elsey and Keith Williams have both had an enduring impact on the course of tourism development on the Gold Coast. Through his hotel developments, Elsey increased the appeal of the Gold Coast to a broader Australian domestic market, while his flare for entertainment accentuated the Gold Coast's reputation as a place where nightlife is an integral part of the holiday experience. Williams initiated the emergence of the Gold Coast as the theme park capital of Australia. There was an earlier generation of theme parks on the Gold Coast prior to his ventures, but none of these could compare with his Sea World in terms of scale and international appeal.

7 Conclusion

The traditional approach to research on tourism destination development has tended to obscure the significance of entrepreneurs because of a preoccupation with order and continuity, and its corresponding inability to cope with the essentially chaotic nature of entrepreneurial activity. Chaos Theory and the allied complexity perspective has therefore been presented as an alternative framework which can be used in conjunction with the well-established Destination Life Cycle Model. The Gold Coast case study was used to illustrate the utility of this approach and this example provides a basis for discussing potential future research directions.

Although it is experiencing some of the problems common to tourist resorts at the mature stage of development, the Gold Coast remains Australia's premium holiday destination. While the region's natural assets continue to feature as one of its main attractions, these have been augmented by an array of man-made attractions (integrated resorts, large-scale theme-parks, a casino, and tourist-oriented shopping centres), which have transformed it both in terms of the scale and nature of tourist activity. All of these developments are, to varying degrees, attributable to the actions of movers and shakers like Bernard Elsey and Keith Williams, whose entrepreneurial flare, determination and creativity brought about a sequence of changes that enabled the Gold Coast as a whole to adapt to changing external conditions and opportunities. These changes, however, seldom involved a smooth transition from one phase to another as the mover and shaker's modus operandi is to both capitalise on, and create, chaos in the process of achieving their goals. The fact that the Gold Coast has flourished as a tourist destination over a long period of time might be attributable to the relatively benign regulatory environment, at least to Australian standards, and the possibility that this has been instrumental in attracting movers and shakers to the area.

A long-term perspective on the history of tourism on the Gold Coast produces the impression that the intensity of mover and shaker activity (as it appeared in the past), has waned. While we can only speculate on the reasons for this, such speculations provide the fuel for future research questions:

- Is the apparent demise of the lone mover and shaker a reflection of globalisation in the ownership and control of the tourism industry, especially in large-scale destinations such as the Gold Coast? That is, do larger corporations control the scene to such an extent that there is no latitude for individuals to have an impact?
- Is this decline simply a reflection of the 'small fish in a big pool' syndrome? With the increasing scale of tourism on the Gold Coast it is more difficult for a single entrepreneur's initiative to have the same relative impact and, therefore, be noticed.
- Alternatively, the Gold Coast may have lost its appeal to movers and shakers owing to the tightening-up of the regulatory regime, which has been both a consequence of and necessitated by the urban growth in the area. Population growth has had the effect of increasing the range of stakeholders, who are now present in sufficient numbers to form viable pressure groups. Through the political process, regulators are therefore more readily influenced in a manner that restricts the activities of movers and shakers. It may well be that movers and shakers, such as Keith Williams, have moved on to other areas precisely because of this trend.

So far as the positive role of Chaos and movers and shakers is concerned, the scale of tourism development on the Gold Coast appears to have two contradictory implications. Firstly, there is a lock-in effect to the extent that the scale of tourism activities has reached a point where it generates its own momentum. The volume of business has the ability to sustain such conditions as regular air services and a marketing infrastructure that ensures the availability of the product and a high level of awareness of the Gold Coast as a tourist destination. The tourism system has therefore reached a dynamic-equilibrium point, whereby shifts in consumer demand require only minor adjustments in marketing strategies in order to maintain levels of business. Within this setting it would appear that the role of movers and shakers is limited. On the other hand, however, any change in the market place also has the potential to initiate significant disruptions within the system, which require drastic remedial action. The impact of the recent Asian economic crisis on the Gold Coast tourism industry has demonstrated how vulnerable it has become owing to the heavy dependence of some enterprises on particular Asian markets. With this shock, a more fundamental realignment of product and re-focusing of marketing activities will be necessary if the viability of the destination is to be maintained. Within this environment, however, new opportunities will emerge and the future vitality of the destination depends on the extent to which there are entrepreneurs present who have the creativity and energy to identify and pursue these opportunities.

References

Barr, T. (1990) From quirky islanders to entrepreneurial magnates: The transition of the Whitsundays. *Journal of Tourism Studies*, 1(2), 26–32.

Bauman, Z. (1988) Sociology and postmodernity. *Sociological Review*, 36, 790–813.

Butler, R. W. (1980) The concept of a tourist area cycle of evolution: Implications for management of resources. *Canadian Geographer*, XXIV(1), 5–12.

Bygrave, W. D. (1993) Theory building in the entrepreneurship paradigm. *Journal of Business Venturing*, 8, 255–280.

Capra, F. (1982). *The Turning Point*. London: Flamingo.

Courier Mail, 18.2.1985.

Domestic Tourism Monitor (1997) *Summary Report*. Canberra: Bureau of Tourism Research.

Drucker, P. F. (1985) *Innovation and Entrepreneurship: Practices and Principles*. New York: Harper and Row.

Echtner, C. M. (1995) Entrepreneurial training in developing countries. *Annals of Tourism Research*, 22(1), 119–134.

Faulkner, B. (1998). Introduction. In E. Laws, B. Faulkner, and G. Moscardo (eds), *Embracing and Managing Change in Tourism: International Case Studies* (pp. 1–10). London: Routledge.

Faulkner, B. and Russell, R. (1997) Chaos and complexity in tourism: In search of a new perspective. *Pacific Tourism Review*, 1(2), 93–102.

Gleick, J. (1987) *Chaos: Making a New Science*. London: Heinemann.

Gold Coast Bulletin, 30.1.1987; 12.5.1992; 21.6.1989; 31.3.1988.

Graburn, N. H. H. and Jafari, J. (1991) Tourism social research, special issue. *Annals of Tourism Research*, 18(1).

Gunn, C. (1994) A perspective on the purpose and nature of tourism research methods. In J. R. B. Ritchie, and C. R. Goeldner (eds), *Travel, Tourism and Hospitality Research: A Handbook for Managers and Researchers* (2nd ed., pp. 3–11). New York: Wiley.

Hall, C. M. (1995) In search of common ground: Reflections on sustainability, complexity and process in the tourism system – a discussion between C. Michael Hall and Richard W. Butler. *Journal of Sustainable Tourism*, 3(2), 99–105.

International Visitors Survey (1997) *Summary Report*. Canberra: Bureau of Tourism Research.

Interview with Mr. Denis Pie (Mayor of Gold Coast City 1985–1988), 2.4.1998.

Janesick, V. (1994) The dance of qualitative research design: Metaphor, methodology, and meaning. In N. K. Denzin, and Y. S. Lincoln (eds), *Handbook of Qualitative Research* (pp. 209–219). California: Sage Publications.

Jones, M. A. (1986) *A Sunny Place for Shady People: The Real Gold Coast Story*. Sydney: Allen and Unwin.

Kaspar, C. (1989) The significance of enterprise culture for tourism enterprises. *The Tourist Review*, 44(3), 2–4.

Kibedi, G. B. (1979) Development of tourism entrepreneurs in Canada. *The Tourist Review*, 34(2), 9–11.

Koh, K. Y. (1996) The tourism entrepreneurial process: a conceptualisation and implications for research and development. *The Tourist Review*, 51(4), 24–41.

Lewis, R., and Green, S. (1998) Planning for stability and managing chaos: The case of Alpine ski resorts. In E. Laws, B. Faulkner, and G. Moscardo (eds), *Embracing and Managing Change in Tourism: International Case Studies* (pp. 138–160). London: Routledge.

McRobbie, A. (1988) *The Real Surfers Paradise*. Surfers Paradise: Pan News Pty. Ltd.

Mullins (1991) Tourism urbanization. *International Journal of Urban and Regional Research*, 15(3), 326–342.

Peat, F. D. (1991) *The Philosopher's Stone: Chaos, Synchronicity and the Hidden Order of the World*. New York: Bantum.

Penrose, R. (1989). *The Emperors New Mind: Concerning Computers, Minds and the Laws of Physics*. New York: Oxford University Press.

Prigogine, I. and Stengers, I. (1985) *Order Out of Chaos*. London: Flamingo.

Russell, R. and Faulkner, B. (1998) Reliving the destination life cycle in Coolangatta: An historical perspective on the rise, decline and rejuvenation of an Australian seaside resort. In E. Laws, B. Faulkner and G. Moscardo (eds), *Embracing and Managing Change in Tourism: International Case Studies* (pp. 95–115). London: Routledge.

Schumpeter, J. A. (1949) *The Theory of Economic Development*. Cambridge, MA: Harvard University Press.

Smilor, R. W. and Feeser, H. R. (1991) Chaos and the entrepreneurial process: Patterns and policy implications for technology entrepreneurship. *Journal of Business Venturing*, 6, 165–172.

Snepenger, D. J., Johnson, J. D., and Rasker, R. (1995) Travel-stimulated entrepreneurial migration. *Journal of Travel Research*, 34(1), 40–44.

Sofield, T. H. B. (1993) Indigenous tourism development. *Annals of Tourism Research*, 20(4), 729–750.

Stacey, R. D. (1992) *Managing Chaos: Dynamic Business Strategies in an Unpredictable World*. London: Kogan Page.

Stanworth, M. J. K. and Curran, J. (1976) Growth and the small firm – an alternative view. *Journal of Management Studies*, 13, 95–110.

Stevenson, H. and Harmeling, S. (1990) Entrepreneurial management's need for a more "chaotic" theory. *Journal of Business Venturing*, 5, 1–14.

Stevenson, H., Roberts, M. J., and Grousbeck, H. J. (1994) *New Business Ventures and the Entrepreneur* (2nd ed.). Illinois: Irwin.

Storey, D. J. (1994) *Understanding the Small Business Sector*. London: Routledge.

Sunday Mail, 27.11.1983; 11.10.1987.

Timmons, J. A. (1989) *The Entrepreneurial Mind*. Massachusetts: Brick House Publishing Company.

Toohey, B. (1994) *Tumbling Dice*. Melbourne: Heinemann.

Waldrop, M. (1992) *Complexity: The Emerging Science and the Edge of Order and Chaos*. London: Simon and Schuster/Penguin.

Weick, K. E. (1977) Organization design: Organisations as self-designing systems. *Organizational Dynamics*, 6, 31–46.

Chapter 11

Towards a Framework for Tourism Disaster Management

Bill Faulkner

1 Introduction

To the casual observer exposed to the plethora of media that currently inform our daily lives, it appears that we live in an increasingly disaster prone world. This perception has some foundations, at least to the extent that the number of disasters (defined in terms of declarations of disaster areas, economic value of losses and the number of victims) has, in fact, increased in recent decades (Blaikie *et al.* 1994). However, the same authors point out that the incidence of natural hazard events (earthquakes, eruptions, floods or cyclones) has not increased, while others have suggested that the definition of disasters has become too fluid for statistical time series purposes (Horlick-Jones *et al.* 1991). Notwithstanding statistical uncertainties, there is a body of opinion which has attributed the apparent increase in the human toll of disasters to a combination of population growth, increased urbanisation and global economic pressures (Blaikie *et al.* 1994; Berke 1998; Brammer 1990; Burton *et al.* 1978; Donohue 1982; Hartmann and Standing 1989). In particular, it is suggested that these factors have either resulted in human settlement and activity being extended into areas which have increased exposure to hazards, or these activities have actually been instrumental in inducing hazards.

In observing that our environment appears to have become increasingly 'turbulent and crisis prone', Richardson (1994) has suggested this might be so not only because we have become a more crowded world, but also because we now have more powerful technology that has the capacity to generate disasters. As the spectre of the Millenium Bug illustrates, for instance, computer failures can bring major computer-driven systems to a standstill instantaneously. The complexity of technology-based systems means that they are more prone to the 'butterfly effect' described by Edward Lorenz (1993) and presented as one of a centre-pieces of chaos theory (Gleick 1987). Small changes or failures in the system can precipitate major displacement through mutually reinforcing positive feed back processes. Mitroff (1988) has alluded to this in his reference to the role of the interaction between information technology and economic systems in creating wild swings in the financial system. The role of technology in exposing humankind to 'natural' disasters is succinctly described in the following remarks by Burton *et al.* (1978: 1–2):

> In a time of extraordinary human effort to control the natural world, the global toll from extreme events of nature is increasing … It may well be that the ways in which mankind deploys its resources and technology in attempts to cope with extreme events of nature are inducing greater rather than less damage and that the process of rapid social change work in their own way to place more people at risk and make them more vulnerable. … To sum up, the global toll of natural disaster rises at least as fast as the increase in population and material wealth, and probably faster.

Whether the incidence of disasters is increasing, or it is simply a matter of each disaster having more devastating effects, as the above summary suggests, it is apparent we live in an increasingly complex world and this has contributed to making us more crisis or disaster prone (Richardson 1994). Complexity, in this context, refers to an intricacy and coherence of natural and human systems, which complicates the process of isolating cause and effect relationships in the manner so often assumed as being possible in traditional research. For this reason, the boundaries between natural disasters and those induced by human action are becoming increasingly blurred, and this element of disaster situations needs to be taken into account in any analysis of such phenomena (Capra 1996; Waldrop 1992). As an area of human activity, tourism is no less prone to disasters than any other. Indeed, it has been suggested that the increased volume of global tourism activity has combined with the attractiveness of high-risk exotic destinations to expose tourists to greater levels of risk (Drabek 1995; Murphy and Bayley 1989). Despite this, relatively little systematic research has been carried out on disaster phenomena in tourism, the impacts of such events on the tourism industry and the responses of industry and relevant government agencies to cope with these impacts. Such research is an essential foundation for assisting the tourism industry and relevant government agencies to learn from past experiences, and develop strategies for avoiding and coping with similar events in the future.

One of the reasons so little progress has been made in the advancing of our understanding of tourism disasters is the limited development of the theoretical and conceptual frameworks required to underpin the analysis of this phenomena. The purpose of the current study is to fill this gap, by using the broader literature relating to crises and disaster management as a foundation for such a framework. The first step in this process involves the establishment of a distinction between crises and disasters, which goes some way towards clarifying the complexity issue alluded to above. Community (and organisational) responses to disaster situations are then examined with a view to providing some insights into the essential ingredients of disaster management strategies. Finally, aspects of tourism disasters are examined as a step towards providing a model for developing tourism-specific disaster management strategies.

2 The Nature of Disasters and Crises

Much early management theory assumed relative stability in both internal and external environments of organisations and, therefore, did not provide a firm foundation for coping with change and crises (Booth 1993). If the implications of change were considered at all, this was viewed in terms of the challenge of coping with gradual (relatively predictable) change, rather than sudden changes which might test the organisation's ability to cope. Such situations might be described as crises or disasters, depending on the distinctions referred to below. Given the specific focus of this paper on tourism sector adjustments to disasters at the destination level, it should be borne in mind that references to 'organisations' in this section apply equally to destinations and host communities.

One perspective on the nature of crises is provided by Selbst (1978), who refers to a crisis as "Any action or failure to act that interferes with an (organisation's) ongoing functions, the acceptable attainment of its objectives, its viability or survival, or that has a detrimental personal effect as perceived by the majority of its employees, clients or constituents". There are two dimensions of the crisis situation emphasised in this definition, which shed light on the distinction between crises and disasters, and the ramifications of these two situations with regard to the responses of organisations and communities. Firstly, by referring to 'any action or failure to act', Selbst implies that the event in question is in some way attributable to the organisation itself. Secondly, it is implied that the event must have detrimental or negative effects on the organisation as a whole, or individuals within it.

Selbst's definition of crises seems to exclude situations where the survival of an organisation or community is placed in jeopardy because of events over which those involved have little or no control. For example, tornadoes, floods and earthquakes can hardly be regarded as self-induced, although communities in vulnerable areas can take steps to minimise the impacts of such events. Thus, for the purposes of this analysis, it is proposed that 'crisis' be used to describe a situation where the root cause of an event is, to some extent, self-inflicted through such problems as inept management structures and practices or a failure to adapt to change. On the other hand, 'disaster' will be used to refer to situations where an enterprise (or collection of enterprises in the case of a tourist destination) is confronted with sudden unpredictable catastrophic changes over which it has little control. We can therefore envisage a spectrum of events such as that depicted in Figure 11.1, with crises located at one extreme and disasters at the other. However, as implied in the introduction, it is not always clear where we locate specific events along this continuum because, even in the case of natural disasters, the damage experienced is often partially attributable to human action.

Good management can avoid crises to some degree, but must equally incorporate strategies for coping with the unexpected event over which the organisation has little control. Frequently, the recognition of a critical problem that might eventually precipitate a crisis becomes a matter of too little too late largely because, as Booth (1993: 106) observes, "standard procedures tend to block out or try to redefine the abnormal as normal". This problem is probably more relevant to the genesis of crises, where organisations fail to adapt to gradual change, but it might apply to disaster situations to the extent that the tendency to ignore warnings of an impending disaster often leaves communities unprepared when it actually happens.

Crises and disasters epitomise chaos phenomena as it is described by such authors as Gleick (1987), Peat (1991), Prigogine and Stengers (1985)

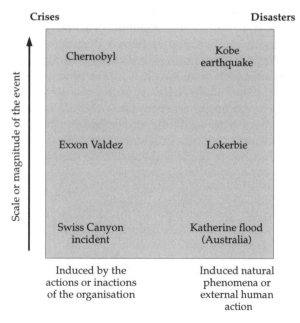

Figure 11.1 Crises and disasters

and Faulkner and Russell (1997) in the tourism context. In terms of Chaos Theory, even apparently stable systems are frequently "at the edge of chaos", whereby a seemingly insignificant event may be enough to precipitate instability and change on such a scale that the integrity and coherence of the system appears to be threatened. Fink emphasises the ubiquity of the 'edge of chaos' condition in business when he suggested that businesses generally are a crisis waiting to happen – i.e. "any time you're (i.e. managers) are not in crisis, you are instead in a pre-crisis, or prodromal mode" (Fink 1986: 7). In his view, the essence of crisis management thus becomes "the art of removing much of the risk and uncertainty to allow you to achieve more control over your destiny" (Fink 1986: 15).

The other aspect of Selbst's definition highlighted above concerns its emphasis on the negative and threatening impacts of the event, rather than the possibility of it representing a turning point or opportunity. As Fink (1986) emphasises, the Webster dictionary definition of a crisis refers to such events as "a turning point for better or worse". Crises and disasters therefore have transformational connotations, with each such event having potential positive (e.g. stimulus to innovation, recognition of new markets, etc.), as well as negative outcomes. This is illustrated by seasonal floods in riverine areas of Peninsula Malaysia, which are seen as both hazards and resources (Chan 1995). The floods bring disruption to communities within the area, but at the same time they replenish the productive capacity of riverine alluvial soils upon which the region's agricultural industry is so dependent.

Again, this is consistent with elements of Chaos Theory, which see chaos as essentially creative, rather than a destructive process. Once a system is pushed past some point of criticality by some crisis or disaster, it may well be destroyed as an entity, it might be restored to a configuration resembling its pre-crisis/disaster state, or a totally new and more effective configuration might emerge. The potential for both destructive and positively creative forces being unleashed by the chaos associated with crises and disasters is illustrated in Berman and Roel's (1993: 82) description of reactions to the 1985 Mexico City earthquake:

> Crises bring about marked regressions as well as opportunities for creativity and new options. They are turning points in which regressive tendencies uncover discrimination (and) resentment about ethnic and socioeconomic differences ...: yet they also trigger progressive potentials and solidarity.

The above discussion has provided an explanation of the distinction being drawn between crises and disasters for the purposes of the current study, along with a description of the general characteristics of these phenomena. However, we are no closer to precisely defining crises and disasters in a form which would enable us to empirically identify when such situations occur. In turning to this issue, it is important that we be reminded that, from an organisational point of view, crises and disasters are essentially very similar and the main distinction between them is a root cause of the problem. The former represent situations where the causes of the problem are associated with on-going change and the failure of organisations to adapt to this, while the latter are triggered by sudden events over which the organisation has relatively little control. Notwithstanding this distinction, most of the features attributed to disasters in the following discussion are equally applicable to crises.

Carter (1991: xxiii) defines a disaster as "an event, natural or man-made, sudden or progressive, which impacts with such severity that the affected community has to respond by taking exceptional measures". In his definition of crises, Booth (1993) places a similar emphasis on the necessity of "exceptional measures" in the community's response by referring to the necessity of non-routine responses, but he adds that stress is created by the suddenness of the change and the pressure it places on adaptive capabilities. Thus, a crisis is described as "a situation faced by an individual, group or organisation which they are unable to cope with by the use of normal routine procedures and in which stress is created by sudden change" (Booth 1993: 86).

Several other authors have attempted to distill the essential characteristics of disaster or crisis situations (Fink 1986: 20; Keown-McMullan 1997: 9; Weiner and Kahn 1972: 21). A synthesis of these contributions produces the following key ingredients:

- a triggering event, which is so significant that it challenges the existing structure, routine operations or survival of the organisation;
- high threat, short decision time and an element of surprise and urgency;
- a perception of an inability to cope among those directly affected;
- a turning point, when decisive change, which may have both positive and negative connotations, is imminent. As Keown-McMullan (1997: 9) emphasises, "even if the crisis is successfully managed, the organisation will have undergone significant change";
- characterised by "fluid, unstable, dynamic" situations (Fink 1986: 20).

Another approach to defining disasters is provided by Keller and Al-Madhari (1996: 20), who applied arbitrary statistical benchmarks. Thus, disasters were defined in terms of a threshold number of fatalities (10), damage costs (US $1 million) and number of people evacuated (50). On the basis of this definition, they claim there has been 6000 disasters since 1970, with 4 million deaths and widespread economic costs. This approach has the appeal of providing a solid, unambiguous foundation for defining disasters, and it is appropriate in the context of studies concerned about statistical issues, such as probabilistic prediction of frequency and magnitude of disasters. However, it loses sight of the qualitative factors referred to above, which are present in disaster situations irrespective of whether or not the fatality, damage cost and evacuation thresholds are reached.

3 Community Responses and the Ingredients of Disaster Recovery Strategies

The reference to both crises and disasters, and the subtleties of the distinction between them, has been useful for the purpose of highlighting how disasters, or at least the severity of their impacts, are to varying degrees influenced by the actions of the individuals, organisations or communities that are affected by them. This section focuses on disasters specifically. That is, those situations where the event which disrupts the routine of the community concerned, and in response to which adjustments have to be made, is triggered externally. We are interested in how communities and individuals respond to these events, and the implications of this for the development of disaster strategies.

From a sociological perspective, the immediate response to a disaster situation has been observed as including several phases (based on Arnold (1980) in Booth 1993: 102–103).

- shock at both the individual and the collective level, where the unexpected nature of the event and the severity of its impacts cause stress and a sense of helplessness and disorientation. While the stressfulness of the situation may initially impair adaptive responses, it is also a mobilising factor for those involved;
- denial or defensive retreat. Denial being an attempt to reach back to the safety of the known, or an attempt to avoid the crisis by repressing it. Defensive retreat may involve either evacuation from the effected area, or a strategic withdrawal to safe places within the area. Evasive action is taken to ensure safety and this enables those concerned to regroup;
- an acknowledgement represents a turning point whereby the community accepts the reality of the change; and
- adaptation, where the community learns from the crisis, develops new ways of coping and rebuilds.

This sequence is probably as much applicable to the individual level as it is at the collective (i.e. organisational and community) level. Chan (1995) suggests that, beyond the immediate occurrence of the disaster, responses might take one of several broader courses:

- to protect (prevent or modify disasters);
- to accommodate (change human use systems to suit disasters);
- to retreat (resettlement elsewhere);
- to do nothing.

It is hard to envisage situations where the "do nothing" strategy provides a viable alternative. Even in the case of the random, one-off event, which has a very low probability of recurrence, some sort of recovery plan needs to be implemented so that lingering longer-term impacts of the disaster can be ameliorated. The applicability of the remaining three strategies will clearly depend on the extent of damage caused by the disaster, the probability and frequency of recurrence and the adaptability of the impacted community.

At some point in a disaster situation there needs to be an assessment of the capacity of the community to cope so that the appropriate level of emergency relief can be determined. A more than appropriate level of relief involves wastage and the unnecessary straining of resources, while insufficient external support will exacerbate the effects of the disaster. However, according to Granot (1995), there are few objective measures for assessing a community's resilience in this regard. Geipel (1982) ranked levels of community impact in a manner that implies a continuum between minimal effects and total collapse. The following categories were therefore identified:

- communities which have not suffered and therefore have the capacity to support others which have;
- communities which escape with only limited loss of life and property – community systems remain largely intact and normal built-in elasticity of resources permits self-recovery;
- communities that sustain so much damage that they can only recover with outside help. With such help their own systems are capable of coping and ultimate recovery;
- communities that are devastated so much that community systems collapse.

Granot challenges the notion of a continuum, however, by suggesting that the effect of a disaster on a community might be more appropriately represented in terms of the percolation principle, which sees changing states as being non-linear. He suggests that, "once a certain threshold is crossed in a sufficient number of constituent subsystems, a basic change takes place in the community system as a whole, affecting its overall capacity to cope" (Granot 1995: 6). It is suggested that factors affecting a community's capacity to cope include:

- community background factors (relevant demographic, socio-economic, political, cultural, organisational and resource level characteristics);
- event factors (objective factors precipitating the cause or causes of the incident); and

- impact factors (immediate discernible outcome, as reflected in such factors as number of casualties, property damage, etc.).

Richardson's (1994) analysis of crisis management in organisations provides another perspective on community adjustment capabilities by distinguishing between "single" and "double loop" learning approaches. In the former, the response to disasters involves a reorientation "more or less in keeping with traditional objectives and traditional roles" (Richardson 1994: 5). Alternatively, the "double loop" learning approach challenges traditional beliefs about "what society and management is and should do". This approach recognises that management systems in place can themselves engender the ingredients of chaos and catastrophe, and "organisations must be prepared to manage through the crisis driven era that is, in one sense, given to them but managers must also be more aware and proactively concerned about organisations as the creators of crises" (p. 6).

For the purposes of exploring these issues further and examining the ingredients of disaster management strategies in more detail, it is useful to look at the frameworks that have been used to describe the stages in response to disasters at the community level. Two such frameworks have been produced, one by Fink (1986) and the other by Roberts (1994). These are described in Table 11.1, where a composite set of stages drawing upon both frameworks is also presented in the first column. The latter set will be utilised as the basis for further discussion because it is more comprehensive.

Community responses to disasters, both during the emergency and afterwards in the recovery period, involve many different organisations (Granot 1997; Huque 1998). In this situation, it is not uncommon for competition and rivalry among these organisations to become a major impediment to both coordination and the ability of organisations to respond effectively (Comfort 1990). In their examination of emergency services responses to the 1989 Newcastle earthquake, for instance, Kouzmin *et al.* (1995) have noted that ambiguities in the division of responsibilities and the rivalries between various emergency service agencies undermined the effectiveness of their response collectively. These problems arise from, and are intensified by, the scarcity of public resources and the necessity of each organisation to justify its existence in order to obtain a share of these resources.

In addition to this problem, different internal cultures and modus operandi become barriers to communication and co-operation between organisations. As Granot (1997: 309–310) has observed, "Old jurisdictional disputes can often be set aside and left unresolved in normal times, but in emergencies they have a way of returning as conflicts that prevent coordination" and as "these situations are difficult to resolve in

Table 11.1 Stages in a community's response to a disaster

Composite stages	Fink's (1986) stages	Robert's (1994) stages
1. Pre-event		*Pre-event:* where action can be taken to prevent disasters (e.g. growth management planning or plans aimed at mitigating the effects of potential disasters)
2. Prodromal	*Prodromal stage:* when it becomes apparent that the crisis is inevitable	
3. Emergency	*Acute stage:* the point of no return when the crisis has hit and damage limitation is the main objective	*Emergency phase:* when the effects of the disaster has been felt and action has to be taken to rescue people and property
4. Intermediate		*Intermediate phase:* when the short-term needs of the people affected must be dealt with – restoring utilities and essential services. The objective at this point being to restore the community to normality as quickly as possible
5. Long term (recovery)	*Chronic stage:* clean-up, post-mortem, self-analysis and healing	*Long-term phase:* continuation of the previous phase, but items that could not be addressed quickly are attended to at this point (repair of damaged infrastructure, correcting environmental problems, counselling victims, reinvestment strategies, debriefings to provide input to revisions of disaster strategies)
6. Resolution	*Resolution:* routine restored or new improved state	

the heat of the moment, it is clear inter-organisational relationships need to be planned ahead and exercised before the actual need occurs". Quarantelli (1982) also sees this as a major challenge in the disaster preparation. However, while coordination between emergency services in the development and implementation of disaster strategies is given lip service, it is seldom reflected in actions (Hills 1994). On the other hand, Granot (1997) also suggests that inadequate resources often force agencies into a collaborative arrangement under emergency conditions. The extent to which pressure to react to the disaster might force organisations to work together, and thus provide a catalyst for breaking down institutional barriers in the longer term, is not clearly addressed in the literature.

The degree to which emergency services and other organisations can be prepared for disasters is questioned by Huque (1998), who notes that policies and decision-making structures that govern an organisation's activities in normal times may not be appropriate in disaster situations. For example, the hierarchical structure and chain of command under normal conditions is necessary for internal coordination purposes, but the tight time lines for decisions and actions during emergencies may make this structure too unresponsive. Bureaucratic structures and power relationships restrict the ability of organisations to respond promptly and effectively to emergency conditions, and this in itself constitutes a barrier to inter-agency cooperation. Heath (1995) observed how response times of emergency services and government agencies in the case of the 1995 Kobe earthquake were affected by bureaucratic procedures. In this case Japanese cultural orientation toward bottom-up consensus in decision-making also affected the timeliness of the response.

Other factors cited by Heath (1995) as impeding the timeliness and effectiveness of the response in the Kobe case provide some useful insights into some of the key considerations in the development of disaster plans. These included:

- communication failures;
- availability of resources (a common problem as governments and response agencies rarely set aside resources in reserve for infrequent and unpredictable crises);
- deployment of resources at a distance from the impact area can be slow – aggravated by damage to infrastructure;
- the attention and efforts of many affected by the disaster shifts from the big picture to immediate, more local concerns and they resist efforts to redirect their attempts towards more coordinated action. Dispersion of resources becomes a related problem;
- "Even without blocked roads and dispersed response demands, a large magnitude impact will create demands for service that exceeds the capabilities of response agencies." (Heath 1995: 17);

Also, on the basis of his analysis of responses to the Kobe incident, Heath has emphasised the need to incorporate a "cascaded strategic priority profile" (CSPP), in the disaster planning phase. This approach involves "a rank ordering of tasks and activities that need to be undertaken, moving from the highest to lowest priority" (Heath 1995: 18). CSPPs need to be developed at various levels of managerial operation, from overall to the local level, to provide multiple layers. Furthermore, these must be articulated with each other to avoid waste, duplication and mutually antagonistic actions.

The role of media in disaster management strategies can be crucial to such an extent that it might make the difference between whether or not a difficult situation evolves into a disaster (Fink 1986; Keown-McMullan 1997). Media outlets can help by disseminating warnings in the lead up to impending disasters (i.e. where these are predictable) and providing information during the recovery stage. However, they can also hinder emergency operations by spreading false information or criticising these operations in a manner that distracts the emergency service personnel from their task. Thus Fischer and Harr (1994) found that up to 20 per cent of emergency operating centre staff's time in the Andover, Kansas tornado incident was spent on media damage control. Furthermore, adverse media reports had an impact on the decisions made by these staff. In Australia, Christine (1995) has noted the effect of misleading reports exaggerating the extent of the 1993 Sydney bushfires. These experiences highlight the necessity of a media communication strategy involving the early establishment of a centralised source in order to ensure that misleading and contradictory information is not disseminated (Riley and Meadows 1997).

On the role of the media in disasters in the US, Quarantelli (1996) has observed:

- disaster preparedness planning in mass media is generally poor;
- some of the coordination problems attributed to emergency services agencies are also evident in the press as "local mass media systems consider disasters in their own community as "their" disasters" and "this is sometimes manifest in tension ... between local mass media and national network staff members" (Quarantelli 1996: 6);
- there is a tendency for selective reporting focusing on the activities of formal organisations (with whom the media has established links), rather than emergent and informally organised volunteers;
- television, in particular, is prone to perpetuate disaster myths, such as the persistence of disruption, panic, looting, etc.

Disaster strategies clearly need to articulate a set of appropriate actions for each of the stages described in Table 11.1. Quarantelli (1984) and Turner (1994) have each commented on the essential ingredients of disaster strategies from two different, but complementary, perspectives. As reflected in Table 11.2, while the latter provides useful guidelines for the production of the strategy, Quarantelli concentrates more on its actual ingredients and the systems that need to be in place to make it work. By amalgamating the analyses of both authors, therefore, it is possible to produce a more comprehensive structure for producing a disaster survival strategy.

From this brief overview of community responses to disasters, and on the basis of other insights provided by analyses of disaster situations, a number of conclusions can be drawn about important considerations in disaster preparedness generally. These will be revisited in the next section after aspects of tourism disasters have been explored, so that they can be related specifically to tourism disaster strategy development considerations.

4 Tourism Disasters

Several authors have emphasised the vulnerability of tourist destinations, and thus tourists, to disasters and some have suggested that, in these situations, tourists might be more exposed to danger than anyone else (Drabek 1995). Murphy and Bayley (1989) suggest that the exposure of tourism to natural disasters is linked with the attractiveness of many high-risk exotic locations, where events such as hurricanes, avalanches and volcanic activity are common. They are also at risk from hijacking and terrorism because, as Lehrman (1986) observes, tourists have become soft targets in a period when increased security measures have made traditional targets (politicians, embassies, etc.) less attractive for terrorists. Furthermore, tourists themselves are often more vulnerable than locals in disaster situations because they are less familiar with local hazards and the resources that can be relied on to avoid risk, and they are less independent (Burby and Wagner 1996; Drabek 1992, 1994).

Despite the potentially devastating effect natural and man-made disasters can have on tourism, few tourism organisations at the enterprise or destination level have properly developed disaster strategies as an integral part of their business plans (Cassedy 1991). In studies of disaster preparedness among tourism industry enterprises in the US, Drabek (1992, 1995) has reported that, while there was a relatively high degree of disaster preparedness among tourism executives, this was qualified by the observation that many had essentially informal (undocumented) strategies in place and these strategies addressed only one type of hazard. Also, the level of staff turnover had not been taken sufficiently into account in the consideration of the frequency of staff education and some misconceptions about disaster effects (e.g. inflated expectations regarding the potential for looting) influenced the planned response. Furthermore, larger firms with more professional senior managers and

Table 11.2 Ingredients of a disaster survival strategy

Strategy development (Turner 1994)

- Form disaster recovery committee and convening meetings for the purpose of sharing information
- Risk assessment (identify potential threats/disasters and prioritise in terms of probability of occurrence – real, likely and historical threats. Perhaps stimulated by a definition and classification of potential disasters)
- Analysis of anticipated short- and long-term impacts
- Identification of strategies for avoiding/minimising impacts, critical actions necessary, chain of command for coordination, responsibilities and resources
- Prepare and disseminate manual and secure commitment from responsible parties and relevant agencies. Relevant contact information must be included

Implementation (Quarantelli 1984)

- Holding disaster drills, rehearsals and simulations
- Developing techniques for training, knowledge transfer and assessments
- Formulating memoranda of understanding and mutual aid agreements
- Educating the public and others involved in the planning process
- Obtaining, positioning and maintaining relevant material resources
- Undertaking public educational activities
- Establishing informal linkages between involved groups
- Thinking and communicating information about future dangers and hazards
- Drawing up organisational disaster plans and integrating them with overall community mass emergency plans
- Continually updating obsolete materials/strategies

planning resources tended to be more prepared than the many smaller establishments. Elsewhere, Burby and Wagner (1996) reported a high degree of preparedness among hotel establishments in New Orleans, but this preparedness was compromised by similar reservations as those raised by Drabek.

The critical role of the media in disaster situations has been referred to in the previous section. In tourism context, the impacts of disasters on the market are often out of proportion with their actual disruptive effects because of exaggeration by the media (Cassedy 1991; Murphy and Bayley

1989; Drabek 1992). As Young and Montgomery (1998: 4) have observed, "... a crisis has the potential to be detrimental to the marketability of any tourist destination, particularly if it is dramatised and distorted through rumours and the media". Meanwhile, disaster situations provide a fertile ground for misinformation, as disruptions to communications systems combine with publication deadlines to inhibit the verification of reports and the ratings game fosters sensationalism (Milo and Yoder 1991).

Media reports have the potential to have a devastating impact on disaster-affected destinations because pleasure travel is a discretionary item and, within the mind of the consumer, the "quest for paradise (can) suddenly transform into a dangerous journey that most travelers would rather avoid" (Cassedy 1991: 4). This effect is expressed in econometric terms by Gonzalez-Herrero and Pratt (1998: 86) when they suggest that "tourism demand presents a higher elasticity index per level of perceived risk than any other industry because of the hedonistic ... benefits customers ascribe to its products and services". By virtue of the power of the media and the tendency for negative images to linger, the recovery of destinations usually takes longer than the period required for the restoration of services to normalcy. This has been observed in a number of case studies, including the 1987 Fiji Coup, the 1989 San Francisco Earthquake, the 1989 Tiananmen Square incident (Cassedy 1991) and Hokkaido's Mt Usu volcanic eruption (Hirose 1982). The effectiveness with which the tourism industry in a disaster area handles a crisis, and therefore the degree to which it is prepared for it, has a bearing on how quickly services are restored to normal. However, the speed of the destination's recovery ultimately hinges on the degree to which market communication plans have been integrated with disaster management strategies.

The above observation perhaps explains why some models for tourism disaster plans (see, for example, Young and Montgomery 1998) tend to emphasise market communication considerations at the expense of other aspects. This approach, however, involves the risk of a counter-productive over-reaction, which is illustrated by Cammisa's (1993) observations regarding the response of Florida tourism authorities to Hurricane Andrew in 1992. Cammisa suggested that, in their eagerness to assure the market that Florida's hotel accommodation had not been affected by the hurricane, tourism authorities overlooked the fact that the rest of the tourism infrastructure in the area had been devastated. Thus, he pointed out that, "rather than face up to this reality, unfortunately "denial" communication emanated from the area" (Cammisa 1993: 294). A similar denial pattern was observed in the response of authorities to the Miami tourist crime incidents in 1992 and 1993. Another form of denial is noted by Murphy and Bayley (1989: 38) who highlight the reticence of tourism operators to bring attention to hazards and the need to take precautions, yet "safety drills and messages have become standard features of sea and air travel".

Bearing in mind the distinction drawn between crises and disasters earlier in this paper, many disasters are not predictable and their disruptive effects are generally unavoidable. However, through the development of a disaster management strategy, many potential hazards can either be totally avoided, or at least their impacts can be minimised as a consequence of the prompt responses facilitated by the plan. Furthermore, confusion and the duplication of effort can be avoided, leading to a more efficient response, while the establishment of a preset plan to guide the responses of those involved results in the potential for panic and stress being reduced (Cassedy 1991).

As mentioned previously, Young and Montgomery (1998) have provided a model for a detailed crisis management plan, although this tends to emphasise communication aspects. Other more balanced models have been developed by Cassedy (1991) and Drabek (1995). The main ingredients of each of the latter models are identified in Table 11.3, which reveals contrasting orientations in these two contributions. Cassedy emphasises aspects of the process of developing effective strategies, while Drabek's approach is structured around the sequence of responses that is necessary to cope with the emergency. While each of these authors provides a useful contribution, the cross-fertilisation between their respective contributions has been limited and few insights have been drawn from the substantial literature on disaster and crises management responses referred to in the earlier sections of this paper.

Another approach to analysing responses to crises is based on operations research, whereby linear programming techniques are used to identify optimal responses (Arbel and Bargur 1980). While this approach has been effective in systems where the parameters can be tightly specified in quantitative terms (e.g. a manufacturing organisation and individual hotel chain operations), it would appear to be less applicable to a tourist destination. A tourist destination encompasses more loosely connected systems (social, economic, environmental, physical infrastructure) than in the case of a single firm and responses to externally induced shocks must take into account the more fluid relationships between the various parties concerned.

Both the linear programming approach and, to a lesser extent, the other approaches described so far implicitly assume that the events creating the crisis situation are invariably temporary aberrations, and that the primary objective is to restore the system to the pre-existing (pre-shock) equilibrium. However, insights from Chaos Theory perspective described earlier in this paper suggest that this view of crises and disasters may be deficient in two respects. Firstly, some shocks have lingering effects that make the pre-shock equilibrium a redundant (or at least sub-optimal) approach with regard to longer-term sustainability. That is, in terms of the chaos framework, systems are often "at the edge of chaos" and a single event can set in train a series of positive feedback loops (or chain reaction) which make the pre-event status-quo no longer viable. Secondly, the chaos created by crises can be a creative process, with the potential for innovative new configurations emerging from the "ruins". In this sense, crisis can act as a trigger or catalyst for a more vigorous and

Table 11.3 Ingredients of tourism disaster strategies

Cassedy (1991)

- Selection of a team leader: a senior person with authority and able to command respect (ability to communicate effectively, prioritise and manage multiple tasks, ability to delegate, coordinate and control, work cohesively with a crisis management team, make good decisions quickly)
- Team development: a permanent and integral feature of strategic planning; able to identify and analyse possible crises, develop contingency plans
- Contingency plan: including mechanism for activating the plan, possible crisis, objectives, worst-case scenario, trigger mechanism
- Actions: action plan assignment of tasks, including gathering information and developing relationships with other agencies/groups (govt. agencies, other travel providers, emergency services, health services, the media, the community, the travelling public)
- Crisis management command centre: a specific location and facility with relevant communication and other resources for the crisis management team

Drabek (1995)

- Warning
- Confirmation
- Mobilisation
- Customer information
- Customer shelters
- Employee concerns
- Transportation
- Employee sheltering
- Looting protection
- Re-entry issues

adaptable tourism industry at a destination. This effect is alluded to in Murphy and Bayley's (1989) reference to the aftermath of the Mt St Helens eruption. Here, recovery measures put in place after the emergency led to additional resources being devoted to tourism development in the affected area, and thus an overall improvement over pre-disaster conditions. The site of the disaster became an attraction in its own right.

Insights derived from the general analysis of disaster and crises management strategies in earlier sections have been combined with those obtained from the more specific examination of tourism disaster strategies in this section to produce a generic framework for tourism disaster strategies in Figure 11.2. The details of this table have been largely dealt with in the preceding discussion. However, the underlying rationale of the framework hinges on several fundamental principles, which warrant some emphasis at this point because they summarise the main conclusions emerging from the study and highlight important implications for future research. These principles are outlined below in terms of the prerequisites for, and ingredients of, effective disaster management strategies.

Prerequisites of effective tourism disaster management planning include:

- *Coordinated, team approach.* Given the range of private and public sector organisations that are directly and indirectly involved in the delivery of services to tourists, the development and implementation of a tourism disaster strategy requires a coordinated approach, with a designated tourism disaster management team being established to ensure that this happens. This team needs to work in conjunction with various other public sector planning agencies and providers of emergency services in order to ensure that the tourism industry's action plan dovetails with that of these other parties.
- *Consultation.* To achieve the maximum cohesion, both within the tourism sector and between this sector and the broader community, disaster planning should be based on a consultative process that is both on-going and integrated with other areas of strategic planning (e.g. tourism marketing strategies, urban planning and broader regional economic plans). Apart from the bearing plans in these other areas might have on the exposure of the tourism sector to risk and the measures that might be implemented in the response to a disaster, the individuals directly involved change over time and this affects the 'chemistry' of the coordination process.
- *Commitment.* No matter how thoroughly and skillfully the disaster management plan may be developed, and regardless of the level of consultation that takes place in the process, it will be of limited value

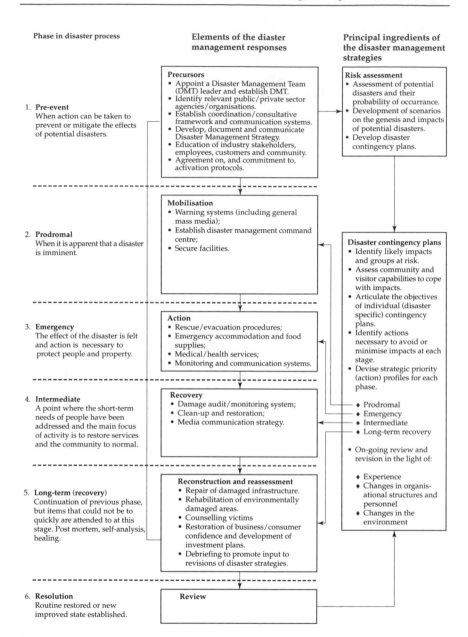

Figure 11.2 Tourism disaster management framework

if the various parties involved are not committed to it and all individuals who are required to take action are not aware of it. As highlighted below, the plan must therefore contain clearly articulated protocols regarding the activation of the strategy and communication/education programme aimed at ensuring that all parties understand what is expected of them.

Ingredients of the tourism disaster management planning process and its outcomes should include:

- *Risk assessment.* An assessment of potential disaster situations that may emerge and their relative probability of occurrence is an essential first step. This should involve an analysis of the history of natural disasters in the region, along with a scanning of the current and emerging environment and alternative scenarios.
- *Prioritisation.* A cascaded strategic priority profile (CSPP), needs to be prepared, with a rank ordering of tasks and activities that need to be undertaken in response to high-risk events identified in the previous step. Part of this process also involves the prioritisation of actions and the articulation of these across organisations so that a coordinated response can be developed. In this context, it needs to be recognised that tourists are vulnerable in unfamiliar surroundings and high priority must be placed on their safety.
- *Protocols.* A clearly enunciated set of protocols to ensure the activities of emergency agencies, tourism authorities and operators are properly coordinated needs to be established and accepted by all parties.
- *Community capabilities audit.* An assessment of the community's capacity to cope with specific types of disasters needs to be carried out so that the appropriate level of emergency relief from external sources can be determined. This should involve an inventory of relevant community (physical, financial and organisational) resources, which is also necessary to address other considerations referred to above.
- *Disaster management command centre.* A properly resourced disaster management command centre, as the focal point for the disaster management team's operations is essential. The location and procedures for setting up this facility must be specified in the plan.
- *Media and monitoring activities.* A media communication strategy involving the early establishment of a centralised source is essential in order to ensure that misleading and contradictory information is not disseminated, and to support the coordination of responses. The media often plays a central role in tourism disaster situations, both in terms of providing important information to tourists during the emergency and in the recovery stage when other sectors of the

industry and the consuming public need to be informed about the restoration of services. Systems for monitoring the impacts of disasters, and providing reliable information on safety matters and the status of tourism services are therefore necessary.

- *Warning systems.* Once a disaster strategy is in place, the conditions necessary to activate it must be specified, along with the types of hazard in relation to which it is designed (Huque 1998). Systems for communicating warnings are also important. The incidence of denial among executives (e.g. "the floods can't affect us because we are on high ground") highlights the need for definitive warning advice (Drabek 1992).

- *Flexibility.* Certain elements of disaster strategies are applicable to all types of emergencies and might therefore be included as part of a generic framework. However, the exposure of some destinations to certain types of disaster is greater than others and it is essential that these be identified so that responses to the specific impacts and requirements of high-risk events can be planned. Some flexibility is also important, as the precise sequence of actions that are necessary may vary between different types of emergency. Flexibility is also required in the sense that it may be necessary for some organisations to perform functions they do not normally carry out.

- *Involvement, education and review.* The effectiveness of disaster response and recovery plans will be very limited unless those who are required to implement them are directly involved in their development (Quarantelli 1984). Organisations and the community in general need to be informed about the strategy, and the strategy should be periodically reviewed in the light of reactions to it and new developments. Disaster strategies therefore need to be updated and refined on a continuous basis in order to ensure that new information and/or organisational changes are taken into account. In particular, debriefings after disasters have actually occurred are important so that lessons can be learned from experience.

The final point is particularly pertinent with regard to the longer-term disaster preparedness of a destination. It is to be expected that individuals and communities who have experienced a particular type of disaster are better equipped to respond to similar situations in the future, at least to the extent that, with the benefit of hindsight, they have a better knowledge of the actual impacts of the disaster and how to cope with it. However, as Burling and Hyle (1997) have noted, in the case of disaster planning in the US schools system, few administrators who had actually experienced a disaster transferred the knowledge gained into the disaster strategy development process. This knowledge can only be effectively tapped through a systematic debriefing procedure, with a "post-mortem" of the event being conducted as a basis for evaluating reactions and refining the strategy.

Conclusion

Natural and human induced disasters alike are neither absolutely predictable nor avoidable. Furthermore, while disasters are, fortunately, relatively rare occurrences and they are to some extent random, it is also true that no destination is immune from such events. In response to the near certainty of experiencing a disaster of some type eventually, tourism organisations can devise means for minimising the damage of, and accelerating the recovering from, such events through the development of disaster management strategies. By studying past events, the responses of those affected and the recovery measures adopted, and retrospectively evaluating the effectiveness of these responses, we can develop strategies for coping with similar events in the future. However, the progress made on this front has been limited because the field has lacked the conceptual framework necessary to structure the cumulative development of knowledge about the impacts of, and effective responses to, tourism disasters. This paper has attempted to address this problem by drawing upon the insights from previous research on disaster (and crisis) management in general, in order to construct a generic model for tourism disaster management specifically.

Within this framework, a distinction has been drawn between crises and disasters. The former have their origins in planning and management deficiencies, and in this sense they are self-inflicted. On the other hand, disasters are triggered by events over which the victim has little control and their impacts are, therefore, to some degree unavoidable. However, the distinction between crises and disasters is often somewhat blurred and it is for this reason it has been suggested that they represent opposite poles of a continuum, rather than a dichotomy. While many disasters are attributable to random natural events, which are beyond the control of the most advanced technology, the impacts of these phenomena can be moderated by planning and management practices. Thus, for instance, various tourism destinations are more or less prone to certain types of natural disasters than others, and in these instances action can be taken to either avoid or at least diminish the harmful effects of the event. Apart from avoiding high-risk locations altogether, one of the more obvious steps that can be taken is to assess the risks an individual destination is exposed to and develop management plans for coping with disaster situations in advance.

A logical step in extending the research described in this paper is to use the framework as a basis for examining and analysing actual cases of tourism disasters. This will enable the generic model to be tested and refined, and provide further insights into the peculiarities of tourism disasters. The methodology for doing this will be described in a companion paper, in which the case of the Katherine (Australia) flood will also be examined.

References

Arbel, A. and Bargur, J. (1980) A planning model for crisis management in the tourism industry. *European Journal of Operational Research*, 5(2), 77–85.

Arnold, W. (1980) in Booth, S. (1993) *Crisis Management Strategy: Competition and Change in Modern Enterprises*. New York: Routledge.

Berke, P. R. (1998) Reducing natural hazard risks through state growth management. *Journal of the American Planning Association*, 64(1), 76–87.

Berman, R. and Roel, G. (1993) Encounter with death and destruction: The 1985 Mexico city earthquake. *Group Analysis*, 26, 89–91.

Blaikie, P., Cannon, T., Davis, I. and Wisner, B. (1994) *At Risk: Natural Hazards, People's Vulnerability and Disasters*. London: Routledge.

Booth, S. (1993) *Crisis Management Strategy: Competition and Change in Modern Enterprises*. New York: Routledge.

Brammer, H. (1990) Floods in Bangladesh: A geographic background to the 1987 and 1988 floods. *Geographical Journal*, 156(1), 12–22.

Burby, R. J. and Wagner, F. (1996) Protecting tourists from death and injury in coastal storms. *Disasters*, 20(1), 49–60.

Burling, W. K. and Hyle, A. (1997) Disaster preparedness planning: Policy and leadership issues. *Disaster Prevention and Management*, 6(4), 234–244.

Burton, I., Kates, R. W. and White, G. F. (1978) *The Environment as Hazard*. New York: Oxford University Press.

Cammisa, J. V. (1993) The Miami experience: Natural and manmade disasters 1992–93. In *Expanding Responsibilities: A Blueprint for the Travel Industry*. 24th Annual Conference Proceedings of Travel and Tourism Research Association, Whistler, BC (pp. 294–295).

Capra, F. (1996) *The Web of Life*. London: Harpers Collins Publishers.

Carter, W. N. (1991) *Disaster Management: A Disaster Manager's Handbook*. Manila: Asian Development Bank.

Cassedy, K. (1991) *Crisis Management Planning in the Travel and Tourism Industry: A Study of Three Destinations and a Crisis Management Planning Manual*. San Francisco: PATA.

Chan, N. W. (1995) Flood disaster management in Malaysia: An evaluation of the effectiveness of government resettlement scheme. *Disaster Prevention and Management*, 4(4), 22–29.

Christine, B. (1995) Disaster management: Lessons learned. *Risk Management*, 42(10) 19–34.

Comfort, L. K. (1990) Turning conflict into co-operation: Organizational designs for community response in disasters. *International Journal of Mental Health*, 19(1), 89–108.

Donohue, J. (1982) Some facts and figures on urbanisation in the developing world. *Assignment Children*, 57(8).

Drabek, T. E. (1992) Variations in disaster evacuation behaviour: Public responses versus private sector executive decision-making. *Disasters*, 16(2), 105–118.

—— (1994) Risk perceptions of tourist business managers. *The Environment Professional*, 16, 327–341.

—— (1995) Disaster responses within the tourism industry. *International Journal of Mass Emergencies and Disasters*, 13(1), 7–23.

Faulkner, B. and Russell, R. (1997) Chaos and complexity in tourism: In search of a new perspective. *Pacific Tourism Review*, 1(2), 91–106.

Fink, S. (1986) *Crisis Management*. New York: American Association of Management.

Fischer, H. W. and Harr, V. J. (1994). Emergency operating centre response to media blame assignment: A case study of an emergent EOC. *Disaster Prevention and Management*, 3(3), 7–17.

Geipel, R. (1982) *Disaster and Reconstruction*. London: Allen and Unwin.

Gleick, J. (1987) *Chaos: Making a New Science*. London: Heinemann.

Gonzalez-Herrero, A. and Pratt, C. B. (1998) Marketing crises in tourism: Communication strategies in the United States and Spain. *Public Relations Review*, 24(1), 83–97.

Granot, H. (1995) Proposed scaling of communal consequences of disaster. *Disaster Prevention and Management*, 4(3), 5–13.

—— (1997) Emergency inter-organisational relationships. *Disaster Prevention and Management*, 6(5), 305–310.

Hartmann, B. and Standing, H. (1989) *The Poverty of Population Control: Family Planning and Health Policy in Bangladesh*. London: Bangladesh International Action Group.

Heath, R. (1995) The Kobe earthquake: Some realities of strategic management of crises and disasters. *Disaster Prevention and Management*, 4(5), 11–24.

Hills, A. E. (1994) Co-ordination and disaster response in the United Kingdom. *Disaster Prevention and Management*, 3(1), 66–71.

Hirose, H. (1982) Volcanic eruption in northern Japan. *Disasters*, 6(2), 89–91.

Horlick-Jones, T., Fortune, J. and Peters, G. (1991) Measuring disaster trends part two: Statistics and underlying processes. *Disaster Management*, 4(1), 41–44.

Huque, A. S. (1998) Disaster management and the inter-organizational imperative: The Hong Kong disaster plan. *Issues and Studies*, 34(2), 104–123.

Keller, A. Z. and Al-Madhari, A. F. (1996) Risk management and disasters. *Disaster Prevention and Management*, 5(5), 19–22.

Keown-McMullan, C. (1997) Crisis: When does a molehill become a mountain?. *Disaster Prevention and Management*, 6(1), 4–10.

Kouzmin, A., Jarman, A. M. G. and Rosenthal, U. (1995) Inter-organisational policy process in disaster management. *Disaster Prevention and Management*, 4(2), 20–37.

Lehrman, C. K. (1986) When fact and fantasy collide: Crisis management in the travel industry. *Public Relations Journal*, 42(4), 25–28.

Lorenz, E. (1993) *The Essence of Chaos*. Washington: University of Washington Press.

Milo, K. J. and Yoder, S. L. (1991) Recovery from natural disaster: Travel writers and tourist destinations. *Journal of Travel Research*, 30(1), 36–39.

Mitroff, I. 1. (1988) *Break-Away Thinking*. New York: Wiley.

Murphy, P. E. and Bayley, R. (1989) Tourism and disaster planning. *Geographical Review*, 79(1), 36–46.

Peat, F. D. (1991) *The Philosopher's Stone: Chaos, Synchronicity and the Hidden Order of the World*. New York: Bantam.

Prigogine, I. and Stengers, I. (1985) *Order Out of Chaos: Man's New Dialogue with Nature*. Hammersmith: Flamingo.

Quarantelli, E. L. (1982) Social and organizational problems in a major emergency. *Emergency Planning Digest*, 9(7–10), 21.

—— (1984) Organisational behaviour in disasters and implications for disaster planning. *Monographs of the National Emergency Training Center*, 1(2), 1–31.

—— (1996) Local mass media operations in disasters in the USA. *Disaster Prevention and Management*, 5(5), 5–10.

Richardson, B. (1994) Crisis management and the management strategy: Time to "loop the loop". *Disaster Prevention and Management*, 3(3), 59–80.

Riley, J. and Meadows, J. (1997) The role of information in disaster planning: A case study approach. *Disaster Prevention and Management*, 6(5), 349–355.

Roberts, V. (1994) Flood management: Bradford paper. *Disaster Prevention and Management*, 3(2), 44–60.

Selbst, P. (1978) in Booth, S. (1993) *Crisis Management Strategy: Competition and Change in Modern Enterprises*. New York: Routledge.

Turner, D. (1994). Resources for disaster recovery. *Security Management*, 57–61.

Waldrop, M. (1992) *Complexity: The Emerging Science and the Edge of Order and Chaos*. Penguin: Simon and Schuster.

Weiner, A. J. and Kahn, H. (1972) Crisis and arms control. In C. F. Hermann, *International Crises: Insights from Behaviour Research* (p. 21). New York, NY: The Free Press.

Young, W. B. and Montgomery, R. J. (1998) Crisis management and its impact on destination marketing : A guide to convention and visitors bureaus. *Journal of Convention and Exhibition Management*, 1(1), 3–18.

Chapter 12

Katherine, Washed Out One Day, Back on Track the Next: A Post-Mortem of a Tourism Disaster

Bill Faulkner and Svetlana Vikulov

1 Introduction

On the evening of Sunday 25 January 1998, Parks and Wildlife staff at the picturesque Katherine Gorge in the Northern Territory's Nitmiluk National Park observed rising river levels apprehensively and informed emergency services personnel in Katherine, 29 km downstream. In the previous week, cyclonic weather patterns had dominated the area, bringing with them the downpours that are typical at the height of the wet season in that part of Australia's tropical north. With this being part of the normal seasonal pattern, nobody anticipated what happened downstream at Katherine on the following day. In fact, the extent and intensity of rainfall over the Katherine river's catchment area had been greater than that experienced at any time over the period of European settlement in the region and, as a consequence, Katherine experienced its biggest ever flood the following day. The flood has since been named the Australia Day Flood, as the 26th of January is celebrated as Australia's national day.

For the Katherine community and its tourism industry, the Australia Day Flood was a disaster of huge proportions, with half of the resident's homes, the whole of the town's Central Business District (CBD) and most of its tourism business premises being inundated, and extensively damaged or destroyed. In terms of the definitions commonly used in the literature, the event exhibited all the features normally associated with natural disasters. It was a natural phenomenon that impacted on the community with such severity that exceptional measures were necessary (Carter 1991: xxiii). Rain and some local flooding may be a routine element of wet season life in Katherine, but flooding of this magnitude is not. From the tourism industry's perspective, the flood epitomised all the essential ingredients of a disaster, as identified by Fink (1986),

269

Keown-McMullan (1997) and Weiner and Kahn (1972). Most notably, it involved:

- a triggering event (flooding), which was so significant that it challenged the existing structure, routine operations and survival of tourism businesses and the regional tourism association (the Katherine Regional Tourism Association or KRTA);
- the flood presented businesses and the KRTA with a high threat situation, involving a short decision time and an element of surprise and urgency;
- there were perceptions of an inability to cope among those directly affected;
- the flood represented a turning point in the evolution of the destination, with both positive and negative connotations; and
- at the height of the flood, and in the period afterwards, both the management environment and personal circumstances of those involved could be described as 'fluid, unstable, dynamic' (Fink 1986: 20).

How the tourism sector adjusts to disaster situations has not received a great deal of attention in tourism management research, even though it is arguable that all destinations face the prospect of either a natural or human-induced disaster at some time in their history. The vulnerability of many tourist destinations has been noted by several authors, who have emphasised the attractiveness of high-risk exotic locations (Murphy and Bayley 1989) and the exposure of visitors to injury owing to their unfamiliarity with local hazards (Burby and Wagner 1996; Drabek 1995). Despite this, tourism businesses and organisations are generally unprepared for disaster situations even in high-risk areas (Cassedy 1991; Drabek 1992, 1995), while many have played down the actual or potential impacts of disasters for marketing reasons (Cammisa 1993; Murphy and Bayley 1989). The latter reaction is largely a response to the importance of safety considerations within the market and the tendency of press reports to exaggerate the impacts of disasters in tourism areas.

The limited amount of progress in the analysis of tourism disasters, and the associated failure of the tourism industry to embrace the notion of disaster management planning, is possibly a consequence of two inter-related deficiencies in the approach that has been adopted so far. Firstly, the theoretical and conceptual foundations for analysing tourism disaster events and developing disaster management plans have not been properly developed. Secondly, as a consequence of this, there has been very little systematic analysis of previous events upon which a cumulative understanding of this phenomenon can be based. A step towards providing a framework for analysing tourism disasters has been taken in an earlier paper (Faulkner 1999, 2001). The present paper's aim is to operationalise and test this framework by applying it to the Katherine floods experience. In the process, a more detailed framework for tourism disaster management plans applicable to flood situations is produced.

2 Katherine as a Tourist Destination (in Normal Times)

Katherine is a town of 11,000 people situated on the Stuart highway 320 km south of Darwin in Australia's Northern Territory (NT). As a tourist destination, Katherine's most well-known attraction is the magnificent Nitmiluk Gorge, where the Katherine River winds between shear sandstone cliffs that rise 20–60m above the water level. The scenery and wildlife of the many spectacular gorges that make up this system can be enjoyed in the comfort of a powered craft or, for the more adventurous, in a canoe safari. With over a quarter of a million visitors in 1997/98, Nitmiluk was the third most visited natural attraction in NT after Ayers Rock (508,000) and Kakadu National Park (300,000) (Northern Territory Tourism Commission 1998: 23).

In addition to this significant attraction, the town also provides a convenient base for experiencing a diverse range of outback attractions in all directions. Within a day trip to the south, one can visit Cutta Cutta Caves, with their unusual limestone formations and the rare Ghost Bat and Orange Horseshoe Bat. A short distance further south is the historic Mataranka, the inspiration for Jeannie Gunn's "We of the Never Never", the thermal springs in Elsey National Park and the historic Daly Waters Pub. Also in this direction is Manyallaluk, the "dreaming place" where visitors can enjoy one of Australia's most highly regarded Aboriginal cultural educational experiences. To the northwest is the historic mining town of Pine Creek, the southern gateway to Kakadu National Park, while to the northeast is Edith falls and Arnhem Land. To the southeast can be found the Gulf country, where the vast savanna is punctuated with magnificent rock formations and, beyond this, extensive wetlands are fed by massive tidal rivers. To the west can be found the Victoria River Gorges, the ancient aboriginal art sites of the Keep River National Park and the Daly River region, where the fishing enthusiast can test their skill against the elusive Barramundi.

In 1997/98 the Katherine region received around 178,000 (overnight staying) visitors, of whom 49 per cent were domestic visitors from other states of Australia and 24 per cent were international visitors, predominately from the United Kingdom and other parts of Europe (NTTC 1998: 12). The remaining 27 per cent of visitors were residents of the NT itself. The number of visitors to Katherine Gorge actually exceeds overnight stayers because of the large number of day-trippers to the area. The main forms of tourist accommodation in the region are hotels and caravan parks, with 14 hotels providing 684 rooms and 20 caravan parks with the potential to accommodate over 1800 vans. Seasonal fluctuations in visitation to the top end are quite pronounced, as large visitor influxes are experienced during the June and September quarter's dry season, while fewer visitors are received during the December and March quarter's wet season. Thus, in the Katherine region, hotel occupancy rates of up to 86 per cent are experienced during the former period, while levels of less than half this occur in the wet season (NTTC 1998). Historically, the region has relied on the drive market, with two-thirds of visitors arriving by road (with or without a caravan) and a substantial 12 per cent arriving by coach. Forty-one per cent of visitors stay in caravan parks.

3 The Australia Day Flood

In mid-January 1998, tourism activity in Katherine was like any other year. The normal wet season trough was being experienced and tourism operators accepted this philosophically in the same manner they had in previous years. However, in the week leading up to Australia Day (Monday 26 January), the remnants of Cyclone Les meandered back and forth across Arnhem Land and dumped 430 mm (17 in) of rain onto the Katherine River's catchment area and Katherine itself. On Sunday 25 January, Parks and Wildlife staff at Katherine Gorge observed dramatic rises in the river to levels that normally produced local flooding downstream at Katherine within 12h. Emergency services authorities were informed and, by 11.00a.m. Monday, 26 January, the river rose to 17m further downstream at Katherine. Police warnings were being broadcast as early as 8.15 a.m., advising motorists that the Stuart highway had been cut and residents should evacuate flood prone areas.

At this stage, tourism operators and residents alike were confused, not knowing whether or not they were in flood prone areas. Many knew that the so-called "100 year flood" had occurred in 1957 and the 19.29m rise of the river produced a flood line which had been used over the ensuing 40 years as a reference point for building purposes. But many did not know precisely where that flood line was and how they might be affected.

Elements of the denial reaction encountered in other disaster situations (Booth 1993) were also evident in reactions at this stage among residents, tourism operators and visitors alike. The owner of tourism facilities that were eventually inundated and seriously damaged by flood waters said "We did not really consider the possibility of a flood like that. The house is 1.5 m above the 100 year flood level." Another operator observed the strange reaction of a tourist to instructions to evacuate her camping ground: "One gentleman sat there in his tent waiting for the rain to stop, so he could fold his tent, but when there was two inches of water in the park, I suggested it was not going to dry up, and may be he should pack and go, which he did." Residents exhibited a similar reticence to evacuate as many continued to enjoy a beer while watching the Australia Day one-day cricket match on television, despite the rising flood waters around their homes.

By the evening of Monday, the water level at the high level bridge had reached 18.62 m and was continuing to rise. Personnel at the nearby Tindal Airforce base had been mobilised for the emergency and were deployed in helicopter rescues of 12 people in outlying areas. Flood waters were beginning to encroach on the Central Business District, where volunteers and defence staff had been engaged in the sandbagging of premises. Later in the evening, flooding in the Gorge area necessitated 58 people (including Parks staff and 15 tourists) to be evacuated to higher ground at the visitor information centre. In the early hours of Tuesday morning, 150 people had to be evacuated by Unimog vehicles from the Knotts Crossing tourist resort on the northern outskirts of the town. As the water level approached 20m by 6.30 a.m. on Tuesday 27th, the NT Minister for Police, Fire and Emergency Services (also the local member and a resident of Katherine) declared a state of emergency. The flood levels continued to rise until 7.15 p.m., when a peak of 20.4 m was reached.

The flood waters in Katherine did not begin to retreat until almost a day later (i.e. 5 p.m. Wednesday, 28 January). In the meantime, 1100 dwellings and every business and government office in Katherine's CBD was inundated, and 1250 people had been rescued and transported to evacuation centres at several schools in East Katherine. An indicator of the effectiveness of the emergency services response is provided by the fact that, despite the extent and ferocity of the flood (see below), only three people lost their lives. The logistical dimensions of the emergency task are reflected in the following statistics on the engagement of personnel and resources at the height of the emergency and in the subsequent clean-up:

- 1100 armed services personnel were deployed in rescues and subsequent clean-up activities;
- 18 helicopters and four Hercules transport planes were used in rescues, evacuations and emergency supply operations;
- 4403 air movements were directed by Airforce air traffic controllers at the Police Operations Centre over the period from 26 January to 1 February.

Apart from the swift and effective reaction of the emergency services, and despite denial reactions among visitors, tourism operators and residents, several factors combined to make the task of securing the safety of residents and visitors more manageable. Firstly, as the flood occurred during the low tourist season, rescue resources were not over-extended to the extent they might have been in the peak period. Secondly, the proximity of Katherine to Tindal air base meant that armed services personnel and equipment were immediately available. This proximity was also advantageous in the sense that the reaction of Tindal personnel was not held up by jurisdictional considerations. As the base commanding officer has the authority to deploy resources within his region, it was not necessary for clearances to be obtained from senior officers elsewhere. Finally, the Katherine Region Counter-Disaster planning group had only recently (November 1997) conducted exercises in which the disaster scenario was a flood associated with the river surpassing the 20m level.

Although the efficiency of rescue operations and follow-up support systems contributed to minimising the discomfort of residents and visitors to the extent that this is possible under such circumstances, the event was nevertheless traumatic for all concerned. Many of those affected by the flood were not only surprised by the height of the water, but also by its ferocity and the life-threatening nature of the currents as they swept through the town. An insight into the traumatic nature of the experience is captured in Minister, Mike Reed's description: "Rescue workers negotiated treacherous waters choked with debris, including fridges, freezers, washing machines, lounge chairs, wheelie bins and other large objects which were washed up in the flood waters, and which made the rescue tasks extremely dangerous.... I vividly recall the anguish of parents, young children and elderly people I collected from flooded homes.... Residents experienced a feeling of numbness, disorientation and disbelief as they evacuated their homes" (Reed 1998).

It might be argued that visitors to Katherine at the time were potentially more vulnerable when the disaster hit because they were in a strange and unfamiliar environment, and less independent in terms of the action necessary to ensure their personal safety. On the other hand, it may have been a less traumatic experience for them, because they did not have the same emotional attachment to the place (Katherine) as the residents, and they were not witnessing the destruction of everything they owned. Again, this aspect of the residents' experience was captured by Mike Reed: "People watched as the flood waters rose in their homes and businesses waiting for the water to peak. The river kept rising and the level of the water carried off peoples' treasured possessions including children's toys, photographs, cars, caravans, fridges, pets and livestock ..." (Reed 1998). Also, many locals, including those working in the tourism industry, were put in a position where their own self interest had to be put aside so that they could attend to the needs of others. As Mike Reed observed, "many of the key players (in the rescue efforts) were victims of the flood, and they worked day and night despite the losses they had suffered, their houses and personal possessions in ruins" (Reed 1998).

With the recession of the floodwaters, the people of Katherine were left standing among the ruins of their businesses and homes, with a massive clean-up task ahead of them. Offices, shops and homes had been totally inundated, with the contents ruined or lost, and structural damage rendered many buildings uninhabitable. A large-scale clean-up operation, involving volunteers and armed services personnel, was mounted to clear away the silt, debris and putrefying food that the flood had left behind. For businesses and home owners alike, the shock of learning that, in most cases, their insurance policies did not cover flood damage remained ahead of them. Personal assistance was provided through the Federal Government's Natural Disaster Relief Fund, while $1.1 million was raised in a Red Cross appeal to assist flood victims. A grant of $5 million in Federal Government funds was provided for repairs to the Stuart Highway, while a $10 million Katherine Region Redevelopment Program, jointly funded by the Federal and NT Governments and the corporate sector, was announced. A Reconstruction Task Force, comprising representatives of key public sector agencies, was set up to coordinate the rehabilitation of infrastructure.

4 Putting Katherine Tourism "Back on Track"

The damage to the infrastructure of Katherine and the surrounding area presented a daunting reconstruction challenge to the public sector agencies and businesses. Damage to public sector infrastructure was estimated at over $60 million, while the corresponding figure for the private sector was tens of millions (Reed 1998). As indicated above, a Reconstruction Task Force was formed immediately after the flood waters receded to oversee the clean-up process and the restoration of key infrastructure to the extent necessary for the community to return to some degree of normalcy. The longer-term reconstruction task was taken over by a Regional Coordination Committee (RCC) in early February. The Chair of the RCC has remarked that the committee faced the dual challenge of maintaining the impetus of adrenaline fueled activity of the immediate clean-up phase over a longer period and bureaucratic mindsets within the public sector agencies involved (Walsh 1999). As observed by some authors in other settings (Heath 1995; Huque 1998), the policies and decision-making structures that governed the behaviour of these organisations in normal times were not appropriate in the disaster recovery situation and, as a consequence, tasks were initially viewed more in terms of the segregation of responsibilities and resource constraints, rather than the teamwork that was necessary to achieve reconstruction objectives. That these obstacles were overcome is evident in the fact that the ambitious target of 80 per cent restoration of infrastructure (i.e. relative to pre-flood standards) by 1 April was achieved.

Against this backdrop of events, the tourism industry was faced with the huge challenge of restoring operations to normal. As many of these businesses soon discovered that flood damage was not covered by their insurance policies, the refurbishment of their infrastructure depended on a rapid re-establishment of cash flows. Major hotels in the area had suffered varying degrees of damage and many were inoperable. Key tourism attractions, including Katherine Gorge and the historic Springvale homestead, sustained serious damage, which neutralised them as tourism assets. A year after the flood, Springvale homestead remained a mere shell, as its owner struggled with the financial burden of re-establishing his various tourism businesses without the assistance of an insurance pay-out. Meanwhile, the same operator's Katherine Gorge boat tours were able to return to normal operations relatively quickly, although this was only possible after the Parks and Wildlife authority had mounted a major clean-up operation around the Nitmiluk visitors' centre at the head of the gorge. In particular, sand deposits produced by the flood resulted in sheds and jetty facilities being buried. However, while shifting sandbanks and debris may have required some adjustments in the navigation of the river, the gorge ecosystem has exhibited remarkable resilience in every other respect. The flood may have been a dramatic and catastrophic event within the context of the area's relatively brief (150 year) European settlement history, but floods of this magnitude have been part of the ebb and flow of the river system over an extended period of geological time.

The Katherine Regional Tourism Association's (KRTA) office and visitor information centre in the CBD had been extensively damaged by flood waters, with most of the equipment and materials required for its operations destroyed or lost. One of the first priorities of the KRTA was to re-establish its office so that its staff could function effectively in providing the local industry with the support it required. This was achieved within 15 days only after substantial external support had been received from the NT Tourism Commission (NTTC), through the provision of personnel, office requisites and funds. Other priorities at this stage included:

- Provision of a relief KRTA manager by the NTTC so that the General Manager could concentrate on marketing activities at trade and travel shows.
- An audit of local tourism businesses to assess the extent of damage and recovery potential. It was necessary for the progress of the reconstruction process to be monitored on an ongoing basis so that the needs of the industry could be continuously assessed, and to ensure that marketing communications were consistent with the capabilities of the industry to deliver services.
- The cancellation of advertisements so these could be replaced by messages relevant to the recovery situation. For example, it was important to communicate the necessity of other operators and consumers to re-book tours and accommodation because the records

of most Katherine-based operators had been destroyed. This procedure was also necessary so that consumers could be informed whether or not the services they required were, in fact, available.

- Employment of a journalist to report on the restoration of services and counteract misleading and damaging press coverage.
- Develop and implementation of the "Katherine Back on Track" tourism promotional campaign in order to reinstate Katherine's image as a tourist destination.

The primary objective of the Katherine Back on Track campaign was to counter tourism consumer and industry perceptions of Katherine having been "washed off the map". There was a danger of this perception lingering, and thus affecting market reactions, as events at the height of the flood were being screened on national television to support the Red Cross campaign for a prolonged period. Elements of the Back on Track campaign included flyers emphasising that, with the restorations, Katherine was now better than ever and attendances at trade and travel shows, where this message was reinforced. Katherine also featured on the national TV show, "Hey Hey Its Saturday". The compere of this show, Daryl Sommers, has been associated with the NT's national advertising campaign for some years. The launch of the NT's $7 million advertising campaign early in February was fortuitous for Katherine, as it provided further exposure for the region and reinforced the back on track message. Apart from the support to Katherine provided through these and other actions previously mentioned, the NTTC also assisted by waiving co-operative marketing fees for Katherine operators and, in some instances, provided financial assistance for key operators to participate in travel shows.

On the basis of the comparative performance of Katherine as a destination in 1997 and 1998, it would appear that the combined marketing efforts of the KTRA and the NTTC were reasonably effective. The NTTC's Telephone Occupancy Survey reveals that, despite the flood, the Katherine region had nearly 60,000 more guest nights in 1998, compared with 1997. This represents a 15 per cent increase. It has been suggested that this figure may have been affected by the influx of trades-people drawn to the area in the reconstruction phase over the first two quarters of 1998. However, when we compare the change in guest nights in this period (i.e., relative to the corresponding period in 1997) with that in the second half of the year, this argument is not sustainable. The first half of 1998 experienced a decline in guest nights of 1.8 per cent, compared with a 27 per cent increase in the second half of the year. It may well be that, in some perverse way, the media exposure Katherine received as a consequence of the flood enhanced its appeal as a destination. As Sharyn Innes, the General Manager of the KTRA has suggested, "We are not just Katherine anymore, we are Katherine, the place that got flooded, the place where that crocodile swam down the main street" (Sunday Herald, 17 May 1998: 63). However, the potential for the flood to become an attraction has been quickly dismissed, in the short term at least. Memories of the trauma associated with the event linger in the minds of those affected, and insensitive inquiries from tourists about the floods has frequently offended staff at the Visitors' Centre and in some tourist operations. Indeed, this became such a problem at the Visitors' Centre that signs were erected requesting clients not to ask personal questions about the flood.

The above analysis describes, in broad terms, the marketing efforts in the recovery stage and indicates that the approach adopted was reasonably effective. In this sense, other destination marketing organisations can improve their preparedness for disasters by drawing on the insights provided by the Katherine example. However, much more can be learned from the Katherine experience by examining the evaluations of those who were directly involved.

5 Evaluation Methodology

Interviews were conducted with individual tourism operators, representatives of key agencies associated with destination marketing and emergency services personnel. The main objectives of these interviews were:

- To gain insights into how events associated with the disaster unfolded, from the individual respondent's perspective.
- To develop a chronology of actions taken by individuals and their organisations in response to these events, and the reasons for these actions.
- To establish the extent to which the actions taken were pre-planned and/or a response to the actions of other parties.
- To engage individuals in a post-mortem of the event in order to identify how, with the benefit of hindsight, they may have coped more effectively with the situation.
- Through the post-mortem process, to identify how other parties might have reacted more effectively to the emergency.

While the focus of the study is on the impacts of the disaster on tourism activities and responses within the tourism sector, these need to be considered in the context of the personal circumstances of the individuals involved. The safety of staff and management, and their immediate family and property, has a bearing on their response to the emergency situation and must be taken into account in the consideration of effective disaster management strategies. Also, it was recognised that the conduct of the interview had the potential to revive memories of what was a highly traumatic and stressful event for many participants. Without some sensitivity to these considerations in the conduct of interviews, the post-mortem could be instrumental in encouraging individuals to become defensive or predisposed to apportioning blame for any 'mistakes' made during the emergency. This could become counter-productive by discouraging the free exchange of views on improvements to disaster strategies in the future. Thus, it was considered important that the interviewer emphasise that no one can make mistakes in a disaster situation, especially if they are not prepared for it by previous experience, and decisions must often be made instantaneously without any opportunity for reflection. It was emphasised that the only mistake is when we fail to learn from the experience and thus, in effect, risk repeating the 'mistakes' of the past. It was suggested that the most effective way to avoid these traps is to systematically re-examine the actions of those involved in retrospect and, with the benefit of hindsight, identify those instances where a different response may have produced better results.

Each interview was loosely structured through the use of the disaster incident response evaluation (DIRE) grid described in Figure 12.1. This grid provides a framework for the respondent's recollection of the sequence of events during the disaster, and their reactions to these events. The stages of the disaster identified in the grid are based on an amalgamation of those used by Fink (1986) and Roberts (1994). The responses of all respondents were then consolidated into a composite record for consideration in the next (workshop) phase of the process.

The workshop phase of the research was aimed at:

- validating the composite record of events. The composite DIRE was presented for scrutiny, with any apparent contradictions in the record of events being highlighted for clarification. Entries on the grid were also cross-checked against official reports and media records prior to the conduct of the workshop;
- conducting a post-mortem of the event by evaluating the effectiveness of the responses of individual tourism operators and the tourism association. At this stage, instances where respondents had suggested alternative actions were highlighted; and
- identifying ways in which the flood has triggered enduring changes in either approaches to tourism management and marketing in the area, or the nature and competitiveness of tourism product.

6 Results

As certain elements of the industry's response have been discussed previously, this section concentrates on those outcomes of the evaluation process that provide additional insights into the details of tourism disaster management. These insights provide a basis for elaborating on, and refining, the generic model for tourism disaster management

Initial instructions:

- We would like to reconstruct a history of the Katherine Floods based on your recollections of what happened.
- We need to learn specifically about the sequence of the events, how you reacted to each development and to what extent your reactions were influenced by those of other individuals and agencies.
- To assist you in this exercise, we will construct a summary record of your recollections on this table. Also we will use the stages identified in the table as a guide.

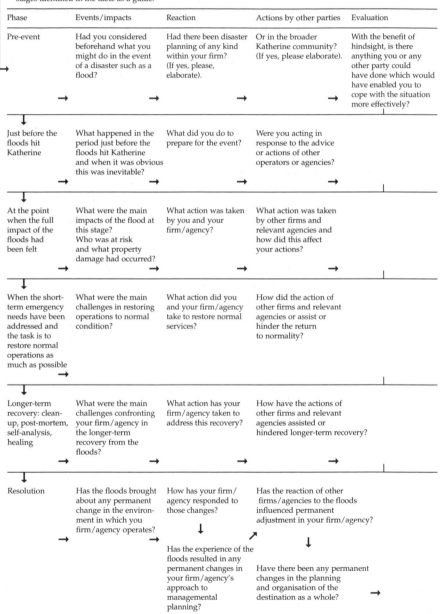

Phase	Events/impacts	Reaction	Actions by other parties	Evaluation
Pre-event	Had you considered beforehand what you might do in the event of a disaster such as a flood?	Had there been disaster planning of any kind within your firm? (If yes, please, elaborate).	Or in the broader Katherine community? (If yes, please elaborate).	With the benefit of hindsight, is there anything you or any other party could have done which would have enabled you to cope with the situation more effectively?
Just before the floods hit Katherine	What happened in the period just before the floods hit Katherine and when it was obvious this was inevitable?	What did you do to prepare for the event?	Were you acting in response to the advice or actions of other operators or agencies?	
At the point when the full impact of the floods had been felt	What were the main impacts of the flood at this stage? Who was at risk and what property damage had occurred?	What action was taken by you and your firm/agency?	What action was taken by other firms and relevant agencies and how did this affect your actions?	
When the short-term emergency needs have been addressed and the task is to restore normal operations as much as possible	What were the main challenges in restoring operations to normal condition?	What action did you and your firm/agency take to restore normal services?	How did the action of other firms and relevant agencies or assist or hinder the return to normality?	
Longer-term recovery: clean-up, post-mortem, self-analysis, healing	What were the main challenges confronting your firm/agency in the longer-term recovery from the floods?	What action has your firm/agency taken to address this recovery?	How have the actions of other firms and relevant agencies assisted or hindered longer-term recovery?	
Resolution	Has the floods brought about any permanent change in the environment in which you firm/agency operates?	How has your firm/agency responded to those changes? / Has the experience of the floods resulted in any permanent changes in your firm/agency's approach to managemental planning?	Has the reaction of other firms/agencies to the floods influenced permanent adjustment in your firm/agency? / Have there been any permanent changes in the planning and organisation of the destination as a whole?	

Figure 12.1 Tourism disaster accident response grid

strategies described in Faulkner (1999, 2001). The revised model is described in Figure 12.2, where new elements are represented in italics. Observations arising from the evaluation process are outlined below in terms of each stage of the event.

6.1 Pre-event stage

With the benefit of hindsight, the tourism sector recognised that, the notion of the "100-year flood" was instrumental in perpetuating complacency in the attitude to disaster preparedness. Apart from the evacuation plans of premises that are required as a routine component of local planning regulations, no operators had disaster management plans in place and there was no destination-wide plan. In the immediate aftermath of the event, there is now a widespread appreciation of the need for a tourism-specific disaster management plan to assist individual establishments, and the destination as a whole, to cope with such situations more effectively. It is also recognised that any tourism specific plan produced by, and for, the tourism sector needs to be articulated with the broader counter-disaster plans developed by emergency services organisations. Indeed, it is arguable that the failure of the latter to consult with the tourism organisations in the development of their plans contributed to the low level of preparedness in this sector. At the individual operator level, many are now particularly conscious of the dangers of less than detailed attention to their insurance coverage and most have upgraded this to include protection from flood damage.

There are three specific initiatives at the industry-wide level that have emerged from these observations. Firstly, the KTRA is proceeding with the development of a destination-wide tourism disaster management plan, in conjunction with emergency services agencies. Secondly, as an adjunct to this action, the KTRA has decided that it will actively engage in developing an awareness among operators of potential disasters, their likely impacts and counter-disaster measures. This will include the dissemination of flood alert information to operators and visitors as a routine responsibility of the KTRA during the wet season in particular. Finally, beyond Katherine itself, the caravan parks sector organisation is actively considering the development of disaster management plans at the individual park level as a requirement for accreditation.

6.2 Prodromal Stage

There were some lapses in the early warning system, which reduced the reaction time of operators. While, to a certain extent, these problems were attributable to denial reactions and a lack of preparedness that made operators less responsive to warnings received, it was also suggested that

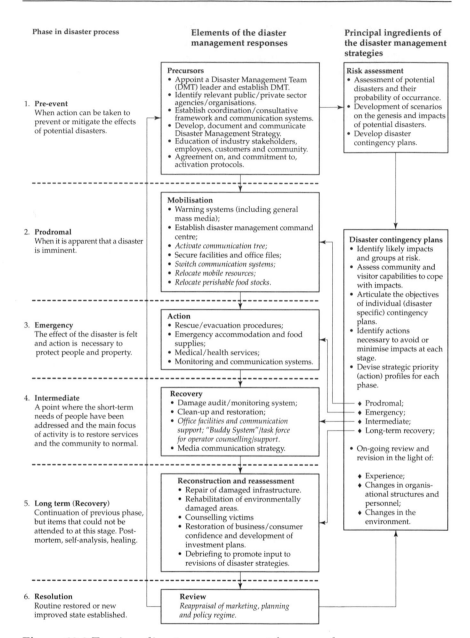

Phase in disaster process	Elements of the diaster management responses	Principal ingredients of the disaster management strategies
1. Pre-event When action can be taken to prevent or mitigate the effects of potential disasters.	**Precursors** • Appoint a Disaster Management Team (DMT) leader and establish DMT. • Identify relevant public/private sector agencies/organisations. • Establish coordination/consultative framework and communication systems. • Develop, document and communicate Disaster Management Strategy. • Education of industry stakeholders, employees, customers and community. • Agreement on, and commitment to, activation protocols.	**Risk assessment** • Assessment of potential disasters and their probability of occurrence. • Development of scenarios on the genesis and impacts of potential disasters. • Develop disaster contingency plans.
2. Prodromal When it is apparent that a disaster is imminent.	**Mobilisation** • Warning systems (including general mass media); • Establish disaster management command centre; • *Activate communication tree;* • Secure facilities and office files; • *Switch communication systems;* • *Relocate mobile resources;* • *Relocate perishable food stocks.*	**Disaster contingency plans** • Identify likely impacts and groups at risk. • Assess community and visitor capabilities to cope with impacts. • Articulate the objectives of individual (disaster specific) contingency plans. • Identify actions necessary to avoid or minimise impacts at each stage. • Devise strategic priority (action) profiles for each phase. ◆ Prodromal; ◆ Emergency; ◆ Intermediate; ◆ Long-term recovery; • On-going review and revision in the light of: ◆ Experience; ◆ Changes in organisational structures and personnel; ◆ Changes in the environment.
3. Emergency The effect of the disaster is felt and action is necessary to protect people and property.	**Action** • Rescue/evacuation procedures; • Emergency accommodation and food supplies; • Medical/health services; • Monitoring and communication systems.	
4. Intermediate A point where the short-term needs of people have been addressed and the main focus of activity is to restore services and the community to normal.	**Recovery** • Damage audit/monitoring system; • Clean-up and restoration; • *Office facilities and communication support; "Buddy System"/task force for operator counselling/support.* • Media communication strategy.	
5. Long term (Recovery) Continuation of previous phase, but items that could not be attended to at this stage. Post-mortem, self-analysis, healing.	**Reconstruction and reassessment** • Repair of damaged infrastructure. • Rehabilitation of environmentally damaged areas. • Counselling victims • Restoration of business/consumer confidence and development of investment plans. • Debriefing to promote input to revisions of disaster strategies.	
6. Resolution Routine restored or new improved state established.	**Review** *Reappraisal of marketing, planning and policy regime.*	

Figure 12.2 Tourism disaster management framework

industry-wide communication systems could be improved to facilitate the activation of counter-disaster measures. In particular, it is believed that the community-wide early warning system needs to be supplemented by a tourism-sector system based on a communication tree. The communication tree involves messages and instructions being relayed through a predetermined sequence of tourism agencies and operators, with cross checks and alternative media contingencies in the event of system failures.

A fundamental element of the disaster management planning process is the production of a "cascaded strategic priority profile", involving a rank ordering of tasks and activities that need to be undertaken, moving from the highest to the lowest priority (Heath 1995). Reflecting on what should have been done at the prodromal stage of the Katherine flood, operators and KRTA staff have suggested the following as the most important measures at this point:

- Activation of the communication tree as mentioned above.
- An adequately resourced tourism command centre needs to be established in a safe location in order to coordinate and monitor tourism related actions and developments. This facility should be located in close proximity to the counter-disaster command centre so that the implementation of the tourism disaster strategy is synchronised with the broader counter-disaster strategy.
- Many operators and KTRA staff took action to relocate office records and equipment, but in many cases these efforts were in vain because everyone underestimated the level of flooding. It was conceded that business operations would have been more readily restored to normal after the emergency if duplicate copies of office records had been routinely stored in safe locations.
- Mobile resources, such as buses, caravans and other vehicles, should be relocated to previously designated safe areas. The tourism disaster management plan should not only identify these areas, but should also have a specific communication strategy for informing operators and visitors about them.
- In order to ensure that clients and elements of the tourism industry elsewhere can receive information on the status of tourism facilities and services, communications to/from all operators should be switched to the command centre. Also, arrangements should be in place to enable communications to be switched to an alternative central communication point in the event of total communication system failures. In this case, the NTTC headquarters in Darwin or the Darwin Regional Tourism Association provide possible options for back-up communication centre.
- To avoid wastage and health problems associated with rancid food

at the clean-up stage, establishments with large food supplies should evacuate this stock in refrigerated trucks.

6.3 Emergency stage

It is notable that no definitive points were raised in the evaluation process regarding actions at the height of the emergency. This was mainly because there was little tourism operators or the KRTA could do at this stage. Attention was focused almost exclusively on safety matters and, at this point in particular, emergency services agencies had total control over rescue and safety procedures. As mentioned previously, some operators had evacuation and other safety procedures in place, in accordance with the requirements of local government and other industry regulatory agencies. However, they conceded that the tourism industry, as a whole, was generally ill-prepared for emergencies and involvement in the development of tourism specific counter-disaster strategies would greatly enhance their capacity to respond appropriately.

6.4 Intermediate stage

Some of the marketing action taken in the intermediate and longer term recovery stages has already been outlined in an earlier section, where it was also noted that these measures appeared to have been reasonable effective in achieving their objectives. However, a number of observations made during the evaluation process suggest that some minor adjustments to this approach might be considered in the refinement of the disaster management plan:

- As mentioned previously, staff from the NTTC carried out a series of damage assessments over a period of time in order to establish the level and nature of assistance required, and to enable progress in the restoration of services to be monitored for the purposes of advising consumers and industry clients. Participants in the evaluation exercise stressed the importance of using outsiders with the required expertise for this process in order to ensure objectivity and accuracy.
- Once the emergency is over, the role of the tourism disaster command centre should be extended to include the provision of equipment and facilities to help individual operators to re-establishment of their office operations and communications with clients. In particular, operators need functional computers and access to telephone and/the internet communications at this stage.
- During the intermediate and longer-term recovery stages, professional counsellors were brought into the community to assist business people and residents to recover from the stress of the event. Many tourism operators felt that this support would have been far more effective if those involved had been industry colleagues, and

especially colleagues who had themselves experienced similar disasters in the past. It was therefore suggested that, in the longer term, tourism industry associations should consider establishing a "buddy" system to facilitate the provision of such support. As an extension of this approach, a "recovery task force" system could be developed, whereby a team of (disaster) experienced operators would be formed to assist colleagues in disaster-affected destinations.

6.5 Recovery

As mentioned previously, during the implementation of the "back-on-track" campaign, a staff member of the NTTC was provided to stand-in for the General Manager of the KRTA so that the latter could be free to concentrate on representing the Katherine region in travel shows. At the time the floods hit Katherine, the GM was on holiday in Hong Kong and she returned to Katherine immediately after learning about the crisis via the global media. The fact that she was required to again be absent during much of the clean-up and rebuilding period made this a frustrating and stressful period for her in two respects. Firstly, it was important that the KRTA maintain a presence in the market in order to restore confidence among industry partners in Katherine's ability to return to normal operations within a short period of time. At the same time, however, there was a general lack of understanding about what everyone in Katherine had been through and an expectation that they could indeed function like normal people within a month of the event when conditions were far from normal. Secondly, the enforced absence from Katherine at a critical stage of the recovery was stressful because the GM would have preferred to have been with her team at the Visitor's Centre and there were aspects of her personal life (i.e. a flood-ravaged home) that needed to be attended to in the aftermath of the flood.

Management and staff in both the KRTA and the tourism industry more generally observed how the challenge of the emergency and the subsequent clean-up required an extraordinary physical effort on everyone's part over an extended period of time. This, along with the psychological stress associated with exposure to the threatening conditions of the flood and the loss of businesses and personal belongings, meant that many of those involved reached a point of physical and mental exhaustion once the task of getting their lives and business operations back to some degree of normalcy was completed. As one operator commented, "up to this point we were sustained by adrenalin, but once the task was done the pent-up emotions and fatigue overwhelmed us". It is at this point, weeks and months after the event, that many were in need of an opportunity 'to recharge their batteries' by taking a break. However, this opportunity did not come because, the high season for tourism was already upon them and it was essential that the cash flows of their businesses be restored. The provision of support through the "buddy system" or task force approach referred to above would have been very timely at this point.

7 Longer-Term Advantageous and Detrimental Effects

It is commonly claimed that, out of adversity experienced by a community (or individual), beneficial changes often emerge which make that community (or individual) stronger and better able to cope with the challenges that confront them in the longer term. In the literature, some authors have followed this theme by emphasising the transformational nature of crises and disasters, and the fact that such events often represent a turning point in the history of the organisations and individuals affected (Fink 1986). Meanwhile, others have stressed that these turning points often have positive, as well as negative, connotations. For instance, Berman and Roel (1993: 82) have observed how the Mexico City earthquake triggered both "regressive tendencies" and "progressive potentials and solidarity" within certain sectors of the affected community. Chan (1995) has also observed that, while periodic flooding in parts of Peninsula Malaysia frequently devastates rural communities, agricultural production in the region relies on this natural phenomenon to maintain the fertility of riverine soils.

Although it may be too early to identify longer-term changes in Katherine's tourism development as a consequence of the flood, a range of actual and potential shifts in the destination's focus have been observed.

The most commonly mentioned positive impacts of the flood include:

- The refurbishment of both general community and tourism specific infrastructure necessitated by damage caused by the flood is seen by many as a major positive outcome of the event. This perception is reflected in the following comment by one of the tourism operators involved in the evaluation: "Before the flood the town was a very tired town. We needed an update. Now we have a lot of upmarket services and hotels (that) had to be refurbished. I would not get on a pedestal and say it, but the flood did us a lot of good. Even the streets are cleaner."
- The Katherine flood was a stressful experience in many respects. It was life-threatening at the height of the emergency, many witnessed their livelihood and personal belongings being literally washed away, while everyone faced the daunting task of restoring their lives and businesses back to normal afterwards. This shared experience was instrumental in galvanising a team spirit and a preparedness to

provide mutual support, which has strengthened the coherence of both the tourism sector and the broader community in the longer term. Also, the flood was seen to be a significant leveler in the sense that the larger operators lost more than their smaller counterparts and, with everyone being reduced to near bankruptcy, a greater willingness to work together is now apparent.

- As suggested in the examination of the "back on track" campaign, media coverage of the event raised the profile of Katherine in the market place. Initially this exposure was counter-productive because it prolonged the perception of Katherine as a flood-ravaged region, and therefore deterred potential visitors. However, as this aspect of the image becomes less significant, positive awareness might be enhanced and the flood itself may become part of the region's attraction.

- While many tourism businesses have suffered substantial financial losses owing to insurance policies that did not cover damage by flood, most now have more appropriate policies that allow for this contingency. Also, at the destination level, there is now a greater appreciation of the need for disaster preparedness within the industry and this is being translated into action involving the development of a disaster management plan.

- It has been suggested that attitudes towards tourism within the community have improved since the flood because, in the struggle to return businesses to viable levels of activity, the dependence of this on fluctuations in visitor numbers has become more apparent.

- Some tourism operators feel that the flood was an "acid test" for staff, which enabled them to distinguish between those staff who could be relied upon in difficult times and those who could not.

It may well be that a combination of the above positive changes in the tourism sector may have reinforced elements of the "back on track" campaign in achieving the relatively strong performance of the industry in the period since the flood. Whether this is true or not, there are other factors which have the potential to limit the longevity of some of these effects. For instance, as memories of the flood fade and the migration of people into and out of the community eventually dilutes the core of "flood veterans", positive effects on teamwork and preparedness to work cooperatively together might not be sustained. The appreciation of the need for disaster preparedness might also erode for the same reason, while any positive promotional effects might be equally short lived. On the other hand, the recognition of these benefits may result in them becoming more permanent if an approach to destination management aimed at ensuring their longevity is put in place.

Negative effects identified in the evaluation process included the following.

- Despite the effectiveness of the Katherine "back on track" campaign, significant short-term financial losses were incurred by tourism operators because the perception of Katherine being washed-out lasted for some time beyond the reality. However, losses associated with this effect were minor when compared with those attributable to the refusal of insurance companies to cover damage associated with the effects of the flood. In the longer term, this will result in operators putting off investment plans for the expansion of their activities. Reduced asset values of properties have detrimentally affected borrowing capabilities.
- The trauma of the flood experience was so intense for many people living and working in Katherine that they have decided to move elsewhere. The loss of experienced staff and continuing high levels of staff turn-over has, in many instances, affected the efficiency of operations, and more resources for staff training has been necessary.
- The focus on reconstruction in the Katherine tourism industry over the last 12 months has meant that strategic marketing and development issues have not been addressed. Also, the increased workload for KRTA staff during the recovery stage, combined with the loss of experienced staff, has meant the tourism industry's interests could not be represented on various public sector and community committees.
- While it has been suggested that the effects of the flood may have been instrumental in improving the awareness of tourism's contribution to the local economy within the community, it is also true that tensions over priorities in the use of funds for reconstruction within the business community has resulted in plans for a much needed new visitors' Centre being shelved. Funds had been earmarked for the construction of a new visitors' centre and KRTA headquarters prior to the flood. However, when the construction of the new centre was mentioned with other expenditures associated with the post-flood reconstruction programme, the business community perceived this as being preferential treatment for the tourism sector and the allocation was rescinded in response to widespread resentment.

A summary of these tourism impacts of the flood is produced in Figure 12.3, where five broad dimensions have been recognised: marketing, investment, disaster preparedness, cohesion and human resources. This framework highlights the complexity of the flood's aftermath by showing that, in each of these areas, the impacts of the flood can be viewed from different angles to produce conclusions that appear to be contradictory. Thus, the impact of the flood on the marketing of the destination appears to have both positive and negative effects, although it might be argued that the diversion of attention away from strategic issues has the potential to eventually nullify any marketing benefits in the longer term. Unless the balance of KRTA activities can be swung more towards addressing strategic issues soon, the destination could struggle on this front in the near future. While the flood has been instrumental in increasing public and private sector investment in the refurbishment of infrastructure, this has been at the expense of investment in new initiatives that might have contributed to the expansion of tourism infrastructure. The flood experience has contributed to increased cohesion within the tourism sector and improved awareness of tourism's economic importance in the local community, but issues associated with the allocation of funds during the reconstruction phase have increased tensions between tourism and other business sectors. In the human resources area, one of the consequences of the flood has been increased staff turnover problems, which have in turn reduced the efficiency and productivity operations. The "acid test" effect appears to be a small consolation in the context of

	POSITIVE	NEGATIVE
Marketing	• Media profile due to flood coverage; • Flood history a potential attraction in its own right.	• Focus on flood impacts delays market response beyond restoration of services; • Focus on recovery diverts attention/resources from strategic issues.
Infrastructure and investment	• Refurbishment of infrastructure.	• Curtailment of investment in expansion of infra-structure.
Improvement in disaster preparedness	• Development of tourism disaster management plan; • Upgrading of insurance policies to allow for flood damage.	• Losses incurred as a consequence of the flood represent a high price for a "wake-up call".
Cohesion	• Team spirit and cooperat-iveness galvanised within tourism sector; • Improved community awareness of tourism benefit.	• Tensions between tourism sector and business community over allocation of resources.
Human resources	• "Acid test" for staff.	• High staff turnover and loss of experienced staff.

Figure 12.3 Longer-term positive and negative tourism impacts of the Katherine flood

this problem. Similarly, the flood has sharpened the industry's appreciation of the need for disaster preparedness, although this has been achieved only after the inordinate financial and personal costs of the flood have been experienced.

By drawing attention to enduring positive and negative impacts of the flood, the above synthesis highlights two aspects of disaster situation, which have been alluded to earlier in this paper and elsewhere (Faulkner 1999). Firstly, conventional approaches to disaster management implicitly assume that the events creating the crisis situation are invariably temporary aberrations, and that the primary objective is to restore the system to the pre-existing (pre-shock) equilibrium. However, as elements of the chaos theory perspective suggest, some shocks have lingering effects that make the pre-shock equilibrium a redundant (or at least sub-optimal) approach with regard to longer-term sustainability. Also the chaos created by crises can be a creative process, with the potential for innovative new configurations emerging from the "ruins". Secondly, Richardson's (1994) distinction between "single-" and "double-loop" learning approaches to disaster situations is insightful, because it emphasises the importance of a fundamental reassessment of the destination's management and planning approaches at the post-disaster stage if the positive enduring effects are to be accentuated and the negatives ameliorated. It is for this reason that the revised model in Figure 12.2 includes a reappraisal of the destination's tourism marketing, planning and policy regime as a part of the resolution phase.

8 Conclusion

For the Katherine community generally, and its tourism industry in particular, the 1998 Australia Day flood represented a situation which embodied all the features commonly associated with a disaster. The magnitude of the flooding was so significant that the routine operations of the tourism industry were not only disrupted, but the future survival of the industry was jeopardised. In addition to the threatening nature of the event, there was an element of surprise that left those affected with very short decision times and a feeling of being unable to cope. The urgency of the disaster situation means that operators and the RTA did not have the luxury of reflecting on the most appropriate action to take. Nor was there time to engage in the consultations necessary to produce a fully coordinated response. Furthermore, as the threat presented by the disaster and the surprise factor made the experience a highly stressful one for those involved, decision-making capabilities were inevitably impaired under such circumstances. These characteristics of the disaster situation highlight the need for the development and ongoing review of destination disaster management plans to become a routine component of the

RTAs' agenda. A prompt and effective response to a disaster is more likely if tourism operators, the RTA and relevant public sector agencies engage in a systematic process of canvassing and evaluating alternative responses to various disaster scenarios in advance. Once this process is completed, the responses agreed to should be incorporated in official disaster management plans that codify responsibilities and coordination requirements.

In many respects, the reaction of the KTRA and NTTC to the Katherine flood was very effective. In particular, the design and implementation of the "back on track" marketing campaign produced the desired results and, in this regard, the approach adopted is a model for others to follow. However, with the benefit of hindsight, there are aspects of the Katherine tourism industry's response at both the individual and the destination level that those directly involved would change. Many of these changes reinforce the above point regarding the necessity of planning for disasters because they require arrangements to be in place in advance of the event. For instance, the communication tree must be pre-arranged, and arrangements for the command centre facility and the switching of communication systems must be made in advance. The Katherine case study, and the retrospective evaluation by those directly involved in tourism at this destination, has provided a rich source of insights for testing and refining the generic model for tourism disaster management developed previously (Faulkner 1999). The revised version in Figure 12.1 contains details that are particularly relevant to disaster situation produced by flooding. The extent to which these changes are potentially applicable to other types of disasters needs to be tested through the examination of more case studies involving a range of different types of disaster.

The focus of this paper has been on how the destination as a whole can cope with disasters, rather than on the measures individual operators might adopt in these situations. This emphasis reflects the view that, as in the case of destination marketing, a coordinated approach involving mutual support among operators will enable them to confront the challenges of the emergency more effectively than if they were each behaving independently. Also, at the destination level, the RTA is in a better position to take the initiative and drive the development of a tourism-specific disaster management strategy in a manner that simultaneously educates operators, brings them into contact with relevant counter-disaster agencies, and involves the degree of ownership of the plan that is necessary for ensuring their full commitment to it. Thus, while the regional counter-disaster plan developed by emergency services agencies deals with many of the issues associated with ensuring the safety of visitors and employees, and comprises the framework for tourism disaster management, the latter provides the vehicle for effectively implementing the plan in the tourism sector. In addition to this, however, there are specific problems affecting the tourism sector in disaster situations that are not addressed in the more general regional counter-disaster plan. These include, in particular, tourism marketing strategies in the recovery phase.

Some destinations experience disasters that have a high probability of recurring. Examples of this include tropical destinations in cyclone belts and, to a less extent, destinations like Katherine where tropical weather patterns increase the incidence of major floods. Such destinations have the dubious benefit of being in a position to refine their disaster management strategies through experience. Meanwhile, where tourism plays a major role in the regional economy, it is more likely that tourism-specific issues will be addressed in the regional counter-disaster plan and related procedures will become more routinised within tourism businesses. One of the challenges of tourism disaster management is to ensure that destinations develop a degree of preparedness for events that have a low probability of occurring. The generic model in Figure 12.1 is equally relevant to such situations. Being prepared for the unexpected requires a process where a broad spectrum of disaster scenarios is identified and contingency plans are developed to cope with these. However, the difficulty of convincing tourism operators to invest their time into a process aimed at considering responses to events that have a low probability of occurring represents one of the major barriers to disaster preparedness in this sector.

Finally, the Katherine flood story has emphasised how disasters can produce potentially enduring changes in the destination with both positive and negative connotations. The expectation of returning the destination to a situation that exactly replicates the pre-disaster equilibrium is therefore neither realistic, nor necessarily desirable. It is not realistic because some of the negative impacts (e.g. financial losses and downstream impacts on investment capacity) are unavoidable, while it is not desirable because there are positive impacts (e.g. improved cohesion of the tourism sector) that can contribute to the longer-term sustainability of the destination. Within the disaster management framework, the implication of this is that the resolution phase should involve the establishment of a post-disaster management and planning regime that reinforces the positive and nullifies the negative changes produced by the disaster.

Acknowledgements

The research described in this paper has been funded by Australia's Cooperative Research Centre for Sustainable Tourism. The authors also appreciate the support provided by the Katherine Regional Tourism Association and, in particular, this organisation's General Manager, Sharyn Innes.

References

Berman, R. and Roel, G. (1993) Encounter with death and destruction: The 1985 Mexico City earthquake. *Group Analysis,* 26, 89–98.

Booth, S. (1993) *Crisis Management Strategy: Competition and Change in Modern Enterprises,* New York, Routledge.

Burby, R. J. and Wagner, F. (1996) Protecting tourists from death and injury in coastal storms. *Disasters,* 20(1), 49–60.

Cammisa, J. V. (1993) The Miami experience: Natural and manmade disasters 1992–93. In *Expanding Responsibilities: A Blueprint for the Travel Industry.* 24th Annual Conference Proceedings, Travel and Tourism Research Association, Whistler, BC (pp. 294–295).

Carter, W. N. (1991) *Disaster Management: A Disaster Manager's Handbook.* Manila: Asian Development Bank.

Cassedy, K. (1991) *Crisis Management Planning in the Travel and Tourism Industry: A Study of Three Destinations and a Crisis Management Planning Manual.* San Francisco: PATA.

Chan, N. W. (1995) Flood disaster management in Malaysia: An evaluation of the effectiveness of government resettlement schemes. *Disaster Prevention and Management,* 4(4), 22–29.

Drabek, T. E. (1992) Variations in disaster evacuation behaviour: Public responses versus private sector executive decision-making. *Disasters,* 16(2), 105–118.

—— (1995) Disaster responses within the tourism industry. *International Journal of Mass Emergencies and Disasters,* 13(1), 7–23.

Faulkner, B. (1999) *Tourism Disasters: Towards a Generic Model.* CRC Tourism Work-in-Progress Report Series, report 6.

—— (2001) Towards a framework for tourism disaster management. *Tourism Management,* 22, 135–147.

Fink, S. (1986) *Crisis Management.* New York: American Association of Management.

Heath, R. (1995) The Kobe earthquake: Some realities of strategic management of crises and disasters. *Disaster Prevention and Management,* 4(5), 11–24.

Huque, A. S. (1998) Disaster management and the inter-organizational imperative: 'The Hong Kong disaster plan'. *Issues and Studies,* 34(2), 104–123.

Keown-McMullan, C. (1997) Crisis: When does a molehill become a mountain? *Disaster Prevention and Management,* 6(1), 4–10.

Murphy, P. E. and Bayley, R. (1989) Tourism and disaster planning. *Geographical Review,* 79(1), 36–46.

Northern Territory Tourist Commission (1998) *Territory Tourism, Selected Statistics 1997/1998,* Darwin: NTTC.

Richardson, B. (1994) Crisis management and the management strategy: Time to "loop the loop". *Disaster Prevention and Management,* 3(3), 59–80.

Reed, M. (1998) Northern Territory Legislative Assembly, 17 February.

Roberts, V. (1994) Flood management; Bradford paper. *Disaster Prevention and Management,* 3(2), 44–60.

Weiner, A. J. and Kahn, H. (1972) "Crisis and arms control". In C. F. Hermann (ed.), *International Crises: Insights from Behaviour Research* (p. 21). New York: The Free Press.

Walsh, B. (1999) *The Aftermath: Critical Aspects. Address to the Northern Territory Employee Assistance Service Annual General Meeting.* Northern Territory: Darwin.

Part 4

Tourism Research Agendas

Introduction

The tourism research effort in Australia up to the mid-late 1980s was both limited and fragmented. Limited in terms of the scale and scope of the research being carried out, and fragmented because of the disparate and relatively isolated groups who were involved in research activities. This situation was largely a reflection of the magnitude, profile and status of the tourism industry at the time. Tourism continued to suffer from the inertia of the 1950s mindset, whereby the prevailing attitude of policy makers and the general public alike had difficulty accepting any area of economic activity that did not produce commodities or manufactured goods that could be physically exported as a legitimate sector of the economy. Without such legitimacy, tourism was marginalised in the policy agenda and there was little motivation for government to fund or otherwise encourage research on tourism issues.

The formation of the BTR in 1987 sent out a clear message that tourism research was to be seen as a serious pursuit, fundamental to the development of an internationally competitive tourism industry. Bill was appointed as the foundation Director of the BTR in recognition of the fact that he had the ability to establish and deliver a tourism research agenda for Australia, and because he was seen to have the skills to foster the development of tourism researchers in Australia. For the remaining 15 years of his life, Bill was dedicated to this cause.

In his role as Director of the BTR, and then later as Deputy CEO and Director of Research for the CRC, Bill led the way in setting and updating tourism research agendas that helped establish Australia as a world leader in tourism research. He also played a vital role as a teacher and mentor to students and research colleagues alike, and took every opportunity to promote research as the most appropriate basis for informed tourism planning and decision-making.

The first chapter in this section was written as an editorial, which appeared in the 1991 September quarter 'BTR Tourism Update', along-side the usual statistics on arrivals, visitor nights, and occupancy rates. Although this type of comment was not customary in these 'Updates', Bill felt compelled, as Director of the BTR, to reflect upon what he felt was an increasing trend toward 'advertising fundamentalism'. He felt that this was diverting funds away from activities that would provide a more thorough understanding of the market, such as research and strategic market planning. Bill enjoyed challenging practices, such as these, that he felt were inappropriate and his views had substantial influence on sub-sequent actions. As a government employee, however, Bill felt somewhat constrained in his ability to express his views on some practices that he considered to be misguided, and this prompted his return to academe in 1992.

In the early 1990s, the Council of Australian University Tourism and Hospitality Education (CAUTHE) was established to represent the interests of universities involved in tourism and hospitality education and research. Bill became one of the key drivers in this organisation that sought to establish a tourism education and research framework within the growing number of universities that had introduced tourism programs. However, Bill's concern about the quality and quantity of tourism research output, and the supportiveness of the environment in which research takes place was still evident in a paper he co-authored with senior colleagues within the CAUTHE organisation. This paper, which was presented at the annual CAUTHE research conference in 1994, is included as the second chapter in this section. The chapter documents the progress made to that date in tourism research, particularly within the academic context, but also highlights some of the impediments facing researchers, many of which are still an issue today. In the period since this chapter was written, however, tourism research has progressed substan-tially, and this is in no small part due to Bill's influence.

The final chapter in this section was one of the last documents that Bill produced. It provides a vision for the new research agenda to underpin the CRC for Sustainable Tourism's bid for re-funding in 2003. Like many of Bill's visions, this one was comprehensive and ambitious and it aimed to develop a research program that informed the planning and manage-ment of growth of Australia's tourism industry over the 20 years until 2020, at which time some forecasts expect inbound tourist numbers to Australia to reach 20 million. The genesis of this vision arose in discus-sions that Bill had with senior staff at the Australian Tourist Commission and the Tourism Forecasting Council about Australia's ability to meet the forecast growth in tourism numbers in a sustainable fashion. Bill developed this comprehensive vision during his illness when he was forced to take time away from day-to-day work pressures.

The proposed agenda combines Bill's interests in forecasting with his awareness of the importance of a holistic approach to destinatio. management through the monitoring of economic, environmental and social impacts. He refers to the importance of identifying and developing strategies to manage 'hotspots', which are areas where the impacts of tourism threaten the sustainability of the destination. The proposal also identifies the potential impact of crises and disasters in tourism ('flash-points'), and the planned research is underpinned by Bill's curiosity and desire to explore alternative research methods. As such, the paper represents a confluence of Bill's interests and is a fitting conclusion to this volume.

↵ Role of Research in Tourism Development

Bill Faulkner

There is an emerging trend among tourism agencies in Australia towards an increasing emphasis on advertising at the expense of research, strategic marketing and other activities which provide the ingredients of a more balanced and rational approach to the development of the tourism industry. The rationale of this approach, which for the purposes of this exercise I will refer to as 'advertising fundamentalism', appears to hinge on four basic propositions:

- That the key to gaining the competitive edge in the quest for maximising market share resides in the manipulation of consumer awareness and choice through advertising programmes. In the context of limited funding and the high cost of maintaining elec- tronic media exposure, therefore, the diversion of funds from research and other areas is justified;
- That research is generally incomprehensible to decision makers, and unless the benefits of tourism research in increasing visitor numbers are immediate and obvious, it is of no value;
- That market forces should be allowed to determine research priorities – i.e., only that research which the industry is prepared to pay for should be carried out; and
- That corporate research needs can most effectively be addressed through the use of external consultants.

The first of these propositions encapsulates the key tenet of 'advertising fundamentalism', while the others have been used to justify the down- grading of research functions which has generally accompanied the shift to the advertising approach. The Bureau of Tourism Research (BTR) would fall short of fulfilling its charter if these trends towards 'advertising fundamentalism' were allowed to gain momentum without comment. Reactions to each of the underlying propositions are therefore provided below.

Advertising Fundamentalism

While it is plausible that an increased commitment to advertising will increase market share, this will only occur if these programs are integrated with a broader strategy encompassing product development and the effective identification and targeting of potential market segments. Also, the impacts of advertising and the marketing programme as a whole need to be continuously monitored and evaluated so that deficiencies can be remedied and adjustments made in response to changing circumstances. Without a sound research basis to these aspects of the total marketing process, the tourism development ship will be under the control of a blind pilot.

The advertising fundamentalists will appear to be vindicated in the short term, as inbound and domestic tourism demand is likely to pick up in response to improving international and domestic economic conditions over the next year or so. The extent to which increased visitation levels are actually attributable to the new emphasis on advertising will therefore be open to question, and will certainly not be verifiable if research functions are downgraded. More importantly, however, problems will be encountered in the future as the effectiveness of longer term (i.e. strategic) planning is jeopardised by the downgrading of research input.

Incomprehensibility of Research

The criticism that research reports are generally incomprehensible, and therefore useless, cannot be lightly dismissed by the research community. Researchers in general need to become more sensitive to the needs of decision makers in terms of both the focus of research projects and the user friendliness of their output. However, there are limits to how far researchers can go in this regard, and the extent to which research is effectively used in the future will depend on the preparedness of key decision makers to provide a meaningful input to the planning of research programmes and to becoming more familiar with technical issues.

Immediacy of Benefits and Market Forces

While market forces provide a valid basis for determining research priorities, reliance on this, approach alone will result in an over emphasis on activities that can be translated into immediate commercial gains, at the expense of giving due consideration to longer term issues of relevance to the broader community and the industry as a whole. It is unlikely that research into, for instance, the environmental and social impacts of tourism would be carried out under the market forces regime, even though problems in these areas could eventually render the tourism product of particular regions unsaleable. The over-reliance on market forces as a guide to tourism research priorities could therefore be counter-productive even in terms of commercial criteria.

Another problem with the application of the market forces rationale to tourism research concerns the difficulty of identifying the specific beneficiaries of research in order to determine who should pay for it. Consideration of the funding options for the Australian Tourist Commission (ATC), in the context of the Industry Commission Inquiry, has demonstrated the difficulty of establishing mechanisms for appor-tioning industry funding contributions to generic promotions programs in relation to which of the benefits are generalised. The problem of funding research is similar in this regard.

Reliance on External Consultants

The use of external consultants to provide research support to agencies obviously creates efficiencies in the deployment of staff when dramatic peaks in workload are involved and/or where staff lack the expertise required for specific tasks. However, they should be used to supplement rather than replace in-house resources. The replacement of in-house resources by external consultants can be counterproductive where on-going projects or services are concerned because this introduces the potential for continuity problems. The external consultant is also required to respond to competing demands from other clients. In any case, some degree of in-house research expertise is essential in order to assist in the specification of corporate research requirements, and to brief and supervise consultants on behalf of the organisation.

Conclusion

Part of the success of Australian tourism in recent years is undoubtedly attributable to the commitment of the Commonwealth and State/Territory governments to tourism research. This commitment is particularly mani-fest in the joint funding of the BTR and, as a consequence of this, Australian tourism statistical and research facilities are arguably far superior to those of other developed countries against whom we are competing for market share. Superiority in research is an integral part of our competitive advantage, particularly if the sound research which is already being carried out can be translated into the strategic positioning of the Australian product. We cannot exploit this advantage if a narrow focus on advertising as a panacea to tourism development is allowed to erode our commitment to the funding and use of research.

Chapter 14

Tourism Research in Australia: Confronting the Challenges of the 1990s and Beyond

Bill Faulkner, Phil Pearce, Robin Shaw and Betty Weiler

1 Introduction

Tourism is now, indisputably, one of Australia's major growth industries, poised to make an increasingly significant contribution to Australia's export income and employment growth. Expectations regarding the role tourism can play in Australia's economic future were expressed by the then Federal Minister for Tourism, The Honourable Alan Griffiths, in a press release associated with the launch of The National Tourism Strategy ('Tourism-Australia's Passport to Growth') on the 5th of June 1992:

> Tourism is one of the nation's biggest and fastest growing industries with the potential to generate major economic benefits for Australia. This strategy provides a framework for realising that potential by providing a co-ordinated and sustainable approach to the industry's future development.

After drawing attention to the potential for overseas visitor arrivals to more than double to between 4.8 and 6.5 million by the year 2000, and the expectation of an accompanying increase of at least 200,000 new jobs over this period, the Minister emphasised that:

> To cater for this growth, we need to ensure that the right policies are in place to provide for the industry's infrastructure needs. We also need to ensure that the industry develops in an environmentally and socially acceptable manner.

An appreciation of the important role research has to play in this process was implied by the Minister's reference to the improvement of 'the industry's research base' as an important element of the Government's strategy. Yet, neither the recent history of developments in this field, nor the content of the published strategy, indicate a commitment to this

303

objective which is sufficient for the aspirations articulated by the Minister to be realised.

This chapter has been prepared in response to widespread concern among tourism researchers over the role of, and approach to, research in tourism development in Australia. An overview of the status of tourism research in Australia is provided as a basis for elaborating on these concerns. Emphasis is placed on university based research, although the research activities of government tourism agencies and the tourism industry are also considered to put this analysis into context. An examination of inquiries into aspects of tourism at the national level also adds perspective by highlighting the breadth of national tourism research needs. Impediments to addressing these requirements are then discussed and options for remedial action are considered.

2 University-Based Tourism Research

2.1 Growth of Tourism Research by the Australian Academic Community

There are many ways to measure the growth in the level of sophistication of research in a particular discipline. The first subsection relates the history of the development of undergraduate and postgraduate programs in universities and the former Colleges of Advanced Education (CAEs), which resulted in the employment of academic staff specialising in tourism teaching and research. This is followed by a discussion of a second and parallel phenomenon, the occurrence of national tourism research workshops and conferences, which have continued to increase in frequency, size and scope. The development of publishing outlets in Australia, and the initiation and expansion of international networks, are discussed in the final two subsections.

2.1.1 The study of tourism in academic institutions
The following five components of tourism education in tertiary institutions are discussed:

- The existence of undergraduate programs in tourism.
- The existence of university research centres engaged in tourism research.
- The existence of postgraduate programs in tourism.
- The completion of postgraduate theses in tourism.
- The establishment of an organisational framework to enable university academics to speak with one voice to industry and government.

With respect to undergraduate tourism degree programs, it is common knowledge that the study of tourism at the tertiary level is new to

Australia. Tourism as a subject was offered in European universities as early as the 1930's, and in the U.S. as early as 1963 at Michigan State University.

In Australia, the first university degree in hospitality management was offered by Footscray Institute of Technology, now a part of Victoria University (VU), and Gatton Agricultural College, now a campus of The University of Queensland in 1976. In 1978, Footscray initiated the first tourism degree program. Bushell and Robertson's (1993) study identified some twenty-two universities offering twenty-six bachelor's degrees in hospitality and/or tourism studies. Not surprisingly, the main players were universities in New South Wales, Victoria and Queensland. Several institutions also had postgraduate programs, with the University of Technology, Sydney (UTS) (Kuring-gai), Victoria University, James Cook University and Griffith University all offering studies up to the Master's and PhD level in the tourism field.

Of course, the growth of university degree programs in tourism does not necessarily indicate the growth of tourism research. Indeed, many tertiary institutions were scrambling in the late 1980's to find academic staff who were suitably qualified to teach in their programs, let alone qualified and motivated to do research. The vast majority of those hired did not have PhD's, and many did not have higher degrees. Perhaps one indication of the lack of research emphasis is provided by a study undertaken in 1990, which found that most degree courses in tourism in Australia which included research methods in the curriculum did not teach these subjects internally, but instead utilised staff in departments and schools outside the tourism programs (Weiler *et al.* 1991).

However, the growth of undergraduate programs would suggest that there is a growing number of academic staff members as well as students learning and able to conduct tourism research. It is estimated that there are some 20 individuals with doctoral qualifications and another 20 with Master's or other research degrees related to tourism in Australia (Pearce 1993).

Paralleling the growth of tourism courses was a second development in tertiary institutions – the creation of tourism research centres and institutes at many of these institutions. These were, in every case, single-institution efforts, the most well-known being perhaps the National Centre for Studies in Travel and Tourism, which was established with industry funding at James Cook University in 1987. Some have combined leisure and tourism emphases, such as UTS's Centre for Leisure and Tourism Studies. Since these centres operate in a competitive market place, their work is not widely available or subject to independent scrutiny. The direction of the research of these organisations is shaped by industry and client support. Consultancy work in the tourism field, particularly in the early 1990's, was frequently directed by the funding available from government agencies such as State tourism organisations and departments. Since tourism consultancy centres attempt to be self-funding, independently viable consulting operations, they have little incentive to conduct fundamental or academic research. Accordingly there is little development of new methods, few new conceptual approaches and a paucity of long term contributions to an understanding of tourism. At James Cook University, for example, the different goals of a consulting centre and a tourism research department were recognised after two years of operation and a division of activities was effected with the National Centre for Studies in Travel and Tourism undertaking commercial work and the Department of Tourism at the University taking responsibility for student education and fundamental academic work.

A third indicator of tourism research growth in Australia is the development of postgraduate degree courses. Bushell and Robertson's (1993) survey identified no less than seven universities in Australia that offered Master's degrees with at least some tourism content, be it coursework or research. This is a new development, as there were no postgraduate programs in tourism as recently as 1988 (King 1988).

Even before such programs existed, of course, there were students undertaking postgraduate research in tourism. Indeed, a fourth and very good indicator of research output from universities is the publication of theses on tourism. Hall (1991) completed a survey of all higher degree (Master and Doctoral) theses in which tourism was the subject, up to 1988. According to Hall's study, the first postgraduate thesis focusing on tourism was completed in 1968. In the 20 years that followed, there were 31 tourism-related theses, an average of only 1.5 a year, and only three of these were PhD dissertations. In 1993, Pearce (1993) estimated that there were something like 30 students in Australia undertaking higher degrees with a tourism focus. Because of these small numbers and the size of the country, and because postgraduate research in tourism is carried out in a wide variety of disciplines, there has not been a lot of networking between these student researchers.

Tourism education, and therefore tourism research, within tertiary institutions in Australia is thus at a very early stage, with almost no institutionalisation and little opportunity for networking and professional development. The need for both publishing outlets and networking has contributed to a second phenomenon that has shown steady growth over the past decade: tourism research workshops and conferences. These are discussed in the next section.

The final indicator concerns the realisation that there exists a community of interest among university-based tourism researchers and educators, and that there is a need for this group to have a common voice in dealings with industry and government. Accordingly, the Council of Australian University Tourism and Hospitality Education (CAUTHE) was formally established in 1993, with the explicit purpose of facilitating networking among its membership and representing their collective interests. Within the title of this organisation, the term 'education' is used in the broadest possible sense to incorporate the nexus between teaching and research.

2.1.2 National tourism research workshops and conferences

With respect to research workshops, the intergovernmental committee known as the Australian Standing Committee on Tourism (ASCOT) has organised an Australian Tourism Research Workshop (ATRW) annually since the late 1970's, with the main objective being to foster the development of research techniques and skills. For this reason, many of the workshops have been restricted in numbers of participants, and their role as a networking medium or as an outlet for the publication of research findings has therefore been minimal. Nonetheless, they have played an important role in keeping tourism research on the national agenda and hopefully raising the standards of research conducted by those who participate in the workshops.

A much better indicator of the growth and scope of tourism research in Australia, particularly academic research, is the staging of and attendance at national tourism research conferences. These provide one useful measure of not only the growth of tourism research, but its strengths and weaknesses in this country. Attendance at these conferences provides one of the few opportunities for a tourism researcher to interact and develop his/her research ideas and expertise, and the only opportunity to network in an environment that is entirely tourism research oriented.

The first national tourism conference was held in Canberra in 1988 and was attended by 104 delegates, many of whom were non-academic. The Bureau of Tourism Research (BTR) in conjunction with The University of Queensland can be credited with taking the initiative to host this conference focusing on tourism research in Australia. However, clearly this conference, called Frontiers of Australian Tourism, had more on its agenda than tourism research. The conference was only partially research-oriented, for three reasons. Firstly, its aims were much broader than research and included, for example:

- The delineation of key policy issues for the upcoming decade; and
- The encouragement of co-operation between government and the private sector in tourism development.

Secondly, the conference was organised in conjunction with ASCOT, and thirdly, the conference was held in Canberra; as a result, the conference attracted a large number of politicians and government bureaucrats, and included many non-research based, policy-oriented papers.

Notwithstanding these limitations, a full-day was devoted to the

Australian Travel Research Workshop (ATRW) and a few research papers were also presented outside this workshop. The objectives of the ATRW included:

- To identify research priorities;
- To explore the application of alternative analytical frameworks and techniques; and
- To establish a network of researchers in tourism.

Of the 46 papers published in the proceedings, 18 were research-oriented.

It is significant and worth noting that the BTR published the proceedings, which has since given the conference its 'research' image. It was therefore an important conference from the perspective of tourism research in Australia.

The strengths and weaknesses of tourism research were assessed based on a content analysis of the authors, titles and abstracts in the proceedings of the first three Australian tourism research conferences.

A profile of the 'typical' researcher publishing in these conference proceedings is male, from an academic institution in New South Wales, and based in the disciplines of Economics or Business. Areas of strength and particularly areas of weakness are as follows:

- There are very few researchers representing the social science disciplines other than economics and business studies;
- The pattern seems to be that conference presenters are most likely to come from the city hosting the conference. This is not a problem, provided that the conference continues to move to new locations each year. All three conferences have been in the vicinity of the Canberra/Sydney/Newcastle triangle, so researchers outside this geographic area have been disadvantaged; and
- Research topics have been heavily dominated by economic and demand issues at all three conferences, with a moderate shift toward marketing, behaviour and perception research.

There are two particularly interesting trends that are worth highlighting and comparing to a study of tourism research trends published in Annals of Tourism Research in 1988 (Dann *et al.* 1988). In this article, the authors note that tourism research is becoming increasingly sophisticated methodologically, but its theoretical development has been much less evident. If we look at the brief period of time represented by the three national tourism conferences held in Australia, we see a trend that seems to be consistent with Dann *et al.*'s (1988) findings:

- There was a moderate but steady increase in the percentage of papers that were empirically-based, from 44% to 52% to 58% of the published papers.

- There was a marked decline in the percentage of papers that made a theoretical contribution to the literature, that is, that tested a theory or offered a new conceptual or analytical framework for the study of tourism, from 67% to 48% to 32% of the published papers.

A second useful measure of tourism research in Australia is the existence and rise of tourism specific sessions and even specifically tourism-related conferences in the 1980's and 1990's. For example, within the discipline of Geography there were only very occasional papers on tourism in the 1970's. In 1984 1988 and 1991 whole sections of Australian Geographical Society conferences featured tourism sections. Similarly, in psychology and social psychology, sections of the 1985 1986 1988 and 1990 Australian Psychological Society and Australian Social Psychology conferences had at least one multiple paper session on tourism. This kind of 'within a discipline' activity, and a similar documentation could be made in areas of economics, anthropology, architecture and planning, business and managerial studies, raises the issue that there are 'hidden' tourism researchers in Australia, that is, individuals who make occasional contributions to tourism from within the frameworks of their own disciplines. Only some of these individuals have been represented at the tourism research conferences discussed earlier. Strategies to develop tourism research in Australia should recognise the existence of these hidden researchers and attempt to develop their broader understanding of tourism while benefiting from their specialist knowledge base and analytic skills.

Additionally, some tourism-specific conferences have been organised which broaden our consideration of the status of Australian tourism research. The Australian Tourism Outlook Forum, conducted annually has featured some academic speakers, and offers the prospect of linking academic research with industry concerns about the future of Australian tourism.

Further, conferences on tourism themes such as transport, tourist attractions, theme parks, national parks and world heritage areas, have all featured academic tourism speakers. One emerging area of interest is that of ecotourism including interpretation and visitor evaluation. These themes have been embraced in such conferences as the Visitor Centres conference (James Cook University, Townsville, April 1991), Ecotourism (Brisbane 1991), Interpretation conference (Deakin University, November 1992) and Open to Interpretation (Newcastle University, November 1993).

The recency of these developments and the variety of conference topics pertaining to tourism suggests that a small set of active researchers is emerging against a background of a much larger group of researchers with occasional 'within discipline' interest in tourism.

2.1.3 The development of Australian tourism publishing
As might be expected from the review of academic programs and
conference activity, there is a small core of committed tourism researchers
involved in publishing their research and a larger body of occasional
contributors. Until 1990 there was no peer refereed academic tourism
journals in Australia. The Journal of Tourism Studies, published twice
a year since 1990, now fills this role with over 56% of authors being
Australian in the first three years of operation. The production of The
Journal of Tourism Studies provides a clear stimulus to fundamental
research, not only in terms of publishing but in involving Australian
academics in the critical review process of appraising other Australian
and international work.

Table 14.1 illustrates the importance of The Journal of Tourism Studies
in stimulating Australian research. The data reported in Table 14.1 indicate
that the existence of *The Journal of Tourism Studies* (1990–1992) has already
doubled the number of articles produced by Australian authors in the
period 1987–1992 and raised the overall percentage contribution in
leading tourism journals from 3% to 5.5%.

A consideration of Australian tourism publishing would not be
complete without reference to the role of the Bureau of Tourism Research
in publishing tourism research conference proceedings and also local
publishing houses, such as Hospitality Press, in encouraging Australian
authors to write introductory tourism text books. Again, these developments are a positive sign of a growing contribution to the tourism research
presence in Australian universities.

2.1.4 International connections and networks
A final measure of the status of tourism research in Australia lies in the
connections between Australian researchers and their international
colleagues. Three Australian academics are members of the International
Academy for the Study of Tourism (an organisation whose elite 50 person
membership is determined by election on the basis of international
scholarly activity). James Cook University is recognised by the World
Tourism Organisation as an international tourism education and training
centre and is a member of the network of world wide education and training centres. Six Australian universities and 20 academics are involved
with the US based Travel and Tourism Research Association, 11 individuals
and 12 institutions are members of the international organisation CHRIE
(for Hospitality and Tourism Educators) while there are three elected
academic members of the prestigious European organisation AIEST
(International Association of Scientific Experts in Tourism).

In addition, several Australian academics are now members of
the editorial boards of the major international tourism research journals.
The consistent image which emerges from this snapshot of Australian

Table 14.1 Analysis of journal publication by place of residence of tourism authors 1987–1992 (All entries refer to the number of articles contributed, not the number of authors)

Place of Residence of Author (11 leading contributors)	Leading International Tourism Journals (Country of Publication)				Percentage of Total Number of Articles	Australian Journal	Percentage of JTS	Adjusted Percentage of Total Number of Articles
	Annals of Tourism Research (US)	Journal of Leisure Research (US)	Journal of Travel Research (US)	Tourism Mange-ment (UK)		Journal of Tourism Studies		
U.S.A.	127	200	144	47	57	12	24	55
U.K.	32	4	9	104	16	4	8	16
Canada	41	16	29	24	12	3	6	12
Australia	10	2	7	7	3	28	56	5.5
New Zealand	2	1	4	7	1.5	2	4	1.5
West Indies	6	1	3	5	1.5	—	—	1.5
Israel	10	2	0	1	1.5	—	—	1.5
Spain	2	0	1	2	0.5	—	—	0.5
Germany	3	0	0	1	0.5	1	2	0.5
Hong Kong	1	1	1	1	0.5	—	—	0.5
Italy	2	0	0	2	0.5	—	—	0.5

academics and their international recognition is that there is a small body of tourism scholars who have nevertheless achieved some recognition and integration with the international tourism research community.

2.2 Current Research Funding Schemes

The present tourism research funding situation in Australia may be referred to as a 'drought'. Despite the increased number of tourism scholars, the rising presence of tourism research in the academic community and the general growth of the industry, the research funding agencies have failed to fund tourism studies in any significant manner.

Researchers seeking funds for tourism studies constantly find themselves marginalised, misclassified and misunderstood. These highly negative and undesirable outcomes, which are currently suppressing the activity of tourism scholars in Australia, derive from multiple sources of influence.

A leading problem is the inadequate classification of tourism research, both in the Australian Bureau of Statistics (ABS) classification of research fields and the associated system of research classification employed by the Australian Research Council (ARC), the leading Government funding agency for academic work. Tourism researchers are forced to classify themselves as 'other social science' or 'other business' or 'other ecology' in their description of their field. This process marginalises tourism research by putting it into a category where it is not seen as a separate reputable field. Additionally, these marginal 'other' areas do not have a consistent reviewing panel; it has been the experience of several applicants that the tourism applications may be variously reviewed by geographers, humanists, scientists and economists, all talented individuals but often lacking any depth of knowledge of tourism questions and an appreciation of tourism as a system.

The problem of being 'marginal' also applies when tourism researchers apply to other agencies such as State and Commonwealth Departments of Agriculture or for the Queensland Government's Business, Industry and Regional Development grants, where research for traditional agricultural and manufacturing industries are usually the successful applicants.

Additionally, the need for fundamental research in tourism is not well understood. Tourism is seen by many funding agencies, such as the ARC, as an applied area of study and frequently the question of 'why doesn't industry fund this work?' is asked. By way of contrast, industry sees a good deal of academic work as too remote from its immediate concerns of maximising profitability. Thus, academic tourism scholars wishing to develop new ideas and new methods in, for example, tourism planning, tourism impact assessment, tourist attitude and satisfaction measurement, destination image studies and community-tourism development find themselves either too academic for industry or too industry oriented for the academics.

Further, it is disturbing to note that the Commonwealth Department of Tourism is not contributing positively to raising the profile and value of academic tourism research. Despite a clear statement that research was an important goal of the first round of Forest Ecotourism grants, not one research proposal was given funds in 1993. Additionally, the documents on rural tourism and visitor expectations and management are notably deficient in referring to or benefiting from the tourism research community (both in Australia and overseas).

The incentive for industry to fund research in many areas of Australian economic activity is provided in the 150% tax incentive for Research and Development. At the present time this tax incentive is not available to any form of social science research nor is it applicable to market research. This policy reveals a rigid interpretation of the sort of research effort required to stimulate industrial growth (notably 'hard science' research) and fails to appreciate that in a service industry such as tourism the product being developed is intimately connected to social change and marketing research analysis. Again, substantial lobbying to change this position on the tax incentives for research and development for tourism is needed.

Further, the current 'drought' has been recognised in a host of tourism inquiries. The 1989 IAC Inquiry, the 1991 Senate Standing Committee Inquiry into Tourism, the 1991 Final Report of the Working Group for Ecologically Sustainable Development – Tourism, the 1993 ASTEC Report on Research in Northern Australia, as well as a number of related state government reports and BTR submissions have all recognised the limited research profile on tourism in Australia. Recognition, however, has not yet led to any action in the areas described above. It is depressing to predict that the current Industries Commission report on Research in Australia is again likely to recognise the lack of tourism research when what is needed are powerful recommendations for change and specific actions.

One notable exception to the funding drought for tourism studies applies to the involvement of tourism researchers in Co-operative Research Centres. While the funding for the tourism programs is in each case a small part of the total program, there is importantly a recognition of tourism researchers in these projects. The findings and activities of these CRC efforts deserve careful monitoring by the Commonwealth Department of Tourism to learn from and benefit from this integration of tourism and other disciplines of study in assessing national assets.

Some implications resulting from this analysis of tourism research funding include the following suggestions:

• Establish a dialogue with the ARC and the ABS to provide a classification of tourism studies. A suggested scheme is as shown in Table 14.2.

Table 14.2 Suggested classification of tourism studies

Field of Research	1300	Tourism
	1301	Tourism statistics
	1302	Economic issues
	1303	Tourism behaviour
	1304	Tourism planning and development
	1305	Tourism impacts (biophysical and socio-cultural)
	1306	Tourism marketing
	1307	Tourism resource appraisal
	1308	Tourism policy analysis
	1309	Tourism management
Socio-Economic Objective		
Economic Development:	1200	Tourism, leisure and recreation
	1201	Sport
	1202	Entertainment industries
	1203	Tourism attractions and tours
	1204	Accommodation and tourism transport
	1205	Leisure
	1206	Recreation
	1208	Environmental presentation and interpretation
National Welfare:		
Social Development and *Community Services*:	1506	Holiday and tourism objectives

- Suggest to the ARC a short list of leading Australian tourism academics to act as reviewers for tourism projects.
- Write to a large number of general research funding agencies (such as Industry councils and specific sector funding groups) highlighting the value of including and stimulating tourism work as a part of their funding profile.
- Establish formal links between the University research community, the Commonwealth Department of Tourism and the BTR so that existing research is used and stimulated by the Commonwealth Government as a part of its policy formulation process.
- Establish links between the University research community and ASCOT's Tourism Research Committee (TRC) to enable a more co-ordinated approach to tourism research development to be established.

- Develop an industry scholarship scheme for PhD programs which has an applied, but nevertheless intellectually rigorous, basis to target some long term strategic study projects of interest to industry.
- Encourage State and Commonwealth Government departments (including the Australian Tourist Commission) to view the academic community as potential users of, and partners in, their research. At present, the Queensland Travel and Tourism Corporation has, under a trial arrangement, allowed James Cook researchers to re-analyse an existing data set (the Domestic Market Segmentation Study). This special arrangement has enabled researchers to add extra information to the consultants' report as well as stimulating student and international academic interest in the perception of Queensland as a tourist destination. The BTR is beginning the process of releasing data through the CD-ROM system for researcher analysis, but the ATC has shown no initiatives in this area. Concerns about any of the competitive advantages inherent in the data can be overcome with written agreements and organisational controls (as has been done at several U.S. and Canadian Universities). The issue of providing data for detailed academic analysis is a valuable approach because it brings refined academic and statistical skill to large task sets which are not normally available to academics but which are usually not fully explored in terms of the complexity and explanation of the results.

3 Government Involvement in Tourism Research

At both the Federal and State/Territory levels, government has become directly involved in research mainly through the activities of its respective tourism agencies. Relevant organisations within the Federal sphere include the Commonwealth Department of Tourism (DofT), The Australian Tourist Commission (ATC) and the Bureau of Tourism Research (BTR). Meanwhile, statutory authorities (variously referred to as Commissions or Corporations) have been established in most States and Territories to carry out a tourism marketing role similar to that performed by the ATC at the national level.

A major step towards the development of a coordinated approach to tourism research among these organisations occurred in 1987 with the establishment of the BTR. Accordingly, the following analysis is structured in terms of pre- and post-1987 developments.

3.1 Pre-1987

Prior to the establishment of the BTR in 1987, a piecemeal approach to tourism research prevailed at the national level. A common interest in monitoring levels of domestic tourism among the State and Territory governments resulted in them pooling their resources to conduct the Domestic Tourism Monitor (DTM) on a co-operative basis under the auspices of the Australian Standing Committee on Tourism (ASCOT). With the ATC's funding of the International Visitors Survey (IVS) as an adjunct to its overseas marketing activities, these various agencies managed to provide a comprehensive monitor of tourist activity in Australia. Some State agencies (notably, Queensland, Tasmania, Western Australia and Northern Territory) had also initiated their own regular (destination based) surveys of visitors at this stage in order to allow the provision of more reliable regional data.

Meanwhile, the Australian Bureau of Statistics (ABS) maintained key tourism related statistical series such as Overseas Arrivals and Departures (OAD) and the Survey (really a census) of Tourist Accommodation (STA). By this time work was also under way on the inclusion of tourism activities (eg. tourist accommodation, car rental services and travel agents) in its periodic Service Industries Surveys (SS). However, arrangements between the Commonwealth and State/Territory Government tourism agencies with regard to the IVS, DTM and tourism research in general were unsatisfactory in several respects:

Firstly, with responsibility for the DTM being rotated among State/ Territory agencies, there was a lack of continuity in the management of this survey. Progress towards the improvement of quality control and the enhancement of output was hindered as a consequence.

Secondly, as the IVS was funded totally by the ATC, its continuation on a year to year basis was dependent upon it being regarded as remaining a priority in that organisation's program vis a vis other research and marketing requirements. Thus, the survey was not conducted in 1982 and 1987 owing to the diversion of funds to other areas of the ATC's activities.

Finally, as neither the Commonwealth nor the State/Territory agencies at the time regarded research as being even a minor reason for their existence, research functions (and particularly research which might be beneficial to the broader community) were marginalised within these organisations. Consequently, both the State/Territory agencies (with respect to the DTM) and the ATC (with respect to the IVS) lacked the staff resources in their research areas which was required to properly maintain these surveys. Similarly there were insufficient resources to carry out the analysis and interpretation necessary to ensure that the data available could be effectively utilised by decision makers in industry and government.

Arrangements in place prior to 1987, therefore, were not conducive to quality tourism research outcomes. Deficiencies in resources and, in the case of the DTM, a lack of continuity in management meant that the two key monitors of tourist activity were sub-standard, while a piecemeal approach to individual research projects meant that conditions were not conducive to the cumulative development of research expertise within the public sector. The marginalisation of research functions within the bureaucracy compounded this problem as the dearth of career opportunities in the research field hindered the retention of talented, upwardly mobile staff in this area.

3.2 Post-1987

The impetus for the development of a more coordinated approach arose out of the Kennedy review of the ATC in 1986 (Kennedy 1992) and simultaneous consideration of the issue by ASCOT. The BTR was established as a consequence of these deliberations in September 1987, after a joint (2:1) funding arrangement between the Commonwealth and State/Territory governments had been agreed to. In effect the pre-existing DTM funding arrangement between the State/Territory agencies was carried over into the funding of the BTR.

Throughout its existence, the mission statement of the BTR has been more or less as articulated in its most recent Annual Report (BTR 1992a: 3):

> To enhance the contribution of tourism to the Australian community, through the provision of accurate, timely and strategically relevant statistics and analysis to the tourism industry, government and the community at large.

The same report (page 3) outlines the key objectives which have structured the organisation's program over the last five years. These are:

- To provide a national focus for the collection, analysis and dissemination of tourism and related data;
- To upgrade the quality, relevance and timeliness of tourism statistics;
- To analyse and distribute tourism data in such a way as to encourage its widespread and effective use in tourism industry development;
- To undertake or co-ordinate research on priority issues in the tourism field; and
- To promote an understanding and awareness of the role of research in Australian tourism development.

The creation of the BTR clearly represented a significant step forward in the development of tourism research in Australia. With the concentration of resources into a single research agency, a 'critical mass' of expertise was established and economies of scale in the deployment of resources could be achieved. Furthermore, it has provided a focus for the development of a more co-ordinated approach to tourism research between the Commonwealth and State/Territory tourism agencies, while some progress towards improved co-ordination at a broader level was achieved through the staging of research conferences and joint projects with some tourism industry bodies.

In addition to the above advantages, there is also now greater potential for government tourism agencies to achieve some degree cost of recovery from their funding of research and thus, theoretically, enable more resources to become available for research. However, as noted elsewhere (Faulkner 1993), the adoption of user-pays and cost recovery principles as the basis for the administration of research leads to distortions in research priorities which may be contrary to both the broader community interest and the longer term sustainability of tourism development. Also, a closer analysis of BTR funding will reveal its relatively strong cost recovery performance has worked against efforts to secure higher levels of government funding.

Another negative implication of the cost recovery/user pays regime is that it inhibits the conduct of research in academic institutions by making this process more expensive. The full value of expensive data collection activities funded by government agencies is therefore not being realised because those data are not being analysed to the extent necessary for underlying patterns, relationships and processes to be identified.

Despite limited resources, the BTR was able to make a substantial contribution to the progress of tourism research in Australia during its initial years. The main areas of progress were recognised in the 1992 formal evaluation process (BTR 1992b) and summarised in the December Quarter edition of the BTR Tourism Update later in the same year (BTR 1992c). Apart from improvements in the instruments for monitoring levels of tourist activities, these documents draw attention to advances in the analysis of the economic impacts of tourism, demand forecasting, and the dissemination of key research data.

While acknowledging the progress the BTR has made in its initial years, the evaluation report concluded that:

> the BTR has reached a stage at which extensions of its activities are necessary if it is to more effectively service the planning needs of government and industry in the 1990's. (BTR 1992b: 2).

Specifically, the report identified the following areas in relation to which action is required:

- Unmet demand for the continuous provision of domestic tourism expenditure data;
- Conduct of more predictive and analytical research, including the development of leading indicators;
- Supply side monitoring and forecasting;
- Monitoring and evaluation of social and environmental impacts of tourism;
- Provision and interpretation of more regional level information;
- Research on topical issues;

- Qualitative market segmentation research; and
- Upgrading the BTR's tourism research coordination role.

Many of these demands are long standing and substantial progress has already been made towards addressing some of them. For instance, work is already well advanced on the establishment of a system for monitoring changes in domestic tourist expenditure. Also, the development of the Regional Tourism Monitor (RTM) kit and the planned provision of regular reports on regional tourism will go some way towards addressing the regional information problem.

The BTR evaluation process served to draw attention to the simple reality that the research needs of government, industry and the community could not be addressed without a major increase in resources. Indeed the report estimated that an additional $1.5 million and 13 staff would be required for the BTR to fulfil its functions. This would bring the BTR funding to $2.8 million and its staffing level to 28. The priorities of the Commonwealth Government were reflected in subsequent decisions which resulted in the BTR's request for additional resources being denied; while, at the same time, the ATC's funding was increased by $10 million (to just under $80 million) and the Department of Tourism received an additional $5.7 million to bring its funding to $30 million. Thus, despite the substantial increases in the level of funding of the Federal Tourism Portfolio over the last five years, research funding has remained static at less than two percent.

An appreciation of the impediments to achieving appropriate levels of funding for tourism research requires an understanding of the motivations of those operating in the upper echelons of public policy making and the paradoxes of this setting. While the senior bureaucrats are the first to complain about the lack of research material to support the policy formulation process, they assiduously resist any additional allocation of resources to research, especially if this is at the expense of their programs and thus, implicitly, involves an erosion of their power. Meanwhile, as Ministerial 'vision' is circumscribed by the three year electoral cycle, research proposals are invariably unpopular because of the long lead time often involved before their results can be translated into policy initiatives. Furthermore, Ministers are predisposed to favouring projects that heighten their visibility and create the impression that positive action is being taken on behalf of the electorate. Within this environment, it is difficult for research to compete for scarce resources against expensive, high profile advertising campaigns (Faulkner 1991) and projects that have the potential to attract a favourable response from an influential industry constituency. Not only is research less visible, but also it involves the risk of potentially embarrassing discoveries.

Other areas of government are, of course, afflicted by the anti-research mindset described above. However, few are affected to the same degree. One of the reasons for this is historical. Most sectors of the Australian economy have been recognised as distinct industries for many years and have thus been accommodated within the government administrative structure. Through bureaucratic inertia alone, therefore, the traditional industries (i.e. rural industries, manufacturing and mining) generally have substantial funding support through a diversity of targeted programs. The scale of these programs means that ample research funds can be made available without disrupting bureaucratic powerbases or jeopardising political visibility. Furthermore, the scientific and engineering bias of major research funding schemes, such as the ARC and the Co-operative Research Centre's program, reflects the dominance of the traditional industries.

On the other hand, tourism has only been recognised as an industry in its own right relatively recently and associated government programs largely came into being since the mid-1980's. Unfortunately for those involved in tourism, this was a period when the trend towards fiscal conservatism gained momentum, resulting in severe constraints being placed on the funds available for new initiatives. Thus, the pool of funds available for tourism programs has been limited and, in this context, research does not feature among the priorities.

Apart from the historical factors mentioned above, there also appears to be a greater appreciation of the value of research to competitiveness and long term survival among key decision makers in the traditional industries. Government funded research initiatives are therefore appreciated within this constituency and Ministers and bureaucrats are 'rewarded' accordingly.

The irony of the tourism industry's situation is that, if tourism oriented government programs have a lower funding base, then the importance of research driven policy development is accentuated. The effective deployment of limited resources hinges on an informed (i.e. research based) assessment of tourism development needs. Also, as alternative destinations to Australia become more competitive and the international tourism market becomes more discerning in its choice of tourism product, a research based approach to tourism management will become even more essential.

The conclusion that can be drawn from the above observations is a simple, but daunting, one. Before Australia's tourism research resources can be mobilised and utilised more effectively for tourism development purposes, a fundamental shift in attitudes towards research within the political leadership, bureaucracy and industry must take place. This shift will not take place of its own accord. Researchers themselves must work towards changing attitudes. This conclusion applies equally to the State/Territory level of government.

3.3 State/territory tourism authority research activities

Apart from their involvement in research initiatives at the national level owing to their association with the BTR, State/Territory tourism authorities also maintain separate research programs aimed at meeting individual organisational and State/Territory specific industry needs. As noted previously, some States conduct their own destination based surveys in order to compensate for the limitations of national surveys at the regional level. In general, the State/Territory tourism authority approach to tourism research can be summarised in terms of several trends.

Firstly, there has been a tendency to minimise in-house resources and expertise, and to rely instead on consultants. While this approach reduces on-going research overheads and is apparently cost efficient as a consequence, the reduced in-house capabilities often means that these organisations do not receive good value for money in their research consultancy budgets. Precision in the terms of reference of research projects often suffers owing to limited research capabilities within the organisation, and consultancy selection and quality control measures are less than adequate.

Secondly, most States have tended to give priority to advertising and related marketing programs at the expense of research. This syndrome, described elsewhere as 'advertising fundamentalism' (Faulkner 1991), resulted in a number of state authority research units being virtually dismantled in the second half of the 1980's. Meanwhile, recent funding decisions at the Federal level (described in the previous section) suggest that this distortion of priorities is not restricted to the states. However, some state bodies have apparently realised the folly of such an approach and reinstated their research functions.

Finally, partly as a reflection of the 'advertising fundamentalism' syndrome, much of the research funded by State/Territory authorities has become narrowly focused on the promotional elements of marketing. While this is understandable, given that the charter of these organisations generally emphasises their promotional role, this is often at the expense of other facets of the marketing process (e.g. product development, price effects, factors affecting tourism demand). Also, there has been a tendency to become overly sensitive to industry requirements, at the expense of broader community obligations. This is illustrated in the review of the Northern Territory Tourist Commission (Kennedy 1992) which actually proposed a substantial (i.e. almost threefold) increase in research, but at the same time indicated that priority should be given to 'commercial aspects of the industry'.

It is essential that problems associated with advertising and business viability be included on the research agenda. However, broader marketing and community issues must also be addressed if a balanced approach to tourism management is to be developed.

4 Tourism Industry Research

It is particularly difficult to compile a comprehensive review of tourism studies conducted for the Australian tourism industry. There is the obvious problem of the confidentiality of much of the material generated for individual operators in the various sectors (transport, attractions, accommodation, etc.). Additionally there is a 'file drawer' problem in that staff and executive changes often ensure that studies conducted in the past are not well understood or readily accessed by new personnel. While it is difficult to generalise, some broad trends may be noted. Much of the work done is carried out by consultants rather than 'in house' research staff. There are few continuous research programs, except possibly in the Airline sector, with much of the work being episodic. Typically, research contributes to businesses in either the feasibility and start-up phases or at times of crises or management rejuvenation. Nevertheless, the accommodation and attractions sector (notably the theme parks) conduct some visitor evaluation and quality assurance programs, although the ability of the consultants to condense statistics into clear information for executive decision making is an enduring management issue.

Tourism consultants who are responsible for the majority of industry driven research are not required to have any formal qualifications nor is there any extensive program of advanced training or professional development for such personnel. The work of tourism consultants in the private sector is not subject to scrutiny by other researchers and quality control is purely through market forces and client satisfaction rather than any process of review. (This may be contrasted with public management agencies such as the Great Barrier Reef Marine Park Authority which routinely reviews all consultancy work usually with a mix of Australian and international referees.)

Selective opportunities do exist for academic researchers to provide advice to the tourism industry either through consultancy work or through research grants. The distinction between these two mechanisms is that in the first case a specific answer to an industry question is required, whereas in the latter the questions are generated by the researcher and the answers may be insightful for tourism industry personnel but may not address the most immediate industry issues.

One significant and still evolving tourism industry endeavour to stimulate Australian tourism industry research deserves special mention. The Australian Tourism Research Institute was founded with industry support in partnership with James Cook University. Initially ATRI was designated as a fund raising organisation which could channel industry money to tourism research. The industry difficulties of 1989 and other factors limited the effectiveness of the organisation in raising funds and an attempt to refocus ATRI to serve as a professional research membership group was made. This met with some success and over 100 research members, notably consultants, academics and tourism students, became members. It proved difficult, however, to generate sufficient funds to pay a Secretariat to run such an organisation with an array of member services and this formal membership function was discontinued in 1992. The organisation still exists and remains as a potential funding channel for industry concerns in tourism research.

An important research oriented joint initiative of ATRI and the BTR was the staging of annual Tourism Outlook Fora. Conferences in this program differ from those referred to previously in that they are aimed specifically at drawing insights derived from research to the industry's attention. Thus, the audience of this series tends to be more industry based and there is a focus on the interpretation of research for management purposes, rather than on research per se.

5 Tourism Research Funding vis-à-vis Other Industries

Reliable data on the aggregate level of tourism research funding are not generally available from published information on research and development expenditure. This is because tourism is not an 'industry' as defined in the Australian and New Zealand Standard Industrial Classification, nor has it been regarded as a socio-economic objective or product field as defined in classifications of research and development expenditure. Estimates of the level of tourism research funding can, however, be made from known spending by government agencies and inferences drawn from official data on research and development expenditure.

The purpose in this section is to compare the level of research funding for tourism with that provided for selected other industries, and to draw some conclusions as to the adequacy of this level of funding. Table 14.3 illustrates that the R&D effort for tourism is well below that for other industries of comparable or even lesser size. A disproportionately large share of R&D expenditure relative to industry size goes to the 'production' industries of mining, manufacturing, transport and communications. For government R&D in particular, the agricultural sector gains the most from these funding discrepancies. By contrast, the tourism industry, which is larger than either the agriculture or mining sectors and is growing faster than the agricultural sector, receives an extremely small share of total and government R&D expenditure.

6 Research Needs in the 1990s

Although several recent reports on, and inquiries into, tourism and related issues allude to tourism research needs (eg. Brokensha and

Table 14.3 Research and development by industry 1990–91 Australia

Industry	Share of GDP (A) (%)	Share of Total R&D Expenditure (B) (%)
Agriculture	4.3	14.2
Mining	4.6	7.0
Manufacturing	15.3	32.1
Transport and Communications	7.2	22.4
Tourism	5.4	0.3

Sources: (A)ABS Cat. No. 5206.0 and BTR Estimates (B)ABS Cat. No. 8104.0

Guldberg 1992; Commonwealth Department of Tourism 1992; ESD Working Group on Tourism 1991; Senate Standing Committee on Environment, Recreation and the Arts 1992), all of these have a particular focus which prevents them from providing a comprehensive and balanced assessment of research needs and priorities. Indeed, the conclusions one can draw from these documents highlights, if anything, the need for a more specific inquiry into national tourism research needs.

The nearest we have to a comprehensive document is the 'National Tourism Strategy' prepared by the Commonwealth Department of Tourism (1992). As pointed out in this statement, research has a crucial role to play in effective policy development and industry planning and, accordingly, numerous specific research needs are implied by the many elements of the overall strategy. Some of these are elaborated, for illustrative purposes, in Appendix A.

Apart from demonstrating the diversity of research needs associated with the Commonwealth policy arena alone, Appendix A highlights the difficulty of determining research priorities in the context of a statement of the national policy agenda which does not itself attempt to identify priorities. A clearer indication of priorities might perhaps be obtained by identifying those recommendations arising from other recent reports/ inquiries which refer specifically to research needs. A summary of these is provided in Appendix B.

The only consistent theme arising from these various perspectives is the notion of sustainable tourism development. The explicit recognition of sustainable tourism development as one of the underlying principles of the National Tourism Strategy is a significant benchmark in the evolution of Federal tourism policy and mirrors the emergence of more general Ecologically Sustainable Development (ESD) guidelines in the Federal policy arena. Sustainable tourism development, according to the Strategy document (Commonwealth Department of Tourism 1992: 60):

recognises that environmental issues should be an integral part of economic decisions

and involves

development that does not jeopardise the future productive base of the industry's resources and which sustains ecological processes necessary to maintain quality of life for present and future generations.

Though not suggested explicitly in the strategy statement, it could be argued that sustainable development principles should take precedence in the National tourism policy agenda. There is less value in the achievement of growth targets in visitor numbers and high levels of profitability, employment growth and improved balance of payments outcomes if this is at the expense of significant negative social and environmental impacts. Apart from their intrinsic relevance to welfare, equity and conservation considerations, such impacts jeopardise long term economic viability by undermining the quality of the tourism product. Accordingly, the pursuance of the economic and even the social goals defined above needs to be moderated by an appreciation of the social, cultural and environmental impacts of tourism, and the necessity of ensuring that the negative aspects of these impacts are avoided and/or ameliorated.

However, recognising that most tourism activity occurs at the level of the individual tourism enterprise, there is clearly a need to focus on the pragmatic, managerial issues which confront operators as they formulate and implement their strategies. It is somewhat idealistic to think that simply expressing the desire for 'harmless' tourism growth will somehow change both the principles and practices of operators to achieve that objective. It will always be a case of achieving net benefits from tourism, after deducting the various costs from the various benefits. The challenge for researchers is to assist managers in improving the ratio of benefits to costs.

7 Conclusions

The increase in the number of Australian Universities offering tourism and/or hotel management degree courses has provided impetus to the development of university based tourism research in Australia. Despite this growth, however, advancement in both the quantity and quality of tourism research conducted has been hindered by a combination of factors.

Firstly, there has been a shortage of tourism oriented academics with advanced (i.e. PhD) research qualifications to provide the leadership required. Secondly, a large number of academic tourism researchers are either new to tourism (i.e. coming from other fields of academic research) or new to academic research altogether. Thirdly, the effects of these factors on the progress of tourism research are compounded by the inertia of competitive research funding schemes (ARC and university based schemes), which result in the failure to recognise tourism as a field of study in its own right. Not only are university based tourism researchers generally less equipped to attract funds through competitive grants schemes, therefore, but also these schemes are structured in such a way that the tourism field is disadvantaged in any case.

Within this environment, many researchers have resorted to consultancies as a means of funding their research activities. On one hand, it could be claimed that this trend has the advantage of ensuring the relevance of university based research to industry and government needs. On the other hand, much of the research being conducted under these conditions is simply replicating established research and, as a consequence, it is not contributing to the development of innovative techniques or the advancement of knowledge in the field. Also, there is an obvious undue emphasis on applied, as opposed to theoretical, research.

Whatever form of tourism research is being funded by industry and government, comparisons with other industries reveal that the commitment to research in tourism is not commensurate with this industry's contribution to the economy. This is despite the broad range of research needs that have been identified as requiring attention if tourism development in Australia is to be sustainable. The recent history of government and industry involvement in tourism research indicates that the essential role of research in tourism management, planning and policy development is not being recognised.

Action is clearly required if the problems identified in this paper are to be addressed. First and foremost, it needs to be recognised that, as a community with a common interest, university based tourism researchers need to become organised so that the case for promoting and using research in tourism development can be effectively articulated. An important step towards mobilising the research community, and pursuing this objective in a co-ordinated way, has been taken with the establishment of CAUTHE.

Within the CAUTHE framework, the following initiatives have been proposed as a basis for future action:

- Formation of a small 'task force' or steering committee to frame and implement an action plan;
- Establish links with the Commonwealth Department of Tourism, BTR, TRC and ATIA with a view to:
  - establishing a more co-ordinated approach to tourism research development nationally;
  - addressing problems associated with the administration of competitive grants schemes.

- Facilitate the continuation of annual research conferences for the purposes of enhancing networking, collaboration and co-ordinated action;
- Consider other networking options such as newsletters, databases etc., and the adoption of the Journal of Tourism Studies as the primary vehicle for research communication in Australia;
- Consider linkages with overseas research organisations (e.g. TTRA, CHRIE etc.,); and
- Develop schemes for encouraging and supporting both under-graduate (Honours) and postgraduate tourism research.

Appendix A. Indicative Research Needs Associated with Actions Identified in the National Tourism Strategy

Strategy component
Marketing, research and co-ordination

International marketing
- In conjunction with industry, enable the ATC to promote Australia effectively overseas as an international tourist destination.
- Ensure that the Australian Government's participation in World Expositions maximises the opportunities for the promotion of Australia's tourism product.

National awareness campaign
- Co-ordinate the development of a National Tourism Awareness Campaign in conjunction with the States and Territories and the industry.

Policy co-ordination
- Monitor and assess the effects of international developments on Australia's tourism industry
- Establish a consultative forecasting framework to provide a more co-ordinated approach to long-term industry planning.

Economic and business issues
- Recognise tourism as a key industry in Australia's future development and help to create an economic environment conducive to sustaining its competitiveness and optimising its contribution to the economy.

Examples of research requirements
- Overseas marketing research

- segmentation
- market potential assessment
- Evaluation research
  - tracking studies to gauge impact of advertising
  - overall program evaluation
- Evaluation of effectiveness and efficiency of expositions as a vehicle for tourism promotion.
- Attitudinal surveys and other marketing research required for the design and targeting of communication strategy.
- Evaluation.
- Implications of international economic, social and political trends and events.
- Domestic and international tourism demand modelling and forecasting.
- Development of methodologies for measuring:
  - net economic impact of tourism at National, State and regional levels.
  - direct and indirect impact on other sectors of the economy.
- Profitability of various segments of the tourism industry and factors affecting profitability.

Investment finance
- Encourage the availability of long-term equity finance for investment in the tourism industry and increase investor confidence in the industry.

Foreign investment
- Continue to permit foreign investment in the tourism industry that is consistent with the national interest.

Small business
- Promote the creation and growth of competitive small business enterprises.

Taxation issues
- Provide for accelerated depreciation of tourism buildings ...
- Encourage investment in large tourism projects through the development of a development allowance.

Business regulation
- Minimise regulations impeding tourism growth.

Transport and facilitation
International aviation policy
- Implement a policy of multiple designation for Australian international carriers which will facilitate competition ... and provide benefits for Australian consumers, the tourism industry and the economy generally.
- Ensure international charter guidelines give adequate recognition to the needs of the tourism industry and the benefits to Australia to efficient charter operations.
- Impediments to investment in tourism.
- Profitability of tourism investment.
- What are the social, economic and environmental implications of foreign investment in tourism?
- Are there areas or conditions of investment where positive/negative impacts are accentuated/minimised?
- Are there particular impediments to small business profitability in tourism?
- What measures are likely to be most effective in improving the performance of small business in tourism?
- What are the effects of the taxation requirements on investment in tourism?
- Evaluation of impact of tourism related adjustments in the taxation system.
- Are there specific aspects of the Commonwealth, State or Local government regulatory environment which impede tourism growth and, if so, what are the broader (economic, social, environmental, etc.) implications of changing these?
- What role does the cost/nature of international airline services play in long haul destination choice?
- What are the net benefits to Australia of additional air services under liberalised regime?

Domestic aviation
- Ensure that in the deregulated domestic aviation environment barriers to effective competition are minimised.

Roads
- Ensure that tourism interests are properly reflected in benefit – cost analysis of road funding proposals and the broader determination of road funding priorities.

Training, employment and standards
Labour force planning
- In conjunction with the industry, document its skills needs across

each industry sector, assess the developmental needs of the existing workforce and continue to provide adequate funds for tourism education and training programs.

Specific training needs
- Encourage education and training institutions to develop courses that are responsive to the sectoral and cross sectoral needs of the industry.

Language and cultural skills
- Identify the language and cross cultural skills needs of the tourism industry and develop a strategy to meet those needs.
- What impact has the deregulated domestic aviation environment had on tourism opportunities/cost for the domestic and international markets?
- What impact have these changes had on patterns of domestic/ inbound tourist behaviour?
- What have been the impacts on various tourist destinations?
- How significant are roads, and variations in the standard of surfaces, in influencing access to/ attractiveness of tourist destinations?
- How can tourism related costs/benefits be factored into cost benefit assessment of road funding proposals?
- Are there specific attitudes to, or conditions of, employment in tourism which contribute to high attrition rates? If so, what are the training and management implications?
- What are the implications of projected changes in the level and nature of tourist activity with regard to future labour force profiles?

Labour market program
- Ensure that the government's labour market programs continue to take account of specific skills needs of the tourism industry.

Workplace reform
- Encourage employers, unions and employees to introduce workplace reforms aimed at embracing industry competitiveness, standards, management practices and career opportunities.

Tourism shopping
- Maximise economic returns from tourism shopping.

Environmental and social issues
Commonwealth's environmental role
- Through the Intergovernmental Agreement on the Environment and liaison with industry and conservation groups, seek a co-operative

approach to the management of environmental issues in tourism contexts.

Sustainable development
- In response to the Tourism Working Groups on ecologically sustainable development and other relevant inquiries, formulate and implement policies to ensure the ecologically sustainable development of the tourism industry.

Coastal tourism
- Develop a Commonwealth coastal policy and a Commonwealth approach to a national coastal strategy that takes account of tourism and other interests.
- Periodic industry skills needs analysis and projections of related training requirements.
- To what extent do workplace practices in the tourism industry:
  - impede competitiveness
  - reduce profitability
  - stifle career paths?
- Are there particular patterns of tourist shopping that reduce or enhance Australia's export income?
- What are the environmental impacts of tourism, how do they vary by type of tourism and destination, and what are their management and policy implications?
- What policy and management strategies for ecologically sustainable development have been adopted overseas, and what have been their respective outcomes?
- What are the particular environmental impacts of tourism in coastal environments?

Great Barrier reef marine park
- Continue to provide for the ecologically sustainable development of tourism within the Great Barrier Reef Marine Park.

Climatic change
- Support increased research into the extent and impact of future climatic change and encourage tourism planners and developers to take account of the likely effects of climatic change on tourism activity.

Regional issues
- Encourage the adoption of a regional approach to tourism planning and management that recognises the importance of integrated land-use plans based on ecological systems.

Environmental impact assessment
- Encourage environmentally sensitive tourism development.

Economic instruments
- Support the equitable application of the 'user pays' principle to offset the cost of public management and environmental impacts of tourist activity and to provide additional resources for the management of increased visitor numbers.

Education and research
- Endeavour to raise tourists' awareness of the environmental impact of tourist activity.
- Effective management of such parks requires the design and implementation of systems for monitoring tourist numbers, activities and the environmental impact of these activities.
- How will climatic change affect tourist destinations and the activity patterns of tourists?
- What are the implications of these changes with respect to the future distribution of tourism demand, and infrastructure and design requirements?
- How do the impacts of tourism vary on a regional basis?
- What monitoring and planning systems need to be put in place to anticipate and control these impacts?
- To what extent can existing environmental impact assessment procedures cope with:
  - tourism related development.
  - the broader, social dimension of ecological sustainability.
- What are the equity implications of the application of 'user pays' principles in tourism?
- To what extent can the user pays instrument be used to ration resources and control demand pressure?
- What are the current levels of awareness of environmental impacts of tourism among the various categories of tourist?
- Do variations in levels of awareness affect behaviour?
- What are the most effective ways of influencing awareness and behaviour?

Social impacts
- Encourage tourism planners and developers to take account of the social costs and benefits of development proposals and support research into the social impacts of tourism development.

Services for disabled travellers
- Seek to improve tourism opportunities for the disabled.

Women and tourism
- Promote and encourage the development of employment and training opportunities for women in the tourism industry.

Accommodation and market segments
Forecasts of accommodation needs
- Define a model for reliably forecasting tourist accommodation needs on a regional basis and develop the Australian Tourism Investment Database to service the industry's information needs.

Conventions and incentive travel
- Promote Australia more vigorously as a convention/incentive travel destination and develop an adequate database for this sector to assist marketing initiatives.

Cultural tourism
- Improve the co-ordination and promotion of cultural tourism and encourage greater co-operation between tourism and cultural organisations so as to enhance tourists' access to cultural experience.
- What are the social costs and benefits of tourism development and how does the potential for these occurring vary by different types of tourism as a tourist destination?
- What are the equity implications of these costs and benefits and how can they be reconciled in different situations?
- How do the patterns of tourist behaviour among different disability groups vary?
- Do these variations reflect variations in taste, affordability or accessibility?
- Is there gender bias in access to training and employment opportunities in tourism?
- Requires the development of methodologies for more effectively monitoring and forecasting demand at a regional level.
- What is the economic significance of the conventions/incentive sector?
- Is the public investment into incentive/convention travel marketing and infrastructure justified?
- What is cultural tourism?
- What is the role of cultural tourism in tourism generally?
- Are there particular impacts (costs and benefits) which are specific to cultural tourism?

Aboriginal involvement
- Encourage increased involvement by indigenous people in the tourism industry so as to enhance visitors' experiences and generate

wider understanding and acceptance of the cultures of indigenous peoples.

Special events/interests
- Encourage the industry to maximise the benefits of special events and special interest tourism by developing and marketing tourist packages linked to these activities.

Ecotourism
- Promote the development of ecotourism that enhances visitor exposure to and awareness of the ecology of our unique natural attractions.

Farm tourism
- Encourage the effective development of farm tourism by the establishment of national standards, a co-ordinated marketing network and the provision of tourism advisory services to the rural sector.
- What is the actual and potential contribution of aboriginal involvement in tourism?
- What are the actual and potential costs/benefits/risks of greater aboriginal involvement in tourism?
- Are there specific markets in relation to which aboriginal culture has particular value in the tourism product?
- Methodologies need to be developed to more effectively monitor and evaluate the impacts of events.
- How effective are events as instruments for long-term tourism development/promotion?
- What are the pros and cons of ecotourism with respect to ESD objectives?
- To what extent, and under what conditions, can farm tourism be an effective strategy for farm viability?

Appendix B Research Priorities Suggested by Federal Government Inquiries and Reports

Statistical and Research Support

Priority	Source				
	ESD Report	Senate Inquiry	Cultural Tourism	Industries Commission	Tourism Strategy
• Standardisation-of definitions used for statistical purposes between ABS and BTR.		•			
• Funding of IVS and DTM should be maintained and adoption of Regional Tourism Monitor (RTM) encouraged to enable regionally specific monitoring/evaluation of impacts.					
• Ensure that the BTR continues to function effectively and efficiently in meeting Government and industry statistical and research needs.	•				
• Expand the scope and improve the co-ordination and funding of tourism research.					•
• Provision of additional funds to BTR to strengthen strategic research.					•
• Institution of a wide ranging review of the funding of tourism in research.	•				
• Develop a convention/incentives industry database to assist marketing initiatives in this sector.	•				•

Economic Research

	Source				
	ESD Report	Senate Inquiry	Cultural Tourism	Industries Commission	Tourism Strategy
• Upgrading of economic models for the assessment of the net benefits of tourism and the impacts of tourist activity on other sectors of the economy.					•
• Establish a consultative framework for tourism demand forecasting.		•			
• Refine models for forecasting tourist accommodation needs on a regional basis and develop the Australian Tourism Investment database to service the industry's information needs.					•
• Upgrading of statistics on foreign investment proposals.		•			
• Ensure sound market research basis for foreign investment proposals (FIRB).		•			
• Improved methodologies for assessing economic and employment implications of foreign investment.		•			
• National transport infrastructure implications of the ATC's targets.		•			
• Assessment of infrastructure needs in the context of integrated regional land use plans.	•				

	ESD Report	Senate Inquiry	Cultural Tourism	Industries Commission	Tourism Strategy
			Source		
Management and equity implications associated with the application of user-pays principles to tourists' access to national parks etc.					
Evaluation of appropriateness, effectiveness and efficiency of publicly funded tourism promotion.				•	
Social Culture					
Guidelines and methodologies for extension of tourism Environmental Impact Assessment to incorporate social and cultural impacts.	•	•	•		
BTR and ATC should give priority to maintaining domestic and international visitor expectations (and post visit satisfaction) regarding interaction with local communities.			•		
Methodologies and systems to enable export value of tourist shopping involving costs and crafts to be measured.			•		
Degree and nature of indigenous people involvement in tourism and impacts of this involvement on indigenous communities.	•				

Social Culture (continued)

	ESD Report	Senate Inquiry	Source		
			Cultural Tourism	Industries Commission	Tourism Strategy
• Market research into tourism opportunities for indigenous people and tourist expectations of indigenous involvement.	•				
• Economic impacts of tourism on indigenous communities and factors affecting financial success of indigenous tourism ventures.	•				
• Education and training needs of indigenous people in tourism.	•				

Environmental

(Note: some items in previous section also refer to environmental considerations)

	ESD Report	Senate Inquiry	Source		
			Cultural Tourism	Industries Commission	Tourism Strategy
• Methodologies for monitoring and evaluating the effects of international tourism on Australia's natural environment and society.		•			
• Empirical studies of the effects of tourism developments on environmentally sensitive sites.		•			

- Developing of methodologies and systems for post-development environmental audits.
- Research into the potential impacts and implications of climatic change with regard to tourism.
- A research funding and co-ordination body should be established to prioritise and support, on a competitive basis, the conduct of research specifically oriented to ESD objectives in tourism.

References

Brokensha, P and Guldberg, H. (1992) *Cultural Tourism in Australia, A Study Commissioned by the Department of the Arts, Sport, the Environment and Territories*, Australian Government Printing Service, Canberra.

Bureau of Tourism Research (1992A) *Annual Report: 1991–92*, Bureau of Tourism Research, Canberra.

—— (1992B) *BTR Evaluation Report*, Bureau of Tourism Research, Canberra.

—— (1992C) *BTR Tourism Update, December Quarter*, Bureau of Tourism Research, Canberra.

Bushell, R. and Robertson, R.W. (1993) *Credit Transfer Practice in Tourism and Hospitality Programs*. A Report prepared for the Australian Vice-Chancellors' Committee, Credit Transfer Project. July.

Commonwealth Department of Tourism (1992) *Tourism: Australia's Passport to Growth: A National Tourism Strategy*. Commonwealth Department of Tourism, Canberra.

Dann, G., Nash, D. and Pearce, P. (1988) Methodology in Tourism Research. *Annals of Tourism Research* 15 (1): 1–28.

Dartnall, J., and Store, R. (1990) The Literature of Tourism. *The Journal of Tourism Studies* 1 (1): 49–53.

Ecologically Sustainable Development Working Groups (1991) *Final Report: Tourism*, Australian Government Printing Service, Canberra.

Faulkner, H.W. (1991) *The Role of Research in Tourism Development*, BTR Tourism Update, September Quarter, Bureau of Tourism Research, Canberra: 2–3.

—— (1993) The Tourism Research Two-Step: Reflections on the Progress of Tourism Research in Australia. In A.J. Veal and B. Weiler, Editors. *ANZALS* Monograph Series, Issue 1.

Hall, C. (1991) Post-Graduate Research in Leisure, Tourism and Recreation in Australia: A Review. *Australian Journal of Leisure and Recreation* 1 (1): 26–31.

Jafari, J. (1990) Research and Scholarship: The Basis of Tourism Education. *The Journal of Tourism Studies* 1 (1): 33–41.

Kennedy, J. J. (1992) *Northern Territory Tourism: The Way Ahead* (Review of the Northern Territory Tourist Commission), Northern Territory Tourist Commission, Darwin.

King, B. (1988) Current Developments in Tourism Education – the U.K., Australia, and New Zealand Experiences, in McSwan, D. (ed.) *Education for Tourism.* Proceedings of the Conference held at Canberra. James Cook University Publication, Townsville: 21–24.

Pearce, R L. (1993) Issues in Australian Tourism Research. Paper presented to the Tourism Research Workshop, University of Western Sydney, May.

Senate Standing Committee on Environment, Recreation and the Arts (1992) *The Australian Environment and Tourism Report*, Commonwealth of Australia, Canberra.

Weiler, B., Shaw, R. and Faulkner, W. (1991) Research in the Tourism Curriculum: Extra or Essential? In Ward, B. *et al.*, (eds) *Tourism Education: National Conference Papers*. University of Canberra 1990: 144–150.

Chapter 15

Destination Australia: A Reseach Agenda for 2002 and Beyond

Bill Faulkner

Introduction

A common expectation shared among opinion leaders within the tourism industry is that Australia will receive around 20 million international visitors by the year 2020 (or 10 million by 2010). While such an expectation may appear to be realistic on the basis of an extrapolation of recent trends, this is nevertheless a risky foundation for long term planning. This is especially so when the implications of 'flashpoint' events such September 11 have to be taken into account. Apart from the obvious flaw of assuming that tends of the last 50 years will necessarily continue over the next 20 years, there are two cautionary caveats that warrant consideration. Firstly, once we take into account the level of growth that will also occur in domestic demand during this period, the potential social, environmental and economic impacts of his level of activity may be such that the target is both undesirable and self-defeating. Secondly, if it can be established that these impacts can be effectively managed, such a target will not be achieved without a concerted effort on the part of industry and governments to make it happen. The following question therefore stands out as possibly the most fundamental issue confronting the Australian tourism industry:

> How can we grow Destination Australia to 20 million international tourists by 2020 (or 10 million by 2010), while at the same time managing this growth in a manner that is consistent with sustainability objectives?

This question provides the focus for a proposed new framework for the CRC for Sustainable Tourism's research agenda.

Fundamental Questions Affecting Australia's Tourism Future

The above question can be more effectively addressed by being considered in terms of the following more specific questions:

- How feasible is a growth target for Australia of 20 million international visitors by the year 2020 (or 10 million by 2010)?
- Are there obstacles to this target that need to be addressed, and what planning, management and marketing strategies need to be put in place to overcome these obstacles and respond to opportunities?
- Is this level of growth sustainable? Bearing in mind the fact that domestic tourism accounts for 70 per cent of demand and growth will also be experienced in this sector, what are the likely social, environmental and economic impacts of the combined level of inbound and domestic tourist activity?
- How manageable are these impacts, and what planning, management and policy measures are necessary to ensure sustainable tourism outcomes?

This set of questions clearly needs to be addressed, in the first instance, at the national level, although ultimately the interrelated set of issues associated with growth potentials, impacts and actions must be embraced at the individual destination level. Equally, these are questions that require the engagement of the private sector and relevant public sector agencies from the outset if any research program we develop is to be translated into effective action. This paper concentrates on a research strategy in particular, rather than the strategy for engagement that is necessary to drive and complement the research program.

Objectives

In broad terms, the objectives of the proposed 'Destination Australia Research Agenda' are:

- To provide national and international leadership in research on medium to long-term future trends in tourism and their implications for sustainable tourism development;
- To build capacity within the Australian tourism sector to develop innovative and sustainable responses to emerging opportunities and threats associated with an increasingly volatile global environment;
- To assess the feasibility of a 20 million international visitor target for Australia in 2020 (or 10 million in 2010), and to identify both obstacles to, and opportunities that support, the achievement of this target;

- To provide analysis of investment, marketing, infrastructure, planning, development, management, and policy measures necessary to realise this target within a sustainable framework;
- To develop a suite of models for identifying sustainable tourism 'hotspots' and sustainable management best practice gaps, at the destination and enterprise levels respectively throughout Australia;
- To develop technologies, models, tools, expert systems, best management practices, planning and monitoring systems to enhance competitiveness and sustainability of destinations. Such tools will be applicable to destination management at various levels, including the States and Territories, and down to the individual regional destination in particular; and
- To develop technologies, models, tools, expert systems, best management practices, planning and monitoring systems to enhance competitiveness and sustainability of individual enterprises, with a focus on the many SMEs that make up the bulk of the tourism industry.

Within this context, the term 'tourism sector' is used in the broad sense to encompass individual commercial enterprises, destination management organisations, relevant public sector agencies and communities. Similarly, the examination of tourism trends needs to be informed by a broader appreciation of social, political, economic, technological and environmental change issues because of both their bearing on tourism demand and supply trends and their relevance to the development of a holistic perspective on sustainable tourism development. Background on the dual notions of 'hotspots' and 'flashpoints' is provided in the next section.

What is Sustainable Tourism Development?

For the purposes of clarifying the focus of the research program, the interpretation of sustainable tourism development has been drawn from a range of international conventions (eg. WTO Manila and Hague Declarations of 1980 and 1989; Globe 90' Conference, Vancouver; World Commission on Environment and Development 1987) and the plethora of academic papers on the issue. Accordingly, for the purposes of the current exercise, sustainable tourism development has been defined as a form of tourism that:

- Safeguards and enhances to natural and cultural assets of the destination;
- Safeguard and enhances the resident population's quality of life and life opportunities;
- Satisfies the needs and expectations of the tourist market;
- Is economically viable and achieves a return on investment for tourism operators; and

- Achieves equity in the distribution of costs and benefits of tourism between different segments of the community and between the current and future generations. That is, outcomes are considered beyond the relatively short term horizon of the current generation to ensure that both inter and intra generational equity is taken into account.

This definition clearly requires an inter-disciplinary research program, involving a balanced approach to the examination and evaluation of the social, economic and environmental impacts of tourism.

Flashpoints and Hotspots as Integral Foci in the Research Agenda

Change, and the effective management of change, are fundamental to contemporary management thinking. The one certainty of modern society is that we live in a changing world, where individuals, business enterprises, government agencies and communities are constantly challenged to anticipate, respond to and influence events that impact on their existence in one way or another. The magnitude of this challenge has been accentuated by recent developments triggered by the events of September 11. Such events might be referred to as 'flashpoint'. They illustrate the reality of 'the certainty of the unexpected' by being intrinsically unpredictable, and they are often global in the extent of the dislocation and devastation they cause. Without diminishing the significance of September 11's impacts on the tourism industry globally, however, it is equally important that we do not lose perspective by becoming preoccupied by this single event. September 11 is one of a string of flashpoints that have afflicted the tourism industry over a period of time (e.g., the 1970s Oil Shock, Chernobyl, Lockerbie, Exxon Valdez, the Australian domestic pilots dispute, the Gulf War, Kosovo, Mad Cow Disease, cyclones, the Asian Financial Crisis, airline collapses), and it is arguable that they have become 'normal' elements of the environment in which we operate. Indeed, it might be argued that these events are to tourism what droughts, flood and bushfires are to the agricultural sector and as such the industry needs to develop a higher degree of resilience and adaptability within such an environment.

To a large extent, the fact that often distant, and sometimes seemingly remote, events can have an impact on the Australian tourism industry is a reflection of the impacts of globalisation on national and regional economies generally, and the associated revolutions in information technology and telecommunications that have supported this process. This technology has not only made it possible for activities and trans-action across the globe to be more inter-connected, but also it has made the chain reactions that precipitate crises more instantaneous. Within this context, the apparent increased volatility of the global environment and the exposure of the tourism industry to flashpoints is attributable to such developments as:

- The paradoxical increase in tribalism along side the trend towards globalisation (Kosovo, the Gulf War).
- The reduced insularity of national economies brought about by free trade arrangements and the internationalisation of business corporations and financial markets (Asian Financial Crisis, Ansett collapse).
- Increased capacity of technology (and technological malfunctions) to precipitate environmental and human disasters (Chernobyl, Exxon Valdez, air disasters).
- Extension of human settlement and tourist operations into increasingly fragile and natural disaster prone areas (cyclones).

The genesis and aftermath of September 11 is arguably a reflection of elements of the first three points mentioned above. Despite our inevitable and frequent exposure to flashpoints, government agencies and the tourism industry alike have tended to react to them in an ad-hoc and piecemeal fashion, with little accumulated knowledge being developed on how to cope with such situations in the longer term. Indeed, the standard response involves industry lobbying for short-term financial assistance for troubled enterprises and increased marketing, while governments usually oblige in order to be seen to be doing something. In the long run, this approach is at best ineffective and potentially counter-productive. A longer-term approach underpinned by a firm research foundation is necessary to increase the resilience, and therefore sustainability, of the Australian tourism industry. The 'paradigms and techniques' component of the research programme described later in the paper addresses this particular problem. It involves:

- A more systematic approach to gathering industry intelligence and environmental scanning on an ongoing basis;
- Improved methods of interpretation and dissemination of information at the time flashpoints are experienced;
- The installation of scenario based planning to complement traditional forecasting;
- The development of improved models for coping with charge and uncertainty within strategic planning frameworks, including better risk management; and
- Adoption of models and techniques for creative engagement, innovation and the introduction of a learning organisation culture in the interface between research and planning.

'Hotspots' refer to situations where projected levels of growth in visitor levels and tourist industry activity have the potential to produce negative economic, social or environmental impacts that threaten to undermine the sustainability and competitiveness of the destination concerned. In such situations, action will be required to manage impacts. The global conditions that make us more prone to flashpoints are also adding to the potential increased incidence of hotspots, although the extension of tourist activities into areas that are increasingly environmentally and/or socially fragile is an important additional condition. In contrast to flashpoints, however, hotspot situations are often the consequence of more gradual changes over a period of time. They are therefore more insidious in the sense that the crisis is often not detected until it is either too late or inordinately expensive to remedy the situation. A premium must therefore be placed on installing systems that enable potential hotspots to be detected well in advance of the critical threshold being reached.

Within the more turbulent and uncertain environment highlighted by flashpoint and hotspot phenomena, decision-makers at all levels need to develop a more sophisticated approach to coping with the future. This approach should be underpinned not only by an improved understanding of the dynamics of change, but also by a capacity to construct scenarios about possible futures in a manner that will enable decision-makers to learn, adapt and respond creatively to opportunities and threats as they emerge. In this context, the test of a 'good' scenario is not so much whether it portrays the future accurately, but rather the extent to which it:

- Makes the forces that push the future in different directions more visible;
- Clarifies the challenges confronting decision-makers and communities; and
- Highlights the opportunities, threats and risks associated with alternative strategic options.

Along with such areas as information technology biotechnology and knowledge generation through research and education, tourism is at the forefront of the national agenda for developing innovative responses to global change. Tourism is seen as both an opportunity for economic development that has emerged as a consequence of the changes alluded to above and a vehicle for economic adjustment in areas that have suffered from structural change. Whether the potential of the industry in both these respects is realised, however, depends on the capacity of the stakeholders in tourism development to cope with change. The focus of the Destination Australia Agenda will be to build this capacity.

Currently, the only source of information on likely future trends in tourism at the national level is provided by the Tourism Forecasting

Council (TFC), a Federal Government funded body that relies on technical support from the Bureau of Tourism Research (BTR). The scope of this body's activities is limited in two respects. Firstly, it concentrates on forecasting international visitor demand levels only and, therefore, does not look at broader contextual issues such as those the Destination Australia Agenda will consider. Secondly, its methods restrict it to short-term (3–5 years) forecasting horizons, rather than the 10–20 year horizon intended by this programme.

Proposed Research Agenda

In considering the planned approach, it is important to note the following clarifications at the outset:

- The 2020 horizon will be examined in terms of two time frames (2010 and 2020), because it is likely that the growth in tourism will produce some impacts that are more immediate than others;
- The examination of future scenarios will initially focus on social, economic, technological and environmental change in general because these provide the context for changes in tourism demand, supply and impacts; and
- Scenarios in domestic, as well as inbound, tourism demand are necessary if potential infrastructure requirements and impacts are to be fully appreciated.

The underlying rationale of the proposed approach involves two interrelated perspectives on sustainable tourism development issues:

- **The destination management perspective,** which recognises that sustainable tourism development is ultimately a holistic concept. That is, in any particular setting, the social, economic and environmental aspects of tourism development must all be examined simultaneously because the neglect of any single facet will undermine the achievement of sustainability objectives across the board and, in any case, interactions between these various dimensions requires such an approach. It follows that the value of much of the CRC's research output to core stakeholders (especially National, State and Territory tourism authorities, but also the many regional destination marketing organisations) is diminished if it is taken out of the context of the full range of destination-wide factors and interrelationships that impinge on destination sustainability and competitiveness. The destination management focus can therefore provide a vehicle for delivering a more coherent and useful package of outputs to core partners.
- **The tourism enterprise perspective,** which needs to be viewed within the context of the particular destinations where enterprises

operate, but which at the same time recognises that a viable and sustainable tourism industry is ultimately and equally dependent upon decisions and strategies developed at this level. Enterprises that adhere to sustainable business management best practices will have a better chance of survival, but these chances will be diminished if they are located in a destination where a sustainable tourism destination management regime has not been established. Conversely, the principles of sustainability, as enunciated earlier in this paper, need to be embraced by operators as a prerequisite for such a regime at the destination level.

The framework provided by State/Territory boundaries provides a key level of resolution for the destination focus, given that this defines the institutional framework governing relevant responsibilities of State/Territory governments and local governments that impinge on destination management activities. Also, the CRC ST has a national organisational structure largely based on a State/Territory Node framework, and core stakeholders include State and Territory Tourism Authorities.

This dual perspective is reflected in Figure 15.1, where the proposed stricture of the Destination Australia Research Agenda is described. The programme is envisaged to comprise six phases:

- Destination audits;
- Enterprise performance audits;
- Strategic management paradigms and techniques;
- Sustainable tourism hotspots (destination perspective) and sustainable business management best practice gaps (enterprise perspective);
- Technology; and
- Opportunities, options, threats and solutions.

Elements of all phases will need to proceed simultaneously, rather than sequentially in order to ensure that synergies between them are effectively developed and that certain programme deliverables are produced within a time frame that will satisfy stakeholder requirements.

Phase 1: destination audits

In addition to the rationale for a destination focus described previously, it is clear that the geographical frame of reference implied by this approach is necessary if the sustainable tourism management implications of future growth are to be effectively examined. The nature and levels of tourist activity will be variable across destinations, as will the potential environmental, social and economic impacts of this activity. A Geographic Information Systems (GIS) based approach is therefore proposed, whereby the unit of analysis will be individual destinations (perhaps as defined in the International Visitors Survey). As it is necessary to establish the current

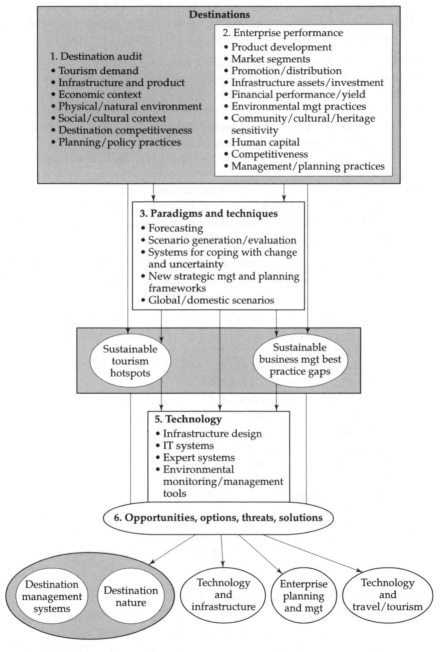

Figure 15.1 Destination Australia research programme

status of destinations in terms of the impacts of tourism in order to provide a benchmark for assessing potential future impacts, a series of 'destination audits' will be conducted in terms of such variables as:

- Nature and levels of tourist activity (tourism demand);
- Infrastructure and product development and the adequacy of this in the light of demand scenarios;
- Economic context of tourism vis-à-vis other sectors of the economy;
- Environmental and cultural assets and the impacts of current levels of tourism-related and other activity;
- The quality of life of resident populations and actual/potential impacts of tourism on this;
- Destination competitiveness situation; and
- Institutional, planning and policy frameworks that have the potential to affect the responsiveness of destinations to competitive and sustainable development challenges.

A range of existing spatial analysis techniques will be employed and extended, and new methods will be developed in this phase. These will include:

- Infrastructure demand-supply modelling (TARDIS Model);
- Environmental impacts assessment (limits of acceptable change and carrying capacity);
- Utilisation and extensions of the CRC's Green Globe environmental best practice accreditation model;
- CSIRO stocks and flows models;
- Modelling economic impacts (I-O and CGE models);
- Social impact assessment modelling using such parameters as economic opportunities indicators, limits of acceptable change in urban and natural environments, cultural integrity, access to facilities and general quality of life; and
- Destination competitiveness modelling.

All of the above, will be developed within a Geographic Information Systems (GIS) framework to enable spatial variations and concentrations to be identified and will build on systems already developed by such organisations as the CSIRO.

Phase 2: enterprise performance audits

The corresponding activity to destination audits will be the conduct of an audit of enterprise management and planning practices, with a view to establishing the extent to which these are consistent with sustainable management best practice models. Ultimately, such audits will need to be conducted on a destination-by-destination basis because of the nexus between the adoption of sustainable management principles at the enterprise and destination levels emphasised earlier. However, to make this task more manageable, and as a step towards identifying best practice benchmarks, a sectoral approach may be necessary (accommodation, themeparks/attractions, tour operators, hospitality, meeting/conventions, transport, etc.). Dimensions of audits within each sector would cover such factors as:

- Product development;
- Market segmentation;
- Promotion/distribution;
- Infrastructure assets/investment;
- Financial performance and yield;
- Environmental management practices;
- Host community relations and cultural/heritage sensitivity;
- Human capital;
- Competitiveness; and
- Management and planning practices.

Phase 3: paradigms and techniques

There will be an integrated programme of research projects aimed at reviewing, and refining methods of strategic analysis and planning, and providing a foundation for critically evaluating and refining the methods used in futures research. This phase will comprise five basic elements.

- **Coping with change and uncertainty:** What are the perceptual, cognitive and decision-making processes that influence how individuals and groups (business enterprises, community organisations and government agencies) comprehend and adapt to change? This component of the study is a critical foundation for the other elements of this phase of the programme. In particular, it will provide insights for a more in-depth analysis of issues associated with other elements of this phase. In particular, it will inform the examination of methods for generating scenarios, paradigms for coping with change and uncertainty and new concepts in strategic planning/management.
- **Paradigms for understanding and coping with change and uncertainty:** Various theoretical perspectives have been employed in various contexts to provide explanatory frameworks for change. These have included Chaos Theory, Catastrophe Theory, Systems Theory and Evolutionary Theory, all of which have tended to be used in isolation from each other. Yet there are common threads among this set of theories, which implies that, in combination with each other, they promise to provide a richer conceptual foundation for understanding change than has been previously achieved.

- **Methods for generating and evaluating scenarios:** What are the main methodologies and techniques far generating and evaluating scenarios in futures research, and what are the relative strengths and weaknesses of alternative approaches? What methods are most effective for stakeholder engagement in scenario generation and strategic planning in specific settings?
- **New management/planning concepts and frameworks for coping in, and adapting to, turbulent environments:** The previous sections of this phase of the programme provide a background for exploring which of the range of concepts and techniques that have been espoused as effective methods for coping with change and uncertainty offer the best combination of methods in such circumstances. Such methods/concepts include: conventional strategic planning; scenario-planning and strategic conversion; knowledge generation, innovation and entrepreneurship; learning and learning organisations; and hazard assessment, risk management and counter disaster planning.
- **Global and domestic scenarios:** What are the main scenarios regarding change in social, economic, political, technological and environmental domains over the next 10 to 20 years? How have these scenarios been derived and how plausible are they in the light emerging events and the previous assessment of different approaches? Drawing on the more rigorous bass for generating and evaluating scenarios provided by research elsewhere in this phase, a collation of published scenarios will be reviewed in order to produce a refined synthesis of scenarios. This will provide a firmer basis for exploring sustainable tourism implications subsequently.
- **Monitoring systems:** Scenario generating and evaluation processes need to be complemented by systems for monitoring more immediate global and domestic changes so that current developments that signal the possibility of longer-term and more significant changes are detected, and so that timely advice on the immediate consequences of flashpoints can be provided to industry and government.
- **Tourism Implications:** What are the implications of the consolidated set of scenarios derived from the previous steps with regard to the place of travel and tourism in people's lifestyles, and what are the ramifications of these considerations with regard to sustainable tourism development?

Phase 4: sustainable tourism hotspots and sustainable business management best practice gaps

Hotspots

- **Geographical disaggregation of tourism scenarios:** A re-examination of the scenarios produced in Phase 3 will be carried out, with a view to generating a suite of tourism futures scenarios and addressing he question: 'what are the implications of these scenarios in terms of the achievement of sustainable tourism objectives in Australia up to and beyond 2010 and 2020?' As emphasised previously, in addressing this issue, it is essential that the scenarios produced take into account the geographical dimensions of tourist behaviour on both the demand and supply side. Thus, the consideration of this issue for Australia as a whole is to a large extent a summation of assessments at the individual destination level.

- **Identifying hotspots:** A series of more targeted analyses drawing on destination audits will be carried out to identify the potential impacts of the tourism scenarios. This will enable decision-makers in industry, communities, planning agencies and policy makers to be more informed about 'the hot-spots', where specific remedial actions are necessary to avert threats to sustainable tourism outcomes The inevitability of there being spatial variations in the levels of tourist activity, along with similar variations in the vulnerability of areas to impacts, means that different responses will be necessary from businesses, communities and jurisdictions at the local, state and federal levels from location to location. Whatever responses are necessary, coordination within and beyond destinations will be essential to ensure that actions taken at individual destination level are informed by what has been learned in similar situations elsewhere. Similarly, such an approach will enable the 're-invention of the wheel' syndrome to be avoided and the actions of different players will be less likely to be at cross-purposes with each other. This will require a coordinated approach involving the Federal, State and Local levels.

- **Devising strategies for addressing the hot-spots and ensuring a sustainable tourism future.** There are two caveats to the establishment of an effective approach to this problem. Firstly, it must be an initiative of local stakeholders at the individual destination level to ensure that this group has ownership of the plan and that the necessary steps for its implementation are followed through. Secondly, the need for Federal, State and Local government involvement is important for the coordination reasons mentioned above, and such involvement is also necessary to provide the resource support and expertise that is essential for destinations to build the capacity for constructing the sustainability strategy. Government involvement and intervention is also necessary because many of the actions required for the plan to be implemented will rely on government action (policy changes and regulation, commitments to providing ongoing coordination support and resources for support personnel, funding for infrastructure and environmental management, etc.).

Among the potential methods that will be employed include the consultative framework developed by the Gold Coast Visioning Project (see Figure 15.2), perhaps in conjunction with the CSIRO's Futures Simulator.

Business Management Best Practice Gaps

- On the basis of the sectorial audit of business performance (Phase 2), a set of sustainable management best practice models will be produced. These models will in turn provide the basis for assessments of business performance at the individual destination level and the identification of gaps in current practices vis-à-vis the demands of sustainability. They will also support the production of generic kits, training modules, best practice manuals and, in some cases, accreditation schemes. However, a purely generic approach will be inadequate, given the variable challenges to sustainability across destinations implied by the differentiation of hotspots. Specific solutions requiring different emphases in aspects of best practice models may be necessary on a destination-by-destination level.

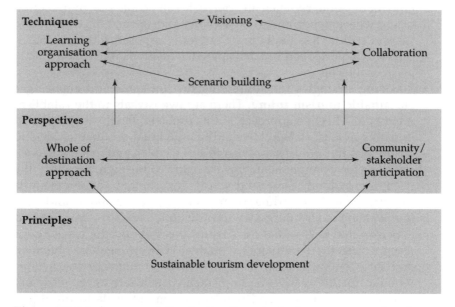

Figure 15.2 A framework for destination strategic management and planning

Phase 5: technology

This phase is fundamentally concerned with the question: how can the options and opportunities presented by technological advances and innovations be expanded to cope with the above scenarios, and support the achievement of sustainable tourism development objectives? A critical element of developing effective responses to the dual challenges of sustainability and competitiveness involves the application of technological innovations in such areas as:

- Engineering and design technology research can be applied to the solution of environmental problems associated with tourist activity and to infrastructure development problems that might otherwise undermine the competitiveness and capacity of destinations.
- Equally, the effective development and adoption of information technology as a tool for enterprise/destination management and marketing has been increasingly recognised as a key to the success of tourist destinations in the future.
- The utilisation and extension of GIS technology for the destination audit process described in Phase 1 also constitutes a major foundation for another stream of work in the technology development area, to the extent that this work will provide the foundation for the development of environmental and asset monitoring/planning systems at the destination level.

A schedule of research projects focusing on technology (engineering and IT) will be necessary to complement other elements of the programme.

Phase 6: opportunities, options threats and solutions

The culmination of the research programme described above will be a synthesis of the opportunities, options and threats confronting Australian tourism over the next 10 to 20 years, and a series of methods, tools and systems to underpin effective responses to these challenges. These responses are envisaged to encompass three main dimensions:

- Destination management systems, encompassing protected area management as a specific type of destination;
- Sustainable infrastructure and IT design systems; and
- Business management and planning systems.

An Alternative Perspective on the Research Structure and Outputs of the Destination Australia Agenda

The flow chart style presentation of the Destination Australia Research Agenda in Figure 15.1 provides a useful reflection of the rationale of the

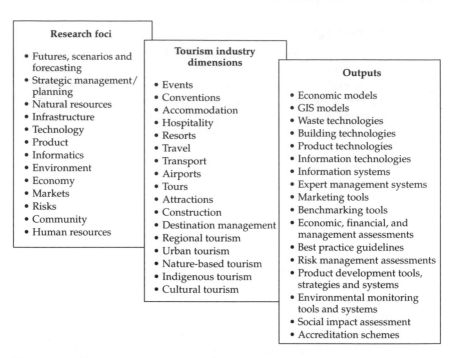

Research foci

- Futures, scenarios and forecasting
- Strategic management/ planning
- Natural resources
- Infrastructure
- Technology
- Product
- Informatics
- Environment
- Economy
- Markets
- Risks
- Community
- Human resources

Tourism industry dimensions

- Events
- Conventions
- Accommodation
- Hospitality
- Resorts
- Travel
- Transport
- Airports
- Tours
- Attractions
- Construction
- Destination management
- Regional tourism
- Urban tourism
- Nature-based tourism
- Indigenous tourism
- Cultural tourism

Outputs

- Economic models
- GIS models
- Waste technologies
- Building technologies
- Product technologies
- Information technologies
- Information systems
- Expert management systems
- Marketing tools
- Benchmarking tools
- Economic, financial, and management assessments
- Best practice guidelines
- Risk management assessments
- Product development tools, strategies and systems
- Environmental monitoring tools and systems
- Social impact assessment
- Accreditation schemes

Figure 15.3 Research structure and outputs

programme, but is less effective in its representation of the programme's research foci, dimensions and output. An alternative schematic summary of the programme is therefore provided in Figure 15.3 to highlight these aspects.

Benefits and Deliverables

The future competitiveness, prosperity and sustainability of the Australian tourism industry hinges on answers to the following questions:

- How will emerging social, economic, political, technological and environmental trends at the global and domestic levels influence the place of travel and tourism in people's lifestyles (and thus demand for tourism opportunities), and what are the implications of these influences with regard to the management and marketing of tourism destinations and product?
- What are the ramifications of foreshadowed changes in the level and nature of tourist activity with regard to the social, environmental and economic impacts of tourism, and how will these impacts vary geographically across Australia?

- In light of the above, what steps are necessary to ensure that the tourism industry, destination management agencies, governments and communities are able to take advantage of, cope with, and manage these changes in a manner that ensures a sustainable tourism future for Australia?

Given the current significance of tourism to Australia's economy and the inevitability that this industry will become even more important as an export earner in the future, its actual and potential future role in supporting the quality of life of Australians is broadly recognised. To the extent that the answers to these questions will have a bearing on the degree to which the industry's potential is realised and, more importantly, on the management of impacts, an examination of them is crucial to the nation's future.

Beyond these general benefits of the programme, its primary contribution will be to enable impacts that will have a significant bearing on the sustainability of tourism in destinations in Australia to be anticipated. Thus, it will be possible for management, planning and policy measures to be put in place in a manner that will enable the impacts to be avoided, rather than requiring remedial action after the event.

The specific outcomes/deliverables of the programme will be:

- A knowledge-based platform for innovation in tourism management, planning and policy;
- Management and planning frameworks for ensuring that the Australian tourism industry adapts to, and takes advantage of, changing global conditions;
- Systems, models, tool, technologies, accreditation schemes etc to improve the competitiveness and sustainability of Australian tourism destinations and enterprises;
- Systems, models, tools, technologies etc for identifying and responding to sustainable touism development threats (hotspots); and
- Technologies for infrastructure and IT systems to support sustainable tourism development.

A Bibliography of Bill Faulkner

2002

Fredline, E. and Faulkner, B. Residents' reactions to the staging of major motorsport events within their communities: A cluster analysis. *Event Management* 7 (2), 103–114.

Fredline, E. and Faulkner, B. Variations in residents' reactions to major motorsport events: Why residents perceive the impacts of events differently. *Event Management* 7 (2), 115–126.

2001

Faulkner, B. Towards a framework for tourism disaster management. *Tourism Management* 22 (2), 135–147.

Fredline, E. and Faulkner, B. *International Market Analysis of Wildlife Tourism*. Gold Coast: CRC Sustainable Tourism.

Tideswell, C., Mules, T. and Faulkner, B. An integrative approach to tourism forecasting: A glance in the rearview mirror. *Journal of Travel Research* 40 (2), 162–171.

Tomljenovic, R., Larsson, M. and Faulkner, B. Predictors of satisfaction with festival attendance: A case of Storsjoyran Rock Music Festival. *Tourism* 49 (2), 123–132.

Faulkner, B. and Vikulov, S. Katherine Washed out one day, back on track the next: A post-mortem of a tourism disaster. *Tourism Management* 22 (4), 331–344.

2000

Faulkner, B. The future ain't what it used to be. Unpublished Professorial Lecture, Griffith University, Gold Coast.

Faulkner, B. and Russell, R. Turbulence, chaos and complexity in tourism systems: A research direction for the new millennium. In B. Faulkner, G. Moscardo and E. Laws (eds) *Tourism in the 21st Century* (pp. 328–349). London: Continuum.

Faulkner, B., Moscardo, G. and Laws, E. (eds) *Tourism in the 21st Century: Lessons from Experience*. London: Continuum.

Fredline, E. and Faulkner, B. Host community reactions: A cluster analysis. *Annals of Tourism Research* 27 (3), 763–784.

Moscardo, G., Faulkner, B. and Laws, E. Introduction: Tourism in the 21st century: Moving ahead and looking back. In B. Faulkner, G. Moscardo and E. Laws (eds) *Tourism in the 21st Century* (pp. xviii–xxxii). London: Continuum.

Tomljenovic, R. and Faulkner, B. Tourism and older residents in a Sunbelt Resort. *Annals of Tourism Research* 27 (1), 93–114.

Tomljenovic, R. and Faulkner, B. Tourism and world peace: A conundrum for the 21st century. In B. Faulkner, G. Moscardo and E. Laws (eds) *Tourism in the 21st Century* (pp. 18–33). London: Continuum.

Faulkner, B., Chalip, L., Brown, G., Jago, L., March, R. and Woodside, A. Monitoring the tourism impacts of the Sydney 2000 Olympics. *Event Management* 6 (4), 231–246.

1999

Faulkner, B. *Tourism Disasters: Towards a Generic Model*. Gold Coast: CRC Sustainable Tourism.

Faulkner, B. and Ryan, C. Innovations in tourism management research and conceptualisation (Editorial). *Tourism Management* 20 (1), 3–6.

Faulkner, B. and Tideswell, C. Leveraging tourism benefits from the Sydney 2000 Olympics. *Pacific Tourism Review* 3 (3/4), 227–238.

Faulkner, B., Fredline, E., Larson, M. and Tomljenovic, R. A marketing analysis of Sweden's Storsjöyran Festival. *Tourism Analysis* 4, 157–171.

Faulkner, B., Oppermann, M. and Fredline, E. Destination competitiveness: An exploratory examination of South Australia's core attractions. *Journal of Vacation Marketing* 5 (2), 125–139.

Russell, R. and Faulkner, B. Movers and shakers: Chaos makers in tourism development. *Tourism Management* 20 (4), 411–423.

Tideswell, C. and Faulkner, B. Multidestination travel patterns of international visitors to Queensland. *Journal of Travel Research* 37 (4), 364–374.

Tomljenovic, R. and Faulkner, B. Tourism and intercultural understanding: A case of Croatian students visiting Spain, Greece and Czech Republic. *Turizam* 47 (2), 108–131.

1998

Faulkner, B. Developing strategic approaches to tourism destination marketing: The Australian experience. In W.F. Theobold (ed.) *Global Tourism* (2nd edn, pp. 297–316). Oxford: Butterworth-Heinemann.

Faulkner, B. Tourism development options in Indonesia and the case of agro-tourism in Central Java. In E. Laws, G. Moscardo and B. Faulkner (eds) *Embracing and Managing Change in Tourism: A Casebook* (pp. 202–221). London: Routledge.

Faulkner, B. and Goeldner, C.R. Progress in tourism and hospitality research (1998 CAUTHE Conference Report). *Journal of Travel Research* 37 (1), 76–80.

Faulkner, B., Tideswell, C. and Weaver, D. (eds) *Progress in Tourism and Hospitality Research: Proceedings of the 1998 Australian Tourism and Hospitality Research Conference*. Canberra: Bureau of Tourism Research.

Faulkner, H.W. and Walmsley, D.J. Globalisation and the pattern of inbound tourism in Australia. *Australian Geographer* 29 (1), 91–106.

Fredline, E. and Faulkner, B. Resident reactions to a major tourist event: The Gold Coast Indy Car Race. *Festival Management and Event Tourism* 5 (4), 185–205.

Harrison-Hill, T. and Faulkner, B. The tyranny of distance: The case of Australia's US Market. *The Australian International Business Review* December, 28–40.

Laws, E., Faulkner, B. and Moscardo, G. Embracing and managing change in tourism: International case studies. In E. Laws, G. Moscardo and B. Faulkner (eds) *Embracing and Managing Change in Tourism: A Casebook* (pp. 1–10). London: Routledge.

Laws, E., Faulkner, B. and Moscardo, G. (eds) (1998) *Embracing and Managing Change in Tourism: International Case Studies*. London: Routledge.

Lawton, L., Weaver, D. and Faulkner, B. Customer satisfaction in the Australian timeshare industry. *Journal of Travel Research* 37 (1), 30–38.

Russell, R. and Faulkner, B. Reliving the destination life cycle in Coolangatta: An historical perspective on the rise, decline and rejuvenation of an Australian seaside resort. In E. Laws, G. Moscardo and B. Faulkner (eds) *Embracing and Managing Change: A Casebook* (pp. 95–115). London: Routledge.

1997

Bushell, R., Faulkner, B. and Jafari, J. *Tourism Research in Australia: Mobilising National Research Capabilities*. Canberra: Bureau of Tourism Research.

Faulkner, B. A model for the evaluation of national tourism destination marketing programs. *Journal of Travel Research* 35 (3), 23–32.

Faulkner, B. On the status of tourism and hospitality management programs in the university education sector. Submission to the (West) Review of Higher Education Financing and Policy on behalf of the Council of Australian University Tourism and Hospitality Education.

Faulkner, B. Tourism development in Indonesia: The 'big picture' perspective. In J. Minnery, M. Gunawan, M. Fagence and D. Low Choy (eds) *Planning Sustainable Tourism* (pp. 7–16). Banding: Penerbit ITB.

Faulkner, B. and Patiar, A. Workplace induced stress among operational staff in the hotel industry. *International Journal of Hospitality Management* 16 (1), 99–117.

Faulkner, B. and Russell, R. Chaos and complexity in tourism: In search of a new perspective. *Pacific Tourism Review* 1 (2), 93–102.

1996

Faulkner, B. and Tideswell, C. Monitoring the social impacts of tourism. Paper presented at the 27th Annual Conference of the Travel and Tourism Research Association, Las Vegas.

Jeong, G.-H. and Faulkner, B. Resident perceptions of mega-event impacts: The Taejon International Exposition case. *Festival Management and Event Tourism* 1 (2), 3–11.

Mules, T. and Faulkner, B. An economic perspective on special events. *Tourism Economics* 2 (2), 107–117.

1995

Faulkner, B. *Canada's Tourism Market Performance: An Evaluation Based on a Shift-Share Approach to Market Share Analysis*. Ottawa: Canadian Tourism Commission.

Faulkner, B. Paribud-Ekoling: Sustainable tourism development in Central Java. *Tourism Management* 16 (7), 545–548.

Faulkner, B. The evaluation of national tourism promotional programs. Global tourism: New rules, new strategies. Paper presented at the 26th Annual Travel and Tourism Research Association Conference.

Faulkner, B. and Raybould, M. Monitoring visitor expenditure associated with attendance at sporting events: An experimental assessment of the diary and recall methods. *Festival Management and Event Tourism* 3, 73–81.

Faulkner, B. and Valerio, P. An intergrative approach to tourism demand forecasting. *Tourism Management* 16 (1), 29–37.

Faulkner, B. and Weiler, B. Progress in Australian tourism research and education (1995 CAUTHE Conference Report). *Tourism Management* 16 (5), 393–395.

1994

Faulkner, B. *Macrolevel Performance Indicators for National Tourism Administration*. WTO Technical Paper. Madrid: World Tourism Organisation.

Faulkner, B. The changing environment of Australian inbound tourism. *Tourism and Travel Review* 2 (9), 12–13.

Faulkner, B. The future ain't what it used to be: Reflections on the nature and role of tourism forecasting in Australia. Paper presented at the Tourism Forecasting: The 1993 Australian Tourism Research Workshop, Canberra.

Faulkner, B. Tourism research lags behind industry growth. *Tourism and Travel Review* 2 (4), 10–11.

Faulkner, B. Towards a strategic approach to tourism development. In W. Theobold (ed.) *Tourism in the 21st Century: Global Issues, Trends, Opportunities* (pp. 231–245). Butterworth-Heinemann.

Faulkner, B. and Davidson, M. Australian research and education examined. *Tourism Management* 15 (5), 390–393.

Faulkner, B., Pearce, P., Shaw, R. and Weiler, B. Tourism research in Australia: Confronting the challenges of the 1990s and beyond. Paper presented at the Tourism Research and Education in Australia: Australian National Tourism Research and Education Conferences, Canberra.

Faulkner, B., Davidson, M., Craig-Smith, S. and Fagence, M. (eds) *Tourism Research and Education in Australia: Proceedings of the Australian National Tourism Research and Education Conferences.* Canberra: Bureau of Tourism Research.

1993

Faulkner, B. All that glitters is not gold: Tourism in Queensland. *Queensland Economic Forecasts and Business Review* 2 (2), 71–78.

Faulkner, B. Costing hallmark events. *Tourism and Travel Review* 2 (3), 9–10.

Faulkner, B. *Evaluating the Impacts of Hallmark Events.* BTR Occasional Paper No. 16. Canberra: Bureau of Tourism Research.

Faulkner, B. Marketing that makes the long term perspective. *Tourism and Travel Review* 1 (8), 10–11.

Faulkner, B. The strategic marketing myth in Australian tourism. Paper presented at the Building a Research Base in Tourism: The Australian Tourism Research Conference 1993, Canberra.

Faulkner, B. The tourism research two-step: Reflections on the progress of tourism research in Australia. In A.J. Veal and B. Weiler (eds) *Australian and New Zealand Association of Leisure Studies Monograph Series* Vol. 1, pp. 35–55.

Faulkner, B. and Bonnett, G. The conventions and meetings industry: Statistical and research requirements. Paper presented at the Building a Research Base in Tourism: The Australian Tourism Research Conference 1993, Canberra.

Faulkner, B. and Kennedy, M. (eds) *Towards a Sustainable Tourism Future: 1992 Tourism Outlook Forum.* Canberra: Bureau of Tourism Research. 1992

Faulkner, B. Existing national tourism data sources: Their relevance to the evaluation of tourism marketing. In H.W. Faulkner and R. Shaw (eds) *Evaluation of Tourism Marketing* (Occasional Paper No. 13, pp. 38–43). Canberra: Bureau of Tourism Research.

Faulkner, B. The anatomy of the evaluation process. In B. Faulkner and R. Shaw (eds) *Evaluation of Tourism Marketing* (BTR Occasional Paper No. 13, pp. 6–9). Canberra: Bureau of Tourism Research.

1991

Faulkner, B. The role of research in tourism development. *BTR Tourism Update,* September Quarter, 2–3.

1990

Faulkner, B. The access versus cost recovery dilemma in the supply of tourism data. *ACSPRI Newsletter* 21, 15–17.
Faulkner, H.W. Swings and roundabouts in Australian tourism. *Tourism Management* 11 (1), 29–38.

1989

Faulkner, B. An overview of tourism research in Australia. In J. Blackwell and L. Stear (eds) *Case Histories of Tourism and Hospitality* (pp. 1–9). Sydney: AIMS Publications.
Faulkner, B. The Bureau of Tourism Research: Establishment, functions and program. In J. Blackwell and L. Stear (eds) *Case Histories of Tourism and Hospitality* (pp. 10–18). Sydney: AIMS Publications.
Faulkner, B. Tourism demand patterns: Australia. *International Journal of Hospitality Management* 7 (4), 331–341.
Faulkner, B. and Poole, M. *Impacts on Tourism of the Disruption to Domestic Airline Services* (Occasional Paper No. 5). Canberra: Bureau of Tourism Research.

1988

Faulkner, B. *Patterns of Tourism Demand in Australia: An Analysis of Recent Trends* (Occasional Paper No. 4). Canberra: Bureau of Tourism Research.
Faulkner, B. and Fagence, M. (eds) *Frontiers of Australian Tourism*. Canberra: Bureau of Tourism Research.

1987

Faulkner, B. *Tourism Statistics: A View from the Australian Perspective*. Tourism Foundation Course, Nuku' Alofa, Tonga: South Pacific/World Tourism Organisation.

1986

Faulkner, B. *Review of Tourism Statistics: Federated States of Micronesia*. Madrid: United Nations Development Program/World Tourism Organisation.
Faulkner, B. *Review of Tourism Statistics: Republic of Palau*. Madrid: United Nations Development Program/World Tourism Organisation.
Faulkner, B. *Review of Tourism Statistics: Western Samoa*. Madrid: United Nations Development Program/World Tourism Organisation.

1985

Faulkner, B. Policy oriented tourism research: A view of future needs. Paper presented at the Institute of Australian Geographers Conference, Brisbane.
Faulkner, B. Simulation games as a technique in information collection: A case study of disabled person transport in Canberra. In T.W. Beed and R.J. Stimson (eds) *Survey Interviewing: Theory and Techniques* (pp. 95–104). Sydney: Allen and Unwin.
Faulkner, B. and Woolmington, E.R. Social atlases of Australia capital cities: The first four. *Australian Geographical Studies* 23 (1).

1983

Faulkner, B. and French, S. *Geographical Remoteness: Conceptual and Measurement Problems* (Occasional Paper No. 54). Canberra: Bureau of Transport Economics.

Faulkner, B. and Nelson, R. The link between transport and unemployment patterns in metropolitan Melbourne. Paper presented at the 8th Australian Transport Research Forum.

1982

Faulkner, B. Campbelltown: A case study of planned urban expansion. In D. Rich, J. Langdale and R. Cardew (eds) *Urban Development and Economic Change in Sydney* (pp. 265–282). Sydney: Allen and Unwin.

Faulkner, B. *Transport of the Disabled in the ACT* (Occasional Paper No. 54). Canberra: Bureau of Transport Economics.

Faulkner, B. and Kunz, M. *Social Aspects of Australian Roads: Position Statement* (Reference Paper 31). Canberra: Bureau of Transport Economics.

Faulkner, B. and Nelson, R. *Unemployment and Transport Availability in Metropolitan Melbourne* (Occasional Paper No. 53). Canberra: Bureau of Transport Economics.

Faulkner, B. and Rimmer, J. An approach to identifying transport gaps: A southwest Sydney case study. Paper presented at the 7th Australian Transport Research Forum.

1981

Faulkner, B. Journey pattern responses on Sydney's metropolitan fringe: An exploratory study. *The Australian Geographer* 15 (1), 17–26.

1979

Faulkner, B. On the human impacts of regions. In B. Faulkner and J. Warhurst (eds) *Western District: Contemporary Issues* (Vol. 1). WIAE: Faculty of General Studies.

Faulkner, B. *Spatial and Social Consequences of Sydney's Metropolitan Expansion: The Macarthur Experience.* University of New South Wales, FMS, Department of Geography Monographs 6.

1975

Faulkner, B. Environmental factors in soil erosion: A systems approach. In G. Connolly (ed.) *Readings in Geographical Themes* (pp. 81–89). Malvern, Victoria: Sorret.